Disorders of Syntactic Comprehension

Disorders of Syntactic Comprehension

David Caplan and Nancy Hildebrandt

A Bradford Book
The MIT Press
Cambridge, Massachusetts
London, England

This book was set in Palatino by Asco Trade Typesetting Ltd., Hong Kong, and printed and bound by Halliday Lithograph in the United States of America.

Library of Congress Cataloging-in-Publication Data

Caplan, David, 1947–
  Disorders of syntactic comprehension/David Caplan, Nancy Hildebrandt.

  p.   cm.—(Issues in the biology of language and cognition)
  "A Bradford Book."
  Bibliography: p.
  Includes index.
  ISBN 0-262-03132-9
  1. Aphasia.   2. Syntax.   3. Neurolinguistics.   I. Hildebrandt, Nancy.   II. Title.
  III. Series: MIT Press series on issues in the biology of language and cognition.
  RC425.C374   1988   616.85'52—dc19   87-21319

Contents

Series Foreword

The MIT Press series on Issues in the Biology of Language and Cognition brings new approaches, concepts, techniques, and results to bear on our understanding of the biological foundations of human cognitive capacities. The series will include theoretical, experimental, and clinical work that ranges from the basic neurosciences, clinical neuropsychology, and neurolinguistics to formal modeling of biological systems. Studies in which the architecture of the mind is illuminated by both the fractionation of cognition after brain damage and formal theories of normal performance are specifically encouraged.

John C. Marshall

Foreword

John C. Marshall

In the Apocrypha we read: "And there shall be lit a candle of understanding in thine heart which shall not be put out." So be it. But the material substrate of understanding in the brain is more fragile. A very substantial proportion of adult patients with acquired aphasia present with comprehension disorders, which range from subtle deficits in following complex verbal reasoning to an almost complete inability to understand the simplest spoken or written communications. Although the group studies by Kertesz (1984) show greater spontaneous recovery of auditory comprehension than of expressive speech, many patients experience residual comprehension impairments that severely restrict their enjoyment of everyday life and their ability to work. Furthermore, the efficacy of current regimens for the behavioral treatment of aphasia is dubious; Howard (1986) provides the best discussion of why attempts to evaluate the success of intervention by randomized controlled trials are inappropriate. And even where unspecified language rehabilitation does appear to have led to gains over and above spontaneous recovery, its effect upon verbal comprehension is equivocal. For example: In the study by Basso et al. (1979), a higher percentage of treated than of untreated patients with severe aphasia showed gains in comprehension; but of those with moderate aphasia, neither the fluent nor the nonfluent patients seem to have had their comprehension improved by therapy.

The notion of "comprehension disorder" covers a vast range of different types of impairment. Thus, a first step toward the theoretical elucidation of miscomprehension, and toward the eventual remediation thereof (see Byng and Coltheart 1986), would be a basic taxonomy of normal processing stages with an associated analysis of the procedures and representations that can be (more or less) independently impaired by brain damage. At the very least, we must distinguish the following components of comprehension.

• Lexical access to the physical form and syntactico-semantic representation of words must be achieved.

Such access can break down in numerous ways. A disorder of "prephonemic hearing" can coexist with normal results on pure-tone audiometry and with a relatively well-preserved ability to recognize environmental noises. A deficit in temporal auditory acuity is often responsible for the failure to achieve a stable phonological percept (Auerbach et al. 1982; Coslett et al. 1984). In other patients, the phonological code assigned to speech input is sufficient to support good oral repetition and good writing from dictation (Ellis 1984); aural comprehension is nonetheless impaired, while comprehension of written material is much better preserved. There may be two forms of such "word-meaning deafness": one in which the phonological code fails to make direct contact with the phonological lexicon and another in which intact lexical phonological representations fail to access semantic representations (Kohn and Friedman 1986). Brain damage can also degrade the stored semantic representations and the encyclopedic knowledge associated with them, either across the board or within restricted conceptual domains (as in the "category-specific" aphasias; see Marshall 1985 and Shallice 1987).

• The information arrayed against base lexical items must be combined with whatever structural cues (word order, closed-class vocabulary, inflectional and derivational morphology) are available to support the assignment of sentential representations.

Many patients whose comprehension of single words is quite adequate (as assessed either by their oral definitions of words or by their ability to point to a word's referent) may nevertheless fail to interpret correctly the thematic roles assigned to noun phrases in rather simple sentences. Such misunderstanding of "who did what to whom" is not confined to patients who fall within the traditional taxonomic classes for which severe comprehension impairment is criterial—global aphasia, Wernicke's aphasia, and transcortical sensory aphasia (Marshall 1986). Caramazza and Zurif (1976) and Heilman and Scholes (1976) demonstrated impaired comprehension in some patients whose primary diagnosis was either Broca's aphasia or conduction aphasia. These patients manifested a striking inability to interpret center-embedded sentences (*The man that the woman is hugging is happy*) and double-object constructions (*The man showed the boys' dog the cages* versus *The man showed the boys the dog cages*) when pragmatic constraints could not determine the correct reading. Simple ("reversible") actives (*The dancer applauds the clown*) or passives (*The cowboy was punched by the man*) cannot always be reliably interpreted by patients whose auditory comprehension appears relatively well preserved when measured on conventional test batteries (Schwartz et al. 1980; Ansell and Flowers 1982). It would seem, then, that some form of "syntactic" or morphosyntactic comprehension disorder is ubiquitous across a wide variety of patients with damage to the perisylvian region of the (language) dominant hemisphere (de Bleser and Bayer 1985).

• The output(s) of the language module *per se* must be integrated with a central database in order to update the belief system and plan appropriate action.

Many aphasic patients have well-preserved extralinguistic knowledge; hence the common finding that semantic and pragmatic plausibility aids sentence comprehension (Kudo 1984). Aspects of discourse structure (including topicalization and given/new constraints) may likewise serve to improve the comprehension of syntactic forms that are misunderstood in isolation (Cannito et al. 1986); more generally, standard measures of sentence comprehension (e.g. Token Test scores) often fail to predict performance on paragraph comprehension (Wegner et al. 1984). By contrast, some patients with *right*-hemisphere damage show impairment in drawing correct inferences from discourse, despite good comprehension and recall of explicit factual information (Brownell et al. 1986). The generality of this finding is, however, open to question (McDonald and Wales 1986); differences in the qualitative nature of the text-based inferences that have been tested, combined with different assessment procedures, have confused the analysis of language breakdown beyond the sentence level. These problems are further complicated by unresolved issues concerning the autonomy of grammatical processing (the assignment of lexical and syntactic structure). The extent to which "contextual" information (either linguistic or extralinguistic) can directly guide the on-line computation of grammatical form remains controversial (Seidenberg and Tanenhaus 1986; Tyler 1987).

But wherever the boundaries of the language module are drawn, the fact remains that the assignment of syntactic representations by purely language-internal algorithms constitutes the core of verbal comprehension. As Merrill Garrett once remarked, it is the grammar that enables us to say the unexpected and to be understood when we do so. And it is the central syntactic processes that are so often compromised by damage to the left perisylvian region of the brain.

Disorders of Syntactic Comprehension is the first major monograph to investigate in detail the nature of aphasic miscomprehension within this core domain. David Caplan and Nancy Hildebrandt set their studies in the context of an explicit, modular theory of grammatical structure (Chomsky 1985) and an equally explicit parsing model for the recovery of syntactic form (Berwick and Weinberg 1985a,b). The relationship between Chomsky's Government and Binding theory and the Berwick-Weinberg parser, whereby the parsing algorithms mirror quite directly the rules and representations of the grammar, allows Caplan and Hildebrandt to analyze the particular representations that a malfunctioning parser may fail to construct in individual patients. Their general (group) results demonstrate that the number of verbs, the number of thematic roles associated with each verb, and the presence of noncanonical word order all contribute additively to sentence difficulty; but Caplan and Hildebrandt can also show, for example, that some patients have specific deficits in the coindexing of phonetically empty categories (*John promised Bill* [PRO *to shave*], where *John* is the subject of *shave*), or that other patients have difficulty in indexing phonetically overt referentially dependent noun phrases (*John kicked himself* versus *John kicked him*, where pronoun and reflexive respectively indicate coreference and noncoreference with the subject of the sentence). The finding that the correct interpretation of pronouns and reflexives can be doubly dissociated in pairs of patients is of particular value, as it is predicted by the Berwick-Weinberg parser, which employs different search algorithms for finding the antecedents of these elements.

Caplan and Hildebrandt's case studies also contribute to the understanding of the role that short-term (working) memory plays in sentence comprehension (see Butterworth et al. 1986). In the case of one patient (B.O.), they provide convincing evidence that parsing *per se* can be intact despite a severe short-term-memory impairment; the comprehension impairment in this case appears to implicate a post-parsing limitation on the ability to hold noun phrases in memory while planning an appropriate response (see Hamburger and Crain 1984). This result, combined with the interactions seen in other patients between general parsing load and difficulty with particular syntactic constructions, strongly suggests that the memory buffering utilized in parsing is specific to the syntactic module.

None of Caplan and Hildebrandt's important results could have been obtained had they not tested an extensive range of theoretically motivated sentence types, had they not used an "acting-out" technique that enables the patient to make his own types of errors (rather than restricting the possible errors by employing forced-choice sentence-picture matching), and had they not derived their processing hypotheses from the operation of a formal deterministic parser.

It will no longer suffice merely to distinguish between heuristically driven and linguistically driven comprehension in the aphasias. Caplan and Hildebrandt have shown how fine-grained proposals about breakdown within particular grammatical modules can be formulated and tested. Their results demonstrate, for example, how the patient's adoption of heuristic strategies for comprehension (e.g., assign the thematic roles Agent, Theme, and Goal to the nouns in linear Noun + Verb + Noun (+ Preposition + Noun) strings, irrespective of phrasal structure) arises when *specific* parsing operations can no longer be carried out. And evidence is outlined to suggest that language-specific parameters may, in part, determine which thematic roles are assigned to linear sequences of lexical categories when hierarchical parsing fails.

Caplan and Hildebrandt's findings also speak to the neuronal realization of syntactic parsing functions. At the level of gross anatomy, their correlations between lesion site and behavioral impairment provide no support for the traditional view that posterior (perisylvian) lesions are more disruptive of comprehension than anterior lesions. Within the perisylvian region, they find no constant association between locus of damage and nature or extent of syntactic-comprehension disorder; neither do they find any correlation between syntactic-comprehension disorder and patients' diagnostic labels within the Wernicke-Lichtheim taxonomy. Caplan and Hildebrandt are thus led to the provocative conclusion that, in terms of both site and extent, the work space for syntactic computations is *variably* localized within perisylvian cortex across the adult population. Mass action, equipotentiality, and the Wernicke-Lichtheim model all seem equally incapable of accounting for Caplan and Hildebrandt's results.

In short, with respect to both functional and anatomical analysis, *Disorders of Syntactic Comprehension* sets new standards for the interpretation of aphasic comprehension disorder.

Ansell, B. J., and C. R. Flowers. 1982. Aphasic adults' use of heuristic and structural linguistic cues for sentence analysis. *Brain and Language* 16: 61–72.

Auerbach, S. H., T. Allard, M. Naeser, M. P. Alexander, and M. L. Albert. 1982. Pure word deafness: Analysis of a case with bilateral lesions and a deficit at the prephonemic level. *Brain* 105: 271–300.

Basso, A., E. Capitani, and L. A. Vignolo. 1979. Influence of rehabilitation on language skills in aphasic patients: A controlled study. *Archives of Neurology* 36: 190–196.

Berwick, R. C., and A. S. Weinberg. 1985a. Deterministic parsing and linguistic explanation. *Language and Cognitive Processes* 1: 109–134.

Berwick, R. C., and A. S. Weinberg. 1985b. The psychological relevance of transformational grammars: A reply to Stabler. *Cognition* 19: 193–204.

Brownell, H. H., H. H. Potter, A. M. Bihrle, and H. Gardner. 1986. Inference deficits in right brain-damaged patients. *Brain and Language* 27: 310–321.

Butterworth, B., R. Campbell, and D. Howard. 1986. The uses of short-term memory: A case study. *Quarterly Journal of Experimental Psychology* 38A: 705–737.

Byng, S., and M. Coltheart. 1986. Aphasia therapy research: Methodological requirements and illustrative results. In *Communication and Handicap*, ed. E. Hjelmquist and L.-G. Nilsson (Amsterdam: North-Holland).

Cannito, M. P., J. M. Jarecki, and R. S. Pierce. 1986. Effects of thematic structure on syntactic comprehension in aphasia. *Brain and Language* 27: 38–49.

Caramazza, A., and E. B. Zurif. 1976. Dissociation of algorithmic and heuristic processes in language comprehension. *Brain and Language* 3: 572–582.

Chomsky, N. 1985. *Knowledge of Language: Its Nature, Origin, and Use.* New York: Praeger.

Coslett, H. B., H. R. Brashear, and K. M. Heilman. 1984. Pure word deafness after bilateral primary auditory cortex infarcts. *Neurology* 34: 347–352.

de Bleser, R., and J. Bayer. 1985. German word formation and aphasia. *Linguistic Review* 5: 1–40.

Ellis, A. W. 1984. Introduction to Byrom Branwell's (1897) case of word meaning deafness. *Cognitive Neuropsychology* 1: 245–258.

Hamburger, H., and S. Crain. 1984. Acquisition of cognitive compiling. *Cognition* 17: 85–136.

Heilman, K. M., and R. J. Scholes. 1976. The nature of comprehension errors in Broca's, conduction, and Wernicke's aphasics. *Cortex* 12: 258–265.

Howard, D. 1986. Beyond randomised controlled trials: The case for effective case studies of the effects of treatment in aphasia. *British Journal of Disorders of Communication* 21: 89–102.

Kertesz, A. 1984. Recovery from aphasia. In *Progress in Aphasiology*, ed. F. C. Rose (New York: Raven).

Kohn, S. E., and R. B. Friedman. 1986. Word-meaning deafness: A phonological-semantic dissociation. *Cognitive Neuropsychology* 3: 291–308.

Kudo, T. 1984. The effect of semantic plausibility on sentence comprehension in aphasia. *Brain and Language* 21: 208–218.

Marshall, J. C. 1985. A fruit by any other name. *Nature* 316: 388.

Marshall, J. C. 1986. The description and interpretation of aphasic language disorder. *Neuropsychologia* 24: 5–24.

McDonald, S., and R. Wales. 1986. An investigation of the ability to process inferences in language following right hemisphere brain damage. *Brain and Language* 29: 68–80.

Schwartz, M. F., E. M. Saffran, and O. S. M. Marin. 1980. The word order problem in agrammatism. 1. Comprehension. *Brain and Language* 10: 249–262.

Seidenberg, M. S., and M. K. Tanenhaus. 1986. Modularity and lexical access. In *From Models to Modules: Studies in Cognitive Science*, ed. I. Gopnik and M. Gopnik (London: Ablex).

Shallice, T. 1987. Impairments of semantic processing: multiple dissociations. In *The Cognitive Neuropsychology of Language*, ed. M. Coltheart, G. Sartori, and R. Job (London: Erlbaum).

Tyler, L. K. 1987. Spoken language comprehension in aphasia: A real-time processing perspective. In *The Cognitive Neuropsychology of Language*, ed. M. Coltheart, G. Sartori, and R. Job (London: Erlbaum).

Wegner, M. L., R. H. Brookshire, and L. E. Nicholas. 1984. Comprehension of main ideas and details in coherent and noncoherent discourse by aphasic and nonaphasic listeners. *Brain and Language* 21: 37–51.

Preface

Syntactic structures are domain- and species-specific mental representations that are crucial to the assignment of important aspects of sentence meaning. The investigation of disturbances in the processing of these structures that are due to neurogenic disease acquired in adult life holds the promise of making two significant contributions to our understanding of human psychology.

First, because the formal aspects of syntactic structure have been characterized in considerable detail, and because we now have computer-implemented models of some of the psychological processes involved in assigning and interpreting these structures, the study of disorders of syntactic comprehension is a domain in which rather detailed theories of psycholinguistic deficits and theories of the functional compensations for these deficits can be developed and empirically justified. Thus, the study of disorders of syntactic comprehension is a domain in which formal aspects of human cognitive psychopathology can be studied in detail. Though this domain is necessarily formally different from other domains of human psychopathology (owing to the structural specificity of syntactic structures and to the attendant unique aspects of their processing), several general principles regarding the nature of breakdowns in other formal domains of human psychology may be suggested by the study of breakdowns in this domain.

The second possible contribution is to our understanding of the neurological basis for the representation and processing of syntactic structures. By correlating deficits affecting specific syntactic structures, specific processing procedures, and the "computational space" in which syntactic comprehension is carried out with specific parameters of neurological lesions, we can begin to develop an empirically supported theory of the neural basis for the representation and processing of syntax. Through the study of how these deficit-lesion correlations vary in subgroups of the human population as a function of organic and experiential factors such as age, sex, handedness, education, and literacy, we can begin to develop a theory of the genetic, maturational, and environmental determinants of the neural basis of the functions involved in syntactic comprehension. To the extent that these functions are uniquely human, representative of other formal computational psychological functions in humans, and crucial to communicative functions, we will thereby be contributing to a theory of the neural basis of a function that is one of the factors making for human intellectual uniqueness and human ecological success.

These two promises—the detailed study of one possibly representative aspect of human cognitive psychopathology and a more detailed understanding of the neural basis for a unique and critical human cognitive capacity—are the principal foci of the work reported in this book. To a lesser extent, our study also bears on the nature of the linguistic representation of syntax itself and on theories of the recovery of syntactic form in the process of auditory comprehension.

This book presents the results of investigations into disturbances of syntactic comprehension undertaken in the Neurolinguistics Laboratory of the Montreal Neurological Institute. The work relies heavily on theories of the linguistic representation of syntactic structure developed in theoretical linguistics and on computer-based models of natural-language parsing, and to a lesser extent on psycholinguistic studies of parsing. Since the mid 1970s a number of studies of syntactic-comprehension disorders have appeared in the literature on aphasia. Though none of these studies are as empirically detailed or as committed to specific parsing models as the work presented here, they do present data and a number of hypotheses that are relevant to the nature and the causes of disturbances in syntactic comprehension. We present our own results in the context of these studies of linguistic representations, parsing, and language disorders. In the introduction we present an overview of our subject and of the basic framework within which we approach the characterization of disorders of syntactic comprehension. In chapters 1 and 2 we present essential background material regarding linguistic theory and parsing models. In chapter 3 we review previous work on syntactic-comprehension disorders, highlighting relevant issues that have arisen in the literature on aphasia. In chapter 4 we present our survey work, in which we explore the basic features of syntactic comprehension in large, unselected aphasic populations. In chapter 5 we present several detailed individual case studies. In chapter 6 we present the principal conclusions of the work, focusing on the basic psychopathological mechanisms involved in determining disturbances of syntactic comprehension, on their neural basis, and on the implications of this research for theories of normal language structure and processing and of the neural foundations of language.

We would like to acknowledge the contributions of many researchers to the genesis of the ideas developed in this book. In particular, we wish to recognize the contributions made by Dan Bub, Alfonso Caramazza, Merrill Garrett, Yosef Grodzinsky, Celia Jakubowitz, John Marshall, Eleanor Saffran, Myrna Schwartz, Mark Seidenberg, Amy Weinberg, and Edgar Zurif to our understanding of the questions we address here. We are indebted to Rhonda Amsel and Francois Dehaut for their help with statistical matters, and to Gloria Waters for her discussions and collaboration on research concerning the nature of short-term memory, its disorders, and the relationship between short-term memory and disturbances of syntactic comprehension. We appreciate the institutional support afforded by the Montreal Neurological Institute and the departments of linguistics and neurology and neurosurgery at McGill University, and the rich and critical interchanges we have had with members of the neurolinguistics group at the MNI. This work was supported in part by grants from the Medical Research Council of Canada (program grant 28, project 7; operating grant MA8602; operating grant MA9761), by an establishment grant from the Fonds de Recherches en Santé du Québec, and by a Chercheur Boursier Senior Award to David Caplan from the Fonds de Recherches en Santé du Québec. We thank our research assistants—Catherine Baker, Karen Evans, and Janet Steer, in particular—for their invaluable help in gathering the data. We are grateful to the speech-pathology staffs of the Montreal Neurological Hospital, the Montreal General Hospital, the Lethbridge Rehabilitation Hospital, the Institut de Réadaptation de Montréal, the Jewish Rehabilitation Hospital of Montreal, the Royal Ottawa Regional Rehabilitation Hospital, and the Ottawa Civic Hospital for referring patients and making testing facilities available. Finally, we wish to thank the patients who participated in these studies, and we hope that these investigations ultimately lead to diagnostic and therapeutic instruments that will help them and similarly affected individuals.

Disorders of Syntactic Comprehension

Introduction

The studies presented in this book consist of a number of investigations of the performance of unselected groups of aphasic patients on a task requiring the comprehension of syntactic form and a series of detailed individual studies of selected patients in which linguistic and processing analyses of performance on these tasks are developed. In this introduction we shall present some of the theoretical and methodological background to these studies from the point of view of aphasiology, leaving more detailed descriptions of linguistic theory, parsing models, previous work in this area, and specific aspects of experimental design to later chapters.

Sentences convey information that is not conveyed by words in isolation. Thematic roles (who is doing what to whom), attribution of modification (which adjectives are predicated of which nouns), scope of quantification (what verbs, nouns, and adjectives fall within the scope of quantifiers such as elements of negation), determination of coreference (what nouns are referred to by pronouns, reflexives, and other referentially dependent noun phrases), and other aspects of sentence meaning are not conveyed by words in isolation; they arise only when words are structured into phrases and sentences. Syntactic structure either determines or significantly constrains the possible assignment of these aspects of sentential semantic meaning. For instance, the assignment of thematic roles in a sentence is a function of the syntax of the sentence and the lexical features of the verb in the sentence. Informally, we may say that, in sentence 1, *John* is taken as Agent and *Mary* as Theme, because *John* and *Mary* occupy the position of subject and object in a sentence with a transitive verb in the active voice.

(1) John kissed Mary.

The syntactic structure in which the proper nouns *John* and *Mary* are found is a critical formal aspect of the representation of sentence form; it determines the assignment of thematic roles. The particular aspects of syntactic structure that determine or constrain thematic roles, attribution of modification, coreference, and so forth are different for different semantic properties of sentences. We shall discuss the structural aspects of syntax that are relevant to the features of sentence meaning we have studied in more formal terms in chapter 1.

The present study is an outgrowth of current work in linguistic aphasiology. In the 1970s, researchers demonstrated that some aphasic patients were unable to appreciate certain aspects of sentence meaning (notably thematic roles) in sentences in which the interpretation of syntactic structure was necessary for these aspects of meaning to be correctly assigned, but that the same patients retained the ability to appreciate these aspects of meaning when they could be inferred directly from the individual meanings of the words in the sentence and knowledge about possible and probable events in the real world. For instance, Caramazza and Zurif (1976) demonstrated that some patients could not understand the thematic roles in the first (relative) clause in sentence 2, but could do so in the first clause of sentence 3.

(2) The boy the girl was chasing is tall.

(3) The apple the boy is eating is red.

In sentence 2, Agency and Theme cannot be assigned on the basis of real-world knowledge and the meanings of the noun phrases *the boy*, *the girl*, and the verb *chasing*, since both boys and girls are capable of chasing the other. Thus, to understand the first clause in sentence 2 a subject must assign and interpret a syntactic structure. In sentence 3, an understanding of the words *the boys*, *the apple*, and *eating*, coupled with an appreciation that boys are animate objects that can eat and apples inanimate objects that can be eaten, is sufficient to allow the pragmatic inference that the boy is doing the eating. Some of the patients described by Caramazza and Zurif were able to accomplish these pragmatic inferences on the basis of individual word meanings but were unable to use syntactic structure to assign meaning correctly when this "lexico-pragmatic" route to meaning was insufficient. We informally term the process of assigning and interpreting syntactic structure *syntactic comprehension*, and we refer to patients who cannot use syntactic structure normally to assign aspects of sentential meaning as having a *syntactic-comprehension disturbance*. The hallmark of a syntactic-comprehension disturbance is the failure to assign aspects of sentential semantic meanings correctly in sentences that are logically and pragmatically semantically reversible when interpreted solely by a lexico-pragmatic route. Thus, disturbances of syntactic comprehension are discovered and explored by investigating patients' interpretations of "semantically reversible" sentences (such as sentence 2). In the work reported here, we examined patients' abilities to interpret these types of sentences by varying the syntactic structure and the semantic feature to be assigned across different sentence types to arrive at more specific accounts of the psychopathogenesis of abnormalities of this function.

In recent years, reseachers have used increasingly sophisticated linguistic descriptions to describe impairments of syntactic comprehension in particular patient populations, such as patients with agrammatism. (See, e.g., Grodzinsky 1984, 1986.) These studies, while moving in the same direction as the present work, fall short of attacking the problem of syntactic comprehension from the perspective of theories of the process of assigning and interpreting syntactic structure (i.e., parsing). In addition, the database in most of these studies is extremely limited, both with respect to the syntactic and semantic features being investigated and with respect to the number and types of patients being tested. The studies reported in this volume extend the syntactic-comprehension database to a large number of patients in many diagnostic groups in the survey work, and to a large number of sentence types in the study of individual cases.

The group studies have several goals. One is to delineate the linguistic regularities in overall group performance of aphasic patients in the area of syntactic comprehension. Another is to determine whether particular disturbances of syntactic comprehension are specific to particular patient groups, and how these disturbances relate to patients' other impairments. A third goal is to determine whether particular disturbances of syntactic comprehension are due to particular types of neurological lesions in particular areas of the brain.

The primary goal of the case studies is to provide detailed descriptions of deficits of syntactic comprehension in linguistic and processing terms. We describe and attempt to formulate generalizations concerning the specific linguistic structures assigned and interpreted by patients and concerning the impairments affecting the assignment of particular linguistic structures and the utilization of particular parsing operations in each case. We focus on the assignment of thematic roles to noun phrases, on the coindexation of referentially dependent noun phrases (pronouns, reflexives, and more abstract, "empty" NPs in Chomsky's [1981, 1982] theory), and on the construction of hierarchically organized phrase markers—all critical, core aspects of syntactic structure.

In both the group studies and the case studies we are concerned about the ultimate psychological origin of the deficits we describe. In the group studies we approach the question of the origin of these syntactic-comprehension deficits by searching for particular patterns of impairment in groups of patients with other aphasic impairments. The goal of these correlational analyses is to determine whether particular disturbances of syntactic comprehension always occur in conjunction with other aphasic impairments, since such correlations, if they exist, would suggest that the two sets of impairments are related. In the individual case studies, we seek to identify impairments as either "primary" or "secondary" through a detailed internal analysis of each case. We consider primary impairments to be those that are due to intrinsic disturbances and limitations affecting the parsing system, and secondary impairments to be those that arise because of the inability of the parser to utilize other cognitive systems. The particular system that is of special interest is the short-term-memory system, which several researchers have suggested is involved in sentence comprehension. Since auditorily presented sentences consist of sequentially presented words, it is *a priori* reasonable to consider that the short-term-memory system, which stores and allows for retrieval of auditorily presented words, might be involved in sentence comprehension. Part of our study of individual cases is devoted to the question of how these two systems are related.

Thus, the group and single-case portions of our work bear on some similar questions. However, they involve different methodologies. For the most part, group performances are analyzed in two ways: Significant differences in mean correct scores on different sentence types are ascertained for unselected groups of aphasic patients and, in some instances, selected groups of patients; and cluster and discriminant-function analyses of patients and normal control subjects are performed on the basis of performances on individual sentences and sentence types. Informal correlational analyses of groups identified by these cluster and discriminant-function analyses with other parameters (such as aphasia type and neurological lesion) and analyses of predominant error patterns of these unselected groups as a whole and of identified subgroups are also part of the analysis of group data. In contrast, the detailed individual case analyses are based on comparisons of individual patients' performances on particular sentence types with normal performance, on analyses that determine whether the particular pattern of interpretations seen in an individual patient for sentences of a particular type is significantly different from chance, and on analyses that determine whether particular responses and patterns of responses of an individual patient on different sentence types are significantly different from one another in frequency of occurrence. Though a presentation of specific details of statistical methods is not appropriate at this juncture, the basic logic of using group and single-case data in linguistic aphasiology and disorders of syntactic comprehension merits a review at this point.

Group data have two roles to play in the development of theories of cognitive psychopathology.

The first role has to do with the relative complexity of particular structures that are related to "markedness" effects in linguistic theory. Statistically reliable differences in the mean performances of brain-damaged patients with respect to different stimuli reflect the relative complexity of processing of the stimuli in question. Statistically significant differences in mean performance on different structural stimuli do not, in and of themselves, tell us why one stimulus is more difficult than another. There are two possible answers to the question why one stimulus is harder to process than another. The first possible answer is that the processing required by one stimulus consists of the processing required by the second plus some additional processing steps. In this case, we would predict that whenever there is a disturbance in the processing of the second stimulus there will necessarily be a disturbance in the processing of the first. In this case, not only should mean group performance reflect the relative difficulty of the processes associated with these two stimuli, but the generalization that a processing disturbance affecting the second stimulus necessarily entails a disturbance in the processing of the first should hold at the individual-case level as well. For this type of relationship, *any* functional impairment that leads to a deficit affecting the second stimulus will lead to a disturbance of the first. Consequently, establishing the specific deficits that lead to impairment on the second stimulus in each patient in a group is not necessary to establish the relationship between the two stimuli. (This point regarding the use of group data has not been appreciated by the theorists who have recently argued that the only inferences regarding normal function that can be drawn validly from pathological performances are based on analyses of deficits in single cases—see, e.g., Caramazza 1986; in press a; in press b). Group data may play an important role in determining whether a difference truly exists between the processing of two stimuli, since differences may be too small to be revealed by any reasonable number of observations in a single case. The second possible answer is that the processing associated with the first stimulus makes greater demands on "working space" or "processing time" than the processing associated with the second stimulus because the two stimuli are processed in qualitatively different ways. In this case, though we would expect that performance on the first stimulus would be worse on average than performance on the second, we would not necessarily expect every individual patient to show such an effect. Disturbances affecting particular processing mechanisms could, in principle, selectively impair the processing of either the first or the second stimulus in any particular case. Group data may play an important role in determining whether the processing of one structure requires more processing resources than the processing of another, because of the possible existence of specific deficits affecting each stimulus in different patients. We shall discuss this possibility in greater detail immediately below.

The second role of group data is to establish the occurrence of some deficit in a particular population. Suppose we analyze a particular observable performance, O_x, as implying a functional lesion, L_x, in some cognitive system in an individual patient. Then the statistically significant occurrence of O_x in a population establishes the statistically reliable occurrence of L_x in that population. The most important use of these "group deficit analyses" is to establish the co-occurrence of two deficits in a population. If O_x implies L_x and O_y implies L_y in a particular cognitive system, then the co-occurrence of behaviors O_x and O_y in a population implies the co-occurrence of the functional lesions L_x and L_y in that cognitive system in that population. These co-occurrences of deficits have suggested shared components of processing of linguistic structures and/or joint reliance of two separate processes on a single neuroanatomical structure. It is possible to correlate functional deficits with organic parameters directly. Data of this sort can be crucial in fashioning a theory of the neurological basis for a particular language-processing subcomponent.

In the individual case studies, analyses establishing differential frequencies of correct interpretation of different sentence types and statistically significant occurrences of particular error patterns are the basis for an account of the functional deficit in each individual patient in linguistic and parsing terms. These deficit analyses are relevant to linguistic aphasiology as well as to linguistics and parsing, but they are not easy to establish. The account of an observed impairment in syntactic comprehension requires a theory of normal language structures, a theory of normal language processing, a theory of possible deficits, and a theory of adaptations to deficits. We shall briefly outline the role of each of these theories.

The first step in developing an account of an aphasic disturbance of syntactic comprehension is the linguistic description of each patient's performance on syntactic-comprehension tasks. A linguistic description of the aphasic language behavior observed in each patient is important for three reasons. (1) Linguistic theory itself provides a powerful, constrained, and independently motivated basis for describing the observed impairment. This description has a bearing on the nature of any processing (parsing) analysis of the deficit in the following way: A parser assigns syntactic structure to an incoming string of words, assigns thematic roles and other syntactic features, and transfers completed phrases to a semantic level at which further operations (inferential, etc.) can occur. A linguistic theory may be related to a parser in many ways. Berwick and Weinberg (1984) have proposed a relationship between linguistic theory and a parser which they call *type transparency*. In such a relationship, the parser preserves the broad distinctions of linguistic components (phonological, morphological, syntactic, semantic), produces phrase markers (syntactic trees) that are provided by the linguistic theory, and simulates the linguistic constraints specified to apply at each particular linguistic level; however, each linguistic rule need not correspond to a parsing rule. A description of an aphasic patient's performance in linguistic terms has a direct bearing on any parsing analysis of the deficit on the assumption that the parser maintains at least a type-transparent relationship to the linguistic theory. (2) Linguistic theories are sufficiently rich that, once a hypothesis concerning a linguistic impairment has been made, further predictions can be made concerning linguistic items that should also be impaired in a particular patient. (3) A description in linguistic terms is required in order to decide whether a deficit is due to an impairment of linguistic representations (resulting in the patient's losing knowledge of a particular item or class of items) or whether it is due to an impairment at the level of the parsing algorithms that compute these representations.

The characterization of a patient's deficit must refer to a theory of normal processing. This is necessary in order to characterize what processing operations exist that may be impaired and retained in an individual patient. For instance, in some cases a processing operation may be unique to a particular linguistic element or structure; in other cases a processing operation may be performed over a variety of linguistic structures. A deficit affecting a processing operation of the first sort would have consequences in only a restricted domain of linguistic representations, whereas an impairment affecting a processing operation of the second sort would be expected to affect many linguistic structures.

The characterization of an individual patient's deficit must be undertaken within a general theory of possible aphasic deficits. Our approach to such a theory initially recognized three different types of possible impairments: (1) A patient who shows a consistent inability to comprehend sentences with a particular linguistic element or structure has an impairment affecting the linguistic representation itself. (2) A patient who shows consistent inability to comprehend sentences requiring a particular parsing operation is analyzed as having difficulty at the level of parsing algorithms; a patient who shows variable difficulty with respect to a particular linguistic representation also is said to have a disturbance affecting processing, not permanent linguistic representations. (3) A patient may have a limitation in the overall "capacity" or "work space" that can be devoted to the task of parsing. With such a limitation, a patient would produce correct responses with respect to particular linguistic items or parsing operations in simple sentences but not in more complex structures, and in such a case it would be of interest to examine what the particular sources of complexity are in the sentences that cause difficulty and whether particular processes are more likely than others to break down when the capacity is exceeded.

Finally, an analysis of a patient's performance must include a specification of the adaptations a patient makes to his primary deficit, and such a characterization must fall within the domain of a theory of adaptations. For example, a patient's use of a particular heuristic to compensate for an inability to assign structure in a particular sentence might happen to generate the correct response to that sentence. In this case, the patient would be achieving the right result for the wrong reason, and the conclusion that he was able to parse a particular sentence correctly would be unwarranted despite a high level of accuracy on that sentence type. Thus, before concluding that an observed dissociation in response accuracies for two different sentence types reflects selective impairment of different functional components of a parser, one must eliminate the possibility that, in a sentence type with high accuracy, a heuristic is fortuitously producing the correct response.

Once an analysis of an individual patient's performance in terms of linguistic and parsing theory and the theory of deficits and adaptations is available, the portion of the analysis that pertains to the deficit itself can be used to verify aspects of the initial theory of linguistic structure and parsing on which the analysis was based. In this task, dissociations in the ability to interpret sentences that can be analyzed as reflecting deficits pertaining to particular linguistic representations or to particular parsing processes constitute empirical evidence of the separate existence of the affected representations and processes.

A series of contrastive case studies enhance the conclusions that can be drawn from the data by constraining the number of possible accounts for each case to those that are compatible with all relevant cases. Furthermore, two contrastive cases are required to reveal "double dissociations," in which (for example) one patient shows a deficit referable to one parsing operation but sparing a second and a second patient shows a deficit affecting the second parsing operation but sparing the first. Double dissociations indicate that each of the two parsing operations contains at least one processing subcomponent not found in the other. A single dissociation, in which a patient (or a series of patients) shows a disturbance in one linguistic representation or one parsing process but retains the ability to accomplish another parsing operation, shows that one subcomponent of the first process is separately disturbable, but not that the two processes each have separate subcomponents.

The implications of single and double dissociations of performances on particular sentence types are interpretable with respect to components of the normal system of representations and processing only when these dissociations in performance can be analyzed as deficits affecting representations or processes. Thus, raw data in the form of dissociations of performance over sentence types does not, in and of itself, speak to the nature of normal systems. Such data must be entered into a theory of normal language structure and processing and of aphasic deficits and adaptations before the deficit analyses that result from the data can be said to constitute evidence relevant to linguistic and parsing theory. In this study, we analyze cases in sufficient detail for such implications to be drawn.

In summary: This book presents the results of a number of group and case studies of disorders of syntactic comprehension—studies that employed different analytic techniques and revealed a variety of features of these psychopathological phenomena. The results illustrate how one formal domain of human cognitive psychology breaks down, and may serve as a model of the general nature of breakdown in other functional spheres. They have implications for aspects of normal language structure and processing, and for models of the neural basis of syntactic representations and their processing.

Chapter 1

Syntactic Structures in Linguistic Theory

In linguistic theory there are a number of different levels at which operations occur. Levels are distinguished by the fact that operations occur on different sets of representations, which may be subject to different sets of principles and constraints. The phonological level deals with relations among sounds, the morphological level with relations among subcomponents of words, the syntactic level with hierarchical relations among words in a sentence, and the semantic level with meaning; the lexical level refers to the permanent representation of words, with their associated meanings and their inherent grammatical properties.

The syntactic level of representation exists as the means of relating a linear string of words to the semantic reading of a sentence. Chomsky (1957) argued that a distinction between syntactic and semantic levels is necessary in order to distinguish between violations of subcategorization restrictions and violations of selectional restrictions. For example, *Colorless green ideas sleep furiously* is grammatical but violates selectional restrictions (e.g., that the thing sleeping must be animate), whereas *John danced Mary* violates the subcategorization of the verb (*dance* is intransitive).

This distinction between syntax and semantics is strictly upheld in the Government and Binding (GB) theory of syntactic structures (Chomsky 1981). Lexical items are inserted into a syntactic D-structure. Generalized transformations occur freely to produce an S-structure. This S-structure is converted into a restricted semantic representation (at the level of Logical Form) and a phonological representation (at the level of Phonological Form). At the levels of Logical Form and Phonological Form, various constraints apply that will eliminate ungrammatical and uninterpretable sentences that may have been generated by the free occurrence of operations at the syntactic level.

The semantic values of lexical items must be carried through the syntax in order to be utilized at the level of Logical Form. The distinction between the grammatical and semantic functions of thematic roles provides a good illustration of the distinction in levels. In an intuitive sense, sentences represent the relations between predicates and their arguments. For example, in a sentence like *John ate the apple, eat* is the predicate, the thing doing the eating is *John*, and the thing being eaten is *the apple*. These relations of the noun phrases (NPs) to the verb are called *thematic relations*, or *thematic roles*. In the sentence under discussion, *John* is the Agent of the verb, and *the apple* is the Theme of the verb. At the lexical level, each item that can be used as a predicate bears information concerning the number and type of thematic roles it must assign. At the syntactic level, once a D-structure has been created, the predicate assigns its associated thematic roles to particular grammatical positions in the sentence, but this assignment is not contingent on the thematic roles' semantic content (Levin and Rappaport 1986; Williams 1981). For example, a transitive verb will have two thematic roles to assign: one to a noun phrase within the verb phrase and the other to a noun phrase outside the verb phrase (the subject). These roles can be assigned to structural positions without any knowledge of the semantic content of these thematic roles. At the level of Logical Form, the semantic values of the thematic roles are interpreted along with selectional restrictions (e.g., the requirement of animacy) and the semantic features of the arguments themselves. We will use the term *theta role* to refer to the assignment that occurs at the syntactic level, and *thematic role* or *thematic relation* to refer to the interpretation that occurs at the semantic level. (Because of the unimportance of the semantic content of the thematic roles at the syntactic level, we will use the term *Agent* to refer to the NP doing the action throughout, even in cases in which another name may be more appropriate on semantic grounds. For example, we will call *John* the Agent in *John believes* and *John dances*. With the sentence types we tested, nothing hinges on this relaxation of terminology.)

There are many linguistic lines of evidence that show that a syntactic level of representation is necessary and that this separation between syntactic and semantic levels is desirable. We will concentrate on three: displaced constituents, hierarchical organization of constituents, and referential dependencies. We will then concentrate on how referential dependencies are treated within Government and Binding theory and other linguistic theories.

Displaced Constituents

Thematic roles such as Agent and Theme can be associated with arguments that appear in a number of different grammatical positions. For instance, *John* is the Agent and *apple* is the Theme of the verb *eat* in each of sentences 1–5.

(1) John ate the apple.   (active)
(2) It was John that ate the apple.   (cleft subject)
(3) It was the apple that John ate.   (cleft object)

(4) I provided the apple that John ate.   (relative clause)
(5) The apple, John ate (but not the pear).   (topicalized)

If *what* is substituted for *the apple*, as in sentence 6, we still know that it is the Theme, even though we do not know the referent.

(6) What did John eat?

Moreover, *what* can be separated from the verb by an indefinite distance, and we still know that it is the Theme of *eat*, as sentence 7 shows.

(7) What did Bill believe that Mary thought that Peter suspected that John ate?

These examples show that in linguistic theory (and, ultimately, in a parsing model), there must be some mechanism of theta-role assignment to ensure that the thematic roles of the predicate are associated with the correct NPs. This mechanism cannot be based merely on pragmatic likelihood, since it applies even when the NPs are semantically reversible (as in sentences such as *John kissed Mary*). Theta-role assignment differs according to different theories of syntactic structure. In GB theory (Chomsky 1981, 1982), theta roles are assigned to particular grammatical positions. For example, *eat* will assign one of its theta roles (Agent) to the subject NP and its other theta role (Theme) to the direct-object NP, thus producing the correct interpretation for sentence 1. However, in the surface strings shown in sentences 2–5, at least one of the NPs is not in the proper structural position to receive the proper assignment of Agent and Theme. In GB theory, each NP argument is inserted at D-structure into the grammatical position in which the proper theta role is directly assigned. These NPs can then undergo movement to a new position, and at S-structure they remain linked with their previous NP positions by means of an empty (phonologically null) place holder, called a *trace*. For example, the phrase markers (syntactic trees) for the two levels of representation for sentence 6 are shown in diagrams 8 and 9. (Details of the representation of the inflection and auxiliary verbs have been omitted.)

As diagram 8 shows, *what* originates in the direct-object position, which is assigned Theme by the verb *eat*, and subsequently moves to the complementizer position (abbreviated as COMP) in diagram 9, leaving behind an empty trace (t), with which it is linked. Thus, the theta role of *what* in sentence 7 is determined through its link with the direct-object position at S-structure. Because of the movement of the *wh*-word, it is called a *displaced constituent*.

Sentences 2–5 are handled in the same fashion. In each case, an NP moves to a position that is not directly assigned a theta role—either a COMP or a TOPIC position—and is linked with a trace in a position that

(8) D-structure:

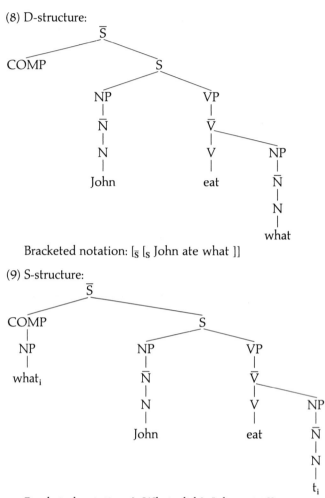

Bracketed notation: [s̄ [s John ate what]]

(9) S-structure:

Bracketed notation: [s̄ What$_i$ did [s John eat t$_i$]]

has been assigned the correct theta role. The S-structure representations of (2)–(5) are given in (10)–(13), respectively.

(10) Cleft subject:
It was John [s̄ that$_i$ [s t$_i$ ate the apple]]
(11) Cleft object:
It was the apple [s̄ that$_i$ [s John ate t$_i$]]
(12) Relative clause:
I provided the apple [s̄ that$_i$ [s John ate t$_i$]]
(13) Topic:
[TOPIC The apple$_i$ [s John ate t$_i$]]

In addition to the coindexing between the NP in COMP and the trace in (10)–(12), the NP in COMP must be linked to the head of the subordinate clause (*John* in example 10 and *the apple* in examples 11 and 12). In GB theory, this linking between head and complement occurs through a semantic rule of predication.

In summary: In Government and Binding theory, theta roles are assigned to particular positions in the syntactic structure, and moved NPs are linked to these positions. The surface string of words in a sentence is related to two levels of syntactic representation: S-structure and D-structure. The entire set of representations allows for a parsimonious statement of how NPs are associated with the proper thematic roles. We shall return later in this chapter to how other theories deal with the surface variation in the realization of theta roles, and in the next chapter we shall describe the Berwick-Weinberg parser, whose output is the set of S-structure representations in GB theory.

Hierarchical Constraints on Linking

In considering example 7, we noted that a constituent can apparently move far from the position to which its theta role is assigned. Not all such long-distance movements result in grammatical sentences, however. Reference to a syntactic level of representation must be made in order to discriminate between grammatical and ungrammatical cases of "unbounded dependencies." An NP can move into a remote COMP position and result in a grammatical sentence in some cases, such as (7), but not in others, such as (14).

(14) *What$_i$ did John throw the picture of t$_i$ into the trash?

In GB theory, an NP may move freely into any position, and a set of interlocking filters and conditions rules out structures in which such free movement would result in ungrammatical sentences. One of these conditions is the "subjacency condition," which states that an empty NP and a moved NP cannot be linked over more than two "bounding nodes." In English, both S and NP are bounding nodes. As can be seen by the phrase marker in diagram 15, the sentence will be rejected as ungrammatical because the NP *what* and the empty NP are more than two bounding nodes apart. (The bounding nodes are circled.)

However, sentence 7 is not rejected, because *what* has moved into each successive COMP node in the embedded sentences and has left behind a trace, with the result that there are two or fewer bounding nodes between each two links in the chain. The existence of a "chain" of traces in successive COMP positions is evidenced by the fact that the sentence becomes ungrammatical when another *wh*-word fills one of the necessary COMP

(15) *What did John throw a picture of into the trash?

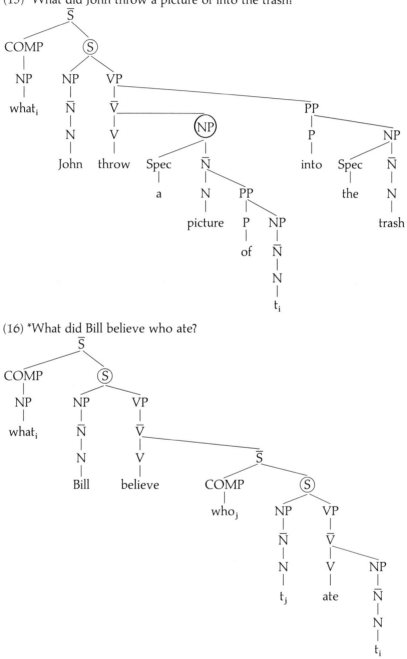

(16) *What did Bill believe who ate?

positions and results in one of the links crossing more than two bounding nodes, as diagram 16 shows.

In summary: Not only can the constraints on the distance over which an NP may move be formulated in terms of hierarchical features of syntactic structure, but it is difficult to imagine a set of constraints at some other level that would account for the ungrammaticality of sentences like that in diagram 16.

The existence of hierarchical organization in syntactic structures can also be seen by considering how certain linear sequences of words are interpreted. In sentence 17, for instance, the substring *the cat ate the cheese* is not understood as a proposition, despite the fact that, by itself, it constitutes a well-formed and interpretable structure.

(17) The dog that chased the cat ate the cheese.

This is so because *the cat* is structurally separated from *ate the cheese*, in that it is part of a relative clause and has been assigned the theta role of Theme by the verb *chased*. Thus, hierarchical aspects of syntactic structure determine aspects of sentence meaning (thematic roles, in this case—we shall consider coreference below) as well as aspects of sentence well-formedness.

Referential Dependencies and the Binding Theory

In the first section of this chapter it was shown that in Government and Binding theory some NPs must be related to an empty grammatical position in order to determine their thematic relation to the verb. The linking between the moved NP and the empty trace can be called a *referential dependency*. A referential dependency, for purposes of this book, will be defined as an NP that depends on another NP for its interpretation. For the empty NPs described above, the interpretation of the correct thematic role of the moved NP depends on its link with the empty NP.

There are other types of referential dependencies than that between a moved NP and its trace. The referents of certain words (which we will call overt NPs, in distinction to the empty NPs discussed above), such as the reflexive *himself*, can be determined only through their relation with an antecedent. For example, in the sentence *A friend of John's kicked himself*, *friend* is the Agent and *himself* is the Theme, but the referent of *himself* can be determined only from the knowledge that the antecedent of *himself* is *friend*.

Overt referentially dependent NPs can be divided into two broad types —reflexives and pronouns—by virtue of the fact that they obey different syntactic constraints on the choice of an antecedent. The possible antecedents of a reflexive and a pronoun are generally in complementary distribution, in that a reflexive *must* be coindexed with a specified NP in the sentence while a pronoun can be coindexed with any pragmatically acceptable NP except this NP, as examples 18–22 show. (Ungrammatical sentences due to disallowed coreference are indicated by an asterisk.)

(18) John told Bill [$_{\bar{s}}$ that [$_s$ a friend$_i$ of Peter's shaved himself$_i$]]
(19) *John told Bill [$_{\bar{s}}$ that [$_s$ a friend of Peter's$_i$ shaved himself$_i$]]
(20) *John told Bill$_i$ [$_{\bar{s}}$ that [$_s$ a friend of Peter's shaved himself$_i$]]
(21) *John$_i$ told Bill [$_{\bar{s}}$ that [$_s$ a friend of Peter's shaved himself$_i$]]
(22) *John told Bill [$_{\bar{s}}$ that [$_s$ a friend$_i$ of Peter's shaved him$_i$]]

In sentence 18, *himself* is correctly coindexed with another NP in the embedded sentence. Sentence 19 shows that not just any antecedent in the embedded clause is appropriate. Sentences 20 and 21 show that *himself* cannot have an antecedent outside the embedded sentence. On the other hand, sentence 22 shows that the antecedent of the pronoun cannot refer to *friend*, the same NP to which the reflexive must refer. Beyond this restriction, the pronoun can refer to any other NP in the sentence, or to an NP mentioned in a previous sentence, or directly to a pragmatic antecedent (one that was not mentioned but can be inferred from the situation).

These constraints on possible NPs for reflexives and pronouns can be stated with respect to the hierarchical structure of the constituents in the sentence. Reflexives must have as their antecedent a c-commanding NP within a specified local domain. The term *c-command* refers to a dominance relation. There are several definitions of c-command; for the present level of exposition we will adopt the simple definition given in (23).

(23) Node A c(constituent)-commands node B if and only if the branching node most immediately dominating A also dominates B.   (Reinhart 1983, p. 18)

Diagram 24—the phrase marker of sentence 18—illustrates c-command.

The nodes have been numbered for convenience. Each node labeled N is the head of the NP dominating it, just as each V is the head of the dominating VP. The first branching node dominating NP3 is S2; in turn, S2 dominates VP2 and all the rest of the nodes under VP2. Therefore, NP3 c-commands NP5. In this sentence, the local domain consists of all the nodes dominated by S2. (We will describe below how the local domain is determined.) NP1 also c-commands NP5, but NP1 lies outside the appropriate local domain. The genitive NP4 *Peter's* does not c-command NP5, since its first dominating branching node is the PP, which does not dominate NP5; therefore, the NP4 *Peter's* cannot be the antecedent of *himself*. Thus, *himself* must have *friend* as its antecedent. The constraint on pronouns, informally stated, is that a pronoun may have as its antecedent any NP except a c-commanding NP within a specified local domain. Thus, if *him* is substituted for *himself* in (24), the local domain is still the set of nodes domi-

(24)

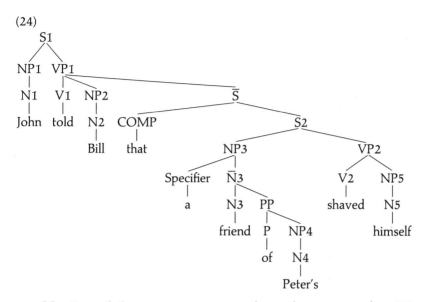

nated by S2, and the pronoun may not refer to the c-commanding NP3 (namely *friend*). As mentioned above, it is difficult to imagine a formulation of these constraints that does not make reference to a syntactic level of representation.

These constraints on various types of referential dependencies have been set down in a subset of the grammar called the Binding theory, which defines the syntactic domains within which particular types of referentially dependent NPs must be or may not be bound. The principles of the Binding theory (Chomsky 1982, p. 20) are the following.

(25) Principle A: An anaphor is bound in its governing category.
     Principle B: A pronominal is free in its governing category.
     Principle C: An R-expression is free.

The term *anaphor* includes reflexives (*himself*) and reciprocals (*each other*), and Principle A states that they must be coindexed with a c-commanding NP within a particular domain—namely, the nodes dominated by the governing category. Government is essentially a structural relation between two nodes. The governing category of a node is defined as the minimal S or NP containing that particular node and the node governing it (Chomsky 1982, p. 20). An NP is bound if it is coindexed with a c-commanding NP. Here, the term is short for *A-bound*, meaning that the c-commanding NP must be in a position that can be assigned a theta role, if the predicate has one to assign. Take as an example the sentence given in (24). V2 governs its complement NP5, and S2 is the governing category for NP5, since it is the minimal S or NP containing both V2 and NP5;

therefore, by Principle A, NP5 must be coindexed with a c-commanding NP that is also dominated by S2. In (24), then, the anaphor *himself* is bound by NP3 within the governing category S2. If this were not the case, the sentence would be ungrammatical, as examples 19–21 show. The term *pronominal* includes pronouns, and Principle B states that they must not be coindexed with a c-commanding NP within its governing category. Other than this syntactic restriction on a pronoun's antecedent, the actual choice of one of the allowable antecedents for a pronoun is considered to be a semantic (not a syntactic) process that occurs at the level of Logical Form. The term *R-expression* denotes overt NPs that are "potentially referential," such as *Ben*, *bird*, or *sincerity* (Chomsky 1981, p. 102). Principle C states, in effect, that an R-expression cannot be coindexed with any NP that c-commands it. Coreference between two full NPs is allowed in sentences like *Whenever Ben$_i$ comes to town, Ben$_i$ gets arrested* because the first *Ben* does not c-command the second *Ben*, and vice versa. Principle C also disallows coreference when the pronoun c-commands the potential antecedent, as in *He$_i$ saw John$_i$*.

In summary: A theory of language must allow a level of hierarchical structural representations in order to account for the correct assignment of thematic roles, the constraints on the distance between a moved NP and its trace, and the choice of an antecedent for a reflexive or a pronoun.

A Typology of Referential Dependencies

Government and Binding theory has generalized the constraints on coindexing reflexives and pronouns and the constraints on coindexing empty NPs into a typology based on the features [± anaphoric, ± pronominal], as shown in (26) (source: Chomsky 1982, p. 78).

(26)	Overt	Empty
[+ anaphoric, − pronominal]	reflexives	NP-trace
[− anaphoric, + pronominal]	pronouns	(pro)
[+ anaphoric, + pronominal]	—	PRO
[− anaphoric, − pronominal]	R-expressions	variables (*wh*-trace)

The typology is based on formal properties of referentially dependent elements (what structures they occur in) as well as on their semantic properties (whether they behave like anaphors or like pronominals), and it determines which principle of the Binding theory each type of referentially dependent NP is subject to.

The displaced constituents in sentences 2–7 are examples of *wh-movement*, in which the *wh*-element always moves into the complementizer

(COMP) position, and the empty NP left behind is called a *wh-trace*. The class of [−anaphoric, −pronominal] NPs into which *wh*-trace falls is subject to Principle C of the Binding theory. *Wh*-trace satisfies Principle C because it is not bound by an NP in an argument position.

There is another type of movement in which an NP moves into a grammatical position that can potentially receive a theta role but in this case does not receive one because the verb does not have one to assign. Consider sentence 27.

(27) It seems that John is dancing.

Even though subjects can be assigned theta roles directly in some structures, in sentence 27 the subject of *seems* is assigned no theta role because *seems* has no theta role to assign. A consequence of this fact is that a pleonastic element (in this case, *it*) acts as a place-filler in the obligatory subject position. Instead of the pleonastic element, *John* could appear in the matrix subject position if the embedded verb were infinitival. In Government and Binding theory, the NP *John* appears in the embedded subject position at D-structure and then moves to the matrix subject position, as shown in (28); nonetheless, *John* is still the Agent of *dance*.

(28) a. D-structure:
　　　e seems to Bill [$_s$ John to be dancing]
　　　(e = empty, noncoindexed NP)
　　b. S-structure:
　　　John$_i$ seems to Bill [$_s$ t$_i$ to be dancing]

This type of movement, in which an NP moves into a "theta position" that is not directly assigned a theta role in that particular sentence, is called *NP-movement*, and the trace associated with this type of movement is called *NP-trace*.

NP-trace is the empty counterpart of reflexives, both of which must also be bound within their governing categories since they are [+anaphoric] elements and hence fall under Principle A of the Binding theory. For example, consider the following sentences:

(29) a. *A friend$_i$ of John's believes [Bill to be shaving himself$_i$]
　　b. A friend$_i$ of John's seems to Bill [t$_{ij}$ to be shaving himself$_j$]

In (29a), *friend* and *himself* cannot be coindexed, because the governing category of *himself* is the embedded S node, and *friend* lies outside the domain dominated by this node. In (29b), *friend* and *himself* are not coindexed but are coreferential because the NP-trace must be coindexed with a c-commanding NP within the matrix (topmost) sentence, and *himself* must be coindexed with a c-commanding NP within the embedded sentence, namely the NP-trace.

Another example of NP-movement occurs with passive sentences (according to Chomsky 1981), as shown in the following:

(30) D-structure: [e was eaten the apple by John]
      S-structure: [The apple$_i$ was eaten t$_i$ by John]

The NP in direct-object position undergoes movement, while the NP that will be assigned Agent is base-generated in the *by*-phrase (i.e., it is already in place at the level of D-structure and undergoes no movement). In the analysis given by Williams (1981), a morphological rule changes a verb's argument structure when it is passivized, such that the arguments will be assigned to NP positions within the verb phrase; hence, the Theme will be assigned to the direct-object NP, and the Agent will be assigned to the NP in the *by*-phrase. Since the matrix-subject position is empty at D-structure and has not been assigned a theta role by the passive verb, the object NP can move into that position.

A third type of empty NP, called PRO, is not created by movement but rather is base-generated (i.e., the empty NP is inserted into D-structure). The distinguishing feature of constructions in which this empty NP appears is that both the empty NP position and the position to which it is related receive independent theta roles. In (31), *John* is assigned a theta role by *promise*, and the empty NP (PRO) is assigned a theta role by *shave*.

(31) John$_i$ promised Bill [$_s$ PRO$_i$ to shave]

The [+ anaphoric, + pronominal] PRO is subject to the conjunction of Principles A and B of the Binding theory, with the result that PRO is limited to grammatical positions that do not have a governing category (i.e., that are ungoverned). The subject of an infinitive is one such position in English.

The empty counterpart of pronouns is *pro* (called "little pro"). This empty category is hypothesized to occur in inflectionally rich languages such as Italian, where the subject of the sentence need not be overt. English, on the other hand, must contain an overt subject. Since *pro* is generally assumed not to exist in English, it will not be considered further here.

As this brief overview of the Binding theory and the typology of empty categories shows, the principles of the grammar in Government and Binding theory interact in highly abstract and complex ways. These interactions extend beyond the domains we have described. For example, government, which played a part in determining the local domain for the binding principles, also plays a role in the assignment of theta roles and in the assignment of Case. These abstract interacting components of the grammar permit broad generalizations about the processes that occur in natural language.

We have focused on a presentation of GB theory (Chomsky 1981, 1982) for two reasons. First, among the major current theories it specifies the largest typology of referentially dependent elements. Therefore, it leads to the prediction of the greatest number of specific impairments affecting these categories. A database resulting from the investigation of a large number of hypothesized types of referentially dependent elements has the potential to reveal impairments involving these categories. If fewer impairments are found, the data may be interpretable with respect to a smaller set of referentially dependent elements consistent with another linguistic theory. An investigation that starts with stimuli designed to document impairments in a smaller number of categories, however, cannot reveal all the impairments that are predictable on the basis of the theory with the larger number of categories. Second, a processing model that has been relatively well specified for the treatment of referential dependencies—the Berwick-Weinberg (1984, 1985) parser—is based on GB theory. (This parser is described in chapter 2.)

Although our work is based on GB theory, we shall briefly outline another theory of syntactic structure, one that contrasts with GB theory in several respects. We present this theory so that the reader can see how different theories handle similar phenomena (e.g. thematic role assignment and passive structures) in different ways. In chapter 6 we will consider the extent to which our data bear on the choice of one theory over another.

Lexical Functional Grammar

In Lexical Functional Grammar (Bresnan 1982b), grammatical functions such as subject and object are considered linguistic primitives. Thus, as part of their lexical representation, words that can function as predicates contain a mapping of thematic roles onto grammatical functions. For example, *kick* has the following lexical representation:

(32) 'kick $\langle$(SUBJ) (OBJ)$\rangle$'
$\qquad$ | $\qquad$ |
$\quad$ Agent   Theme

This notation means that the lexical representation of *kick* associates the two grammatical functions listed within the angle brackets with two particular thematic roles. (In presenting this theory we will use the term *thematic role* to refer to both the assignment and the interpretation of thematic relations.)

Unlike Government and Binding theory, Lexical Functional Grammar contains only one level of syntactic structure (called "constituent structure" or c-structure), which closely mirrors the word order of the surface string. At the level of "functional structure," or f-structure, grammatical functions such as subject and object are read off the c-structure representation and matched with thematic roles, as specified by information associated with the lexical representation of the predicate. Take, for example, a structure that in GB theory is analyzed as containing an NP-trace. As (33) shows, in the Lexical Functional Grammar c-structure the embedded complement is a verb phrase (VP), and hence no empty NP is necessary, since there is no embedded-subject position.

(33) [$_S$ John [$_{VP}$ seems [$_{VP}$ to be shaving]]]

In order to translate this c-structure into an f-structure, the lexical specification of *seems* must be accessed:

(34) 'seem ⟨(XCOMP)⟩ (SUBJ)'

In (34), the complement shown within the angle brackets is a predicate function—i.e., it will form a second-order (embedded) predicate—and hence is not associated with a thematic role. The SUBJ grammatical function, lying outside the angle brackets, is also not associated with any thematic role. It is listed to indicate that a matrix-subject NP is obligatory at the syntactic level. This structure is considered to be a type of control structure, in which a lexical rule of functional control applies to assign a particular grammatical function as the unmarked controller. The order of preference of controllers is as follows: the second object, if there is one, such as in the sentence *Tom will serve you the fish raw* (Bresnan 1982, p. 323); the direct object, if there is one (*John persuaded Bill to shave*); and the subject (*John tried to shave*). In the sentence under consideration in (33), there is no object, and hence the subject will be the controller, with an equation assigned as follows:

(35) (↑SUBJ) = (↑XCOMP SUBJ)

The f-structure representation is then constructed as in (36).

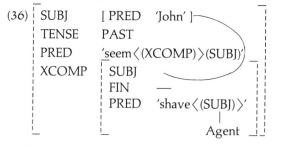

(36)
SUBJ	[PRED 'John']	
TENSE	PAST	
PRED	'seem⟨(XCOMP)⟩(SUBJ)'	
XCOMP	SUBJ	
	FIN —	
	PRED 'shave⟨(SUBJ)⟩'	
		Agent

At f-structure, the embedded clause is given a subject grammatical function because such a function is associated with an argument of *shave*. This subject cannot be filled with the contents of a constituent in embedded-subject position at c-structure (since it does not exist), and the control equation in (35) will cause this subject to be coindexed with the matrix subject. Since the subject NP in the embedded clause depends on another NP for its reference, the representation in (36) contains a referential dependency according to our definition, although not at the syntactic level.

Another type of functional control structure in Lexical Functional Grammar is the obligatory-control structure (i.e., subject-control verbs as in *John promised Bill to shave*, and object-control verbs as in *John persuaded Bill to shave*). The difference between the obligatory-control verbs and the *seems*-type verbs is that both the SUBJ and the OBJ functions of the obligatory-control verb are associated with thematic roles, as shown in (37).

(37) 'promise ⟨(SUBJ) (OBJ) (XCOMP)⟩'
          | |
      Agent Theme
   (↑SUBJ) = (↑XCOMP SUBJ)

The lexical rule of functional control described above would preferentially assign the direct object as the controller of XCOMP. For a verb like *promise*, this lexical rule produces the wrong result; therefore, the information that the subject is the controller must be idiosyncratically stipulated, as shown by the equation in (37). The c-structure for a sentence like *John promised Bill to shave* will be represented with a VP complement at c-structure, and hence there will be no empty NP and no referential dependency at this level, as shown in (38).

(38) [John promised Bill [$_{VP}$ to shave]]

Combining the lexical information from (37) with the c-structure in (38) produces the following f-structure:

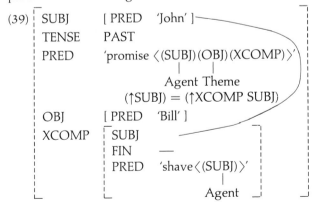

(39)
  SUBJ   [PRED 'John']
  TENSE   PAST
  PRED   'promise ⟨(SUBJ)(OBJ)(XCOMP)⟩'
                    | |
                 Agent Theme
         (↑SUBJ) = (↑XCOMP SUBJ)
  OBJ   [PRED 'Bill']
  XCOMP   SUBJ
            FIN   —
            PRED   'shave⟨(SUBJ)⟩'
                    |
                Agent

The referential dependency in (39) is just the same as that in (36). The difference will be that in (39) each subject position will ultimately be associated with a different thematic role, whereas in (36) only the embedded subject will be assigned a thematic role.

In summary: While Government and Binding theory analyzes *seems*-raising structures and obligatory-control structures as having not only empty NPs but also different types of empty NPs (NP-trace and PRO, respectively), Lexical Functional Grammar analyzes all these structures as functional control structures containing the same type of referential dependency at f-structure and no empty NP at c-structure.

In Lexical Functional Grammar there is one more structure with functional control, which in GB theory is analyzed as not containing a referential dependency at all. Consider the sentence 40.

(40) John believes Bill to be shaving.

In GB theory this structural type is called $\bar{S}$ Deletion, and in Lexical Functional Grammar it is called Raising-to-Object. Its structural analysis within GB theory is shown in (41), and that within Lexical Functional Grammar is shown in (42).

(41) John believes [$_S$ Bill to be shaving]
(42) John believes Bill [$_{VP}$ to be shaving]

In Lexical Functional Grammar, the lexical representation of *believe* is as shown in (43).

(43) 'believe $\langle$(SUBJ) (XCOMP)$\rangle$ (OBJ)'
$$|$$
Agent

Similar to the *seems* analysis, there is one grammatical function that is not assigned a thematic role by *believe*; in this case it is the direct object. As with the other unmarked functional control structures, the lexical rule of functional control will apply and the direct object will be selected as the controller. The f-structure will be obtained in the same way as those described above.

Passives, which are a type of NP-raising in GB theory, are formed by a lexical rule of passivization in Lexical Functional Grammar that changes the associations between grammatical functions and thematic roles, stated as in (44) (source: Bresnan 1982c, p. 20).

(44) Passivization:
Operation on lexical form: (SUBJ) $\rightarrow \emptyset$ / (BY OBJ)
$\qquad\qquad\qquad\qquad$ (OBJ) $\rightarrow$ (SUBJ)
Morphological change: V $\rightarrow$ V$_{[Part]}$

The morphological rule in (44) changes the verb into its participle form, either via a productive rule of affixation or by idiosyncratic stipulation of an irregular form within the lexical entry, and the passivization rule applies to the lexical representation, as shown in (45).

(45) 'love ⟨(SUBJ) (OBJ)⟩' → 'love ⟨(BY OBJ / ∅), (SUBJ)'
       | | | |
   Agent Theme   Agent   Theme

The c-structure will contain a subject NP and a *by*-phase, but no empty NP in direct-object position as would be the case in GB theory. The f-structure would be directly constructed from this c-structure, as is shown in (46) for the sentence *John is loved by Mary.*

(46)
```
┌ SUBJ      [ PRED    'John' 1 ]                    ┐
│ TENSE     PRESENT                                 │
│ PRED      'loved ⟨(BY OBJ / ∅), (SUBJ)'           │
│                        |          |               │
│                      Agent      Theme             │
└ BY OBJ    [ PRED    'Mary' ]                      ┘
```

Thematic roles would be associated with the appropriate grammatical functions in the normal fashion. Thus it can be seen that whereas GB theory includes an analysis of passive (or at least some passives) as a type of referential dependency, in Lexical Functional Grammar the passive contains no referential dependency at any level.

Because thematic roles are assigned at the level of f-structure, only a subset of the empty NPs hypothesized within GB theory are necessary at the syntactic level—namely, "long-distance dependencies," which fall under the heading of *wh*-movement in GB theory. For example, in sentence 47 (source: Pinker 1982, p. 663), the "e" represents an empty NP at the level of (syntactic) c-structure.

(47) The singer [s I like e] is blind.

From the c-structure representation, along with the lexical information concerning the word *like*, the f-structure representation in (48) can be constructed.

In (48), the information associated with each predicate (PRED) is inserted from the lexicon. The values for the "SUBJ" and "OBJ" listings are filled in from the appropriate grammatical positions at c-structure. The referential dependency is represented by the same abbreviatory convention as above.

In summary: Long-distance dependencies are represented with an empty NP at c-structure and with coindexation (or a notational variant) at f-structure. This type of referential dependency is called *constituent control*. Functional control structures, on the other hand, contain a referential dependency at the level of f-structure but have no empty NP at c-structure.

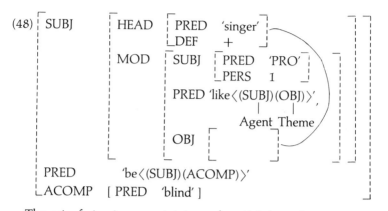

(48)

The set of structures containing referential dependencies is somewhat different in Lexical Functional Grammar and Government and Binding theory, and both the organization of referential dependencies into types and the analysis of these types are different within the two theories, as table 1.1 shows. Passives do not contain referential dependencies in Lexical Functional Grammar, whereas $\overline{S}$ deletion structures (with verbs like *believe*) do not contain referential dependencies in GB theory. The NP(*seems*)-raising verbs and the obligatory-control structures in GB theory are all instances of functional control in Lexical Functional Grammar. In GB theory

Table 1.1
Referential dependencies in English.

Government and Binding Theory (Chomsky 1981)	Lexical Functional Grammar (Bresnan 1982b)
Structures containing an empty NP at the syntactic level	
wh-movement (relative clauses, cleft constructions, topicalized constructions, etc.) NP-movement (*seems*, passive) Control PRO	Long-distance dependencies (relative clauses, cleft constructions, topicalized constructions, etc.)
Referential dependencies for which coindexation occurs at the syntactic level	
Reflexives *wh*-movement NP-movement	Long-distance dependencies
Referential dependencies for which coindexation occurs at Logical Form (Government and Binding theory) or f-structure (Lexical Functional Grammar)	
Pronouns Control PRO (e.g., subject control, object control)	Reflexives Pronouns Functional control (e.g., subject control, object control, raising-to-object (*believe*), raising-to-subject (*seems*))

there are several types of empty NPs at the syntactic level, but in Lexical Functional Grammar there is only one type, used for long-distance dependencies. In GB theory, all referentially dependent elements except the [+ pronominal] NPs (pronouns, obligatory-control PRO) are coindexed at the syntactic level; in Lexical Functional Grammar only the long-distance dependencies are coindexed at the syntactic level.

We have based our work on Chomsky's theory for the reasons outlined above. However, in chapter 6 we will discuss the data with regard to Lexical Functional Grammar as well as GB theory. We now turn to a parsing model based on GB theory and to a number of issues related to the parsing process.

Chapter 2
Parsing Models and On-Line Sentence Processing

The processing models that deal with syntactic aspects of sentence comprehension are known as *parsing models* or *parsers*. Following Government and Binding theory and assuming a type-transparent relationship between linguistic theory and the parser, we define the tasks of the parser as assigning syntactic structure to incoming strings of words, assigning theta roles (but not interpreting them), coindexing anaphoric elements, and converting the completed phrasal constituents into representations appropriate for semantic interpretation. After discussing some general properties of parsing models in the first section of the chapter, we shall present a brief overview of the Berwick-Weinberg parser, a deterministic type-transparent parsing model that is based on GB theory. In the third section we review psycholinguistic experiments that are relevant to on-line syntactic parsing, and in the fourth we review alternative models that do not make use of a parser to extract semantic information from sentences.

Some General Properties of Parsing Models

It is the general objective of parsing models to provide a set of algorithms that act to convert a linear string of incoming words into a propositional representation so that semantic interpretation can occur, while conforming to constraints imposed by limitations on processing capacity. Parsing algorithms make use of two broad types of data: the linear array of words in the particular input string to be parsed (bottom-up information) and the parser's own knowledge of the grammar of the language (top-down information). We shall consider the assignment of empty categories and the coindexation of referentially dependent NPs to illustrate how these sources of information are utilized in parsing a sentence.

There are four types of top-down information that the parser could use to build an empty NP. First, subcategorization information may reveal an obligatory NP position. For a sentence like *Who did you take*, the verb *take* is obligatorily transitive, but there is no overt noun following the verb in the input string, and so an empty NP must be created. Second, the occurrence of a *wh*-word could serve to alert the parser that the sentence contains an upcoming *wh*-trace. Third, in a sentence like *John seems to be dancing*, the subject *John* is not assigned a theta role by the following verb *seems*, which could serve to alert the parser that there is an upcoming NP-trace. Fourth, even with no advance warning of an upcoming empty NP, phrase-structure rules would indicate that sentential complements must have subjects. For example, in the sentence *John promised Bill [PRO to dance]*, *promise* cannot unambiguously signal an upcoming empty NP, because *promise* can also take a non-infinitival complement (*John promised Bill that he would shave*) or no complement (*John promised Bill*). Which of these possible sources of information are utilized by the parser must be determined within each particular parsing model.

In addition to procedures for locating an empty NP, there must be procedures to coindex all referential dependencies, both overt and empty, with an antecedent. There are several ways this can be done. One way is to put potential antecedents into a special storage area. When a gap occurs in the overt string, the parser fills that position with the contents of the special storage area. A second way is to tag potential antecedents in the structure, such that the parser can immediately look back to the appropriate area when a gap is detected. A third way is that a *wh*-word or an NP without a thematic role is not specially tagged but rather triggers a generalized gap-hunting procedure, so that once the empty NP is found the parser must look back to find the appropriate antecedent, just as it does for other types of referentially dependent NPs whose presence is not signaled by an antecedent. In this case, the gap-hunting procedure serves as an aid to gap location rather than to coindexation with an antecedent.

Which procedures a particular parser actually utilizes to locate and coindex referential dependencies is determined by constraints from parsing theory, constraints from linguistic theory, and assumptions about the relationship between the parser and the grammar. We shall outline the Berwick-Weinberg parser, with specific reference to its treatment of referentially dependent NPs.

The Berwick-Weinberg Parser

The Berwick-Weinberg (1984, 1985) parser is a modified version of the Marcus (1980) parser. Both are attempts to provide a functional account of certain linguistic hierarchical constraints, such as subjacency. The Berwick-Weinberg parser incorporates certain changes in the theory of generative grammar presented by Chomsky (1981, 1982). We will present a rough overview of the parser's operations and then work through an example.

The simplifying assumption is made that the stream of speech serving as input to the parser has already been segmented into discrete words (plus their inflectional affixes), that these words have been classified as to grammatical category (noun, verb, and so on), and that lexical information has been accessed for each word (theta roles and selectional restrictions). The string of words is fed into an input buffer with three cells. The parser accesses the word in the first position in the buffer but is allowed to look ahead to see the words in the other buffer cells. The parser is *deterministic* in assigning structure; that is, it is not allowed to backtrack if it makes an error, other than to start all over at the beginning of the sentence. Allowing the parser to look over the next few upcoming words means that most of the local ambiguity is eliminated and the parser can immediately assign the correct structure to the word it is currently parsing. In cases where the lookahead does not disambiguate a structure, the parser sometimes assigns the incorrect structure and is thereby "garden-pathed." For example, in the sentence *The horse raced past the barn fell* the first six words tend to be parsed as a sentence, leaving the parser stranded when it encounters the last word *fell*. The correct analysis is immediately achieved if a relative pronoun is used to signal the relative clause, as in *The horse that was raced past the barn fell*.

A deterministic parser with limited lookahead is considered important for three reasons. First, it represents a constraint from parsing theory that guarantees that the string can be parsed in linear time. Thus, this class of parsers meets a complexity metric in principle. Second, it can potentially provide an independently motivated functional explanation for locality conditions in linguistic theory, which otherwise must be stipulated, either in the parser or in a universal grammar. Third, it reflects human constraints on processing capacity. Thus, this type of parser is a plausible candidate to become the correct model of a human processor.

The parser assigns structure one phrase at a time. For each new phrase, the parser temporarily pushes away the constituent it has been working on and begins on the subconstituent. This "stack" of uncompleted constituents is called a *pushdown stack*. As a subconstituent is completed, it is attached to a constituent in the next-higher stack. It is up to each particular parsing model to specify and define exactly what constitutes a phrase or a constituent in order to specify formally the conditions under which the stack is to be pushed down.

When a phrase has been completed and its NPs have received theta roles, it is removed from the syntactic structure to a "propositional list," a semantic representation of the predicate-argument structure of the sentence. The propositional list corresponds to the level of Logical Form in Government and Binding theory. It is at this level that the semantic reading is extracted and further interpretive processes occur.

Referential dependencies are coindexed with their antecedents at two different levels. In a sentence with a reflexive like *himself*, an NP-trace, or a *wh*-trace, the parser searches for a c-commanding antecedent by looking back through a limited domain over the structure it has created so far. For pronouns, on the other hand, a second-stage processor searches through the propositional list for a possible antecedent. In this way, the parser mirrors the distinction in GB theory between the search for the antecedent of a reflexive or trace as a syntactic process and the search for the antecedent of a pronoun or PRO as a semantic process.

These basic operations of the parser can be illustrated by working through an example. We will use approximately the same level of specificity as Berwick and Weinberg (1984) in the construction of a phrase marker and in the notion of a phrase.

(1) The man who you kicked saw me.

The first three words are fed into the three cells of the input buffer (figure 2.1). The parser begins with an S node for the entire sentence. The first word in the buffer, *the*, unambiguously signals the parser to construct an NP, to which the next word *man* can be attached. This series of steps appears in figure 2.2. (The nodes are numbered for convenience.) The next word in the buffer, *who*, signals the parser to build a COMP position, which entails the creation of an embedded sentence. The parser pushes down the first phrase, constructs a COMP position dominated by $\bar{S}$ at the

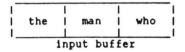

Figure 2.1
Parse of the sentence *The man who you kicked saw me.*

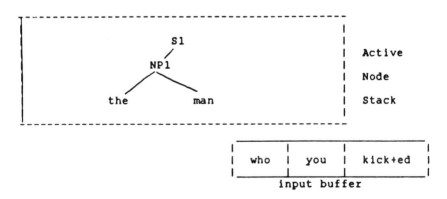

Figure 2.2
Parse of the sentence *The man who you kicked saw me.*

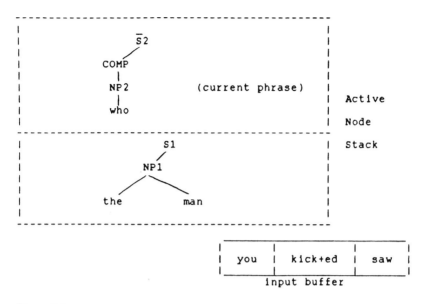

Figure 2.3
Parse of the sentence *The man who you kicked saw me.*

top of the stack, and attaches *who* (figure 2.3). The next word in the buffer, *you*, triggers the creation of a subject position, so the stack is pushed down and a new phrase is started, as shown in figure 2.4.

The next word in the buffer, *kicked*, triggers the creation of a verb phrase (figure 2.5). (The nodes bearing information concerning inflection, tense, and agreement have been omitted.) The lexical information that *kick* is a transitive verb signals the need to create an object NP; however, the next word in the buffer is another verb. The parser therefore creates an empty NP, as shown in figure 2.6. At this point, the search for an antecedent is initiated. In order for the parser to decide whether to search for the antecedent at the level of the syntactic structure or the propositional list, it must decide what type of empty NP is present. Although Berwick and Weinberg do not specify these recognition procedures, one possible simple mechanism for empty referentially dependent NPs is that whenever a gap-hunting procedure has been initiated previously (in this case by the relative pronoun *who*), the parser looks back at the syntactic level.

Once the antecedent is found, both the antecedent and the trace are immediately coindexed. Now the embedded VP is complete and can be attached to the S2 node, which in turn can be attached to the next higher S̄ node, as shown in figures 2.7 and 2.8. After thematic roles are assigned, the entire embedded sentence is converted to the appropriate semantic

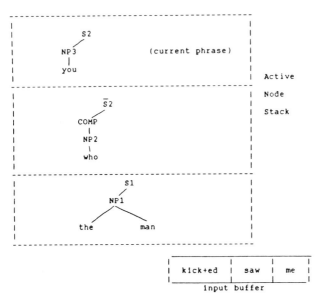

Figure 2.4
Parse of the sentence *The man who you kicked saw me.*

representation and sent to the propositional list, leaving behind a copy of the topmost node, which can then be attached to the next higher phrase, as shown in figure 2.9.

The next word in the buffer is *saw*, and so the parser pushes down the current stack again to build a VP. The last word in the buffer, *me*, is also attached to this VP. These two steps have been conflated and are shown in figure 2.10. Now the second verb phrase is completed and attached to the next higher phrase (figure 2.11), thematic roles are assigned, and the contents of the S1 phrase are converted into the appropriate semantic representation and sent to the propositional list (figure 2.12).

Some of the operations outlined for the example sentence may occur in a different order, depending on the definition of a phrase and when thematic-role assignment occurs (two things not fully specified by Berwick and Weinberg). For example, *kicked* may assign a thematic role to the embedded subject position before embedded object position is constructed. The question of when theta-role assignment occurs becomes more important for a sentence such as *John promised Bill [PRO] to shave.* If the parser looks through the propositional to find an antecedent for PRO as soon as the empty NP is created, then *John* has to be transferred to the propositional list before PRO is coindexed; otherwise an antecedent will not be found. These issues involving thematic-role assignment and the construc-

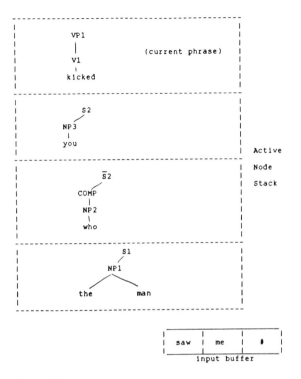

Figure 2.5
Parse of the sentence *The man who you kicked saw me.*

tion of phrases will ultimately have implications for other operations and constraints in the parser.

Another underspecified operation is the exact mechanisms by which obligatory-control PRO is coindexed with an antecedent. Consideration of possible mechanisms reveals a discrepancy between the parser and the formulation of linguistic theory on which it is based. In cases of so-called obligatory control (subject control or object control), the lexical properties of the verb determine whether the empty PRO must be coindexed with the subject NP (for verbs such as *promise*) or with the object NP (for verbs such as *force*). If the parser coindexes PRO at the propositional level, grammatical categories such as subject and object should no longer be available, and the information about obligatory control will have to formulated in other terms, such as obligatory coindexing with the Agent or the Theme.

One solution to this is to distinguish between obligatory-control PRO and optional-control PRO, according to arguments advanced within Government and Binding theory. Williams (1980) and Bouchard (1982) have pointed out that there is a difference between "obligatory control" (which

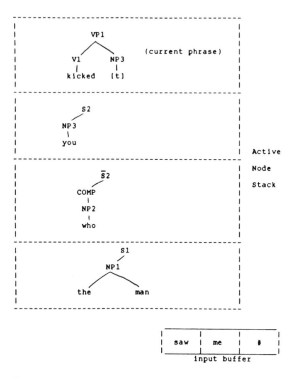

Figure 2.6
Parse of the sentence *The man who you kicked saw me.*

occurs with verbs such as *promise* and *force*) and "optional control" (which occurs in sentences like *PRO feeding lions is dangerous*, in which PRO has an unspecified antecedent, similar to an overt pronoun). Bouchard (1982) has proposed that obligatory-control PRO is anaphoric (like NP-trace and reflexives), while optional-control PRO is pronominal. Stated in terms of Chomsky's (1982) typology, obligatory control would become a type of [+ anaphoric, − pronominal] NP. This analysis would entail that obligatory-control PRO be coindexed at the syntactic level by the parser. Evidence from the individual case studies reported in chapter 5 tends to support this analysis.

In summary: There are two steps involved for referentially dependent elements. First, the parser constructs an NP position for the referentially dependent element. Overt NPs are distinguished from empty NPs in that empty NPs must be created in the absence of information from the actual input string. Second, there is a search for an antecedent at one of two levels. The search for the antecedent of [+ pronominal] elements (overt and empty) occurs at the level of the propositional list, whereas the search for

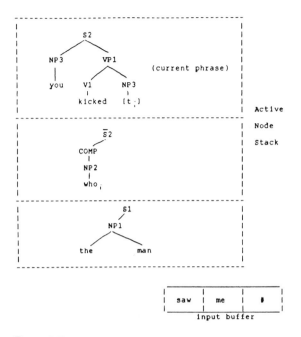

Figure 2.7
Parse of the sentence *The man who you kicked saw me.*

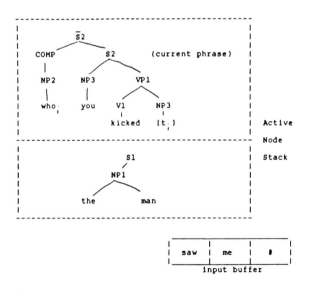

Figure 2.8
Parse of the sentence *The man who you kicked saw me.*

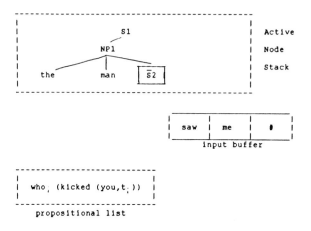

Figure 2.9
Parse of the sentence *The man who you kicked saw me.*

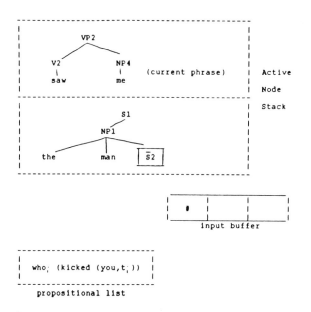

Figure 2.10
Parse of the sentence *The man who you kicked saw me.*

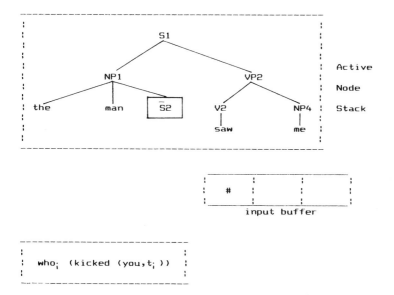

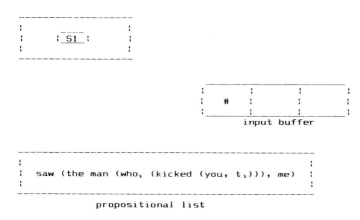

Figure 2.11
Parse of the sentence *The man who you kicked saw me.*

Figure 2.12
Parse of the sentence *The man who you kicked saw me.*

the antecedent of [−pronominal] elements (overt and empty) occurs over the parse tree. Whether obligatory-control PRO is coindexed by the parser at the syntactic level or at the level of the propositional list depends on the linguistic analysis of PRO as [+pronominal] or [−pronominal] and the level at which the coindexation of [+pronominal] and [−pronominal] elements occurs in Government and Binding theory.

At the beginning of the chapter, four types of information by which a parser could be alerted to the existence of an empty NP were mentioned. The Berwick-Weinberg parser makes use of two of these possible types of information: lexical information about subcategorization and phrase-structure rules. Neither *wh*-words nor NPs without a theta role are used to signal the presence of an upcoming empty NP, since this signaling ability would require extra machinery (Berwick and Weinberg 1985). On the other hand, information about subcategorization and phrase-structure rules are required for the parsing of all sentences, not just those with empty NPs, and thus extra machinery need not be stipulated. Thus, in the Berwick-Weinberg model empty NPs must be located purely on the basis of information provided by the subcategorization features of the predicate and the phrase-structure requirement that sentences contain subjects. The coindexing of any referentially dependent NP with an antecedent occurs through a process of lookback, either at the syntactic level or at the level of the propositional list.

The Berwick-Weinberg parser is a theoretical model of natural-language processing that is constrained by linguistic theory and parsing theory. In the next section, some psycholinguistic evidence is presented that either supports aspects of the model or suggests ways in which the model can be further specified.

Some Psycholinguistic Studies of Processing Complexity

Two lines of experimentation in the psycholinguistic literature are relevant to our discussion of natural-language parsing models and to our analyses of patients' performances: the studies dealing with immediacy of processing and the investigations of local processing load and its interaction with total processing capacity.

Immediacy of Parsing/Interpretive Operations

There are many locally ambiguous points in sentences at which a decision must be made before phrase structure can be assigned. At these points, there are two actions that a deterministic parser could take: It could pause at the ambiguous point and look ahead or back to try to resolve the ambiguity, or it could make an immediate parsing decision that might subsequently prove to be wrong. If lookahead and lookback are limited, the parser must adopt the second option in cases where the disambiguating material occurs outside the lookahead or lookback limit.

Several studies have shown that, at least in some cases, the parser adopts the second option and makes a decision immediately, even when the decision may be wrong. Frazier (1978) found that the parser makes immediate principled decisions about certain types of structure assignment at locally ambiguous points. Frazier formulated these principles as the Minimal Attachment Strategy and the Late Closure Strategy. The Late Closure Strategy tells the parser to attach an ambiguous constituent to the current phrase rather than to start a new phrase. This principle accounts for the fact that sentence 2 (source: Frazier 1983, p. 225) tends initially to be parsed incorrectly.

(2) Since Jay always jogs a mile seems like a short distance to him.

The Minimal Attachment Strategy tells the parser to assign the structure with fewest possible nodes. For example, consider sentence 3 (source: Frazier 1983, p. 225).

(3) Tom heard the latest gossip about the new neighbors wasn't true.

Subjects tend to interpret *the latest gossip about the new neighbors* as the direct object of *hear* until the parser encounters *wasn't true*. In other words, local ambiguity occurs after the parser assigns structure to *heard*. *Heard* can either begin a sentential complement or construct a direct-object NP. The Minimal Attachment Strategy will cause the parser to choose to construct a direct-object NP.

Another series of experiments documents the immediacy of decision-making by the parser in relation to assigning antecedents for empty NPs. Frazier, Clifton, and Randall (1983) investigated sentences containing locally ambiguous points where there is more than one possible antecedent for an empty NP. For example, at the point at which the empty NP is constructed in a sentence like *This is the girl the teacher wanted to talk to*, the Agent of *talk to* can be either *the teacher* (which will ultimately be the correct choice) or *the girl* (which would be the correct choice in a sentence like *This is the girl the teacher wanted to talk to Paul*). Locally ambiguous sentences were compared against unambiguous subject-control sentences, such as *This is the girl the teacher decided to talk to* (for which the antecedent of the empty NP preceding *talk* is the nearest overt NP), and against object-control sentences, such as *This is the girl the teacher forced to talk* (for which the antecedent of the empty NP preceding *talk* is not the most recent NP). The sentences were displayed one word at a time at 300-msec exposure durations, with a 50-msec interstimulus interval. Subjects were instructed to respond as soon as possible after the end of the sentence, whether they "intuitively felt they understood a sentence" or had missed it. In addition, they were asked a comprehension question after one-third of the trials. There was a main effect for distance between the NP and the antecedent; in other words, subjects indicated successful understanding less often on the sentences requiring a distant antecedent than on the sentences in which the antecedent was the nearest lexical NP, and their indication of their understanding of the distant-antecedent sentences was slower than that of the near-antecedent sentences. However, there was no main effect of ambiguity (i.e., whether a local ambiguity was present or absent), and there was no interaction between ambiguity and the distance between the NP and its antecedent.

Frazier, Clifton, and Randall take these results as support for the "Most Recent Filler" strategy (the strategy by which the parser immediately chooses the nearest possible antecedent for the empty NP that it constructs, even when subsequent information proves this choice to have been wrong). If the Most Recent Filler strategy applies before the lexical information about obligatory control is made use of, then the sentences for which the most recent NP is the correct answer should be understood correctly on the first pass, whereas the sentences for which the correct antecedent is not the most recent NP should show signs of misunderstanding on the first pass and also take longer to comprehend (owing to the need to revise the choice of antecedent). Furthermore, these effects should show up regardless of the local ambiguity at the site of the gap, since lexical information has not been accessed to indicate ambiguity in any case. These were the results that were obtained. Thus, for example, for the object-control sentence *Everyone liked the woman who the little child forced to sing those stupid French songs last Christmas*, the subject should first choose *the little child* as the antecedent of the empty NP occurring in the subject position before *sing*, and later revise the analysis when the information that *force* requires an obligatory antecedent is made use of. That this information is utilized at some point is suggested by the fact that on the intermittent-comprehension questions the subjects were equally good on both types of obligatory-control structures, and better on these than on the locally ambiguous structures. This interpretation of the results implies that even for a simple subject-control sentence like *John promised Bill to dance* the parser should first coindex the empty embedded subject NP with *Bill* by the Most Recent Filler strategy and then revise the choice of antecedent when the lexical-control information becomes available.

A more recent study (Crain and Fodor 1985) suggests that a Most Recent Filler strategy is used only in locally ambiguous cases, and that sentences with obligatory-control verbs such as *force* and *start* are not included as cases containing locally ambiguous choice points for antecedents. Crain and Fodor used a self-paced reading task in which the subject was forced to press a bar to receive the next word in the sentence. On some trials the subjects were asked to make grammaticality judgments after the entire sentence had appeared, in order to encourage them to pay attention to the task. Modified versions of sentences from the study of Frazier et al. were used, and the number of sentence types was expanded. Instead of cleft structures, *wh*-questions were used. The structures contained either an ambiguous or an unambiguous antecedent at the point where the empty NP was encountered, and the antecedent was either "recent" or "distant." The following are examples of some of the sentence types used.

(4) Who could the little child have started ———— to sing those stupid French songs for ———— last Christmas?
(unambiguous recent-filler question)

(5) Who could the little child have forced ———— ———— to sing those stupid French songs for Cheryl last Christmas?
(unambiguous distant-filler question)

(6) Who could the little child have begged ———— to sing those stupid French songs for ———— last Christmas?
(temporarily ambiguous recent-filler question)

(7) Who could the little child have begged ———— ———— to sing those stupid French songs for Cheryl last Christmas?
(temporarily ambiguous distant-filler question)

Each sentence was matched with its declarative form. For example, the declarative counterpart of sentence 4 is *The little child could have started [ ] to sing those stupid French songs for Cheryl last Christmas*. Increases in latency were computed between the *wh*-question and declarative structures for corresponding words at eleven positions in the sentence. According to the Most Recent Filler hypothesis of Frazier et al. (1983), subjects should initially coindex the empty NP with the most recent lexical NP (*the little child*) in all the *wh*-question structures. For each of the distant-filler sentences, such as (5) and (7), this choice would subsequently prove wrong; therefore, for these sentences, a greater increase in latencies should appear at the point where the incorrect choice is revealed. However, Crain and Fodor, comparing the distant-filler sentences, found that the ambiguous sentences (such as 7) showed a significant increase in latency in the disambiguating region, whereas the unambiguous sentences (such as 5) did not. These results suggest that the Most Recent Filler strategy is applied to sentences in which the choice of antecedent is locally ambiguous, but that where lexical information about obligatory control is available this information is immediately utilized, the correct antecedent is immediately selected, and no later reanalysis is necessary.

In summary: The Crain-Fodor study suggests that the parser uses all the information at its disposal at locally ambiguous points, but that it assigns structure even when the ambiguity cannot be resolved locally.

Other studies have found evidence for immediacy of other parsing/ interpretive operations. Ehrlich (1983) and Ehrlich and Rayner (1983) tested the immediacy hypothesis in an eye-movement study with sentences containing pronouns. In a text passage they varied the distance between the pronoun and the only pragmatically possible antecedent. The antecedent either occurred in the immediately preceding sentence and immediately preceded (and was adjacent to) the pronoun; occurred in the preceding line of text and in the preceding sentence and was separated from the pronoun by one or more NPs; or occurred at least three lines of text away, with one intervening sentence. Neither of these studies found an increase in latency for fixating the pronoun itself; however, latencies did increase over the next few words after the pronoun, as the distance between the pronoun and its antecedent increased. These findings suggest that the search for the antecedent of a pronoun begins immediately, and that greater distance between the pronoun and the antecedent causes a heavier processing load until an antecedent is located. In addition, it shows that processing of the rest of the sentence continues simultaneously with the search for an antecedent.

Just and Carpenter (1980) investigated eye-fixation patterns in the reading of passages in which the local context suggested a particular interpretation of an ambiguous phrase or a pronoun which later proved to be wrong. The subjects did not show longer fixation times at the initial point of ambiguity, but the later discrepancy caused them to return to the originally ambiguous point and spend time shifting their gaze between the mutually inconsistent parts. This finding suggests that information about context can influence semantic interpretation, at least at ambiguous points, and that semantic processing occurs as soon as possible (which further suggests that theta roles are assigned as quickly as possible).

On the basis of these studies, we adopt the working assumption that assigning structure and selecting antecedents of referentially dependent NPs are processes that are initiated immediately, although more complex operations may take longer to complete. In cases of local ambiguity (or at least in those cases in which lookahead or lookback cannot resolve the ambiguity), the parser makes a decision, which may later prove to be wrong.

Other aspects of the immediacy assumption remain to be tested. For example, if theta roles are assigned as soon as possible, then there should be an extra processing load when an NP cannot be assigned a theta role by the nearest verb. For example, in the sentence *John seems to Bill to be dancing,* the word *John* must be held without a theta role until the Agent of *dance* is assigned to the empty NP and thereafter transferred.

Immediacy of processing does not negate the validity of a deterministic parser. Lookahead can potentially occur more quickly than can be measured in these studies, and the incorrect assignment of structure at locally ambiguous points may occur only when the disambiguating information lies beyond the lookahead capability of the parser. In addition, a semantic interpreter can work in lockstep fashion with the parser; in other words, semantic interpretation can begin as soon as the parser begins to assign theta roles and to send subconstituents to the propositional list. Therefore, the finding that semantic processing occurs quickly after the parser encounters a word does not constitute counterevidence to a modular parser that assigns syntactic structure before semantic interpretation begins.

Local Processing Load and Processing Capacity
An important set of studies concerning processing capacity are those showing that both processing and storage operations take up part of the same working-memory capacity that is allotted to sentence comprehension in reading. Less efficient processing will take up more capacity and therefore allow less room for short-term storage of items; conversely, greater storage demands will allow fewer processing operations to occur simultaneously. Daneman and Carpenter (1980) asked subjects to read a list of sentences and keep the last word of each sentence in memory. At the end of the sentence list they had to recall the final words. The length of the sentence list was progressively increased. The working-memory span for an individual subject was taken to be the list length at which the subject could recall all the final words. This individual working memory span was found to correlate well with three reading-comprehension measures and with a listening-span task. Subsequent studies found a significant correlation between the working-memory span and accuracy on specific tests consisting of test passages that required finding the antecedents of pronouns (Daneman and Carpenter 1980), detecting semantic inconsistencies (Daneman and Carpenter 1983), extracting the main theme of the passage (Daneman and Carpenter 1980), and inferring the meaning of an unknown word on the basis of contextual clues (Daneman and Green 1986). The implication of these studies for the present purpose is that, within the overall capacity available for sentence processing, there is an inverse relationship between storage capacity and efficiency of executing parsing procedures. For example, a patient with a specific deficit of certain parsing procedures will be slower in processing and hence may have more difficulty storing necessary items. Conversely, a patient with limited storage capacity may have more difficulty parsing more difficult sentences. Thus,

what looks like a deficit specific to parsing routines may actually be due to a storage limitation, and vice versa.

In studies of local sentence-processing complexity, it is assumed that both processing and storage operations take up a part of the total capacity available for sentence processing, showing up as increases in reaction time or error rate.

Several studies have investigated the complexity of processing sentences with relative clauses. Wanner and Maratsos (1978), working within an Augmented Transition Network model, predicted that object relatives (relative clauses with an empty NP in object position) should display greater local increases in complexity than subject relatives, as reflected by reduced accuracy on two different tasks: a comprehension test and a secondary task of recalling a list of names that had been memorized at an interrupted point in the sentence. This prediction sprang from the assumption that the antecedent is put into a special HOLD cell until the empty NP is encountered. Maintaining an NP in this HOLD cell takes up storage capacity, thereby leaving less space for the list of names. When the empty NP was in object position the material in the HOLD cell would have to be maintained longer, and during the time that other processing operations were occurring, thus causing more errors as a result of greater complexity. The results confirmed the predictions: At the interruption point around the embedded verb, the error rate was higher on both tasks for the object relatives than for the subject relatives.

Ford (1983) similarly found greater processing load for object-relative sentences on a self-paced reading task in which subjects read sentences one word at a time by pressing a bar to receive each next word. Ostensibly primary but actually secondary tasks, such as repetition of the sentence, lexical decision, or judgment of grammaticality, were used to ensure that the subjects paid attention to the sentences. A heavier processing load was assumed to slow the calling up of the next word. On the assumption that the processing of each word is initiated immediately, the greater complexity reflected in increased reaction time could be attributed to the word just encountered. Measuring reaction times to lexical decisions made on every word in the sentence, Ford found longer reaction times for object relatives than for subject relatives at the point of the embedded verb, and the following two words, as shown in (8) and (9). The matched positions across sentences are numbered; longer reaction times were found for positions 5, 6, and 7 in (9) than in (8).

$$1 \quad 2 \quad 5 \quad 3 \quad 4 \quad 6 \quad 7 \quad 8$$
(8) The reporter that attacked the senator admitted the mistake.

$$1 \quad 2 \quad 3 \quad 4 \quad 5 \quad 6 \quad 7 \quad 8$$
(9) The reporter that the senator attacked admitted the mistake.

Psycholinguistic studies have also documented the existence of "gap-hunting" processes in the parser, which would increase the parsing load. Stowe (1983, 1986) found increases in reaction time when the parser encountered an unexpected overt element in the position of an expected gap. She compared sentences without empty NPs such as in (10) and sentences containing empty NPs in various positions, such as (11)–(13).

(10) The young hostess really wondered if Mark had greeted me together with Ann when the party began.
(11) The young hostess really wondered who t had greeted me together with Ann when the party began.
(12) The young hostess really wondered who Mark had greeted t together with Ann when the party began.
(13) The young hostess really wondered who Mark had greeted me together with t when the party began.

This experiment was a self-paced sentence-reading paradigm, like the Crain-Fodor (1985) study; the difference was that the subject was asked to repeat a sentence occasionally after reading it instead of making occasional grammaticality judgments. Although the latencies could not be measured for the empty NP positions, there was no increase in latency for the positions directly following the empty NP in (11), (12), and (13) over the latencies for the same positions in the comparison structure with no empty NP in (10). Thus, there was no evidence that empty NPs involve a greater processing load. However, longer latencies did occur at the direct-object position (*me*) in (13) than at the direct-object position in the declarative and subject-gap sentences (10 and 11, respectively). Stowe called this finding a "gap-nonlocation effect" and suggested that in the sentences with a *wh*-relative pronoun the parser expects a gap (i.e., an empty NP) in the direct-object position, does not find one, and requires some time to recover.

The gap-nonlocation effect suggests that there is some type of gap-hunting procedure, since there is no gap-nonlocation effect in a sentence that contains no *wh*-word. This finding stands in contradiction to Berwick and Weinberg's (1984) proposed gap-recognition process, which should occur whether or not a sentence contains an empty NP. However, it would be possible to incorporate a gap-hunting procedure into a deterministic parser such as that of Berwick and Weinberg. A *wh*-word could trigger a generalized gap-hunting procedure; when a referentially dependent NP was identified, the parser would have to look back to select the proper antecedent. Forcing the parser to look back to search for an antecedent preserves hierarchical constraints on the distance over which an NP may be coindexed with an antecedent.

Stowe's results, as well as those of Crain and Fodor (1985), fail to show greater processing load for empty NPs than for overt NPs in matched sentences. There are several possible reasons for this finding, which bear on the processing load found in such sentences. One is that the linguistic analysis of the structure is wrong and no empty NPs actually exist in the sentence. Another is that constructing an empty NP is actually no more difficult than constructing any other NP, and that the assumptions underlying the predictions are wrong. A third possibility is that the extra processing load does not occur instantaneously at the point at which the empty NP is located but is distributed over the next several words and hence does not reveal itself in a noticeable reaction-time increase. A fourth possibility is that the increase in reaction time is so small that it does not reveal itself as an effect significantly different from noise. A fifth possibility is that the parsing processes associated with reading sentences operate in a highly different fashion from those associated with listening to sentences.

Before more drastic conclusions are drawn, the possibility should be eliminated that normal processing increases in complexity are so minute in normal subjects that they do not show up in a direct reaction-time measure. Wanner and Maratsos (1978) and Ford (1983), who found differences in processing complexity between object relatives and subject relatives, used concurrent-task paradigms—recalling a list of names in the former study, making lexical decisions on each word in the latter. On the other hand, Stowe (1983, 1986) and Crain and Fodor (1985), who found no processing increases for empty NPs, asked subjects to (respectively) repeat the sentence or judge its grammaticality only after the entire sentence had been read, and only on a proportion of the trials. Therefore, in a paradigm in which subjects are forced to operate beyond the limits of their capacity with concurrent task requirements, local reaction-time increases for empty NPs may begin to emerge. The next step in investigating this hypothesis would be to test sentences such as those used by Stowe (1983, 1986) in a concurrent-task paradigm.

In summary: The psycholinguistic literature on sentence processing that is pertinent to the parsing model outlined above offers the following conclusions. First, parsing processes are initiated as immediately as possible, at both the syntactic and the semantic level. The parser even makes decisions about the assignment of structure and coindexation at locally ambiguous points in the sentence, without waiting for the later disambiguating information. Second, the parser has a limited processing capacity that is diminished by both storage and processing requirements. Third, object relatives take up more capacity than subject relatives. Fourth, there is evidence that a gap-hunting procedure is activated for *wh*-words. There is no evidence pertaining to whether a gap-hunting procedure is activated by antecedents of NP-trace. Fifth, there is so far no evidence that the construction of empty NPs requires more capacity than the construction of overt

NPs. More work is needed before the conclusion can be drawn that empty NPs are not constructed or do not increase processing load.

Alternatives to Parsing Systems

Several lines of investigation indicate that, in addition to semantic representations derived from the operation of a parser, subjects also can infer aspects of sentential semantic representations in a more direct fashion. Slobin (1966) presented active and passive reversible and irreversible sentences to subjects in a picture-verification task in which reaction times were measured. He reported an interaction between verb voice and reversibility such that reversible passive sentences produced longer reaction times than reversible active sentences. He concluded that active and passive thematic roles are inferred from the lexical meanings of nouns and verbs in a sentence and from real-world knowledge, and that syntactic structure is computed only if this "lexico-pragmatic" route to meaning fails.

Not all studies have shown similar results. For instance, Forster and Olbrei (1973) attempted a modification of the Slobin experiment in which the dependent variable was reaction time to a grammaticality judgment. They found a main effect of voice (passive sentences producing longer reaction times than active) but no interaction between voice and reversibility. They concluded that syntactic structure is routinely computed, and that a lexico-pragmatic route to meaning is not often employed. The differences between the two experiments may lie in the nature of the task (picture verification versus well-formedness judgments) or in the nature of the stimuli (the sentences of Forster and Olbrei included quantifiers that might have triggered syntactic analysis and diminished reliance on lexico-pragmatic strategies). The data overall suggest that a lexico-pragmatic route to meaning can be used with relatively simple structures (such as passive forms without quantified nouns) in comprehension tasks, if not in grammaticality-judgment tasks.

The lexico-pragmatic route to meaning bypasses a parser, but is ineffective in semantically reversible sentences. Its existence, if established, would not challenge the existence of a parser, although it might reduce reliance on a parser considerably in actual conversational settings. However, another approach to sentence comprehension explicitly denies the existence of a parser, even in the interpretation of semantically reversible sentences. This approach asserts that sentence comprehension is accomplished through a set of "heuristics" or through "direct mappings" between superficial aspects of sentence and word form and sentential aspects of meaning. This approach has been termed a "perceptual" approach to sentence interpretation by Bever (1970) and a "functionalist" approach by Bates and MacWhinney and their colleagues (Bates, McNew, MacWhinney, Devescovi, and Smith

1982; MacWhinney, Bates, and Kliegl 1984). We shall discuss the Bates-MacWhinney model, which, to our knowledge, is the most fully developed one of its kind.

Bates et al. (1982) and MacWhinney et al. (1984) clearly state the fundamental assumption of this approach: that the mapping between form and function is "direct," by which these investigators mean that "it is possible for language to integrate semantic contrasts on an equal footing with syntactic cues in a parsing system" (MacWhinney et al. 1984, p. 128). In their model, "coalitions" of functions map onto formal devices. For instance, the functions of agent, actor, and topic prototypically map onto the formal device of "subject." These coalitions "derive, in large measure, from facts about the ways in which things go together in the world and ways in which the human information-processing system interacts with the conversational task" (MacWhinney et al. 1984, p. 129). Since these coalitions of functions and form are often subject to dissociation (as, for instance, in the passive voice in which the subject is topicalized but would no longer be an agent), the listener may make use of a variety of "cues" to determine aspects of meaning. Cues may be reinforcing (as when all cues map onto the prototypical coalition of functions and form), or they may be in competition (as occurs in the passive). Individual cues are of different importance in different languages, with the strength of any individual cue— word order, agreement, case-marking morphology, stress, etc.—derived from the frequency of that cue in the language and the extent to which that cue definitively maps onto a particular function (called *cue validity*).

This model of mapping sentence form onto meaning is said by Bates and MacWhinney to differ significantly from the way a parser operates. Their approach denies the existence of linguistic representations except insofar as they are involved in processing; in terms of Chomsky's (1965) distinction between "competence" and "performance," this model denies the existence of competence. Moreover, in this theory the "rules" of language processing are simply probabilistic statements regarding the way different superficial cues to meaning yield a semantic reading. Implicit in this view is a denial of the existence of the entire mental apparatus we have described in this chapter and the preceding one. Stated in different terms, this view denies the existence of any mental structures unique to language, except for a few superficial features of sentence and word form, and claims that the rules governing language processing are not derived from a special domain of functioning but are simply part of the more general mental capacities related to the measurement of probability. In short, this view sees language as consisting of a very simple set of structures, and its processing as entirely part of general intellectual functioning.

The evidence in favor of this approach to sentence interpretation is said to be the existence of differences in the importance of different "cues" in comprehension tasks in different languages. Bates et al. (1982) varied word order, animacy, emphatic stress, and topicalization in a study of comprehension in Italian and English. The stimuli consisted of sequences of the form noun-verb-noun, noun-noun-verb, and verb-noun-noun, many of which were ungrammatical in English and uncommon in Italian and others of which constituted grammatical sentences in English and common forms of sentences in Italian. English-speaking subjects showed a strong tendency to take noun-verb-noun (N-V-N) sequences as representing agent-verb-theme, the immediately postverbal noun as theme in V-N-N sequences, and the immediately preverbal noun as agent in N-N-V sequences. Italians, on the other hand, showed only a roughly 70% choice of the first noun as agent in N-V-N sequences, and between 50% and 60% choice of the first noun as agent in the other sequences. Differences between the languages were also found with respect to the degree to which animacy influenced the assignment of thematic roles, with respect to the interaction of animacy and word order, and with respect to the importance of stress and topicalization. In both Italian and English, a "convergence" of cues always produced faster and more consistent decisions regarding thematic roles than resulted when cues "competed." MacWhinney et al. (1984), using the same paradigm, extended these observations to the investigation of the role of word order, verb agreement and case morphology, animacy, and emphatic stress in English, Italian, and German. Again, the languages differed significantly with respect to the importance of word order, subject-verb agreement and case markings, and animacy. In English, 50% of the variance was accounted for by the word-order parameter, as opposed to 1.4% in Italian and 0% in German. Agreement accounted for 54% of the variance in Italian, 0.9% in English, and 10.4% in German. Animacy accounted for 20.2% of the variance in German, 1% in English, and 4.2% in Italian. This hierarchy of cues was used to establish predictions regarding the effects of "competition" and "convergence" on the assignment of thematic roles, and the results were in keeping with the predictions of the model.

In addition to the fact that the data are consistent with their model, Bates and MacWhinney argue that their results deny the existence of a syntactic parser for two reasons. First, the probabilistic nature of determining cue validity leading to the assignment of thematic roles is incompatible with an invariant rule-based parser. Second, the fact that English relies mainly on grammatical cues (word order) whereas Italian relies mainly on semantic cues (animacy, as long as agreement does not disambiguate the sentence) is not consistent with a language-universal notion of a parser that relies on syntactic features to construct a parse tree.

However, the crucial question is whether the model proposed by Bates and MacWhinney can ultimately deal with all the complexities of language for which a parsing model is generally considered necessary. All the sentence structures they tested are extremely simple, consisting of two nouns and a verb. It is not clear how this model could be extended to a larger range of structures in natural language. For instance, the observation that the immediately preverbal noun is taken as Agent in English might be expected to lead to consistent misinterpretation of the following sentences:

(14) The father of the child kissed the woman.

(15) The man who kissed the woman hugged the child.

Normal subjects do not misinterpret sentence 14 as indicating that the child kissed the woman, or sentence 15 as indicating that the woman hugged the child. Bates (personal communication, 1986) claims that part of the mechanism of sentence interpretation depends on a set of probabilities for particular constituents to occur adjacently in the language. For example, in English the NP following the word *of* in sentence 14 would have a high probability of serving as a genitive and a very low probability of serving as Agent of the sentence; therefore, the Agent should be correctly assigned. However, there is a very real question of how far sentence interpretation can go with a set of surface features in the input string and a set of probabilities based on adjacent constituents. In the Bates-MacWhinney model, discontinuous constituents are correctly interpreted when they are recognized as not occurring where they should. However, the more common the occurrence of a particular discontinuous constituent, the lower the probability of that constituent's occurring in a position in which it would normally be assigned the correct thematic role, and the lower the probability of that constituent's being recognized as discontinuous.

Linguistic theory itself is based on hierarchical, not linear, relations. The Bates-MacWhinney model has the potential to account for some hierarchical effects in that the (semantic) predicate-argument representation is hierarchical and could interact with the interpretation of the input string. However, as far as we know, a hierarchical predicate-argument representation cannot account for parsing constraints such as Minimal Attachment (Frazier and Fodor 1978) or linguistic constraints such as subjacency, both of which apply to hierarchical *syntactic* representations. Here it is of interest that, although Italian subjects may base their interpretations of ambiguous sentences on animacy or agreement rather than on word order, Italian obeys the subjacency constraint, just as English does, albeit with different bounding nodes (Rizzi 1978). This fact is accounted for by the existence of a syntactic parser, but not by a language-specific model of assigning thematic roles according to surface features of the language such as animacy.

Despite the claims to the contrary, the cross-linguistic data of Bates and MacWhinney need not be inconsistent with the existence of a parser if surface cues such as word order, animacy, case marking, agreement, and stress are utilized at a pre-parsing level. Consider how a parser would deal with the unambiguous grammatical, the ambiguous grammatical, and the ungrammatical sentences used in the experiments of Bates and MacWhinney. A parser based on a representation of language structures provides the correct structural description of the syntactic structure of a sentence. A parser does not provide a structural description for a nonsentence. Accordingly, a parser would assign unequivocal structures and interpretations to grammatical and unambiguous sentences, would have to choose among competing structures for grammatical but ambiguous sentences, and would not assign structure to any nonsentences. In languages with a higher probability of grammatical ambiguity, it is conceivable that the surface features in question could serve as pre-parsing cues to disambiguate the assignment of structure. The language-specific reliance on certain features over others may come about in the followed way: In English, noncanonical word order is accompanied by some disambiguating feature in the string— a relative pronoun in the case of relative clauses and cleft sentences, or stress in the case of topicalization (*Beans, I hate*). In Italian, however, when the verb agrees with either noun in a sentence the word order does not disambiguate the correct structural assignment; for example, a sentence could be Subject-Object-Verb or Object-Subject-Verb. In Italian, other features, such as pragmatic context and stress, can potentially serve to disambiguate the correct structural assignment for the parser and would serve to reduce the possibility of assigning the wrong structure. The strong claim would be that both pre-parsing cues and assignment of structure by the parser occur in the interpretation of every sentence, rather than occurring only in ambiguous and syntactically complex sentences, respectively.

Conclusion

We have reviewed one implemented model of the parsing process based on one theory of syntactic structure and a number of psycholinguistic experiments that bear on the nature of this process. Though there are models of sentence processing that deny the existence of a parser, we have concluded that these models are overstated. Many aspects of the processing and the final interpretation of sentences appear to result from the operations of the parser. It is, however, likely that a lexico-pragmatic route to meaning is engaged simultaneously with the operation of the parser, and that it may contribute to the assignment of meaning (at least in simple sentences). Similarly, it is likely that many language-specific "cues" trigger parsing rules and are important in the assignment of preferred readings in ambiguous structures. With this background regarding the nature of syntactic representations and their processing in the task of sentence comprehension, we now turn to studies of disturbances affecting these representations and these processes.

Chapter 3
Previous Studies

It has been known for over a century that certain patients have difficulty understanding aspects of meaning that are related to phrases and sentences, despite relatively preserved abilities to understand the meanings of single words. Jackson (1874), Thomas (1908), Goldstein (1948), and others commented on the fact that some patients had an isolated comprehension disturbance affecting propositions but not single words. It was not, however, until the 1970s that the psychopathogenesis of disturbances in the understanding of propositional aspects of meaning was investigated in greater detail. A series of studies demonstrated that one reason for a failure of some patients to understand aspects of propositional meaning in certain sentences was their inability to assign and interpret syntactic structure. In this chapter we shall review the literature on this topic, highlighting the theoretical claims made by investigators regarding the nature and the causes of disturbances of syntactic comprehension.

Documentation of Syntactic-Comprehension Impairments

Though earlier work (e.g. Zurif, Caramazza, and Myerson 1972) suggested that certain patients might have disturbances of language processing that could lead to an inability to interpret syntactic structure, the first and seminal paper documenting disturbances of this function was Caramazza and Zurif 1976. These authors tested Broca's aphasics, conduction aphasics, and Wernicke's aphasics on a sentence-picture matching test, using sentences of the following four types:

(1) The apple the boy is eating is red.
(2) The boy the dog is patting is tall.
(3) The girl the boy is chasing is tall.
(4) The boy is eating a red apple.

Sentences 1–3 contain a center-embedded relative clause. They differ inasmuch as sentence 1 is pragmatically irreversible, sentence 2 has a pragmatically preferred reading that is contrary to the syntactically derived meaning, and sentence 3 is semantically reversible with respect to thematic roles around the embedded verb. Sentence 4 is a control sentence with a simpler syntactic structure. Each sentence was presented with the correct picture and one of four "foils": a picture in which one of the adjectives was altered, one in which the verb was altered, one in which both these changes were made, and one in which the Agent and the Theme of the verb were inverted. Patients were scored on the number of errors they made in selecting the correct picture.

Broca's and conduction aphasics made almost no errors when pictures with incorrect adjectives or verbs were used as foils. Their errors were confined to pictures representing reversals of the thematic roles of the nouns in the sentences. Moreover, these patients made errors only on sentences such as 2 and 3—sentences in which the syntax indicates an event improbable in the real world or in which the thematic roles are reversible. Caramazza and Zurif interpreted these results as indicating that patients with Broca's aphasia cannot construct syntactic structures, argued that the subjects had relied on the meanings of individual content words and on their knowledge of possible and probable events in the real world to determine meaning through a lexico-pragmatic route, and suggested that these results showed that agrammatic patients can use heuristics based on basic word order to interpret sentences.

Though Caramazza and Zurif's results have widely been taken as evidence of the existence of an isolated deficit in the comprehension of syntactic form, several objections to their original interpretations have been voiced. Schwartz, Saffran, and Marin (1980) have pointed out that Caramazza and Zurif presented no semantically reversible sentences in canonical word order, and that therefore the suggestion that the patients tested could use the canonical word order of lexical items in a sentence to derive thematic roles has no empirical basis. We note, furthermore, that testing the assignment of thematic roles in pragmatically constrained sentences such as (1) requires the depiction of impossible events (such as an apple eating a boy), and that in these cases patients may simply have selected the picture that depicted a realistic event rather than matching that picture to sentence meaning. In retrospect, though Caramazza and Zurif's original interpretation of their results may be correct, these data do not prove conclusively that the patients tested had a disturbance restricted to syntactic comprehension, with retention of lexico-pragmatic and word-order-based heuristic routes to assignment of thematic roles. Nonetheless, the Caramazza-Zurif experiment led to a number of subsequent investigations of how patients interpret syntactic structures, including the present study. In addition, it identified the two factors that must be controlled in an investigation of the residual use of a parser by an aphasic patient: lexico-pragmatic factors (which determine aspects of sentential meaning otherwise assigned by the parser) and heuristic strategies (which assign aspects of sentential semantic meaning without reference to the full syntactic representation assigned by a parser).

The Caramazza-Zurif study introduced two questions regarding disorders of syntactic comprehension into linguistic aphasiology: What are the exact natures of the linguistic structures that aphasics can interpret and those they cannot? Is a disturbance of syntactic comprehension secondary to some other aphasic impairment? The first of these questions arose from Caramazza and Zurif's suggestion that word-order-based heuristics were available to their patients who could not interpret more complex syntactic forms such as center-embedded relatives. The second question arose because of Caramazza and Zurif's emphasis on the co-occurrence of the syntactic-comprehension deficit they described with expressive agrammatism in their Broca's aphasics. They argued that the two symptoms were both consequences of a processing impairment affecting the use of the function-word vocabulary and the inflectional vocabulary. Because the question of agrammatism has been so important in directing both the empirical and the theoretical work in this field, we shall explore this aspect of the literature first, although the question regarding linguistic structures is more important.

Agrammatism and Syntactic-Comprehension Disorders

Agrammatism is a disturbance of speech planning in which function words and inflectional morphemes are omitted more frequently than major lexical-class items. The linguistic description of the omitted items and the psychopathogenetic mechanisms involved in their omission and in other features of the speech of patients with this symptom have been discussed in many recent publications (e.g. Kean 1977; Berndt and Caramazza 1980; Bradley, Garrett, and Zurif 1980; Lapointe 1983; Grodzinsky 1984; Badecker and Caramazza 1985; Caplan 1986a). The relationship between expressive agrammatism and syntactic comprehension has been characterized in a variety of ways. We shall consider seven analyses that have led to empirical experimentation, and shall comment on several others that have been enunciated on the basis of existing observations without themselves leading to or directly resulting from new empirical work. We shall consider these theories in order from the most general to the most specific, where by "general" we mean "postulating a more severe deficit."

The theories we shall consider are

• the hypothesis that agrammatic patients cannot construct thematic roles (Saffran, Schwartz, and Marin 1980; Schwartz et al. 1980),

• the theory that agrammatic patients have a global failure of parsing operations (Berndt and Caramazza 1980),

• the theory that agrammatic patients cannot map syntactic structures onto semantic features (Linebarger, Schwartz, and Saffran 1983a),

• the theory that agrammatic patients "trade off" between assignment and interpretation of syntactic structure (Linebarger et al. 1983a; Schwartz, Linebarger, Saffran, and Pate 1987),

• the theory that agrammatic patients cannot use function words and inflectional morphemes to construct syntactic structures in "on-line" tasks (Bradley et al. 1980; Zurif 1982, 1984),

• the theory that agrammatic patients cannot construct hierarchically organized phrase markers (Caplan 1983b, 1985), and

• the theory that agrammatic patients cannot coindex traces in comprehension tasks (Grodzinsky 1986).

Other restrictive hypotheses regarding the relationship between expressive agrammatism and syntactic-comprehension disturbances have been advanced by Kean (1982) and by Rizzi (1985); we shall consider these in passing.

The most severe syntactic-comprehension deficit that has been postulated in agrammatic patients is one presented by Schwartz et al. (1980) and Saffran et al. (1980). As noted above, Schwartz and her colleagues observed that Caramazza and Zurif's claim that their agrammatic patients used heuristics based on word order to establish thematic roles was not directly supported by data from their own experiments. They therefore set out to investigate whether agrammatic patients were able to interpret "word order" by presenting the following types of sentences to five agrammatic patients:

(5) The dancer applauds the actor.
(6) The actor applauds the dancer.
(7) The dancer is applauded by the actor.
(8) The actor is applauded by the dancer.

In a sentence-picture matching task in which there were two pictures from which to select—one representing the meaning of the sentence and one representing a reversal of the thematic roles of the NPs in the sentence—five agrammatic patients interpreted the active sentences 5 and 6 correctly about 75% of the time. On a case-by-case basis, two patients performed well above chance on sentences in the active voice and one patient's performance was exactly at the cutoff point for statistical reliability on sentences in the active voice. In the passive sentences 7 and 8, the patients performed at chance as a group, choosing 68 out of 124 correct pictures. Four of the five patients performed at chance level, and one consistently chose the incorrect picture. Schwartz et al. replicated the study with the same patients using more abstract stimuli in an effort to eliminate any subtle lexical effects and obtained similar results overall, although there was considerable variability in individual patients' performances. They also tested patients' abilities to understand sentences with a postcopula locative phrase, such as

(9) The box is in the cage.

Depending on how lexical errors are estimated, the five patients chose 103 or 114 correct pictures and made 91 syntactic errors.

Schwartz and her colleagues took these results as evidence that agrammatic patients are not able to assign thematic roles in semantically reversible sentences even when they are in canonical noun-verb-noun or noun-verb-prepositional phrase form. They argued that this failure to assign thematic roles correctly in these simple sentences is evidence that these patients do not use heuristics based on word order to assign thematic roles. This, in turn, implies that the comprehension disturbance in agrammatic patients extends beyond any consequences of a failure to utilize the function-word vocabulary and the inflectional vocabulary in both comprehension and sentence production, since it extends to the use of heuristics based on linear sequences of major lexical class items as well as to structure-building and interpretive operations that might utilize the function-word vocabulary.

This interpretation has been questioned by Caplan (1983a), who has pointed out that the group results for the active sentences 5 and 6 suggest that the patients did appreciate the word order of the sentence but were also influenced by the animacy of each noun. The pattern of interpretations could result from the patients' taking either the first noun or any animate noun as the Agent of the sentence with equal probability. Though the intrusion of an "animacy affect" complicates the responses, the results suggest that these patients do appreciate basic SVO or N-V-N word order in active sentences. On one set of assumptions regarding lexical errors, the same conclusion applies to simple locative sentences (such as sentence 9). Caplan (1983a) accepts that the results show that the patients are unable to interpret passive sentences correctly. However, this too could result from several impairments. One possibility is that the patients assign no thematic structure to a sentence at all, as Schwartz et al. suggest. Another possibility is that they take both the subject NP and the NP in the by-phrase as possible Agents, and cannot decide between these possibilities (Grodzinsky 1986). This would imply that they appreciate many syntactic features of sentences, including both word order and the passive construction, but cannot use this information normally.

Agrammatic patients' abilities to understand "word order" have been explored in several other studies. Kolk and van Grunsven (1985) report that one Dutch agrammatic patient was able to assign thematic roles to NPs in active sentences in canonical form at above-chance rates. Bates et al. (in press) report a somewhat similar result, observing that English, German, and Italian agrammatic aphasics made greater use of word-order cues than of agreement and case-marking cues to assign thematic roles to NPs in sentences and nonsentences in experiments patterned after Bates's work with normal subjects (see chapter 2). It thus appears that the ability to utilize canonical word order as a cue to the thematic roles played by NPs around verbs is retained in many agrammatic patients. The patients tested by Schwartz et al. also retained this ability, but they are among the more impaired agrammatic patients reported in the published literature with respect to this ability. On the basis of the available evidence, it appears that most patients with agrammatism retain the ability to map the basic word order of their language onto thematic roles. This entails the denial of the speculation of Saffran et al. that these patients have lost their understanding of the existence of thematic roles.

A second hypothesis regarding syntactic-comprehension impairment in agrammatic patients was formulated by Berndt and Caramazza (1980). These authors reached a conclusion very similar to one of the possibilities entertained by Schwartz et al. (1980): that the parser fails in agrammatism. Their hypothesis differs from that of Schwartz et al. inasmuch as it does not preclude the use of word-order-based heuristics for sentence interpretation, whereas Schwartz et al. were explicit in their argument that such heuristics are unavailable to agrammatics.

The evidence that led Berndt and Caramazza to the conclusion that the parser fails *in toto* in agrammatism is the performance of agrammatic patients on Caramazza and Zurif's experimental materials, described above. The argument that the parser fails in agrammatism is made in two parts. First, it is argued that all patients with agrammatism show syntactic-comprehension disorders. Second, it is argued that patients with agrammatism fail on tests of syntactic comprehension for different reasons than other patients. We shall consider the ubiquity of disorders of syntactic comprehension below, and discuss Berndt and Caramazza's analysis of the different mechanisms leading to disorders of this function here.

In the original experiment by Caramazza and Zurif, agrammatic Broca's aphasics were not the only patients to fail in the sentence-picture matching task when presented with syntactic foils in semantically reversible or improbable center-embedded relative clauses. Conduction aphasics also failed on these types of sentences. Several other studies also showed that patients with impairments other than expressive agrammatism had difficulty in comprehending syntactically complex semantically reversible sentences. Heilman and Scholes (1976), for instance, showed that both Broca's aphasics and conduction aphasics had difficulty understanding sentences such as 10 and 11, assigning to each of these sentences both its own meaning and the meaning appropriate for the other:

(10) Can you show her baby the pictures.
(11) Can you show her the baby pictures.

Indeed, difficulty interpreting these sentences was not confined to brain-injured subjects but was also found in a group of partially hearing-impaired adolescents. The Caramazza-Zurif (1976) results and the Heilman-Scholes (1976) results are typical in this regard: The vast majority of studies in which different patient groups have been tested have failed to show any differences with respect to the syntactic structures that are difficult for agrammatics and other patients to understand. (See Volin 1983 for one exception.)

Prima facie, the similarity of the sentence types that are difficult to understand for different patient groups constitutes an argument against the specificity of any parsing deficit in patients with expressive agrammatism, as Caplan (1985) pointed out. However, Berndt and Caramazza (1982) and Caramazza, Berndt, Basili, and Koller (1981) advanced the hypothesis that patients with different symptomatologies (other than a disturbance of syntactic comprehension), who thus belong to different patient groups, fail on tasks of syntactic comprehension for different reasons. They contrasted the performances of one agrammatic and one conduction aphasic on a number of tasks. Both performed equivalently in the comprehension of reversible passive and center-embedded sentences. However, they showed differences in performance on an anagram task in which the constituent words of a sentence were presented separately on randomly arranged cards. Whereas the agrammatic patient could not construct coherent phrases at all, the conduction aphasic constructed a sequence of short phrases, with several false starts, but finally arrived at a coherent arrangement of words. Berndt and Caramazza argue that the agrammatic patient's failure to solve the anagram task reflected a disturbance in parsing functions, whereas the conduction aphasic's gradual piecing together of words into phrases was a consequence of a short-term-memory limitation in that subject.

Though Berndt and Caramazza are correct that performance on other tasks may be useful in determining the primary psychopathogenesis of a syntactic-comprehension deficit, the particular analysis they propose for agrammatism is contradicted by performance of other agrammatic patients on yet another task. Linebarger et al. (1983a) had four agrammatic patients perform grammaticality-judgment tasks on a number of sentence types and found that, in the great majority of cases, these four patients, who failed on syntactic-comprehension tasks involving reversible passive sentences and did not perform well on reversible simple active sentences, were capable of making accurate judgments regarding the grammaticality of sentences with a large variety of well-formedness violations. Linebarger et al. concluded that parsing does not fail in agrammatic patients. We thus have a situation in which one ancillary task—anagram solution—suggests that an impairment in a parser underlies a disturbance of syntactic comprehension in one agrammatic patient, but a second ancillary task—grammaticality judgment—seems to show that agrammatics retain parsing abilities.

Because the results of Linebarger et al. cast serious doubt on the analysis of agrammatics' syntactic-comprehension deficit as a global failure of the parser, they reopen the question whether agrammatic patients' disturbances in syntactic comprehension are due to a different mechanism than those seen in conduction aphasia. Linebarger et al. (1983a, note 18) suggest that a deficit in "working memory" may underlie the syntactic-comprehension impairments seen in agrammatic patients—an analysis indistinguishable from that advanced by Berndt and Caramazza (and other authors, including Saffran; see below) regarding the syntactic-comprehension deficit in conduction aphasia.

The solution to the question of the mechanistic basis for comprehension failure in any individual patient, or in a group of patients with some common symptomatology such as agrammatism, thus has not been been forthcoming from the correlation of syntactic-comprehension deficits with impairments on other tasks, since these correlations have led to contradictory conclusions: Whereas the co-occurrence of a syntactic-comprehension deficit with difficulty in anagram solution suggests the failure of a parser, the co-occurrence of syntactic-comprehension impairment with intact grammaticality-judgment abilities suggests the intactness of a parser. Reconciling these disparate results, and interpreting each co-occurrence, poses problems because the metalinguistic tasks with which syntactic-comprehension deficits are correlated are ones whose task requirements are not known. Correlations of this sort are of limited utility in determining the mechanistic causes of disorders of syntactic comprehension, unless very detailed task analyses are available for failures on each of the correlated failed tasks.

Linebarger and her colleagues offer two specific hypotheses of their own for the failure of agrammatic patients to perform correctly on tasks requiring syntactic comprehension, both of which take into account their finding that these patients can perform grammaticality-judgment tasks. The first of these hypotheses is that agrammatic patients cannot map syntactic structures created by the parser onto semantic representations; the second is that agrammatic patients "trade off" between an ability to assign and interpret syntactic structures, such that more syntactic structure is computed when the task requires only a "shallow" semantic representation (as in grammaticality judgment). The second of these theories relates the syntactic-comprehension disturbance in agrammatic patients to a limitation of "working memory" that reduces a patient's ability to accomplish two tasks simultaneously or to relate the products of two operations.

Schwartz et al. (1987) attempted to investigate these two possibilities further by presenting sentences such as 12–15 to agrammatic subjects.

(12) The bird ate the seed.
(13) The seed ate the bird.
(14) The seed was eaten by the bird.
(15) The bird was eaten by the seed.

The subjects' task was to indicate whether the sentence was semantically odd or not. Agrammatic patients performed well on simple active sentences but poorly on passive sentences. Since picture interpretation was eliminated in this task, and since the patients continued to show impairments related to the assignment of thematic roles in sentences with more complex syntactic structure, Schwartz and her colleagues inclined toward the view that the deficit that had led to syntactic-comprehension disturbances in the patients affected the assignment of semantic features to a parse; i.e., the first hypothesis.

Before this account can be considered to be the correct analysis of the impairment in agrammatism, three issues need to be considered. The first, which we shall discuss below, is whether all agrammatic patients perform in the same way on these tasks. The second is whether there is an analysis of the pattern of performance on all these tasks, in linguistic terms, that allows the formulation of a deficit affecting a specified set of linguistic structures. The third issue is whether the processing-deficit analysis just presented is the only one compatible with these data.

The second issue has been discussed by Zurif and Grodzinsky (1983), who have argued that the sentences on which grammaticality judgments were well performed by the patients in the study by Linebarger et al. were ones in which the grammaticality violation involved the position of major lexical class categories—nouns, verbs, and adjectives—in surface structures, whereas the sentences in which violations involved only function-word categories were rejected considerably less often. For instance, performance was better on sentences in which a noun phrase occurred in what should have been a gap position, as in (16) and (17), than on sentences in which the auxiliary verb in a tag question did not agree with the matrix auxiliary or in which a reflexive did not agree in number, person, or gender with its antecedent, as in (18) and (19).

*(16) How many did you see birds in the park?
*(17) Mary ate the bread that I baked a cake.
*(18) John is very tall, doesn't he?
*(19) I helped themselves to the birthday cake.

Zurif and Grodzinsky argue that this pattern of relative difficulty of these different sentence violations suggests that the patients were less able to recognize ill-formedness when it resulted from errors limited to the function-word vocabulary than when it involved the major categories, and that this is consistent with an impairment affecting the use of function words in both sentence-interpretation and grammaticality-judgment tasks.

Linebarger, Schwartz, and Saffran (1983b) responded to these observations by acknowledging the differences in patients' performances between these sentence types but emphasizing the extent to which their patients did well on many sentence types in which violations involved only the function-word vocabulary. Specific data regarding performance on sentences with violations of auxiliary verb-subject agreement do not support the suggestion of Zurif and Grodzinsky. The view of Linebarger et al. is that their patients did too well on many of these latter types of violations for their syntactic-comprehension deficits to be attributable entirely to impairments in utilizing the function-word vocabulary to interpret syntactic structure.

This reply is an adequate response to the particular analysis proposed by Zurif and Grodzinsky, but it does not settle the issue of whether the performance of the patients on the grammaticality tests utilized by Linebarger and her colleagues implies that the parser is working in its normal fashion to yield normal structures. For instance, several of the violations these patients detected involved the presence of extra noun phrases that could not be assigned a thematic role by a verb in a sentence (as in *The cake that the woman ate the pie was good*). A patient who simply rejected any sentence in which a noun phrase was not assigned a thematic role would reject these sentences, whether or not he was assigning normal structure to the relative clause. Linebarger et al. suggest that the output of the parsing process that occurs in these patients consists of a "shallow semantic structure," but express uncertainty about what such a structure is. In short, though these results do point to the preservation of some aspects of the parsing process and the sentence-interpretation process in these patients, the exact parsing operations that are being utilized and the exact structures that result from these operations are not known.

Zurif and Grodzinsky also raise the question whether the processing analysis suggested by Linebarger and her colleagues is correct. They argue that the grammaticality-judgment task is "off-line," inasmuch as it does not require responses immediately related temporally to the operation of the parser. In response, Linebarger et al. argue that all the tasks on which agrammatic patients fail—sentence-picture matching, word relatedness, etc.—are off-line tasks (except lexical-decision tasks, to be discussed below). They argue that there is no reason to postulate a separate parsing mechanism that operates only in grammaticality-judgment tasks and not in normal sentence-comprehension tasks, or to assume that the grammaticality judgments were accomplished by the operation of a set of heuristics independent of the normal parser. Our view is that this aspect of the position taken by Linebarger et al. is appropriate. Though it may be the case that good performance on a grammaticality task reflects the operation of parsing or heuristic mechanisms not involved in normal sentence comprehension, the most parsimonious theory would posit that the same parsing mechanism is involved in well-formedness judgment and comprehension tasks. If so, the performance of the agrammatic patients reported by Linebarger et al. is evidence that some of these parsing mechanisms are available to agrammatic patients, subject to the uncertainty we have just expressed regarding exactly which operations are retained.

Before moving on to other hypotheses, we shall suggest another processing analysis of the findings of Linebarger et al. Recall that their results (1983b) and those of Schwartz et al. (1987) were taken as evidence for intact parsing abilities and for impairment in the mapping of syntactic structures onto semantic structures in sentence comprehension in agrammatic patients. However, there is another possible account of this pattern of performance (which is also relevant to the performance of patients with short-term-memory impairments; see below). Not only is it possible that the patients studied by Linebarger et al. are more impaired with respect to normal parsing operations than these authors suggest; it is also possible that they are *less* impaired than these authors suggest with respect to comprehension, to the point that they may be able to assign sentential semantic values, such as thematic roles, on the basis of a constructed syntactic structure. If so, their ability to make grammaticality judgments at above-chance levels requires no explanation, but their poor performance on sentence-comprehension tasks remains to be accounted for. It may be explained as follows: The normal sentence-interpretation system yields sentential semantic information via two routes: a syntactic route and a lexico-pragmatic route. For a semantically reversible sentence, the lexico-pragmatic route will yield two sets of thematic roles, one corresponding to each of the pragmatically possible events in the real world, and the syntactic route will yield the reading that is grammatically licensed. In this circumstance, a post-interpretive "adjudication" process must "decide" which interpretation corresponds to the meaning of the presented sentence, and this process may review the form of the sentence just presented to arrive at this judgment. In the case of a semantically anomalous sentence, such as (13) or (15), the lexico-pragmatic route yields one acceptable semantic reading and the syntactic route yields a second, anomalous reading. In this case, a post-interpretive process deciding which of these two readings corresponds to the presented sentence is also needed. The impairment that leads to poor performance on both sentence-picture matching tests for reversible sentences with complex syntactic structures in which syntactic foils are presented and tasks of anomaly detection in non-reversible sentences with complex syntactic structure may be one in which this putative post-interpretive adjudication mechanism is involved. This analysis bears on the role of components of the "working memory" system in syntactic comprehension, and will be discussed again later in this chapter. The present point is that an analysis along these lines claims that a working-memory deficit affects operations that occur after syntactic structure has been assigned and interpreted, whereas the analysis proposed by Linebarger et al. suggests that a working-memory deficit internal to the parsing/interpretive process underlies agrammatic syntactic-comprehension impairments. We shall return in chapters 5 and 6 to the details of how such a sentence-internal processing deficit related to "working memory" may affect syntactic comprehension.

The fifth analysis of the syntactic-comprehension deficit in agrammatism that we shall consider was suggested by Caplan (1983b, 1985). Basing his analysis on a review of the literature and on a case study (Caplan and Futter 1986), Caplan argued that a feature of both sentence comprehension and sentence production that characterized all cases of agrammatism was an inability to map thematic roles onto hierarchically structured phrase markers and a retention of the ability to map this aspect of semantic structure onto purely linear sequences of major lexical-category nodes—nouns, verbs, and adjectives. This led to the "lexical node hypothesis," according to which agrammatic patients assign thematic roles to linear sequences of major lexical-category nodes. The evidence we have already presented that agrammatic patients can utilize canonical word order to assign thematic roles supports this theory, since it establishes a "lower bound" regarding the features of syntactic form that are utilized in sentence comprehension by agrammatic patients. The remaining aspect of the argument rested on the demonstration that agrammatic patients did not utilize more than these sequences of nouns and verbs for the assignment of thematic roles; case S.P. in chapter 5 below is taken to present such evidence for one agrammatic patient. It is now clear, however, that this characterization, though perhaps true of some agrammatic patients (such as S.P.), does not apply to all agrammatic patients. We shall discuss the range of syntactic-comprehension disturbances in agrammatic patients and the implications of the variability in this function in this population after presenting the remaining hypotheses regarding syntactic comprehension in agrammatism.

The Caplan (1985) hypothesis incorporated one feature of the historically first proposal regarding the relationship between expressive agrammatism and syntactic comprehension proposed in the recent literature—that suggested by Zurif and Caramazza on the basis of their 1976 experiments, which we reviewed at the outset of this chapter. Zurif and Caramazza

(1976) argued that the results they had obtained with Broca's aphasics were attributable to an inability of these patients to utilize the function-word vocabulary for purposes of constructing syntactic phrase markers. They pointed to earlier results of theirs (Zurif et al. 1972; Zurif, Green, Caramazza, and Goodenough 1976) as indicating that Broca's aphasics with expressive agrammatism had a variety of disturbances affecting the use of the function-word vocabulary. Zurif et al. (1973) demonstrated that these patients did not integrate function words into hierarchical clusters on the basis of judgments of the degree of relatedness of pairs of words in word triads taken from sentences; Zurif et al. (1976) showed that agrammatic patients were unable to map the definite and indefinite senses of the articles *the* and *a* onto items in an array in the same way as normals. Post-1976 work by Zurif has also been analyzed as showing abnormalities in the processing of function words by agrammatic patients. Bradley et al. (1980) reported an abnormal frequency sensitivity to function words in a lexical-decision task, and a similarly abnormal presence of a nonword interference effect in lexical-decision tasks when the first few letters of a nonword string constituted a function word. These investigators argued that these abnormalities reflected a disturbance in a lexical-access mechanism specific to the use of the function-word vocabulary in parsing operations. Rosenberg, Zurif, Brownell, Garrett, and Bradley (1985) reported an abnormal detection rate for the letter E in function words in a letter-cancellation task in agrammatic patients. All these results have been taken by Zurif (1982, 1984) as evidence for abnormal processing of the function-word vocabulary in agrammatic patients; Zurif argues that this abnormal processing is causally related to the syntactic-comprehension disturbances he has documented in these patients.

This analysis encounters several serious empirical problems. Critical aspects of the database supporting this analysis have not been replicated; in particular, the lexical-decision results of Bradley et al. were not found in separate experiments by Gordon and Caramazza (1982) and Segui, Mehler, Frauenfelder, and Morton (1982). The range of syntactic-comprehension deficits found in agrammatic patients cannot be related to disturbances affecting the use of the function-word vocabulary and the inflectional vocabulary without considerably more detailed descriptions of the particular impairments postulated in individual cases (see below). Zurif has attempted to distinguish between on-line and off-line utilization of the function word/inflectional vocabulary, and between its use in the construction of syntactic structure and its contribution to sentence meaning through intrinsic semantic features of function words such as prepositions, arguing that the impairment in agrammatism affecting function-word-vocabulary and inflectional-vocabulary items involves the first member of both these pairs of functions. However, as Linebarger et al. (1983b) pointed out, many of the tasks on which agrammatic patients fail are "off-line" tasks. In addition, poor performance on tasks such as that reported in Zurif et al. 1976 must reflect a difficulty patients have in utilizing intrinsic semantic information in function words (in this case, definite and indefinite articles). The problems raised above regarding the interpretation of failure on anagram tasks apply to patients' failures on many of the tasks cited by Zurif: The tasks themselves have not undergone componential analyses, so we cannot know what failure on the task reflects or how such failure is related to impairments in syntactic comprehension.

The final hypothesis regarding the nature of syntactic-comprehension deficits in agrammatic patients we shall review is due to Grodzinsky (1986). This analysis is also part of a more general description of agrammatic patients' difficulties related to Zurif's "function word" account. Grodzinsky (1984) suggested that agrammatic patients misproduce items that are not phonologically specified at S-structure. This analysis is one formalization of the "function word" theory of agrammatism; we shall briefly consider other formalizations of such theories in linguistic terms below. Grodzinsky (1986) argued that agrammatics have difficulty comprehending these same items. Empty categories specified by Chomsky (1981, 1982) are among these items (see chapter 1 above), and Grodzinsky argues that the disturbances of syntactic comprehension that have been documented in agrammatic patients are due to a failure to coindex traces with their antecedent NPs. Grodzinsky (1986) presents data from five agrammatic patients indicating that they randomly assign thematic roles in passive sentences, such as (20), and in sentences with object relativization, such as (21) and (22), but not in sentences with subject relativization, such as (23) and (24).

(20) The dog$_i$ was chased t_i by the cat.
(21) The dog$_i$ that the cat chased t_i followed the rat.
(22) The dog chased the cat$_i$ that the rat followed t_i.
(23) The dog$_i$ that t_i chased the cat followed the rat.
(24) The dog chased the cat$_i$ that t_i followed the rat.

Grodzinsky argues that (20)–(22) require coindexation of traces to be understood, but that (23) and (24) can be understood by a heuristic that takes the head NP of a relative clause as the Agent of the verb of that clause.

We (Caplan and Hildebrandt 1986; Caplan 1987a) argue that, although this failure of Grodzinsky's patients is consistent with an inability to co-index traces, this database is not sufficient to prove that this is the impairment the patients have. Grodzinsky has not shown that his patients can coindex overt referentially dependent items—pronouns and reflexives. He has not shown that his patients can find the antecedent for other empty categories specified in Chomsky's theory, such as PRO. He has not even shown that patients can understand sentences with the same number of noun phrases as there are noun-phrase positions in the sentences with traces that he used (sentences with four noun-phrase positions as controls for the object relative sentences, and sentences with similar structures with three overt noun phrases as controls for the passives). In the absence of these control data, we do not know whether the patients reported in Grodzinsky 1986 have a deficit unique to the coindexation of traces. Their deficit may extend to the coindexation of all referentially dependent items, or to the coindexation of all empty categories, or may be due to memory factors that affect sentences with particular numbers of noun phrases. To determine that Grodzinsky's analysis is correct for even one of his own cases requires more empirical evidence than is available in his report.

Several other specific linguistic analyses of the deficit in agrammatism have been suggested. Kean (1977, 1980, 1982) has proposed that the items subject to omission in expressive agrammatism are those that are not subject to word-level phonological processes (so-called phonological clitics). She argues (Kean 1982) that a processing disturbance affecting these vocabulary items would affect the construction of syntactic structures in both sentence-production tasks and syntactic-comprehension tasks. Like Grodzinsky's (1984, 1986) analysis, this theory provides a formal description of the linguistic items affected in agrammatism and relates this characterization to a very general processing model; and as is the case with that analysis, the database supporting this specific analysis is inadequate to distinguish this proposal from others phrased at the same level of detail. Similar comments apply to the linguistic analysis proposed by Rizzi (1985), which holds that theta-role assignees and assigners are retained in agrammatism and that items accomplishing neither of these functions are subject to omission and do not lead to structures that are interpreted in sentence-comprehension tasks. These highly specific theoretical formulations make minimally different claims regarding syntactic comprehension in agrammatism (minimally different, that is, relative to the existing database regarding these impairments), and more empirical work specifically directed toward verifying these different hypotheses is needed before they can be accepted or rejected.

We must emphasize that all the theories reviewed above have been formulated in terms that suggest that the deficit analysis proposed in each account is true of all agrammatic patients. We have indicated at several points that this assertion is not supported by the available data. Indeed, it has been argued that expressive agrammatism is not a single category, because of the extensive variability in the speech abnormalities seen in patients termed "agrammatic" (Badecker and Caramazza 1985). Though

Caplan has argued elsewhere (1986a) that expressive agrammatism is a reasonable and defensible category of aphasic deficit given the level of theory and the empirical data that now characterize this area of aphasiology, we have also indicated that there may be many "profiles" of agrammatism, each due to different selective deficits, even on the expressive side. When we consider how patients with agrammatism perform on syntactic-comprehension tasks, we see such a wide degree of variation as to preclude the possibility that a single functional disturbance underlies the syntactic-comprehension impairments in many individual patients with agrammatism.

Several patients with expressive agrammatism have shown no disturbances of syntactic comprehension whatsover. Miceli, Mazzucchi, Menn, and Goodglass (1983), Nespoulous, Perron, Dordain, Caplan, Bub, Mehler, and Lecours (1985), and Kolk and Van Grunsven (1985) have reported agrammatic patients without disturbances in syntactic comprehension. The Nespoulous case was tested on a wide range of sentences, including all the sentence types that had proved difficult for the patients we reviewed above. Though some of these patients may be exceptional in certain ways (one of the Miceli patients, for instance, had only a transient aphasic impairment, which resolved within a month), many of them have classic expressive agrammatism and are not distinguishable from other agrammatic patients who do have disturbances of syntactic comprehension. These cases therefore constitute counterevidence to the proposition that there is only one impairment producing expressive agrammatism that necessarily entails a disturbance of syntactic comprehension. The strongest theory relating expressive agrammatism and syntactic-comprehension deficits that can be maintained in the face of these counterexamples is one that postulates several disturbances underlying expressive agrammatism, one or more of which entail a disturbance of syntactic comprehension and others of which do not.

At present, there is no theoretical "fractionation" of the disturbances in expressive agrammatism that allows particular impairments to be related to or separated from syntactic-comprehension disturbances. Any theoretical development along these lines would also have to account for the fact that, to the extent that disturbances of syntactic comprehension and expressive agrammatism can be assessed in terms of degree of severity, there seems to be no correlation between the severity of a syntactic-comprehension deficit and the severity of expressive agrammatism in an individual patient (Caplan and Hildebrandt 1986). Among the patients we have studied, the Nespoulous case was moderately impaired in spontaneous speech but showed no disturbance of syntactic comprehension; the more mildly agrammatic patient (S.P.) described in Caplan and Futter 1986 showed a fairly severe impairment in the construction and interpretation of syntactic form. To the extent that judgments of severity can be made regarding published cases, a similar lack of correlation between expressive and receptive deficits in agrammatic patients characterizes the other cases in the literature. Though these observations do not preclude the development of a theory that would relate certain forms of expressive agrammatism to particular patterns of syntactic-comprehension impairment, it renders the possibility that such an account would apply to more than some agrammatic patients highly unlikely. In most, if not all, agrammatic patients, a co-occurring deficit in syntactic comprehension is probably an unrelated aphasic impairment.

Disorders of Short-Term Memory and of Syntactic Comprehension

Expressive agrammatism is one of two major language-related impairments that researchers have thought might lead to disturbances in syntactic comprehension. The second such impairment is a disturbance of short-term memory (STM). One might expect that any impairment in the ability to maintain lexical items in short-term memory or to retrieve items from an STM system would result in an impairment in the comprehension of sentences, in which words are necessarily presented in sequential order in the auditory modality. However, the matter is more complicated than it at first appears. STM capacities are typically assessed by evaluation of a subject's recall span for lists of digits, nonsense syllables, or words of one sort or another. Depending on the stimulus material, and subject to individual differences, this span is usually between five and nine items. In contrast, subjects are able to recall sentences with a considerably larger number of words verbatim. This indicates that the structure provided by sentence form and meaning is somehow helpful in the task of immediate recall. Sentence form is not the only structure that aids immediate and short-term recall in this fashion. Grouping items into intonational groups— for instance, presenting items in intonationally contoured triads separated by pauses—also greatly increases digit span (Miller 1956). These observations on normals prove that structures above the word level (intonational, possibly syntactic, possibly semantic, etc.) are assigned to incoming auditorily presented material and aid the functioning of STM. In addition, comprehension of sentences and discourse greatly exceeds subjects' abilities to recall these structures verbatim. Thus, if we measure "short-term memory" in terms of the largest number of digits or isolated words that a subject can recall, we can conclude that "short-term-memory span" is more limited than the "span" of words that can be assigned a syntactic structure and sentential semantic features by normal subjects.

From the discrepancy between the number of words that can be inter-preted and the number that can be recalled verbatim in sentences, we can conclude that some portion of the sentence-interpretation process assigns and interprets supralexical structure and can store and retrieve this interpre-tation in a form or a fashion that is not available for the verbatim recall of words in lists or even in interpretable sentences. Psychologists (see e.g. Fodor and Garrett 1967; Fodor, Garrett, and Bever 1968; Fodor, Bever, and Garrett 1974) have suggested that sentences are interpreted in "chunks," each of which is assigned a structure and an interpretion, and that the resulting interpretation is entered into a system other than the system responsible for the verbatim recall of word lists or words in sentences. One psychological characterization of this process holds that successive inter-preted aspects of sentences are placed in "long-term store," as opposed to the "short-term store" primarily responsible for storage and verbatim re-trieval of word lists and sentences.

Some evidence for a distinction between "short-term store" and "long-term store" is derived from the properties of the items that are most easily recalled after short and long temporal intervals. Conrad and Hull (1964) and Baddeley (1966b) have shown that phonological similarities among items in a list reduce recall of those items after short delays, up to several seconds, but do not influence recall of items when recall is delayed for more than several minutes. Conversely, semantic similarity between lexical items in a list has no effect on recall at short post-presentation intervals, but causes recall to deteriorate after several minutes (Baddeley 1966a,b). These observations are consistent with the theory that items that are interpreted are moved to "long-term store," whereas items in "short-term store" are uninterpreted but remain available for verbatim recall. However, this ex-planation affects the account of performance on STM tasks. Since items in lists can be recalled verbatim after a delay of several minutes, it must be possible to retrieve or reconstruct items in verbatim form from "long-term store." This raises the possibility that some aspects of performance in tasks requiring recall after short post-stimulus intervals are due to retrieval from "long-term store," and that other aspects of performance after these short delays are due to retrieval from "short-term store." A characteristic feature of recall of lists that exceed a subject's span is that the first and last items in such lists are better recalled than the items occupying medial positions— the so-called primacy and recency effects. It has been suggested that the primacy effect results from retrieval of items from "long-term store" and the recency effect is due to retrieval of items from "short-term store" (Glanzer, Koppenaal, and Nelson 1972). Since the recency effect is usually limited to three or four items when a list is presented at the rate of one item per second, this view would suggest that "short-term store" either main-tains at most three or four items or is limited to approximately 3 seconds' worth of auditorily presented verbal material. If this is the case, the role in sentence comprehension of what is technically defined as "short-term store"—a memory system that maintains items in phonological form for approximately 3 seconds—may be more limited than the initial considerations stated above suggest.

This analysis, however, is not universally accepted. An alternative account holds that the primacy effect is due to subjects' ability to rehearse items (Atkinson and Shiffrin 1968, 1971; Rundus 1971), whereas the recency effect is due to the rate of decay of phonological representations in one component of an STM system. Since rehearsal is generally taken to be accomplished over phonological (or even articulatory) representations, some theorists prefer to divide "short-term store" into a "phonological store," in which items are represented in phonological form and decay rapidly, and an "articulatory loop," in which the phonological form of items is maintained by a more active rehearsal process. Recent work has questioned the relationship of the primacy effect to rehearsal and the relationship of the recency effect to passive decay of phonological representations. The recency effect has been found in long-term-memory tasks (Baddeley and Hitch 1974; Tzeng 1973) and shown to be influenced by strategies used by a patient (Vallar, 1985), so it is unlikely that it results from passive decay of a phonological form. However, these basic operations of the STM system for verbal material—phonological storage and articulatory rehearsal— have remained important aspects of a new theory of the structure of this system. Baddeley and Hitch (1974) and Baddeley (1981) have suggested that these two components of the STM system are "slave systems" that maintain items in STM when the processing capacity of the cognitive system engaged in assigning further structure to linguistic representations— which Baddeley and Hitch call a "central executive"—is exceeded by the processing demands of the task. Baddeley and Hitch term the entire system consisting of the "central executive," the "phonological store," and "articulatory loop" the system of "working memory." Based on the results of dual-task experiments in normals, Baddeley has concluded that the articulatory loop is automatically engaged in reading tasks, and has suggested that the phonological store is necessary for certain aspects of normal sentence comprehension.

Many neuropsychologists share this assessment of the data. A characteristic view of the role of a phonological (and/or articulatory) memory system in sentence comprehension is that of Caramazza and Berndt (1985), who state that "morphologically interpreted phonological representations are placed in a phonological working memory for syntactic parsing" (p. 46) and who claim that "the evidence that a phonological working memory system is implicated in syntactic parsing comes from studies of both normal and pathological populations" (p. 48).

Some of the basic questions about these formulations pertain to the structure of the STM system (e.g., what is the source of the recency and primacy effects in list recall?); others pertain to the role this system plays in sentence comprehension. The performance of brain-damaged subjects has been related to both these issues. We shall selectively review this literature, advancing critical comments and our own interpretation of the data.

Warrington and Shallice (1969, 1972) were the first investigators to document an isolated disturbance of short-term-memory or "short-term store" functions. Their patient K.F. did well on tests requiring memory of public events and details of his personal history, thus demonstrating an intact "semantic memory" and "episodic memory." His scores on free-recall tests were consistent with an impairment in STM functions. Digit span was reduced to two. Probe-recognition tasks, in which K.F. had to say whether a stimulus following a list of words had been presented in the list, also yielded a very reduced recognition span (about two items). K.F. showed proactive interference effects from semantically related items in STM tests, indicating that he was retrieving items from "long-term store" in these tests. Warrington and Shallice concluded that the pattern of memory performance in K.F. could best be explained by a disturbance in "short-term store," and that this analysis supported the theory of memory that postulated this structural component in STM tasks.

Another patient with an impairment in STM functions was reported by Vallar and Baddeley (1984a,b). P.V.'s memory deficit was analyzed within the framework of the "working memory" theory outlined briefly above. Vallar and Baddeley suggested that P.V. had a selective impairment of the phonological store. This analysis was said to account for her reduced span for auditorily presented materials and her better performance with visually presented language stimuli. However, several aspects of P.V.'s performance are hard to reconcile with this analysis. P.V. showed no effect on her span of word length, which usually influences span (longer words reducing span). Elsewhere, Baddely and his colleagues have claimed that the word-length effect is attributable to the operation of the articulatory loop (Baddeley, Thomson, and Buchanan 1975), not the phonological store. In addition, P.V. showed a normal effect of phonological similarity on span with auditorily presented material, but not with visually presented material; and concurrent articulation (counting from one to eight aloud) had no effect on visual-span performances. Baddeley et al. (1975) and Salamé and Baddeley (1982) have argued that phonological-similarity effects in auditory-verbal span tests are due to the operation of the phonological store, and that the presence of these effects with written stimuli reflects the operation of the articulatory loop (which is engaged by visual material and which feeds the phonological store, on this view). The effect of concurrent articulation on visually presented material also has been related to the operation of the articulatory loop in other papers by Baddeley and his colleagues. Thus, the pattern of performance of P.V. on these tests is actually more consistent with a disorder of the articulatory loop than with a disorder of the phonological store. However, Vallar and Baddeley argue that P.V.'s span was too greatly reduced to result from an impairment in the articulatory loop, since concurrent articulation reduces spans in normal subjects to between five and six items, not the two to three items seen in P.V. They also argue that the discrepancy between auditory and verbal spans seen in P.V. cannot be accounted for by an impairment in the articulatory loop, and that P.V.'s articulatory rate, which correlates with span in normals and is related to the operation of the articulatory loop, is comparable to those of other patients with far better spans. Vallar and Baddeley thus suggest that the impairment in P.V. lies in the phonological store and that it renders the operation of the articulatory loop ineffective.

These two cases, and several others in the literature, establish the partial independence of a short-term-memory system, sensitive to phonological form, from a longer-term-memory system. The existence of patients with the reverse pattern of retained and impaired functional capacities (Warrington and Weiskrantz 1973) documents a "double dissociation" between two such memory systems and argues for the complete independence of at least one aspect of each. On the other hand, these case studies fall short of clarifying the structure of the short-term system. The ascription of the deficit in P.V. to the phonological store, for instance, runs counter to previous analyses of the role of this component of the short-duration-memory system, as we have seen above, and requires a *post hoc* premise that the phonological store can be damaged in such a way as to allow it to retain some of its characteristic properties (e.g., a phonological-similarity effect for auditorily presented material) but to make the operation of another part of the working memory system—the articulatory loop— ineffective. This *ad hoc* and *post hoc* account of the deficit in P.V. saves the theory at the expense of introducing such a large number of degrees of freedom into the accounts of how deficits can affect the system as to make it difficult to test the theory through the use of pathological performances.

The role of the short-term-memory system in sentence comprehension has been addressed by a number of studies in which the sentence-comprehension abilities of patients with STM deficits have been examined. Warrington and Shallice commented that their patient K.F. did poorly on the final section of the token test (DeRenzi and Vignolo 1962). The token test requires the manipulation of colored geometrically shaped objects in response to verbal commands. Its final section includes a variety of syntactic structures and requires that subjects accomplish actions in the reverse order from that in which they are spoken. Though failure on the sixth section of this test may indicate comprehension failure, it also may indicate an inability to retain a propostion in memory long enough to execute another action before the action specified in that proposition is accomplished. If poor performance on this portion of the token test does reflect comprehension failure, the specific aspects of comprehension that are impaired cannot be delineated, because of the heterogeneity of structures on this portion of the test and the small number of examples of each structure. Warrington and Shallice comment on the overall good comprehension of K.F., and suggest that whatever comprehension impairment he has may reflect difficulty in structuring or in interpreting more complex aspects of sentence form.

A similar conclusion was reached by Saffran and Marin (1975) on the basis of their study of I.L. (another STM patient). I.L. was not tested on a sentence-comprehension test directly. Rather, he was asked to repeat sentences, and it was observed that he often produced a semantic paraphrase of a sentence rather than a verbatim repetition. Because of this feature of his responses on this task, Saffran and Marin used his performance in repetition as an index of his comprehension. They pointed out that I.L.'s responses sometimes reflected syntactic ambiguities in the presented sentences. For instance, he paraphrased a sentence that mentioned sailors and "amusing girls" by saying that the sailors had fun with the lively girls. However, they also note that I.L. reversed the thematic roles of Agent and Theme in several passive sentences in the initial stimulus set. Because of this feature, they presented I.L. with a separate set of passive sentences for repetition. He repeated six of ten correctly, reversed the voice and the thematic roles in two, and had incomplete and unscoreable responses to the remaining two sentences. Saffran and Marin interpret this performance as consistent with I.L.'s having a deficit in interpreting passive constructions, and they argue that patients with STM impairments have trouble interpreting complex (or "tortuous") syntactic structures. However, the data supporting the hypothesis that a disturbance of short-term auditory verbal memory impairs I.L.'s ability to interpret complex syntactic structures (especially noncanonical word orders) are weak. I.L. showed considerable sensitivity to syntactic structure, including appreciation of lexical ambiguities. He made frequent errors only under the special circumstance when the passive-voice main clause of a sentence was preceded by a long subordinate clause or prepositional phrase that was semantically unrelated to the main clause. Since I.L.'s task was verbatim sentence repetition, and these lengthy sentences were considerably beyond his STM span, the fact that he failed to interpret passive clauses correctly when his memory abilities were taxed in this fashion does not indicate that he could not interpret syntactic structures when this difficult concurrent task was not imposed. I.L.'s performance on the specially devised test of repetition of passive sentences, which did not require repetition of these long, unrelated phrases and clauses, suggests that he could interpret passive constructions. (Six of eight scoreable responses were correct.)

Patient P.V. (Vallar and Baddeley 1984b) also showed evidence of retained ability to assign and interpret syntactic structure; she performed within normal limits on a test of syntactic comprehension devised by Parisi and Pizzamiglio (1970). This battery tests comprehension of passive sentences, subject-verb agreement, adjective-noun agreement, and other syntactic features of Italian, in sentences whose length greatly exceeds P.V.'s span. P.V. also did well on several other specially designed tests of sentence comp· hension. She did fail on one experimental condition, in which she was ·   .ired to judge whether sentences such as the following were true.

(25) The world divides the equator into two hemispheres, the northern and the southern.

Vallar and Baddeley interpret this failure as evidence of P.V.'s inability to interpret "word order." However, their use of this term is quite distinct from that of other researchers. For Vallar and Baddeley, "word order" refers to the inversion of two nouns within a sentence to yield a semantically false or anomalous reading. They attributed P.V.'s difficulty with these sentences to an impairment in syntactic processing. However, another account is possible. Though the resulting sentences are anomalous when interpreted on the basis of their syntactic structure, a lexico-pragmatic route to meaning would yield a meaningful interpretation of sentences such as (25). If both a syntactic and a lexico-pragmatic route to meaning are available to P.V. and yield conflicting meanings for sentences such as (25), P.V. would have to adjudicate between these two readings by referring to the actual verbatim order of words in the sentence that she heard. It is possible that P.V.'s impairment in STM functions precludes this verbatim review of the form of a sentence. We discussed this possibility above in connection with the analysis by Schwartz et al. of the similar impairment in their agrammatic patients. P.V.'s failure on this sentence-anomaly-detection task is also similar in some ways to I.L.'s failure on a repetition task with long sentences containing verbs in the passive voice. In both cases, the patient failed on tasks that placed great demands on verbatim recall and hence on STM. Neither performance, however, necessarily indicates that the patient cannot assign and interpret the syntactic structure of a sentence.

A fourth STM case was reported by Caramazza, Basili, Koller, and Berndt (1981). Patient M.C. was tested on a sentence-picture matching test using semantically reversible syntactically complex sentences, and failed to choose the correct picture over lexical and syntactic foils on tests of passive and center-embedded clauses with auditorily presented sentences. He did, however, show a decline in his overall error rate from about 50% with auditory presentation to about 25% with visual presentation. Since M.C. had a disturbance of "auditory-verbal" short-term memory and not of "visual" memory, the increased number of errors on these sentences with auditory presentation was interpreted by Caramazza et al. as an indication that auditory verbal STM is required for auditory sentence comprehension when interpretation of syntactic form is necessary.

Again, a close examination of the data makes this analysis less plausible. M.C.'s increased impairment with auditorily presented sentences did not come about because of increased selection of *syntactic* foils, but because of increased selection of *lexical* foils. M.C. had evolved from an initial stage of severe word deafness, and it is quite possible that his poor performance with auditory presentation reflected some residual word deafness. The magnitude of the increase of selection of lexical foils from visual tc auditory presentation is almost the same for syntactically complex semantically reversible sentences as for simple single-word–picture matching. In fact, M.C. selected slightly *fewer* syntactic foils in the auditory presentations of these sentences than in the visual presentations. Moreover, M.C. was allowed to look at the sentence while he selected the picture when sentences were presented visually but nonetheless made about the same number of syntactic errors with visual as with auditory presentation. This also suggests that the source of his syntactic deficit was not an inability to keep a verbatim record of a presented sentence in a memory store but rather some other impairment in the assignment or interpretation of syntactic structure.

One other case sheds additional light on the relationship between STM impairments and disturbances of syntactic comprehension. Saffran (1985) reported a patient, T.I., who failed to understand semantically reversible passive and center-embedded relative clauses. However, Saffran argued that aspects of T.I.'s sentence-comprehension performance suggest that his disturbances in this function are not secondary to his STM impairments. For instance, sentence length did not affect T.I.'s performances; he performed as poorly on "truncated" passives without a *by*-phrase, such as (26), as on full passives.

(26) The dog was chased.

Saffran argued that if this patient's STM impairment underlay his syntactic-comprehension problem, his performance should have improved on short sentences that were within his memory span of three digits. Saffran also investigated T.I.'s abilities to construct syntactic form through the use of the grammaticality-judgment task. The number of words between the elements involved in a violation were varied, as in the following:

(27) The *boy* in the car *are* wearing a hat.

(28) The *boy* in the car parked illegally next to the doughnut shop *are* wearing a hat.

T.I. performed extremely well on the grammaticality-judgment task, and showed no effect of the number of words intervening between the critical items determining grammaticality. Saffran thus concluded that T.I. could assign syntactic structure but could not interpret it. She suggested that auditory-verbal STM functions are not involved in assigning syntactic structure but might be involved in interpreting these structures.

These five cases present a very different picture of the relationship between syntactic comprehension and a short-duration-memory system in which the phonological form of lexical items is retained than that presented by Caramazza and Berndt. Patients with severe limitations on this memory system have been shown to be capable of comprehending many aspects of syntactic form. Only when the memory requirements of the task are increased, through the requirement for verbatim repetition or through the need to review the phonological form of a sentence to determine which of two readings corresponds to that in the stimulus, do STM patients show disturbances of syntactic comprehension.

The assumption with which we began this section—that the fact that words in sentences are presented sequentially in auditory form suggests that a phonology-based short-duration-memory system may be involved in sentence comprehension and, more specifically, in syntactic comprehension—appears to be empirically refuted. Another consideration appears to be more relevant: the fact that the construction and the interpretation of sentence form cannot make direct use of the phonological form of words once lexical access has been achieved, but rather operates on the syntactic and semantic properties of lexical items. Logically, a sentence-interpretation device needs only to maintain a pre-lexical phonological representation of the segmental phonology in an utterance until lexical access is achieved. In some implemented auditory sentence-comprehension systems (Woods 1970; Woods 1982; Lesser, Fennel, Erman, and Reddy 1975), such a representation is maintained for relatively long periods of computational time because identification of phonological segments and lexical items is not unequivocally achieved. Indeed, in these systems, the phonological form of words is also maintained for some time, because hypotheses as to lexical identities are subject to revision on the basis of both top-down and bottom-up information. However, the human lexical-access system appears to be sufficiently fast and accurate to make the recomputation of lexical identity through phonological reanalysis an unusual event in normal sentence processing (Marslen-Wilson and Welsh 1978; Marslen-Wilson and Tyler 1980). Moreover, even if such a process does occur more frequently than it appears at present, this process requires only that the phonological representation of words be available for lexical access and lexical verification processes, not for parsing.

Though a parser cannot make direct use of the segmental phonological representations of lexical items, it nonetheless may be the case that lexical items are maintained in phonological form in some of the representations constructed by a parser, such as constructions in which a constituent has been displaced and thus not assigned (all) its thematic role(s) on the basis of its grammatical role relative to the verb of its clause. Though this is how the parser may operate, the evidence from STM cases indicates that this is not how it does operate. Significant reductions in STM functions do not obligatorily lead to disorders in the comprehension of semantically reversible sentences with a variety of syntactic structures. On the other hand, sentence comprehension is not normal in STM patients. We may identify the locus of this abnormality as a stage of processing that occurs after syntactic structure has been assigned and interpreted. Excluding the cases in which dual task demands (repetition) may have affected comprehension and in which syntactic-comprehension impairments are attributable to independent disturbances of the parser, all the sentence-comprehension impairments that have been documented in STM cases can be attributed to an impairment in a subject's ability to check semantic readings derived lexico-pragmatically and syntactically against the presented sentence. This suggests that an STM system of the type we have discussed above is used in these post-interpretive processes. Evidence in support of this conclusion also comes from dual-task experiments in normals (Waters, Caplan, and Hildebrandt 1987). We shall consider the relationship of STM impairments to syntactic comprehension and post-interpretive processes in one of our own patients in chapter 6.

Our conclusions regarding the nonrole of a phonological STM system in syntactic comprehension do not apply to phonological processing in general. One would expect that patients with impairments in phonological decoding (e.g., disturbances affecting phoneme discrimination) would have disturbances in sentence comprehension. Such disturbances might affect lexical access and thus make for incorrect word recognition, with attendant lexical errors. In addition, whenever decoding deficits slow down the rate of word identification to a point that words in sentences are not identified as they occur in the speech stream, prelexical segmental phonological values and even representations of acoustic features of utterances have to be retained in memory to allow lexical access to occur after a word has been "passed by." This retention of acoustic and lexical phonological features of utterances would be expected to occupy language-processing resources, and could well lead to impairments in assigning and interpreting syntactic structures, which might require processing resources no longer available because of the increased demands made by the impaired lexical-access process. In fact, one patient with a disturbance affecting phonological decoding has been shown to have mild difficulty with comprehension of reversible passive and locative sentences (Friedrich, Martin, and Kemper 1985). However, this difficulty was mild (performance on both these sentence types was above chance), and a similar difficulty was also found with visual presentation of these sentence types, so the conclusion that an impairment in phonological decoding leads to these difficulties in syntactic comprehension must be considered premature. One would predict that a phonological-decoding deficit that led to impairments of lexical access would lead to a syntactic-comprehension deficit when syntactically crucial lexical items were improperly recognized (as well as to abnormal comprehension of irreversible sentences when other lexical items were misidentified), but whether a disturbance of phonological decoding that does *not* lead to incorrect lexical identification ever leads to a disturbance of syntactic comprehension remains unclear.

Conclusion

Several conclusions can be drawn from the work we have reviewed in this chapter. It is clear that many patients have disturbances affecting their abilities to assign thematic roles in semantically reversible sentences with any type of syntactically complex structure (passive verb voice, object relativization, inner dative constructions, and others). These disturbances have been most often documented in patients with expressive agrammatism and impaired short-term memory, but do not appear to be direct consequences of these deficits. The psychopathogenesis of these impairments is largely unknown.

The principal reason that various theories of the psychopathogenesis of the deficits in syntactic comprehension seen in patients with expressive agrammatism and limited short-term memory have not been either verified or clearly rejected is that theory is not making adequate contact with empirical data in this domain of research. In many instances, empirical data have run ahead of detailed modeling of task components. For instance, the correlation of deficits in metalinguistic tasks such as grammaticality judgment, anagram solution, word-relatedness judgment, and letter cancellation with syntactic comprehension is not immediately interpretable because of the lack of detailed component analyses for these tasks. In other areas, theory has advanced beyond an adequate database. Present theories are still either underspecified (as in the case of Zurif's formulation regarding an "overarching" deficit in agrammatism, or Saffran and Marin's claim that STM patients experience difficulty when syntax is "tortuous"), overly general (as in the case of Berndt and Caramazza's claim that a parser fails in agrammatism), lacking in adequate empirical support (as in the case of the analyses of agrammatism by Kean, Rizzi, and Grodzinsky), inconsistent with the data presented (as in the case of the account by Schwartz et al. of the word-order problem in agrammatism and the depiction by Caramazza et al. of the comprehension disturbance in M.C.), or misleading as to what is being claimed (as in the case of Vallar and Baddeley's use of the term *word order*). One conclusion we may draw is that a more detailed database, one focused on specific theoretical questions, is necessary to establish the psychopathogenesis of a disturbance of syntactic comprehension in an aphasic patient or a group of such patients.

Perhaps the most striking aspect of the literature on syntactic-comprehension disorders to date is the nearly complete absence of re-ferences to existing models of the parsing process—both those suggested by implemented parsers and those consistent with the results of psycho-linguistic experimentation. Despite repeated references to the role of the function-word vocabulary or of a short-term-memory system in parsing, almost none of the papers we have reviewed refer to specific aspects of a parsing model related to these vocabulary items or this memory system. In the few cases in which references are made to parsing processes, such as the citation of the two-pass structure of the Frazier-Fodor (1978) parser by Linebarger et al. (1983a), there is no clear connection between the detailed operation of the parsing model and the deficit analysis proposed for a patient or a group of patients. In other cases, parsing constructs have been invented without being related to existing models. For instance, Linebarger et al. refer to the concept of "shallow semantic structure" but provide no definition of this structure in terms of the output of any stage of a parser. No formulation distinguishes between "parsing" and "interpretation" in formal terms, despite the availability of linguistic and parsing models that make this distinction on principled grounds (see chapters 1 and 2 above). The performance of a system in the one "lesion experiment" in an im-plemented parser of which we are aware (Marcus 1982) has not been related to a documented pattern of comprehension impairment in detail. Analyses of syntactic-comprehension deficits have generally not operated within the constraints on description and explanation set by existing models of normal functions, preferring to invent constructs related to normal functioning on the basis of aphasic data. This has, so far, not proved very productive; both deficit analyses and those invented parsing con-structs have for the most part remained suggestive, broad, poorly defined, and inadequately justified. No such constructs postulate specific parsing mechanisms. A few analyses are related to specific linguistic models but make no mention of parsing and are inadequately supported empirically. A tighter relationship between linguistic theory, parsing theory, and a theory of aphasic impairments and adaptations is needed for the nature of impair-ments of syntactic comprehension to be understood in detail, and for the character of these impairments to be useful in constraining linguistic and parsing theory in specific areas.

In the following two chapters, we present the beginnings of such a detailed analysis of syntactic-comprehension deficits. Chapter 4 is relatively general, but provides evidence for a general framework within which to approach these disorders and several suggestions regarding the content of a theory of syntactic-comprehension impairments. Chapter 5 presents nine case studies, which begin the documentation of the details of deficits of syntactic comprehension. Chapter 6 summarizes the conclusions and implications of our studies.

Chapter 4
Group Studies

In this chapter we present the results of group studies done in our laboratory and dealing with disorders of syntactic comprehension in brain-damaged subjects. As we said in chapter 3, two basic questions emerged from the Caramazza-Zurif (1976) study of syntactic comprehension: Are there linguistic patterns to the structures that patients can and cannot interpret? Are certain patterns of syntactic-comprehension disturbance secondary to other deficits, such as the impairment underlying expressive agrammatism? In 1982, when we began the study reported here, the majority of published papers maintained that syntactic comprehension failed totally if it failed at all, leaving only simple heuristics and lexico-pragmatic means of interpreting sentences. No paper published at that time suggested that syntactic-comprehension deficits might be partial in that they might, for instance, reflect specific impairments in individual parsing operations. Though such suggestions have since been made (see chapter 3), the absolute and the relative incidence of "complete" and "partial" impairments in syntactic comprehension have not been explored. Only a few case studies contain the beginnings of the documentation of the specific nature of impairments in syntactic comprehension. The compensations patients make for deficits in this functional sphere, the neuropathological correlates of these impairments, and other basic issues were unexplored when we began our work. Our survey study was thus designed to answer basic questions regarding the incidence and the nature of syntactic-comprehension deficits in aphasia.

The major questions regarding aphasiological aspects of syntactic comprehension disorders which we sought to answer in the survey studies were the following:

• Are aphasic subjects distinguishable from neurologically normal individuals with respect to their syntactic-comprehension abilities?

• Are there significant differences in the frequency with which different syntactic structures and semantic features are correctly assigned after brain damage?

• Are there are identifiable subgroups of patients who differ with respect to their ability to interpret syntactic structures?

• If subgroups of patients exist, do they differ only in the overall severity of their impairments in syntactic comprehension, or do they also differ with respect to the specific syntactic structures they can and cannot interpret?

• If subgroups of patients exist, do they differ with respect to the types of semantic features that can be assigned to syntactic structures?

• If subgroups of patients exist, do they correspond to otherwise defined aphasic groups?

• Are patients' erroneous interpretations of syntactic structures random?

• If erroneous interpretations are not random, are they constrained by the structures of presented sentences?

• Do identifiable subgroups of patients make different types of errors?

Our approach to these questions consisted of presenting batteries of tests requiring the assignment of different sentential semantic features to different aspects of syntactic form to patients with a variety of aphasic impairments. We ascertained the reliability of the results by repeating the protocols (sometimes with minor variations) with different aphasic populations. We analyzed the performances of these patients in several ways. First, we looked for statistically reliable differences in mean correct scores among the presented sentence types, and attempted to relate these differences to aspects of syntactic structure, parsing, and other features of sentences (such as length) that might influence comprehension. Second, we performed cluster analyses of the patients in each population and analyzed the pattern of responses in each cluster in relation to the syntactic structures and parsing processes that might be retained and affected in patients in the cluster. Third, we performed principal-components analyses of the determinants of patient clustering, to determine whether sentence types with similar structural features tended to group together as determinants of patient clustering. Fourth, we analyzed patients' errors to determine what principles, if any, underlay the errors patients made. In some studies, we performed discriminant-function analyses to ascertain whether aphasics were distinguishable from normal subjects, and we looked for correlations between patients in the clusters that emerged from our analyses with parameters of neurobiological interest (e.g. age, sex, educational level, lesion site and size) and aphasiological significance (type and overall severity of aphasia).

The question of the relative complexity of different syntactic structures, the dissociation of abilities to interpret different syntactic structures or to assign different semantic features to syntactic structure in different patient groups, the error patterns seen in syntactic comprehension, and the relationship of particular impairments in syntactic-comprehension processes and particular error patterns to other aphasic symptoms are all questions in linguistic aphasiology, the answers to which provide the beginnings of a characterization of the dominant tendencies in the realm of syntactic comprehension in aphasic patients. The answers to these questions thus constitute a broad empirical basis for situating an individual patient's performance within the entire range of syntactic-comprehension performances of aphasic patients. The group studies we have undertaken do not allow us to provide detailed mechanistic accounts of the breakdown of syntactic comprehension in subgroups of the population studied, because of the limited number of observations that can be made of each patient in group work of this kind. Nonetheless, a number of suggestions regarding basic mechanisms of language breakdown in this sphere emerge from our group studies.

The relationship of identifiable subgroups of patients to features of neurological lesions—in the present study, lesion site and size—is part of a database upon which theories of the neural basis for language can be founded. To the extent that identifiable subgroups of patients in our population are homogeneous with respect to the deficits in syntactic comprehension seen in their members, the locations and the sizes of lesions in patients in the subgroups speak to the location and the amount of the neural tissue that is devoted to the functions that are deficient in these groups. The logic of such inferences has been discussed in several recent papers (Klein 1978; Caplan 1981, 1987d, in press). Briefly, it is as follows: If a performance of an individual subject with a neural lesion is best analyzed as a deficit in an otherwise justified model of normal language processing, then the function that is deficient in that patient can be said to have been partially carried out in the lesioned area of the brain. If all patients with the neurological lesion in question have the deficit in question, and no patients with other neurological lesions have the deficit in question, then we may conclude that the neural substrate damaged by the lesion is responsible for the accomplishment of the function that is deficient in these patients. If there is variation in the neural lesions that produce the deficit in question in different patients, then there is variability in the neural substrate responsible for the function that becomes deficient in these patients. If there are constraints on the variability of the lesion features that occur in association with particular deficits (which emerge as significant correlations of aspects of neurological lesions with functional deficits), then these constraints can be used in conjunction with other neurobiological and socioeconomic factors (age, sex, handedness, literacy, language proficiency, etc.) to fashion a theory of the genetic and environmental determinants of consistency in the neural basis for language functions.

Reliable differences in mean correct scores (or, in some instances, in mean rates of production of certain errors) for different sentence types in unselected aphasic populations can be taken to reflect stable differences in the processing of different sentence types after brain damage. Such differences may bear on the nature of syntactic structures and on their processing. One approach to interpreting such differences is in terms of markedness theory, which specifies that one structure is more difficult than another. As we noted in our introductory chapter, one structure may be more marked than a second structure because it includes all the structural and processing components of the second structure plus additional structures or operations, or simply because the processing components relevant to the first structure are more complex than those related to the second. In interpreting statistically significant differences in mean correct scores for different sentence types in relationship to the relative complexity of the processes and structures underlying comprehension of the sentence types in question, we are not utilizing data from aphasic groups in the same fashion as we do in the development of neurolinguistic theory. In the construction of neurolinguistic theory, we are concerned with a correlation of deficits: a functional deficit in syntactic processing in some group of patients and the organic lesion(s) that occur in association with these functional deficits. In the present instance, we are primarily concerned with *constraints* on deficits—namely, those complexity considerations that make one operation more likely to be affected, on average, than another. The relative complexity of different sentence types revealed by significant differences in mean correct response rates for different sentence types in our survey studies allows us to infer several features of the mechanisms underlying normal sentence processing.

We shall present the results of five studies involving three different patient groups and two different protocols. Some of these results have been reported previously (Caplan, Baker, and Dehaut 1985; Caplan 1986b, 1987c); here we summarize and extend the previous reports.

Methods

We used two means of assessing syntactic comprehension. One was the traditional sentence-picture matching test; the experimenter read a sentence with normal nonemphatic intonation, while a subject viewed two or three pictures: one depicting the meaning of the sentence, one depicting a syntactic misinterpretation of the sentence, and, in some instances, a third depicting a misinterpretation of one of the lexical items in the sentence. The syntactic foils varied, depending on what aspect of sentence form and what semantic feature was under investigation.

Though widely used to test syntactic comprehension, the sentence-picture matching task has important limitations that preclude using it to answer all the questions presented above. The most significant of these limitations is that the syntactic foils (and, for that matter, the lexical semantic foils) must be preselected by the examiner. This precludes investigation of spontaneous errors. Moreover, it can lead to circumstances in which a subject is presented with two pictures (the correct interpretation and a foil), neither of which he judges to be correct—a situation that may not be recognized by the experimenter and whose effect on a patient's performance on the entire task is unknown. For these reasons, we utilized an object-manipulation (enactment) task—a methodology often used in studies of children (Roeper 1978)—as a second means of assessing comprehension in our group studies.

The object-manipulation task requires a subject to use toys to demonstrate semantic features of sentences. In the studies to be presented in this chapter, the semantic feature to be demonstrated is the thematic roles of nouns. The Token Test (DeRenzi and Vignolo 1962; Boller and Vignolo 1966), widely used to assess sentence comprehension, also involves an enactment paradigm. It requires the ascription of adjectives to nouns and, in some sentences, the assignment of thematic roles to noun phrases. Caplan, Matthei, and Gigley (1981) successfully used an enactment test to investigate comprehension of gerundive constructions in eleven aphasic patients.

Several concerns about the object-manipulation task were articulated in the early stages of our work. One was that patients with hemiparesis, hemiplegia, or various forms of apraxia affecting the limbs might find it difficult to enact thematic roles, or that some of their actions might be uninterpretable. A second concern was that spatial-manipulation preferences—taking objects preferentially from left to right or vice-versa—might influence the actions patients generated. A third concern was that errors made by patients on this test might reflect difficulty in mapping sentence meaning onto actions, not difficulty in comprehension itself. In retrospect none of these issues present serious problems, and at the outset of our work the need for a task that would allow patients to demonstrate their own (mis)understandings of sentences and our successful (though limited) previous experience with the object-manipulation task led us to decide to utilize this technique to answer the questions posed above, despite these concerns.

Materials and Methods in the Object-Manipulation Task

As noted above, the questions to which we sought answers require that aphasic patients' comprehension abilities be assessed with respect to a variety of syntactic structures and several semantic features. The object-manipulation test that we devised consisted of nine sentence types, illus-

Table 4.1
Stimulus sentences.

Sentences with one verb

Two-place verb sentences
Active (A): The elephant hit the monkey
Passive (P): The elephant was hit by the monkey
Cleft-subject (CS): It was the elephant that hit the monkey
Cleft-object (CO): It was the elephant that the monkey hit

Three-place verb sentences
Dative (D): The elephant gave the monkey to the rabbit
Dative passive (DP): The elephant was given to the monkey by the rabbit

Sentences with two verbs
Conjoined (C): The elephant hit the monkey and hugged the rabbit
Subject-object relative (SO): The elephant that the monkey hit hugged the rabbit
Object-subject relative (OS): The elephant hit the monkey that hugged the rabbit

---

trated in table 4.1, which tested the assignment of thematic roles in different syntactic structures. Additional sentential semantic features were tested in the sentence-picture matching test (see below).

For each of the nine sentence types, subjects had to enact the thematic roles of noun phrases. In terms of the distinction between grammatical theta roles and semantic thematic roles discussed in chapters 1 and 2, these materials require not only that the theta grid of each verb be completed properly at the syntactic level but also that the particular thematic roles specified by each verb be assigned to the appropriate noun phrases at the semantic level. Most of the particular syntactic structures used in this test had been used previously to test syntactic comprehension in aphasic patients in the literature reviewed in chapter 3. The sentence types examined four fundamental aspects of syntactic organization: the linear order of major lexical categories (nouns and verbs), the hierarchical organization of categories, verb argument structure, and the role of function words and morphological elements in determining syntactic structure.

The linear order of major lexical categories was tested in three respects. First, sentences with both canonical word order (subject-verb-object, or noun-verb-noun) and canonical thematic-role order (Agent-Theme) were presented. In active and cleft-subject sentences, Agency is assigned to the first (preverbal) noun and Theme to the second (immediately postverbal) noun. We also presented dative sentences of the form noun-verb-noun-prepositional phrase, in which a third noun in a prepositional phrase played the thematic role of Goal. In this set of materials, the basic English subject-verb-object-indirect object word-order maps onto the thematic roles of Agent, Theme, and Goal in the canonical manner for English.

A second sentence type—passive sentences—consisted of sentences with canonical word order but noncanonical thematic-role order. In these sentences there is still a single preverbal noun, but the second noun in the sentence is the object of the preposition *by* in the passive of transitive verbs and the object of the locative preposition *to* in dative-passive sentences. These sentences thus make minimal changes in the sequence of major lexical categories compared to active and dative forms, simply changing the immediately postverbal noun from the direct object of a verb to the object of a preposition. However, the mapping of preverbal and postverbal nouns onto thematic roles is altered considerably. In simple transitive passive forms, the noun in sentence-initial preverbal position is Theme and the noun in the prepositional *by*-phrase is Agent; in the dative-passive forms, the second noun, in the prepositional *to*-phrase, is Goal.

The third set of sentence types contained sentences with both non-canonical word order and noncanonical thematic-role order. In cleft-object and subject-object sentences, there are two nouns preceding the first non-copula verb. The first noun in the sentence is assigned the thematic role of Theme, and the second noun is the Agent of the noncopula verb. These sentences thus violate both canonical word order and canonical thematic-role order. In addition, since the second noun is in immediately preverbal position, these sentences can serve to distinguish an interpretive heuristic that assigns Agency to the first noun in the sentence from one that assigns Agency to the noun immediately preceding the verb.

The hierarchical organization of categories is essential for the correct assignment of theta roles to noun phrases by each verb in the sentences with two verbs listed in table 4.1. In conjoined sentences, such as (1), the second verb phrase is conjoined to the first; in object-subject relatives, such as (2), the second verb phrase is part of a relative clause, which is embedded under the second noun.

(1) The elephant kissed the monkey and hugged the rabbit.
(2) The elephant kissed the monkey that hugged the rabbit.

If the relative pronoun signals an embedding and the coordinate con-junction a coordinate structure, patients should distinguish (1) from (2). If the relative pronoun does not signal an embedding and the coordinate conjunction does not signal conjunction, the sentences should receive iden-tical interpretations with respect to theta-role assignment. Subject-object relatives, such as (3), also test the ability of patients to interpret hierarchical structure. If patients do not assign the second noun to a theta role around the final verb in these sentences, this is an indication that they recognize that the first verb is part of a relative clause embedded under the matrix-subject noun phrase.

(3) The elephant that the monkey kissed hugged the rabbit.

If hierarchical structure is assigned and its assignment is itself a source of parsing or interpretive difficulty, patients should show more errors with cleft-subject sentences than with simple active transitive sentences.

The third syntactic feature tested in these materials is the contribution of different verb-argument structures to the determination of sentence meaning. Two argument places must be filled in active, passive, cleft-subject, and cleft-object sentences, and three in dative and dative-passive sentences. In these preliminary and exploratory materials, the contrast between two-place and three-place verbs is confounded by overall sentence length. This confound is partly resolvable on the basis of overall patterns of performance, as will be discussed below.

A final aspect of sentence form which we tested in these sentences was the role of the function-word vocabulary in determining syntactic structure and its interpretation. The function-word and morphological vocabularies play a variety of roles in determining syntactic structures and meaning in the sentences used in this battery. The morphological marking in the passive is one of the indications that thematic roles are not to be assigned in canonical order in these sentences. Relative pronouns signal the presence of embedding in the cleft sentences and in sentences containing relative clauses. Ability to interpret all these sentence types would therefore indicate that the ability to utilize the function-word vocabulary in a variety of ways is intact. Selective disturbances of one or another aspect of syntactic comprehension might follow from selective difficulties in the utilization of the information carried in the function-word and inflectional vocabularies.

Five examples of each of the nine sentence types illustrated in table 4.1 were constructed. The noun phrases referred to toy animals, because these manipulanda seemed natural in the context of an object-manipulation task and because they allowed for alternation between attribution of an animate and an inanimate status to the items in dative sentences, where the direct object is considered inanimate (or, at least, a passive recipient of an action) and the indirect object is considered animate. Six nouns and twelve verbs were used in the pilot experiment, and five nouns and ten verbs in the more controlled second and third experiments. Ideally, a larger number of animals and verbs would have been used, to avoid effects of proactive semantic memory interference over the entire set of sentences. However, many of the patients had single-word auditory-comprehension impairment, and the use of a large number of animals would have likely led to the elimination of large number of subjects from this study. The number of lexical items used represents a compromise that minimizes both these problems.

Sentences were presented in a pseudo-random order, with no more than two examples of a single sentence type in sequence. A higher degree of blocking of sentence types is undesirable; it could lead a patient to interpret successive sentences of the same type in the same way because of the immediately preceding interpretation. A pseudo-random order of sentence types increases the chances that a patient will approach each sentence on the basis of his retained knowledge of language structure and his parsing capacities, rather than on the basis of an immediately preceding decision as to the meaning of that type of sentence. Though list effects cannot be avoided entirely when five examples of each of nine somewhat similar sentence types are presented in a single battery, pseudo-randomization of sentence order minimizes the most undesirable consequences of repeating sentence types.

Procedure

Experimental sessions began with a short introductory conversation and a description of the experiment. Because of variation in patients' abilities to comprehend instructions, no single set of instructions was used. The experimenter indicated that the purpose of the experiment was to test the patient's ability to understand sentences and that the task required that the subject indicate the meaning of a sentence—"who did what to whom"—by acting out the actions in the sentence with the toy animals provided. After this brief conversation, the experimenter briefly tested the patient's ability to identify the animals and his short-term-memory pointing span. In the identification pretest, the five or six toy animals to be used in the experiment were placed in front of the patient and the experimenter read their names individually, going through the list of names in random order twice. The subject was required to point to each animal as it was named. Patients who did not identify all the animals on the first trial were given a short period of additional instruction and practice and then tested again. Patients who did not identify all the animals on the second trial were eliminated from the study. The test of short-term memory consisted of two serial pointing tasks, one testing order recall and one testing item-and-order recall. Subjects were not eliminated from the study because of diminished pointing spans.

After this pretesting, the experimenter repeated the purpose of the test and demonstrated the type of response that was required, using a simple active transitive sentence. A practice session was instituted so that the experimenter could be confident about his scoring of the subjects' responses for all sentence types. With about a quarter of the patients who were tested, this process required that the experimenter work with the patient to achieve a mutually comprehensible action code for the depiction of thematic role in certain sentences. During this period of "training," the subject's responses were positively reinforced if they were interpretable, whether or not they were correct. If the experimenter was required to demonstrate a response, he demonstrated a correct response unless he was reenacting an erroneous response the subject had just made in order to clarify its meaning.

The experimenter then read the 45 sentences in the battery with a normal, neutral intonational contour. If a subject requested a repetition of the sentence, the experimenter returned to that sentence after an interval of about ten sentences, so that each scored response would reflect the subject's interpretation of a sentence presented once. The subjects were allowed to repeat the sentences, but were neither encouraged nor discouraged to do so. Testing was carried out in private rooms, reasonably well insulated from surrounding noise. One or two observers in addition to the experimenter were often present during the testing sessions and, when present, discussed the interpretation of difficult responses and attempted to arrive at a consensus.

Scoring

Responses were scored in a notation designed for easy comparison of responses across difference sentence types. Each noun in a sentence was labeled according to its linear position, and "slots" were assigned for the arguments of each verb in the sentence in the order Agent, Theme, Goal. The noun used for each of these thematic roles was recorded in each slot. This was repeated for each of the verbs in the sentence. Thus, for instance, the nouns in the following sentences are numbered as indicated, and the correct responses are coded as indicated below each sentence:

       1   2
(4) The monkey hit the elephant.
Correct: 1,2 (noun 1 is Agent; noun 2 is Theme);

       1   2   3
(5) The monkey was taken to the elephant by the bear.
Correct: 3,1,2 (noun 3 is Agent; noun 1 is Theme; noun 2 is Goal);

       1   2   3
(6) The monkey hit the bear that kissed the rabbit.
Correct: 1,2;2,3 (noun 1 is Agent of the first verb; noun 2 is Theme of the first verb; noun 2 is Agent of the second verb; noun 3 is Theme of the second verb).

      .

                      1   2   3
(7) The monkey that the bear hit kissed the rabbit.
Correct: 2,1;1,3 (noun 2 is Agent of the first verb; noun 1 is Theme of the
first verb; noun 1 is Agent of the second verb; noun 3 is Theme of the
second verb).

Subjects

For the object-manipulation test, we shall report three separate studies of
three separate populations. Experiment 1 was the first study to use an
object-manipulation task with a large and largely unselected group of
aphasic patients. Its goals were to answer the questions outlined above and
to investigate whether the object-manipulation test could be used effec-
tively to gather data on syntactic comprehension in aphasic patients.
Several minor modifications in the protocol were then instituted, and two
additional studies were run by way of replication. We tested 58 patients in
experiment 1, and 37 and 49 in the two subsequent studies. Experiment 1
contained both English-speaking and French-speaking patients, experiment
2 only native English speakers, and experiment 3 only native French
speakers. In all studies, patients were tested in their native language. The
patients were selected by speech pathologists in hospitals and rehabilitation centers in Montreal and Ottawa, and any patient who had a reasonable single-word auditory receptive vocabulary was considered eligible.
   The data on each patient (gathered from medical charts and interviews)
included age, sex, handedness, familial handedness, languages spoken and
written, verbal proficiency, mother tongue, schooling, and occupation.
Neurological data included the etiology of the disease, the data of onset of
symptoms, the results of a neurological examination, and radiological data.
The radiological data, obtained through chart review, included CT-scan
reports, angiography data, and occasionally data from radionucleotide
scans. Reports of electroencephalograms were also sometimes available.
Patients' medications were recorded. Speech-therapy data were obtained
from the patients' charts and recorded, with emphasis on the quality and
quantity of spontaneous speech and performance on naming, verbal fluency, repetition, auditory single-word comprehension, auditory passage
comprehension, reading aloud, reading comprehension, and writing and
copying tasks. Each patient's diagnostic category and overall level of
severity, as determined by the referring speech pathologist, were noted.

Results

We report the results of these three experiments in a standard format. First,
we describe any features that are particular to the experiment being dis-

Table 4.2
Group results, experiment 1.

Sentence type	Mean	S.D.
Cleft-subject (CS)	3.9	1.6
Active (A)	3.9	1.6
Passive (P)	2.8	1.9
Dative (D)	2.8	2.2
Cleft-object (CO)	2.4	1.8
Object-subject (OS)	1.9	2.0
Dative-passive (DP)	1.8	2.0
Conjoined (C)	1.5	1.7
Subject-object (SO)	1.2	1.5

Results of Tukey's procedure (experimentwise error rate: 0.05)

CS   A   P   D   CO   OS   DP   C   SO

(Sentence types underlined by a common line do not differ from one another; sentences types not underlined by a common line do differ.)

cussed. Then we present the significant differences in mean correct scores per sentence type, followed by the results of the patient clustering analyses and those of the principal-components analyses. The complete set of responses and a more detailed description of the subgroups in each experiment can be found in the appendix.

Experiment 1

A preliminary goal of experiment 1 was to document the utility of the object-manipulation test. Despite the concerns detailed above, only 1.24% of the responses made by patients in experiment 1 were uninterpretable. These uninterpretable responses occurred in approximately 25% of the population, and most of them arose on sentences that were more difficult for the population as a whole. These responses were not entered into the statistical analyses that follow. The means and standard deviations of the 58 subjects' scores for each sentence type on the scorable responses are presented in table 4.2.

An analysis of variance with repeated measures on the sentence-type factor revealed a significant effect of this factor on the number of correct responses: $F(8,456) = 42.1$; $p < 0.001$. Tukey's "honestly significant difference" procedure was applied at an experimentwise error rate of 0.05 to determine which of these means were statistically significantly different

(Winer 1971). The results of this procedure are illustrated in table 4.2. These differences indicate that sentence type affected the correct responses provided by these patients. Whether this effect was due to the syntactic structure of the sentence or to other factors (such as sentence length) will be discussed below.

To look for different patterns of correct responses in different groups in this population, we performed a clustering analysis of the 58 subjects based on their scores on these nine sentence types, and then examined the determinants of this clustering using a principal-components analysis (PCA) and details of each subgroup's performance. We used Ward's (1963) method of hierarchic fusion to cluster patients. The resulting clustering was checked by the RELOCATE procedure of the CLUSTAN program (Wishart 1978), an iterative procedure that considers each subject in turn and transfers it to the cluster it is most similar to, if it is not properly located by the original hierarchical clustering process. This procedure can generate anywhere from two to 58 groups in a population containing 58 subjects. We shall report on the results of clustering of the population into eight subgroups. The reason for the choice of eight subgroups is that it represents the largest number of stable subgroups that emerged from the clustering analysis. Only four subjects changed groups after the RELOCATE procedure when eight subgroups were generated by Ward's method; significantly larger numbers of subjects changed subgroups after the application of the RELOCATE checking procedure when more than eight subgroups were generated by Ward's hierarchical fusion method. Thus, the eight subgroups we shall report here are the largest number of subgroups that have similar memberships under different methods of calculating subgroup membership. This, in turn, indicates that these subgroups represent the optimal compromise between the desire to have homogeneous groupings of patients (which would result in a larger number of subgroups) and stability of subgroup formation under different mathematical approaches to calculating subgroups (which would result in a smaller number of subgroups). Though other approaches to defining subgroups are possible, investigation of the patterns of syntactic comprehension in subgroups formed this way is of interest, as we shall see.

The performance of each of the subgroups is displayed in table 4.3. We present a brief description of these subgroups here; a more detailed account is found in the appendix. Table 4.3 shows that the first three groups performed well on all single-verb sentences but differed in their performance on two-verb sentences. Group 1 interpreted all two-verb sentences quite well; group 2 interpreted object-subject sentences well and conjoined and subject-object sentences poorly; group 3 interpreted conjoined sentences well and subject-object and object-subject sentences poorly. Groups 4 and 5 showed much higher error rates for certain sentences with only a single

Table 4.3
Results by subgroup, experiment 1.

Cluster	Number of subjects	Mean score (and S.D.) for each sentence type								
		A	P	CS	CO	D	DP	C	SO	OS
I	7	5.0	4.9	4.9	4.9	5.0	4.3	4.0	4.1	4.6
		(0)	(0.4)	(0.4)	(0.4)	(0)	(1.0)	(1.0)	(0.7)	(0.8)
II	6	5.0	4.5	5.0	3.8	4.8	4.7	2.0	1.3	4.6
		(0)	(1.2)	(0)	(0.7)	(0.4)	(0.5)	(0.6)	(0.8)	(0.5)
III	5	5.0	5.0	5.0	4.4	5.0	4.2	4.0	2.0	1.4
		(0)	(0)	(0)	(1.3)	(0)	(1.1)	(1.0)	(0.7)	(0.9)
IV	12	4.4	2.9	4.6	2.5	3.8	1.6	0.5	1.2	2.8
		(0.8)	(1.4)	(0.7)	(1.2)	(1.1)	(1.2)	(0.7)	(1.3)	(1.3)
V	4	4.8	0.8	5.0	0.3	4.0	0.5	3.5	1.3	2.3
		(0.5)	(0.5)	(0)	(0.5)	(1.1)	(0.6)	(1.0)	(1.3)	(2.1)
VI	11	3.0	2.7	2.9	1.8	0.8	0.3	0.3	0	0.1
		(1.0)	(1.1)	(1.0)	(0.8)	(1.7)	(0.6)	(0.6)	(0)	(0.3)
VII	7	4.3	1.1	4.6	1.4	0.1	0	0.1	0	0.1
		(0.8)	(1.1)	(0.5)	(1.3)	(1.4)	(0)	(0.4)	(0)	(0.4)
VIII	6	0.2	0.3	0.2	0.2	0.3	0.3	0.2	0.2	0
		(0.4)	(0.8)	(0.4)	(0.4)	(0.8)	(0.8)	(0.4)	(0.4)	(0)

verb than groups 1, 2, and 3. With noncanonical thematic-role order, as in passive, cleft-object, and dative-passive sentences, these groups' performances dropped dramatically. Performance on sentences with two verbs was quite poor, although responses were provided for most of the two-verb sentences. Patients in group 4 interpreted passive and cleft-object sentences more accurately than patients in group 5, and patients in group 5 interpreted conjoined sentences more accurately than those in group 4. Groups 6 and 7 consisted of patients who were able to provide responses to sentences containing one verb with two thematic roles but who failed to provide responses to the majority of sentences with three thematic roles to be assigned by a single verb and to sentences with two verbs. Patients in group 6 assigned Agency and Theme with roughly equal frequency to both nouns in all one-verb, two-argument-place sentences; patients in group 7 provided more correct responses when sentences had both canonical word order and canonical thematic-role order. Patients in group 8 could not perform this task.

Table 4.4 illustrates how the PCA achieves the separation of patients into subgroups. The first vector of the PCA accounts for 64% of the total variance, and each of the sentence types contributes roughly equally positively to this vector. This indicates that the principal determinant of the separation of patients into these subgroups is their overall level of performance on this task, and this overall level of performance is reflected in the

Table 4.4
Principal-components analysis, experiment 1.

Eigenvector	Percentage of total variation	Factor loading, by sentence type									
		A	P	CS	CO	D	DP	C	SO	OS
1	63.6	0.321	0.335	0.310	0.340	0.361	0.365	0.317	0.329	0.318
2	10.5	−0.571	0.184	−0.631	0.164	0.019	0.304	0.142	0.319	−0.019
3	8.4	−0.067	−0.548	−0.053	−0.487	0.214	−0.100	0.388	0.276	0.416

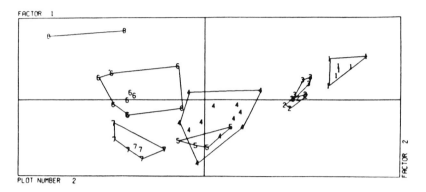

Figure 4.1
Plot of factor 1 versus factor 2, pilot study.

score of each patient relative to all other patients in roughly the same way on each of the sentence types. This vector may thus be considered a "success factor" or, alternatively, a "severity factor." The second eigenvector accounts for 10.5% of the total variance, and is not equally weighted for each of the sentence types. The sentence types with the largest scores on this vector are active, cleft-subject, dative-passive, and subject-object sentences, with the first two sentence types negatively weighted and the last two positively weighted. The third eigenvector accounts for 8.4% of the total variance, and the contributions of the passive and cleft-object sentence types are opposed to the conjoined and object-subject types. These two vectors thus illustrate that there is a different contribution of different sentence types to the determination of some patient clusters, though the principal determinant of patient clustering is a patient's overall severity of impairment on this task, as illustrated in the first vector.

The patterns of performance of the different subgroups are (necessarily) related to the values of the various sentence types in the PCA. The separation of patients into subgroups by the first three factors of the PCA is illustrated in figures 4.1 and 4.2. Each subject is identified by the number of the group to which he belongs, and the groups are outlined by convex figures including all subjects within them. As can be seen, the principal separation into groups is accomplished by the first factor in both these plots. Group 1 is completely distinguished from all other groups solely on the basis of this factor; groups 2 and 3, groups 4 and 5, and groups 6 and 7, though not separated from each other, are separated from the other groups by the first factor alone. The second factor contributes to the separation of groups 2 and 3 and completely determines the separation of groups 6 and 7. The second factor is strongly weighted for active, cleft-subject, dative-

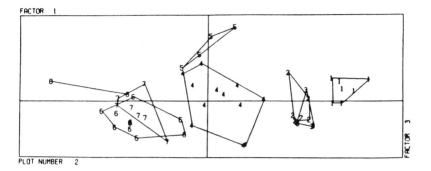

Figure 4.2
Plot of factor 1 versus factor 3, pilot study.

passive, and subject-object sentences. Active and cleft-subject sentences are important in distinguishing groups 6 and 7, and there are some differences between groups 2 and 3 with respect to how they perform on dative-passive and subject-object sentences. The third factor of the PCA completely distinguishes groups 4 and 5 and contributes significantly to distinguishing groups 2 and 3. In fact, all but one subject in group 3 is distinguished from the members of group 2 by the third factor. Factor 3 is heavily weighted for passive and cleft-object sentences (which, we observed above, produced noticeably different scores in groups 4 and 5), and also strongly weighted for conjoined and object-subject sentences, which are the principal sentence types that distinguish groups 2 and 3.

This analysis of the performance of individual subgroups determined by clustering procedures gives tentative answers to some of the questions our study was designed to investigate. First, it is clear that aphasic patients do not all show similar patterns of breakdown of syntactic comprehension. There appears to be a continuum of breakdown of syntactic-comprehension functions; some patients show considerable ability in this sphere of language processing, while others are so impaired that they cannot even accomplish this task. Between these two extremes lies a range of performances. For the most part, this range seems to reflect the overall severity of patients' impairments in this function. However, patients' syntactic-comprehension abilities to some extent also reflect their difficulties with specific sentence types.

Sentences are not all equally easy for subjects to understand, as the significant differences in mean correct responses for the sentence types listed in table 4.2 illustrate. As noted above, these significant differences in mean correct scores can be interpreted within markedness theory as related to linguistic structures and processing. We shall discuss these results in detail after presenting the next two experiments. We can, however, already say that some of the significant differences between sentence types, such as those between the different two-verb sentences, cannot be due entirely to differences in sentence length, but must reflect complexity differences associated with different syntactic structures.

Overall, the results of experiment 1 validate the use of the object-manipulation task as a means of obtaining group data regarding syntactic comprehension in aphasic patients. Before attempting to interpret these results in relation to the questions posed above, we shall report two replications of this experiment, which confirm the basic pattern of results.

Experiment 2

In the second experiment, 37 English-speaking aphasic patients were tested on a slightly modified version of the battery used in the pilot experiment. The modifications were introduced to reduce the possibility that subtle pragmatic factors related to the intrinsic nature of the manipulanda used, or factors related to the spatial array, might influence the results. The first of these factors was better controlled by reducing the number of animals used from six to five and assigning each animal once to each grammatical position (and hence each thematic role) around each verb in each sentence type, with random pairing of animals. This eliminated the possibility that significantly different numbers of correct responses on different sentence types could arise because of the intrinsic pragmatic "force" associated with each animal stimulus, although the possibility of pragmatic factors associated with pairs of animals influencing the results remained. This remaining possibility was investigated in specially undertaken analyses of patients' errors (see below). Animals in each grammatical position in each sentence type were counterbalanced across the spatial array, thus eliminating the possibility that significantly different numbers of correct responses on different sentence types could arise because of a spatially based manipulation strategy. The role of spatial factors in generating responses was also examined in specially designed analyses. The mean and the standard deviation for each sentence in this experiment are given in table 4.5.

An analysis of variance with repeated measures on the sentence-type factor showed a significant effect of this factor on the number of correct responses: $F(8,288) = 22.0$, $p < 0.001$. Tukey's "honestly significant difference" procedure was applied at an experimentwise error rate of 0.05 to determine which of these means are significantly different from the others; the results are displayed in table 4.5. As can be seen, different sentence types were interpreted correctly at significantly different rates, indicating an effect of sentence type on correct interpretation.

As in the previous experiment, patients were clustered according to Ward's method, with the clustering verified by the RELOCATE process in

Table 4.5
Group results, experiment 2.

Sentence type	Mean	S.D.
Active (A)	4.4	1.3
Cleft-subject (CS)	4.2	1.4
Dative (D)	3.2	1.9
Passive (P)	2.9	1.7
Conjoined (C)	2.7	1.9
Cleft-object (CO)	2.6	1.8
Object-subject (OS)	2.3	1.9
Dative-passive (DP)	2.0	1.8
Subject-object (SO)	1.3	1.7

Results of Tukey's procedure (experimentwise error rate: 0.05)

A   CS   D   P   C   CO   OS   DP   SO

(Sentence types not underlined by a common line differ; those underlined by a common line do not.)

Table 4.6
Results by subgroups, experiment 2.

Cluster	Number of subjects	Mean score (and S.D.) for each sentence type								
		A	P	CS	CO	D	DP	C	SO	OS
I	9	5.0	4.8	5.0	4.9	4.8	4.3	4.1	3.7	4.6
		(0)	(0.4)	(0)	(0.3)	(0.4)	(0.7)	(1.2)	(1.2)	(0.7)
II	15	4.7	2.9	4.8	2.5	3.9	2.1	3.3	0.7	2.5
		(0.5)	(1.3)	(0.4)	(1.2)	(0.9)	(1.3)	(1.4)	(1.0)	(1.5)
III	5	5.0	0.6	4.6	0.2	2.2	0.4	2.4	0.6	0.6
		(0)	(0.9)	(0.9)	(0.4)	(1.9)	(0.9)	(1.9)	(0.9)	(0.9)
IV	6	3.7	3.3	2.8	2.3	0.8	0.3	0.5	0	0.7
		(1.2)	(0.5)	(1.0)	(0.8)	(1.3)	(0.8)	(0.8)	(0)	(1.2)
V	2	0	0	0	0	0	0	0	0	0
		(0)	(0)	(0)	(0)	(0)	(0)	(0)	(0)	(0)

Table 4.7
Comparison of subgroups by sentence type, experiment 2.

Sentence type	Pair of groups					
	(1,2)	(1,3)	(1,4)	(2,3)	(2,4)	(3,4)
A						
P	*	*				
CS			*		*	
CO	*	*	*			
D		*	*			
DP	*	*	*			
C			*		*	
SO	*	*	*			
OS		*	*			

*Significantly different by Dunn's procedure at experimentwise error rate of 0.05.

the CLUSTAN analysis. Table 4.6 gives the mean scores and standard deviations of each sentence type for each of the five patient groups identified. A detailed description of the performance of these groups is found in the appendix. Table 4.7 gives the results of applying Dunn's multiple-comparison procedure to the scores of the first four of these groups on each sentence type to determine which sentence types are significantly different across the different subgroups. Table 4.8 shows the principal-components analysis of the sentence-type factors that determine the separation of patients into groups.

Factor 1 of the PCA accounts for 59.9% of the variance, and all factor loadings are approximately equal. Factor 1 may thus be considered an overall severity or success factor. Factor 2 accounts of 14.7% of the variance. There are negative loadings for factors representing active, cleft-subject, dative, and conjoined sentence types. Factors active and cleft-subject have the most strongly negative loadings, and factors passive and cleft-object have the strongest positive loadings on this vector. Factor 3 accounts for 9.3% of the variance. Factors active and passive have the greatest negative loadings; factors dative-passive, conjoined, and subject-object have the strongest positive loadings. In factor 3, all the two-place-verb sentences have negative loadings; the remainder of the sentence types have positive loadings. Figure 4.3 illustrates the partitioning of subjects as a function of plotting the first against the second eigenvector of the PCA; figure 4.4 the partitioning of subjects as a function of plotting the first against the third eigenvector. The two subjects in group 5 are superimposed in the upper left portion of the plot.

It can be seen that the first factor achieves a great deal of separation of subjects; groups 1 and 5 are entirely separated from the other groups by

Table 4.8
Principal-components analysis, experiment 2.

Eigenvector	Percentage of total variation	Factor loading, by sentence type								
		A	P	CS	CO	D	DP	C	SO	OS
1	59.9	0.290	0.296	0.315	0.338	0.359	0.375	0.323	0.334	0.360
2	14.7	−0.493	0.362	−0.518	0.359	−0.183	0.168	−0.240	0.279	0.178
3	9.3	−0.370	−0.567	−0.199	−0.322	0.153	0.344	0.397	0.302	0.091

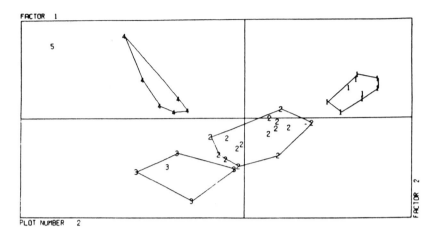

Figure 4.3
Plot of vector 1 versus vector 2 of principal-components analysis, experiment 2.

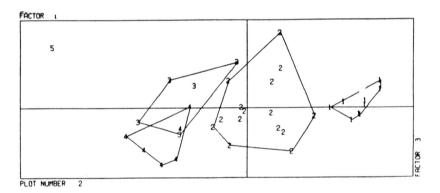

Figure 4.4
Plot of vector 1 versus vector 3 of principal-components analysis, experiment 2.

Table 4.9
Group results, experiment 3.

Sentence type	Mean	S.D.
Active (A)	4.1	1.5
Cleft-subject (CS)	4.0	1.6
Passive (P)	3.2	1.8
Dative (D)	2.9	2.0
Conjoined (C)	2.8	2.0
Cleft-object (CO)	2.7	1.8
Object-subject (OS)	2.1	1.9
Dative-passive (DP)	1.9	2.1
Subject-object (SO)	1.4	1.6

Results of Tukey's procedure (experimentwise error rate: 0.05)

A   CS   D   P   C   CO   OS   DP   SO

(Sentence types underlined by a common line do not differ; those not underlined by a common line do.)

virtue of this factor, group 1 representing the subjects with the best performance and group 5 those with the worst. Groups 3 and 4 are largely overlapped with respect to factor 1, and thre is some overlap between groups 2 and 3 as well. These groups achieve considerable separation on factor 2. The low position of group 3 along factor 2 indicates that this group has relatively low scores for passive and cleft-object sentences and relatively high scores for active and cleft-subject sentences. This situation is reversed for one subject in group 4, who has the highest score on factor 2. Factor 3 contributes to the separation of groups 3 and 4. These analyses indicate that, though most of the grouping of subjects reflects overall severity and is equally affected by all sentence types, a finer division of subjects is revealed by vectors that load unequally for different sentence types. We note that these results are very similar to those of experiment 1, and postpone detailed discussion until after presentation of the results of experiment 3.

Experiment 3
In the third experiment, 49 French-speaking aphasic patients were tested on the French version of the revised battery used in experiment 2. The mean and the standard deviation for each sentence for this group are shown in table 4.9.

An analysis of variance with repeated measures on the sentence-type factor showed a significant effect of this factor on the number of correct responses: $F(8,384) = 28.8$, $p < 0.001$. Tukey's "honestly significant difference" procedure was applied at an experimentwise error rate of 0.05 to determine which of these means are significantly different from the others, and the results are displayed in table 4.9. As in the previous studies, different sentence types were interpreted correctly at significantly different rates, indicating an effect of sentence type on correct interpretation.

As in the previous experiments, patients were clustered using Ward's method verified by the RELOCATE process of the CLUSTAN analysis. Table 4.10 shows the mean score and the standard deviation of each sentence type for each of the resulting seven patient groups. Table 4.11 shows the results of applying Dunn's multiple-comparison procedure to the scores of each of these groups on each sentence type to determine which sentence types are significantly different across the different subgroups. A detailed description of the performance of these groups is found in the appendix. Table 4.12 shows the PCA of the sentence-type factors that determine the separation of patients into these three groups.

The first observation regarding these analyses is that the number of groups yielded by this procedure is compatible with the number of groups yielded by similar procedures in other studies, given the number of subjects in this population. The PCA is also very similar to those of experiments 1 and 2. The first factor accounts for approximately 64% of the total variance (about the same percentage as in the first two studies), and is roughly equally positively weighted for all sentence types, thus constituting a success or severity factor. The second and third factors are unequally weighted for different sentence types, and together contribute about 18% of the total variance, as in the first two studies. The PCA thus shows that the separation of patients into subgroups in experiment 3 also primarily reflects the overall severity of each patient on the task, with some contribution from a patient's performance on individual sentence types to this cluster-formation process. The actual separation of patients into groups by the factors of the PCA is illustrated in figures 4.5 and 4.6.

As can be seen, the first factor is almost entirely responsible for the separation of groups 1,2,3, and 7. Factor 2 primarily distinguishes groups 5 and 6 and contributes significantly to the separation of groups 4 and 5. Factor 3 distinguishes groups 4 and 5. Factor 2 is strongly negatively weighted for active and cleft-subject sentences, and has moderate positive weights for passive and cleft-object sentences, the sentence types on which patients in groups 5 and 6 showed the largest number of responses and which therefore distinguish patients in these groups. Factor 3 is strongly negatively weighted for passive and cleft-object sentences, on which patients in groups 4 and 5 performed differently, and has its strongest

Table 4.10
Results by subgroups, experiment 3.

Cluster	Number of subjects	Mean score (and S.D.) for each sentence type								
		A	P	CS	CO	D	DP	C	SO	OS
I	7	5.0	5.0	5.0	4.4	5.0	5.0	4.9	4.6	4.7
		(0)	(0)	(0)	(1.3)	(0)	(0)	(0.4)	(0.5)	(0.5)
II	9	4.9	5.0	4.8	4.4	4.8	4.4	4.6	1.9	2.9
		(0.3)	(0)	(0.4)	(1.0)	(0.4)	(0.7)	(0.5)	(0.9)	(1.0)
III	7	4.7	3.6	4.6	3.1	4.1	0.7	3.0	1.6	4.6
		(0)	(0.9)	(0.9)	(0.4)	(1.9)	(0.9)	(1.9)	(0.9)	(0.9)
IV	8	4.5	1.5	4.9	0.9	2.5	0.9	3.6	0.3	1.5
		(0.8)	(1.5)	(0.4)	(1.0)	(1.5)	(1.1)	(1.2)	(1.5)	(1.3)
V	8	4.4	2.5	4.3	2.1	1.6	0.5	0.8	0.4	0.3
		(0.5)	(1.2)	(0.7)	(1.1)	(1.3)	(0.8)	(0.8)	(0.5)	(0.5)
VI	5	3.8	3.2	1.2	2.4	0.8	0.8	1.2	0.8	0.6
		(0.8)	(1.5)	(0.8)	(1.5)	(1.8)	(0.8)	(1.3)	(1.3)	(1.3)
VII	5	0.2	0.6	1.0	0.6	0	0	0	0	0
		(0.4)	(0.9)	(1.4)	(0.9)	(0)	(0)	(0)	(0)	(0)

Table 4.11
Comparison of subgroups by sentence type, experiment 3.

Sentence type	Pair of groups					
	(1,2)	(1,3)	(1,4)	(2,3)	(2,4)	(3,4)
A			*		*	
P	*	*	*			
CS		*	*	*	*	
CO	*	*	*			
D	*	*	*			
DP	*	*	*			
C		*	*	*	*	
SO	*	*	*			
OS		*	*	*		

*Significantly different by Dunn's procedure at experimentwise error rate of 0.05.

Table 4.12
Principal-components analysis, experiment 3.

Eigenvector	Percentage of total variation	Factor loading										
		A	P	CS	CO	D	DP	C	SO	OS
1	63.7	0.289	0.343	0.291	0.322	0.372	0.359	0.346	0.328	0.329
2	12.0	−0.534	0.273	−0.596	0.270	−0.037	0.257	0.173	0.334	0.056
3	6.1	−0.281	−0.346	−0.040	−0.647	0.109	0.233	0.443	0.331	0.100

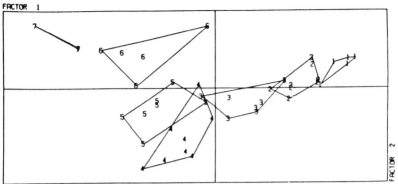

Figure 4.5
Plot of vector 1 versus factor 2 of principal-components analysis, experiment 2.

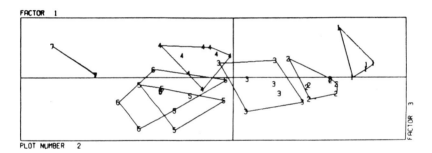

Figure 4.6
Plot of factor 1 versus factor 3 of principal-components analysis, experiment 3.

Table 4.13
Characteristics of subjects.

	Controls		Aphasics	
	Anglophone (N = 23)	Francophone (N = 23)	Anglophone (N = 36)	Francophone (N = 48)
Age	48.4 ± 17.7	45.7 ± 16.2	54.2 ± 14.3	43.4 ± 16.1
Education				
Elementary	5	6	7	9
Secondary	7	9	15	17
Post-secondary	11	8	8	14
Unavailable			6	8

Characteristics of Aphasic Patients

Type of aphasia	A*	F†	Severity	A	F	Etiology	A	F
Broca's	2	11	Mild	7	8	CVA	28	32
Wernicke's	1	5	Moderate	17	14	Trauma	2	8
Conduction	2	3	Severe	7	18			
Dysarthria/dyspraxia	1	15	Unknown	5	8	Other	6	9
Anomia	3	2						
Mixed/other	27	12						
Total	36	48		36	48		36	48

* Anglophones
† Francophones

positive weighting for conjoined sentences, which also were differentially interpreted by patients in these two groups.

Discrimination of Normal and Aphasic Subjects

In experiments 2 and 3, two groups of normal control subjects were also tested—23 native English-speaking and 23 native French-speaking patients. The control and aphasic populations were similar with respect to a number of socio-biological variables, as table 4.13 shows. (For this study, patients over the age of 75 were eliminated, reducing the aphasic population to 36 English-speaking and 48 French-speaking cases.)

For each of the two groups, discriminant analyses (Nie, Hull, Jenkins, Steinbrenner, and Bent 1985) were performed to identify the sentence types that had the greatest power in distinguishing normal and aphasic subjects. The five separate analyses performed were based on the entire set of nine sentence types, the two-place one-verb sentences, the three-place one-verb sentences, the one-verb sentences (including both the two-place and the three-place one-verb sentences), and the two-verb sentences. Standardized canonical discriminant coefficients obtained through these analyses are displayed in table 4.14 for experiment 2 and in table 4.15 for experiment 3. The magnitude and the sign of these coefficients reflect the relative contribution of each sentence type to the discrimination of normal and aphasic subjects for each set of sentences. Dative-passive and Subject-object relative sentences are the most important in discriminating normal and aphasic subjects in all the analyses in which they appear. Cleft-object sentences are the most important sentence type among the one-verb sentences. This pattern is identical in the two studies.

Discriminant analysis also can be used to classify patients; that is, discriminant analyses can determine the likely group membership of an individual subject on the basis of his scores on particular sentence types, once the discriminant-function coefficients for different sentence types are known. This type of analysis is usually used to classify new subjects as belonging to different groups, but it can also be applied to the subjects whose performances gave rise to the original discriminant-function coefficients to compare actual group membership with that produced by the discriminant-function analysis. The assignment of patients and controls to groups on the basis of the classification function obtained by the different discriminant analyses utilized is presented in tables 4.16 and 4.17 for the anglophone and francophone populations.

In experiment 2 assignment varies from approximately 80% to 85% correct; in experiment 3 it varies from 75% to 80% correct. In experiment 2 there is never more than one normal subject who is classified with the aphasic groups in any of the discriminant-function analyses, though the subject is not the same in different analyses. In experiment 3 three normal subjects are classified with the aphasic subjects. In experiment 2, eight to eleven aphasic patients are classified with a group of normal subjects by the various analyses. Eleven to seventeen aphasic patients are misclassified as normal on different analyses in experiment 3.

The discriminant-function analyses conform to those of the clustering analyses reported above. All the patients who are classified with the normal group on one or another of the discriminant analyses are classified in the best- and the second-best-performing group by the clustering analyses, and all the patients in the best-performing clusters are classified with the normal group on at least one, and in most cases all, of the discriminant analyses. Thus, there is considerable overlap between the separation of patients into "normal" and "aphasic" groups as determined by the discriminant-function analyses and the classification of patients on the basis of their correct scores that results from the clustering analyses.

Table 4.14
Discriminant-function-analysis canonical coefficients, anglophone study.

	All sentence types	Two-place-verb sentences	Three-place-verb sentences	One-verb sentences	Two-verb sentences
Active	−0.23	−0.53		−0.23	
Passive	0.27	0.30		0.31	
Cleft-subject	0.03	0.53		0.13	
Cleft-object	−0.06	0.73		0.06	
Dative	−0.26		−0.27	−0.29	
Dative-passive	0.40		1.17	0.99	
Conjoined	0.29				0.26
Subject-object relative	0.53				0.75
Object-subject relative	0.05				0.14

Table 4.15
Discriminant-function-analysis canonical coefficients, francophone study.

	All sentence types	Two-place-verb sentences	Three-place-verb sentences	One-verb sentences	Two-verb sentences
Active	−0.11	−0.11		−0.08	
Passive	−0.08	0.30		−0.24	
Cleft-subject	0.19	0.24		0.03	
Cleft-object	0.23	0.69		0.40	
Dative	−0.04		0.10	0.12	
Dative-passive	0.39		0.93	0.81	
Conjoined	−0.03				0.21
Subject-object relative	0.71				0.95
Object-subject relative	−0.18				−0.11

Table 4.16
Assignment of individuals to groups on basis of discriminant-
function coefficients, anglophone study.

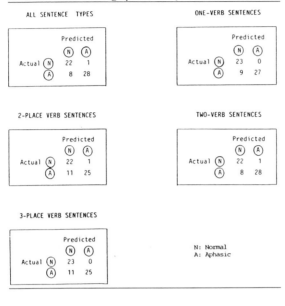

ALL SENTENCE TYPES

		Predicted	
		Ⓝ	Ⓐ
Actual	Ⓝ	22	1
	Ⓐ	8	28

ONE-VERB SENTENCES

		Predicted	
		Ⓝ	Ⓐ
Actual	Ⓝ	23	0
	Ⓐ	9	27

2-PLACE VERB SENTENCES

		Predicted	
		Ⓝ	Ⓐ
Actual	Ⓝ	22	1
	Ⓐ	11	25

TWO-VERB SENTENCES

		Predicted	
		Ⓝ	Ⓐ
Actual	Ⓝ	22	1
	Ⓐ	8	28

3-PLACE VERB SENTENCES

		Predicted	
		Ⓝ	Ⓐ
Actual	Ⓝ	23	0
	Ⓐ	11	25

N: Normal
A: Aphasic

Table 4.17
Assignment of individuals to groups on basis of discriminant-
function coefficients, francophone study.

ALL SENTENCE TYPES

		Predicted	
		Ⓝ	Ⓐ
Actual	Ⓝ	20	3
	Ⓐ	11	37

ONE-VERB SENTENCES

		Predicted	
		Ⓝ	Ⓐ
Actual	Ⓝ	22	1
	Ⓐ	13	35

2-PLACE VERB SENTENCES

		Predicted	
		Ⓝ	Ⓐ
Actual	Ⓝ	22	1
	Ⓐ	17	31

TWO-VERB SENTENCES

		Predicted	
		Ⓝ	Ⓐ
Actual	Ⓝ	20	3
	Ⓐ	11	37

3-PLACE VERB SENTENCES

		Predicted	
		Ⓝ	Ⓐ
Actual	Ⓝ	22	1
	Ⓐ	15	33

Error Patterns

All responses made by patients in experiments 2 and 3 are presented in the appendix (tables A1—A10). Inspection of these tables reveals a surprisingly small number of error types. For instance, of 36 possible responses to conjoined sentences, patients in experiment 2 produced only two response types with any frequency: the correct response (1,2;1,3) and the error pattern 1,2;2,3. Erroneous responses were mainly of the form 1,2,3 in three-place one-verb sentences and of the form 1,2;1,3 and 1,2;2,3 in two-verb sentences. Better-performing groups also produce some partially correct responses. For instance, patients in cluster 2 of experiment 2 produce twelve errors of the form 2,1;2,3 for subject-object relatives, for which the correct response was 2,1;1,3.

Thus, the errors patients made were not random but were largely based on the linear sequence of nouns and verbs in each sentence. When patients made errors, they assigned Agency, Theme, and Goal to successive nouns, filling the argument structure of each verb in turn. The noun immediately preceding a verb was taken as the Agent of that verb, the first noun following a verb as that verb's Theme, and the next noun as Goal (if the verb required Goal to be assigned). In sentences with two verbs, this process was repeated for each verb, except that the first noun in the sentence was occasionally taken as Agent of the second verb.

A striking feature of the responses listed in tables A1—A10 is that errors of these types were found in all the identified subgroups of patients. The better performing subgroups have more partially correct responses, but their errors—including the erroneous portions of partially correct responses—are the same as those of patients in more poorly performing clusters. Random performance may be seen only in the very worst-performing subgroups of patients (e.g. cluster 4 in experiment 2), and, even here, it is limited to the simplest sentences (two-place one-verb sentences).

Thus, it appears that patients' errors are heavily constrained by elementary features of sentence form—the linear sequence of nouns and verbs and the argument structure of the verbs in the sentence. Errors must reflect the failure of normal parsing mechanisms and the adaptations patients make in the face of such failures. We shall discuss the nature of these adaptations in detail in chapter 6, after presenting data from individual cases in chapter 5.

Implications of the Results of Object-Manipulation Test

We begin by considering the implications of these results for the incidence and the nature of aphasic disturbances in syntactic comprehension. First, we note that the incidence of disturbances of syntactic comprehension is very high. Our results indicate that the vast majority of brain-injured patients who carry the diagnosis of aphasia can be distinguished from neurologi-cally intact controls by our test of syntactic comprehension. If we take a very conservative approach to the diagnosis of "aphasic" performance and say that any subject who is classified with the aphasic group on any of the discriminant analyses should be considered as having performed in an "aphasic" manner on this test, then we are left with six English-speaking and eight French-speaking aphasic patients who perform "normally." These fourteen patients are indistinguishable from normals with respect to their performance on any of the subtests of the sentence-comprehension battery we have used. These results set the incidence of disturbance of syntactic comprehension at about 0.85 in this aphasic population. Since about half of the aphasic population was eliminated from this test (either on the basis of being judged by a speech pathologist to have inadequate single-word auditory comprehension to accomplish this test or on the basis of having failed the pretest), we can estimate the incidence of disturbances affecting syntactic comprehension to be over 0.90 in an unselected aphasic popula-tion suffering from cerebro-vascular disease.

Table 4.18 presents educational, sociological, neurobiological, and aphasiological features of the fourteen patients who are grouped with the normal controls on all discriminant-function analyses. Eight of these patients have "dysarthria" or "apraxia of speech"—diagnostic labels associated with aphasic impairments largely or completely restricted to speech output. Given the fact that these patients' speech pathologists distinguished cases with "Broca's aphasia" from others with these two motor speech disturbances, we can assume that these eight patients have primarily output problems and very few disturbances of other "central" aspects of language processing. These eight patients represent 50% of the patients with these diagnoses in the population. Five of the remaining six patients who are indistinguishable from normals are "mixed" aphasics; one is an "anomic" aphasic. These six patients represent 7.5% of the patients with diagnoses other than dysarthria and apraxia of speech in this study. On this basis, assuming an exclusion rate of patients from this study of 50%, we can estimate that the incidence of disturbances affecting syntactic comprehension is close to 0.97 in patients with other aphasic impairments that affect "central" aspects of language processing, but much lower—perhaps only 0.75—in patients with disturbances largely restricted to speech production processes. These numbers indicate that disturbances of syntactic comprehension are common in aphasia.

We now turn to the implications of these results for the nature of syntactic-comprehension disturbances. The first point to be established regards the reliability of the database. We can use the degree to which these three different populations perform similarly on this test as an indi-cation of the generalizability of our results to other unselected aphasic

Table 4.18
Characteristics of aphasics classified as normals on all studies.

SUBJECT	AGE	SEX:M	SEX:F	SCH:Unavail.	SCH:Elementary	SCH:Secondary	SCH:Post-Sec.	HAND:Left	HAND:Right	FAM:Yes	FAM:No	READ:Rare	READ:Same	READ:Consider.	WRITE:Rare	WRITE:Daily	WRITE:Extensive	OCC:Unempl./Retired	OCC:Blue Collar	OCC:Prof./business	OCC:Other/Unavail.	ETIO:Stroke	ETIO:Tumour	ETIO:Trauma	ETIO:Other/Combin.	HEMI:Left	HEMI:Right	HEMI:Both	HEMI:Unavail.*	CT:Frontal	CT:Temporal	CT:Parietal	CT:Subcortical	CT:Uncertain	TYPE:Broca	TYPE:Wernicke	TYPE:Conduction	TYPE:Dysarthria/Dyspraxia	TYPE:Anomia	TYPE:Mixed/Unclassified	SEV:Unavail.	SEV:Mild	SEV:Moderate	SEV:Severe	TIME:1-10	TIME:10-50	TIME:50-100	TIME:>100
1	73	×				×			×		×		×		×			×				×				×						×								×		×			×			
27	73	×					×		×		×			×			×	×				×				×								×						×		×			×			
29	60		×			×			×		×				×				×			×				×				×									×			×			×			
34	59	×					×		×		×			×		×		×				×				×								×				×					×		×			
37	33		×			×			×		×		×		×			×				×						×						×						×		×			×			
64	58		×			×		×		×		×		×		×			×		×					×							×				×			×			×			
90	52		×			×			×		×			×			×		×		×				×		×		×	×			×				×				×			×		
103	21	×				×			×		×	×			×			×	×		×			×		×				×	×		×			×			×			
105	60	×				×			×		×	×			×			×	×		×				×		×		×				×			×			×	×		×
109	19	×				×			×		×	×			×			×	×		×		×							×				×			×	×		
110	20		×	×					×		×	×			×			×	×				×				×				×					×			×			×	×		
119	18		×				×		×		×		×		×		×				×					×	×				×			×			×		×				×
120	35	×			×				×		×			×		×			×			×		×								×				×			×		×		
176	29	×					×	×		×		×		×			×		×					×			×						×			×			×			×

*Lesion site is uncertain in trauma cases

**Lesions listed under a specific lobe are restricted to that lobe on CT scan

Table 4.19
Comparison of mean correct scores on three experiments.

	Sentence type								
	CS	A	P	D	CO	OS	DP	C	SO
Pilot study	3.9	3.9	2.8	2.8	2.4	1.9	1.8	1.5	1.2
	A	CS	D	P	C	CO	OS	DP	SO
Experiment	4.4	4.2	3.2	2.9	2.7	2.6	2.3	2.0	1.3
	A	CS	P	D	C	CO	OS	DP	SO
Experiment 3	4.1	4.0	3.2	2.9	2.8	2.7	2.1	1.9	1.4

(Sentence types underlined by a common line do not differ significantly on Tukey's test set at an experimentwise error rate of 0.05 for each of the experiments; sentences not underlined by a common line do differ significantly.)

populations. There is, in fact, a high degree of consistency from study to study. This can be seen in numerous ways. First, the rankings of mean correct responses for each sentence type in these three groups are very similar, as are the patterns of significant differences between mean correct score per sentence type, as shown in table 4.19. Only the relative ranking of conjoined sentences differs significantly between the three populations. Second, the eigenvectors in the PCAs (tables 4.4, 4.8, and 4.12) are also similar. The first factor accounts for roughly 60–65% of the total variance, and the second and third factors, combined, account for roughly 20–25% of the total variance in all studies. The first vector is a "severity" or "success" vector in all studies, and the second and third vectors indicate some contribution of performance on particular sentence types to patient grouping. The weightings for sentence-type factors on the second and third eigenvectors are very similar in the three studies. The second eigenvector is strongly positively weighted for active and cleft-subject sentences, and has less strong, positive weightings for passive, cleft-object, dative-passive, and subject-object sentences. In all three studies, the third vector is negatively weighted for all two-place one-verb sentence types, and, except for dative-passive sentences in the pilot experiment, is positively weighted for all other sentence types. Finally, the patterns of errors in these studies are similar for the patients as a whole, and the patterns of errors seen in particular subgroups are similar in subgroups that are similar with respect to the nunber of correct responses for each sentence type.

We are aware that certain technical aspects of some of the statistical measures we have used can be questioned. For instance, Tukey's test, used to determine significant differences in mean correct scores in patient groups, requires data to be normally distributed—a requirement not met by our data. Furthermore, the particular clustering algorithms we have used, though correct as far as we know, are only one approach to patient clustering. They themselves could have been used with a different aspect of the database; for instance, clustering could have been done over patterns of correct scores and particular erroneous responses, rather than over correct scores without regard for error types. In each case of a statistical approach where we are aware of alternative methods or limitations of our selection, we have reasons for the our choice of methods. For instance, the non-Gaussian distribution of data points violates the least important prerequisite of Tukey's test, and a measure of statistically significant differences that makes allowance for an experimentwise error rate is crucial in an analysis in which nine factors are all mutually compared. The very limited number of error types found in our population (see appendix) makes it unlikely that using specific errors as part of the basis for patient clustering would have significantly changed the results of the clustering analyses. A minimum-distance clustering algorithm is widely used with data of this sort (see, e.g., Kertesz 1979). The analytic approaches we have used are the most appropriate ones of which we are aware for preliminary, exploratory analysis of data of the sort yielded by the group study.

The most telling argument against the possibility that these analyses are misleading because of technical errors is the observation that the results have been replicated in three different patient groups. The replication of these results makes it highly unlikely that they are simply artifacts due to an interaction of the statistical approaches we used and idiosyncratic features of the performances of the patients we tested. We are confident that this pattern of interpretation of sentence types, and the subdivision of patients into different groups on the basis of their performance on this task, is a reliable reflection of how English- and French-speaking aphasics perform on this particular task.

The pattern of performance on this test is such that we can reasonably conclude that our subjects' performances reflect disorders of syntactic comprehension and adaptive heuristic interpretive strategies, which they apply when parsing fails, and not disturbances of other intellectual functions or the use of adaptive strategies derived from other cognitive domains. We have evidence that rules out the possibilities that these patients' deficits are due entirely to short-term-memory impairments and that their patterns of responses are based on pragmatic or spatial factors. We shall review the evidence regarding these possibilities before developing our account of these results.

The strongest argument against the view that performance on our test reflects short-term-memory abilities alone is the fact that sentences of equal length are not equally easy to interpret. The best examples of this phenomenon are performances on the two-verb sentences, which contain the same number of words, nouns, verbs, and function words and which differ only in syntactic structure. For each of the populations as a whole, and for many identified subgroups within each of the three populations, there are significant differences between the number of correct responses provided for these three sentence types. The same is true of cleft-subject and cleft-object sentences. On the other hand, sentences that are unequal in total length (active and cleft-subject sentences), in the number of nouns in the sentence (dative versus passive and cleft-object sentences), and in the number of function words and informative morphological forms (dative versus passive), are indistinguishable with respect to the number of correct responses they generate for each of the populations as a whole and for many identifiable subgroups. There is no identifiable subgroup whose performance varies on different sentence types solely as a function of overall sentence length. These results strongly suggest that the syntactic structure of a sentence contributes in a major way to determining whether that sentence is correctly interpreted. This does not, of course, imply that memory factors play no role in determining patterns of correct responses or error types. On the contrary, there is evidence that memory also influences performance. For instance, several subgroups perform differently on sentences with different numbers of nouns.

We can also exclude the possibility that the results are due to pragmatic factors. In experiments 2 and 3, animal names were counterbalanced across a grammatical positions so that pragmatic preferences as to thematic roles based on individual animal types would have canceled out across the set of sentences of each type. Analyses of errors also show that pragmatic factors did not determine error patterns. Two naive subjects were asked to assign Agency, Theme, and Goal to each noun phrase in each stimulus sentence on the basis of pragmatic factors—that is, on the basis of their judgment as to which noun phrase would be expected to be Agent, Theme, and Goal given the particular nouns and verbs in sentence. This is obviously a very unnatural judgment to make for most sentences, but it must reflect pragmatic preferences related to the assignment of thematic roles to noun phrases in these stimuli. A very small number of errors correspond to these pragmatic preferences. In experiments 2 and 3, 11 out of 54 dative sentences, 17 out of 171 dative-passive sentences, 4 out of 126 conjoined sentences, 38 out of 195 subject-object sentences, and 37 out of 119 object-subject sentences produce "pragmatic errors." These results overestimate pragmatic effects, because many of these errors are also strictly linear errors and/or spatial errors (see below).

Finally, we can conclude that the position of an object in the spatial array did not determine the use of that object as Agent or Theme to any significant degree in any of the sentence types. The design of experiments 2 and 3 precluded the possibility that significantly different numbers of sentences of different types could have been correctly interpreted with such a spatially based strategy. Calculation of the number of "left-to-right" or "right-to-left" errors in these two experiments was undertaken, and a comparison of the percentage of left-to-right errors as a function of total errors with the percentage of right-to-left errors as a function of total errors was not significant for the entire population or for any identifiable sub-group within the population in either study.

Thus, we can eliminate pragmatic and spatial effects as major determinants of responses on this test, and, despite the likelihood that memory limitations determine to some extent which sentences can be interpreted correctly, we can conclude that a good deal of the pattern of responses is due to patients' retained abilities and impairments in parsing and interpretive operations.

What can be said about the nature of disturbances of parsing on the basis of these results? We begin with the significant differences in mean correct scores for different sentence types in each of the three studies, illustrated in table 4.19. Several features of syntactic form consistently emerge as determinants of sentence complexity, which result in these significant differences in mean correct scores.

The first is the order in which thematic roles are assigned in a sentence. Sentences with noncanonical thematic-role orders—both passive and object-relativized sentences—are more difficult than corresponding sentences with canonical thematic-role order. In all three experiments, active sentences were more accurately interpreted than passive sentences, dative sentences were more accurately interpreted that dative-passive sentences, cleft-subject sentences were more accurately interpreted than cleft-object sentences, and either conjoined or object-subject sentences (or both) were more accurately interpreted than subject-object sentences. On the other hand, the two basic noncanonical thematic-role orders we investigated—passive and object relativization in cleft-object sentences—did not differ significantly in the two-place one-verb sentences in which they could be directly compared, despite the fact that they differ with respect to word order.

Second, verb argument structure seems to contribute to sentence complexity; when matched for word order, dative sentences are more difficult than active sentences, and dative-passive sentences are more difficult than passive sentences. Though this effect may be due in part to the increased length of the three-place one-verb sentences, the considerations discussed above regarding sentence length suggest that the number of arguments that must be assigned to noun phrases around the single verb is likely to add to any effects of length to produce the increased difficulty of the sentences with three arguments assigned by a single predicate.

Finally, the comparison of mean correct scores indicates that sentences with two verbs are more difficult than sentences with one verb, as a comparison of sentences with equivalent word orders shows: conjoined and object-subject sentences are more difficult than active and cleft-subject sentences, and subject-object sentences are more difficult than cleft-object sentences.

Thus, it appears that the presence of a noncanonical order of thematic roles, a third theta role to be assigned around a verb, and a second verb are basic syntactic structural features of sentences that partially determine the complexity of the sentences in which they appear. To a very considerable extent, the relative complexity of a sentence type can be predicted from the number of these features that occur in that sentence. The addition of a theta role in dative sentences increases the difficulty that patients have with these sentences to roughly the same extent that a noncanonical thematic-role order does. The presence of a third theta role and a noncanonical thematic-role order, resulting in a dative-passive sentence, makes for yet more difficulty, as does the presence of a second verb in combination with a noncanonical word order, as in subject-object sentences. It also appears that the presence of a second verb with two argument positions renders a sentence more difficult to understand than either of the two factors associated with a single verb (noncanonical thematic-role order and the presence of a third theta role in the argument structure of a verb): sentences with two verbs with canonical thematic-role order are sometimes significantly more difficult to understand than sentences with one verb with noncanonical thematic-role order (e.g., object-subject sentences are more difficult than passive ones in experiment 1), and sentences with two verbs with canonical thematic-role order are also sometimes more difficult than sentences with one verb and three arguments (e.g., object-subject sentences are more difficult than dative ones in experiments 2 and 3, and both object-subject and conjoined sentences are more difficult than dative ones in experiment 1).

The relative complexity of two-verb sentences, sentences with three argument places to fill around a single verb, and sentences with non-canonical thematic-role order can also be seen by considering the pattern of correct responses found in subgroups identified on this test. The best-performing subgroups in each of the three studies interpreted all sentences well. Slightly more impaired subgroups began to show difficulties with sentences containing two verbs. Subject-object relative sentences were always more impaired in these next-to-best-performing subgroups, and conjoined and object-subject sentences showed variable and lesser degrees of impairment. Yet more severely impaired subgroups of patients began to make errors on three-place one-verb sentences, as well as on two-verb sentences. For all sentence types, errors in each of the subgroups appeared on sentences in noncanonical form before they appeared in sentences in canonical form. In only one subgroup of patients did the ability to interpret sentence types contravene these generalizations regarding the relative complexity of different sentence types: group 4 of experiment 3, which produced more nonresponses to three-place one-verb sentences than to two-verb sentences (see appendix).

These results suggest that these aspects of sentence structure contribute independently and additively to the complexity of parsing in patients with disturbances of syntactic comprehension, both in the population as a whole and in identifiable subgroups. We may think of this feature of aphasic performance as resulting from a reduction in the resources available to a patient for syntactic comprehension. If there is a small reduction in resource availability in a patient, only the more complex sentences will be affected; with a greater reduction in resource availability, simpler sentences will prove difficult.

On the other hand, different patient groups perform differently on different sentence types. This feature shows up in the later eigenvectors of the principal-components analyses. Though the database is too limited for detailed deficit analyses in these groups, the pattern of errors and correct responses does suggest that particular aspects of sentence form are particularly difficult in certain subgroups. This implies that a second component of the deficit in a patient is a disturbance of particular parsing operations. We shall consider this aspect of the psychopathogenesis of these disturbances in greater detail in chapters 5 and 6.

Our final observation regarding overt performances of aphasic patients on syntactic comprehension is that a very restricted number of heuristic interpretive strategies apply to yield thematic roles in sentences in which parsing fails (see appendix for the data upon which this conclusion is based). These heuristics are based on the linear sequence of nouns and verbs in a sentence, and make no reference to the hierarchical organization of constituents in the sentence. For sentences with a single verb, these heuristics assign Agency to the first noun, Theme to the second, and Goal to the third (when present). For sentences with two verbs, these heuristics assign the role of Agent of both verbs of the sentence to the first noun and that of Theme to each of the two immediately post-verbal nouns (that is, a 1,2;1,3 response), or they assign Agency to each immediately preverbal noun and Theme to each immediately postverbal noun (that is, a 1,2;2,3 response). These heuristics occur in all subgroups except those in which the performance is random; this indicates that they apply no matter what the level of overall severity of impairment of syntactic comprehension. These heuristics may contribute to higher accuracy on sentence types in which they yield the correct response (active, cleft-subject, dative, conjoined, and object-subject). These heuristics are not based on pragmatic or spatial factors. Thus, it appears that patients assume that this test requires the assignment of structure to lexical items in sentences, and that they use what structure they can assign—a linear sequence of nouns and verbs—as the basis on which to assign thematic roles. We shall discuss these heuristics in greater detail in chapter 6.

We noted in the introduction to this chapter that significant mean differences in rates of correct interpretations of different sentence types could be interpreted in terms of the complexity of the different parsing operations related to each sentence type. The fact that sentences with noncanonical thematic-role order, sentences with more theta roles to be assigned around a verb, and sentences with two verbs are progressively more difficult may be related to aspects of the parsing process that are relevant to the assignment of thematic roles. If the portion of the parser that assigns theta roles creates a structure into which it places the number of nouns needed to fill the argument structure of each verb of a sentence, and if it assigns specific theta roles as a function of the number of arguments specified by each verb and as a function of the features of syntactic structure that indicate how these arguments map onto lexical items in a sentence, we can expect that the creation of two such structures, the assignment of three rather than two theta roles, and the utilization of a noncanonical mapping will increase the complexity of processing. Thus, our results are consistent with a parsing process that incorporates such structures and operations. We shall discuss the implications of our findings for aspects of the normal parsing process again in chapter 6.

Sentence-Picture Matching Test

Materials
The sentence-picture matching test was used to investigate patients' abilities to assign coreference, scope of quantification, attribution of modification, and thematic roles as a function of verb argument structure. It was decided to use a sentence-picture matching task to assess these aspects of sentence form because the number of possible errors of interest in a preliminary characterization of syntactic-comprehension disturbances was small for these aspects of sentence meaning. Five examples of each of the thirteen sentence types shown in table 4.20 were constructed.

The first four sentence types assess the ability of patients to assign

Table 4.20
Sentence types on the sentence-picture matching test.

I. Sentence types involving category assignment

A. Sentences with lexically ambiguous items

1. Mary has melted the chocolate.
2. Mary has the melted chocolate.

B. Sentences with compound nouns or noun phrases

3. John showed her the baby pictures.
4. John showed her baby the pictures.

II. Sentences types with inchoative and non-inchoative verbs

Inchoative transitive

5. The cup broke the saucer.

Inchoative intransitive

6. The cup broke.

Non-inchoative transitive

7. The lion left the tiger.

Non-inchoative intransitive

8. The lion left.

III. Sentences requiring determination of scope of quantification

9. Show me the second brown bear.

IV. Sentence with referentially dependent NPs

A. Pronominal and R-expression in same clause

10. John read his book.
11. He read John's book.

B. Pronominal and R-expression in separate clauses

12. While she tried on a sweater, Mary noticed a hat.
13. She noticed a hat while Mary tried on a sweater.

lexical categories to words that are lexically category-ambiguous. The first English sentence pair contains items that are ambiguous between an adjectival and a verbal form (eg. *melted*). In the second English sentence pair (modified from Heilman and Scholes 1976), two nouns may be structured either as a compound noun (*baby pictures*) or as two separate noun phrases (*her baby, the pictures*). In both these cases, the function-word and morphological vocabularies critically determine the hierarchical organization of nodes which in turn determines phrase boundaries and the lexical category of a category-ambiguous item. The syntactic foil for these sentence types consisted of a depiction of the meaning of the opposite member of the pair.

The next four sets of sentences contrast the transitive and intransitive forms of "inchoative" verbs with the transitive and intransitive forms of non-inchoative verbs. An inchoative verb assigns the thematic role of Agent to its subject and the role of Theme to its object in the transitive form, and the role of Theme to its subject in the intransitive form. A non-inchoative verb assigns the thematic role of Agent to its subject in both the transitive and the intransitive form. For each of these sentence types, two pictures were presented: one showing the subject noun phrase as Agent and one showing it as Theme. For instance, the pictures for sentences 5 and 6 in table 4.20 contained one picture in which a cup falling onto a saucer was cracked and one in which a cup falling onto a saucer created a crack in the saucer. Similarly, for sentences 7 and 8 the first picture showed a lion walking away from a tiger and the second showed a tiger walking away from a lion. These sentences present a strong test of a subject's appreciation of the contribution of verb argument structure to the determination of thematic roles, since the two transitive and the two intransitive sentence pairs are identical in terms of number of words and syntactic structure, differing only in the way the verb assigns thematic roles in the intransitive form.

The third type of stimuli used in the sentence-picture matching test consisted of a modification of materials used by Matthei (1982) to test scope of quantification. Sentences such as *Show me the second brown bear* were presented. The corresponding picture contained an array of five drawings of bears, colored (from left to right) red, brown, red, red, and brown. The array always contained an appropriately colored object in the position specified by an erroneous "intersective" interpretation (i.e., a brown bear in the second position). This response would be appropriate for a non-quantification adjective (e.g., *the large brown bear*).

The final aspect of sentential semantic meaning tested in these sentences was the coindexation of pronouns and possessive adjectives. Four sentence types were used.

(8) John read his book.

(9) He read John's book.

(10) While she tried on a sweater, Mary noticed a hat.

(11) She noticed a hat while Mary tried on a sweater.

In sentence 8, the possessive adjective *his* can be coreferential with the subject noun phrase *John* because *John* lies outside the governing category of the pronominal (in this case, the NP dominating the phrase *his book*) and thus satisfies principle B of the Binding theory (see chapter 1). In contrast, because the pronoun *he* c-commands the noun phrase *John* in sentence 9, *he* and *John* cannot be coreferential by principle C of the Binding theory. Similarly, because the pronoun *she* occurs in a subordinate clause and does not c-command the noun phrase *Mary* in sentence 10, *she* and *Mary* can be coreferential, whereas they cannot be coreferential in sentence 11 because *she* c-commands *Mary*. It is always correct to interpret the pronoun as disjoint in reference to the noun in these sentences. In each of these cases, the pictures depicted both a coreferential and a disjoint-reference reading for the pronoun in the sentence.

Thus, the sentence-picture matching test extended the set of observations to include a number of sentential semantic features that had not previously been tested in any aphasic population and to test further certain structural features of sentence form (such as the argument structure of verbs) that were also tested in the object-manipulation task.

Procedure
Subjects were told that in this portion of the test they should select the picture that they thought best illustrated the meaning of each sentence they heard. A short practice session with sentence-picture matching materials other than the 65 sentences on the test itself was then held. Sentences were presented in pseudo-random order for the reasons described above. All subjects who performed the object-manipulation test found the sentence-picture matching test easy to perform.

Subjects
The 37 subjects in experiment 2 and the 49 subjects in experiment 3 took part in this test. We shall discuss the results for these groups separately, along with the implications of how the patients performed on this task.

Results: Anglophone Group
The mean scores for each of the thirteen sentence types used in this battery are presented in table 4.21. As can been seen, these mean scores are quite similar and the standard deviations are large. Because of the large number of sentence types in relation to the number of subjects and the lack of

Table 4.21
Mean correct score per sentence type.

Sentence type	Anglophones		Francophones	
	Mean	S.D.	Mean	S.D.
Adjective-verb ambiguity (verb)	3.4	1.3	3.6*	1.6
Adjective-verb ambiguity (adj.)	2.5	1.2	3.6†	1.4
Noun-noun phrase ambiguity (noun)	3.2	1.4	3.4	1.7
Noun-noun phrase ambiguity (NP)	3.2	1.4	3.9	1.5
Inchoative-transitive	3.9	1.3	3.8	1.5
Inchoative-intrasitive	3.6	1.2	3.2	1.5
Transitive	3.8	1.1	3.8	1.5
Intransitive	3.9	1.2	4.0	1.5
Scope of quantifier	3.5	1.8	3.1	2.0
Coreference within clause	4.5	1.0	4.5	1.3
Disjoint reference within clause	2.8	1.3	2.9	1.4
Coreference between clauses	4.5	1.0	4.3	1.3
Disjoint reference between clauses	2.9	1.2	2.6	1.3

*French test used verb version of verb-noun ambiguity.
†French test used noun version of verb-noun ambiguity.

normality in the distribution of scores, it was felt that too many of the conditions for the use of Tukey's test were absent from these data for that test to be used. Though it is possible that some of these scores in fact differ significantly from others, this would be hard to demonstrate for these data.

As was noted above, the sentences of the sentence-picture matching test can be grouped into four different major categories on the basis of the type of syntactic structures and semantic values that have to be assigned. The first four sentences involve syntactic categorization: Sentence types 1 and 2 contain category-ambiguous lexical items that must be disambiguated on the basis of the local syntactic environment, and sentence types 3 and 4 contain sequences of lexical categories that must be assigned phrasal structure as a function of this environment. Once this categorization is accomplished, the NPs in these structures must be assigned thematic roles and adjectives attributed to nouns. Sentence types 5–8 do not require this type of local syntactic computation; in these sentences, the structures are very simple, and the task is to assign thematic roles on the basis of the argument structure of the verb. Sentence type 9 requires appreciation of the extension of the scope of a quantifier over a modifier in a noun phrase. Sentences 10–13 require structuring of hierarchical phrase markers and coindexation of referentially dependent elements (pronouns and possessive adjectives). In order to increase the reliability of statistical treatment of the data on this test, these groups of sentences were treated as separate variables, which we

Table 4.22
Mean correct score per sentence-type grouping, anglophone population.

Score	Mean	S.D.
1 (categorization)	12.4	3.3
2 (verb argument structure)	15.3	3.7
3 (coreference)	14.8	3.4

Tukey's procedure (experimentwise error rate: (0.05)

Score 1	Score 3	Score 2

shall henceforth call sentence-grouping SCORES. Because of the unequal number of observations in these SCORES—twenty trials in the first, second, and fourth SCORES, and only five in the third—we dropped the third SCORE (scope of quantification) from subsequent analyses. We then proceeded to determine whether the three remaining SCORES elicited significantly different correct response rates for the population as a whole or for any subgroup of the population.

The mean correct responses and standard deviations for each of the three SCORES, along with the results of Tukey's test, are displayed in table 4.22. As can be seen, the first SCORE is significantly lower than the other two. This cannot be entirely an artifact of the number of selections available in the pictures for each sentence type, because there were three pictures available in both SCORE 1 and SCORE 3. We thus conclude that these types of sentences are not all equally difficult for the patients in this population.

To determine whether this pattern of differential complexity of different sentence-type groupings is similar in all identifiable subgroups of the population, we performed a clustering analysis of patients and an examination of the determinants of clustering, as in the analysis of the object-manipulation test. The clustering of patients according to Ward's hierarchical method, corrected by the RELOCATE procedure of the CLUSTAN program, yielded four clusters, subject to the conditions regarding stability of groups discussed above. (One patient, whose SCORES were close to zero on all sentence types, was excluded.)

A principal-components analysis of the determinants of patient clustering (table 4.23) yielded two important eigenvectors, the first accounting for 63% and the second for 27% of the variance. The first vector has roughly equally positive weights for each of the three SCORE variables; the second vector is unequally weighted for each SCORE variable. These results indicate that, as in the object-manipulation test, a "success" or "impairment" factor affecting performance on all sentences types determines most of the

Table 4.23
Principal-components analysis of determinants of subgroups as a function of SCORE variables (anglophone population).

Vector	Cumulative variance	SCORE		
		1	2	3
1	62.7	0.621	0.657	0.427
2	90.0	−0.414	−0.186	0.891
3	100.0	−0.664	0.731	−0.157
Variance				
Vector 1	62.7			
Vector 2	27.3			
Vector 3	10.0			

Table 4.24
Mean correct responses for each SCORE variable for each subgroup, anglophone population.

Subgroup	SCORE variable		
	1	2	3
I	15.7	19.3	17.7
II	11.0	15.2	17.0
III	14.2	17.1	13.7
IV	10.9	12.7	13.4

patient clustering, but that some degree of clustering results from patients' abilities to interpret particular sentence types.

The mean correct responses for each of the three SCORES for each of these subgroups are displayed in table 4.24. Tukey's test set at an experimentwise error rate of 0.05 was utilized to determine which of these correct response rates differed from others for each of these groups (table 4.25), and Dunn's multiple-comparison procedure was utilized to determine significant differences between groups with respect to particular SCORES (table 4.26). Examination of these SCORES shows that group 1 did the best on all sentence groupings and group 4 the worst. Groups 2 and 3 performed at intermediate accuracy levels overall, but showed interesting differences in mean correct responses on different sentence grouping SCORES. Group 2 performed better on the third SCORE (that related to coindexation of pronouns and possessive adjectives), and group 3 performed better on the second SCORE (that related to utilization of verb argument structure). This double dissociation suggests that the processing of each of these types of sentences involves independent components. Thus, the results of Tukey's procedure indicate that, for each of these four

Table 4.25
Significant differences among SCORE variables in each subgroup, anglophone population.

Subgroup	Number of subjects	SCORE variable*		
1	7	1	3	2
2	9	1	2	3
3	9	3	1	2
4	11	1	2	3

*Results of Tukey's test applied at experimentwise error rate of 0.05. Variables not underlined by a common line differ significantly.

Table 4.26
Significant differences among subgroups on each SCORE variable, anglophone population.

SCORE	Subgroup pair					
	1,2	1,3	1,4	2,3	2,4	3,4
1	*		*	*		*
2	*		*			*
3		*	*	*	*	

(Results of Dunn's procedure applied at an experimentwise error rate of 0.05.)

groups, different sentence groupings (SCORES) are easier or harder to interpret, and that which set of sentences is most difficult or easiest is not the same in all groups. This pattern is essentially one of multiple dissociations, not entirely attributable to the relative complexity of sentence groupings. Though we cannot analyze these dissociations in any degree of detail, their existence suggests that specific impairments in processing related to the structural and/or semantic features that distinguish these sentence groupings can be separately obtained in aphasia, in a manner that is, to some degree, independent of the patient's overall level of performance.

Results: Francophone Group
The mean correct responses for each of the thirteen sentence types for the francophone group are presented in table 4.21. As in the anglophone study, these means are quite similar, and the standard deviations large. For the same reasons as in the anglophone study, we dropped the sentences dealing with scope of quantification from further analyses, regrouped the remaining twelve sentence types into three sentence groupings (SCORES), and calculated the mean correct response rate for each SCORE for the group as a whole and for six subgroups identified in the fashion used throughout this study. Three subjects with SCORES close to zero were eliminated from these analyses. The mean correct responses for each of the SCORES for the

Table 4.27
Mean correct score per sentence-type grouping, francophone population.

SCORE	Mean	S.D.
1 (categorization)	14.5	5.4
2 (verb argument structure)	14.7	5.2
3 (coreference)	14.3	4.4

(Tukey's procedure reveals no significant differences among SCORE variables at experimentwise error rate of 0.05.)

Table 4.28
Principal-components analysis of determinants of subgroups as a function of SCORE variable, francophone population.

Vector	Cumulative variance	SCORE 1	2	3
1	64.5	0.540	0.653	0.531
2	89.8	−0.694	−0.011	0.720
3	100.0	0.476	−0.757	0.447
Variance				
Vector 1	64.5			
Vector 2	25.3			
Vector 3	10.2			

entire francophone group are presented in table 4.27. The results of a PCA of the determinants of the patient clusters and the mean correct responses for each of the SCORES in each of these clusters are shown in tables 4.28 and 4.29. Tables 4.30 and 4.31 illustrate the results of Tukey's test set at an experimentwise error rate of 0.05 to determine which of these correct response rates differed from others for five of these groups, and the results of using Dunn's multiple-comparison procedure to determine significant differences between groups with respect to particular SCORES.

The PCA for this group is very similar to that for the anglophone population. The first two vectors account for almost 90% of the variance, the first accounting for 63% and the second for 27%. The first vector has roughly equally positive weights for each of the three SCORE variables and thus constitutes a "success" or "impairment" vector affecting performance on all sentences types roughly equally; the second vector is unequally weighted for each SCORE variable, indicating some degree of clustering due to patients' abilities to interpret particular sentence types. The actual values of each of the SCORE factors are highly similar in these first two vectors in the two PCAs.

Table 4.29
Mean correct responses for each SCORE variable for each subgroup, francophone population.

	SCORE		
Subgroup	1	2	3
I	18.4	17.8	17.3
II	16.6	14.6	14.4
III	12.7	16.6	17.0
IV	18.7	18.7	13.3
V	11.0	13.1	13.6
VI	10.5	7.0	10.0

Table 4.30
Significant differences among SCORE variables in each subgroup, francophone population.

Subgroup	Number of subjects	SCORE		
1	16	3	2	1
2	7	3	2	1
3	7	1	2	3
4	6	3	1	2
5	7	1	2	3

(Results of Tukey's test applied at experimentwise error rate of 0.05. Variables not underlined by a common line differ significantly.)

Table 4.31
Significant differences among subgroups on each SCORE variable, francophone population.

	Subgroup pair									
SCORE	1,2	1,3	1,4	1,5	2,3	2,4	2,5	3,4	3,5	4,5
1		*		*				*		*
2	*			*		*				*
3	*		*	*	*				*	

(Results of Dunn's procedure applied at experimentwise error rate of 0.05. Group 6 omitted from this analysis.)

Examination of the responses in table 4.29 and the analyses in tables
4.30 and 4.31 shows that group 1 did the best on all sentence groupings
and group 6 the worst. Groups 3 and 4 show a double dissociation with
respect to correct responses on SCORES 1 and 3. These two groups performed at approximately the same overall level of accuracy, the same level
at which group 2 performed. The fact that different patterns of significant
differences in mean correct responses for these three sentence-grouping
SCORE factors are seen in these three groups suggests that specific impairments in processing related to particular structural and/or semantic
features of sentences are separately obtained in different aphasic patients
independent of the overall level of performance of the patient groups.

Implications of Results of Sentence-Picture Matching Test

Our two aphasic populations performed very similarly on this battery of
tests. This is all the more striking when one considers that, for these
sentence types, there are potentially important differences between features
of English and French. For instance, in English we utilized adjective-verb
category-ambiguous items (*the melted chocolate* vs. *melted the chocolate*),
whereas in French we used noun-verb ambiguities that depended on homo-
phonic identity (*voit la fumée* vs. *la voit fumer*). These language-specific
differences in the protocols had no major effects on the overall level of
performance or on the principal-components analyses of the determinants
of patient clustering.

The results basically reinforce the conclusions we drew from the findings
of the object-manipulation test. Patient clustering is determined primarily by
performance on all sentence types, and to a lesser extent by performance
on sets of sentences sharing particular syntactic or semantic features. Very
few significant differences between mean correct scores on different sentence types or sentence-type groupings were found in this protocol,
though many were found in the object-manipulation test. This is likely to
be due to the fact that the sentence types and sentence-type groupings
used in the sentence-picture matching protocol differ in primarily qualitative ways, whereas the sentence types in the object-manipulation protocol differed from each other in part through the addition of specific aspects
of syntactic form. When sentences were primarily qualitatively different on
the object-manipulation test (as in the case of cleft-object and passive
sentences, which make use of quite different formal devices to achieve what
we have taken to be the important structural change relevant to aphasic
performance—a reversal of the assignment of Agent and Theme to the
first and second nouns in the sentence), the sentence types did not differ on
that protocol either. Thus, this apparent difference in results is due to an
aspect of aphasic performance that was documented in the object-

manipulation test. When sentences are qualitatively different but make roughly equal overall processing demands, differences do not appear in the mean correct scores of the aphasic population at large; however, small groups of aphasics show specific impairments with regard to particular sentence types. Sentences that require more processing because they contain many features of syntactic structure, each of which adds to the processing load, are interpreted correctly at significantly different rates by aphasic patients.

Correlation of Patient Groups and Other Factors

Many of the questions that we posed at the beginning of this chapter require the correlation of specific deficits in syntactic comprehension in sets of individual patients with other deficits—other aphasic symptoms, or aspects of organic lesions. We have argued that a significant component of the functional deficit in the patients we studied consists of the degree of diminution of the work space available for syntactic comprehension in a given patient. To a large extent, this single factor is the most important determinant of performance on our battery of tests. Though many of the subgroups we have identified are likely to contain patients with different specific deficits in parsing, the subgroups primarily reflect patients' overall severity and, we have argued, therefore represent groups of patients with roughly similar, and progressively greater, diminutions in the work space available for syntactic-comprehension processes. Thus, the correlation of subgroups with other deficits, both functional and organic, is relevant to the question of the relationship between the degree of reduction in a syntactic work space and other factors. Correlations of patient subgroups with lesion site, aphasia type, and overall severity of aphasia are presented in tables 4.32–4.34.

The lesion-site data were derived from radiologists' reports of imaging studies, for the most part CT scans. Lesions classified as frontal, parietal, temporal, or subcortical are those exclusively confined to these areas according to these reports, in patients in whom all aspects of neurological examination and other laboratory findings are consistent with the CT reports. For instance, a patient whose lesion site was said in the CT-scan report to be parietal but whose clinical examination showed a hemiparesis would not be classed as having a purely parietal lesion, because the majority of hemipareses follow lesions in the frontal lobe or its efferent fibers, and the conservative criteria we adopted regarding determination of lesion site excluded such a patient from the group of patients with purely parietal lesions. Patients were classified into the standard clinical varieties of aphasia on the basis of examinations by speech pathologists using standard diagnostic batteries, such as the Boston Diagnostic Aphasia Examination

Table 4.32
Lesion site, by subgroup.

	Group	Frontal	Temporal	Parietal	Subcortical	(L) Hemisphere
Pilot study	1	0	0	0	—	4
	2	0	0	0	—	4
	3	2	1	2	—	1
	4	3	2	1	—	4
	5	0	0	0	—	1
	6	0	4	3	—	4
	7	2	0	2	—	4
	8	0	0	0	—	4
Experiment 2	1	2	2	2	0	1
	2	4	3	9	0	1
	3	1	0	2	0	0
	4	1	0	2	0	1
	5	1	0	1	1	1
Experiment 3	1	1	2	0	0	0
	2	2	2	1	1	2
	3	0	2	0	0	2
	4	1	3	3	0	2
	5	1	1	0	0	1
	6	0	0	2	0	2
	7	0	1	1	0	1

Table 4.33
Aphasia type, by subgroup.

	Groups		
	Pilot study	Experiment 2	Experiment 3
Aphasia	1 2 3 4 5 6 7 8	1 2 3 4 5	1 2 3 4 5 6 7
Broca's	1 2 0 4 1 1 2 2	1 1 0 0 0	0 2 4 1 3 1 0
Wernicke's	0 0 0 1 1 4 1 0	0 0 1 1 0	0 3 1 0 1 0 0
Conduction	0 1 0 1 1 1 1 1	0 1 1 0 0	0 0 0 3 0 0 0
Dysarthria/apraxia	6 0 1 1 0 0 0 0	0 0 0 1 0	6 2 0 3 1 1 2
Anomia	0 1 2 0 0 0 0 1	1 2 0 0 0	0 0 0 0 2 0 0
Mixed/other/ unclassifiable	0 2 2 5 0 4 2 2	7 11 3 4 2	1 2 2 1 1 3 1

Table 4.34
Overall severity, by subgroup.

	Group	Mild	Moderate	Severe
Pilot study	1	1	3	0
	2	4	1	0
	3	1	2	0
	4	1	4	5
	5	1	1	1
	6	1	4	4
	7	0	3	3
	8	0	1	3
Experiment 2	1	2	4	0
	2	4	7	3
	3	0	4	1
	4	1	3	2
	5	0	0	1
Experiment 3	1	1	2	3
	2	2	4	3
	3	1	1	0
	4	2	2	3
	5	1	2	2
	6	0	1	2

(Goodglass and Kaplan 1972, 1982) and the Western Aphasia Battery (Kertesz and Poole 1974).

As can be seen from tables 4.32–4.34, the groups that we have identified in this study do not have lesion sites in common, are not homogeneous with respect to particular types of aphasia in the clinical classificatory system, and consist of patients with a considerable variation of overall severity of aphasic symptoms. The failure to find a correlation between subgroups of patients defined by the clustering procedures we have used and clinically identified classes of aphasic patients suggests that a patient's other symptoms do not correlate in any significant and consistent way with the overall diminution in work space available for syntactic comprehension in an individual patient. The wide variety of levels of severity of overall aphasic impairment in each of these subgroups also indicates that, to a large extent, diminution in the work space available to an individual patient for syntactic comprehension may be independent of the number and/or the severity of the patient's other symptoms.

We must express considerable caution about these conclusions, because of uncertainties about the significance of the clinical classification of patients and about judgments of overall severity. As has been recently pointed out (Schwartz 1984; Marshall 1986), the classical aphasic syndromes are themselves quite heterogeneous and "polytypical," so that individual patients vary considerably within a given clinical classification with respect to their symptoms. Thus, it is possible that if we were to seek correlations between specific aphasic symptoms and group membership in the present study, such correlations would exist. Likewise, the clinical assessment of the overall severity of a patient's impairment is a judgment whose significance is hard to assess. Criteria regarding overall severity may shift; a severely dysarthric patient may be rated "severe" despite the absence of other deficits, while a patient with moderate impairments in several functions, whose communicative ability is more disturbed, may be rated as a "moderate" case, because each symptom is "moderate" and the patient is moderately affected in comparison with other patients who have multiple deficits. Moreover, though we are reasonably confident that the patient groups we have identified reflect different degrees of reduction in the work space used for syntactic comprehension, and though this reduction of work space is arguably the most important factor determining the extent of a deficit in syntactic comprehension, patients in each of these subgroups probably differ among themselves with respect to impairments of specific parsing operations. These correlations, therefore, do not necessarily imply that specific aphasic impairments (for instance, those responsible for certain forms of agrammatism) are not systematically correlated with and responsible for specific parsing impairments. However, the present failure to find any correlation between the degree of reduction of syntactic work space with other aphasic symptoms or with clinicians' assessments of overall severity, coupled with the degree of variability in syntactic comprehension seen in patients with agrammatism (the aphasic symptom most likely to be related to a comprehension deficit), strongly suggests that both a reduction in syntactic work space and specific processing impairments affecting parsing are primary psychopathological events, not ones that are usually secondary to other impairments in the processing of the language code.

The fact that lesions confined to different portions of the perisylvian cortex are found in all the subgroups has important implications for the neurological basis of language, which we shall discuss in chapter 6. At this point, we simply note that the degree and probably the type of syntactic-comprehension impairment seen in an individual aphasic patient is not predictable from the location of his lesion within the perisylvian association cortex. Thus, we conclude that the site of the cortex in the perisylvian region devoted to the function of syntactic comprehension is highly variable across adult members of the species.

Conclusions

The following answers to the questions we posed at the outset of this chapter are based on the results of our studies.

• The incidence of disturbances of syntactic comprehension in aphasic patients is very high. If patients with only output disorders are excluded, probably over 97% of patients with other diagnosed aphasic symptoms have disturbances affecting this function.

• Sentences of different types are unequally difficult for aphasic patients. Sentence length may be a factor here, but the effect of syntactic structure on sentence complexity is also a factor. Several different structural factors have been identified as contributing to complexity; sentences increase in complexity as a function of the number of these features they contain.

• Patients can be clustered into subgroups. Different means of clustering yield similar results, and different populations tested with the same materials show similar clusters. The determinants of clustering are similar no matter what aspects of syntactic structure and what semantic representations are being tested.

• Patient subgroups are defined primarily by the patients' overall level of performance on syntactic-comprehension tests, and to a lesser but non-negligible extent by their performance on tests of particular sentence types. Subgroups thus contain patients who perform at a particular overall level and who have difficulty with particular sentence types.

• To the extent that patient subgroups are determined by performances on particular sentence types, these groups include patients with specific impairments affecting the processing of certain syntactic structures and the assignment of certain semantic values more than other structures and values.

• Subgroups are not correlated with aphasic deficits in areas of language processing outside syntactic comprehension, as judged by the noncorrelation of subgroups with other aphasic diagnostic categories.

• Errors partially reflect the use of interpretive heuristics that make use of the linear sequence of major lexical categories in presented sentences. Random errors occur only in the most affected groups, in which both parsing and heuristic approaches to structuring and interpreting sentences have broken down.

• Errors (and, thus, we conclude, interpretive heuristics) are also constrained by structural features of sentences. These structural features include the presence of passive morphology and/or a *by*-phrase, the presence of canonical or noncanonical word order, and the presence of a relative pronoun. These features trigger normal interpretive mechanisms (e.g. assignment of Agency to the object of a *by*-phrase), which may conflict with heuristics based on more general structural features of a sentence, such as its sequence of nouns and verbs.

• Patients in every subgroup all make the same types of errors, which largely reflect the use of heuristics based on the linear sequence of major lexical categories, until performance becomes random.

These results present a general picture of the nature of syntactic-comprehension disorders. These disorders appear to be due to two separate factors: a reduction in the amount of resources available to a patient for parsing and specific impairments in the parsing process. In the general aphasic population, neither of these factors appears to correlate with other aphasic impairments; this suggests that these are primary disturbances of language functioning, not disturbances that are secondary to other processing disturbances.

With this survey work as a general empirical framework within which to view individual cases of syntactic-comprehension impairments, we now turn to the documentation of particular patterns of impairment in greater detail. We shall relate the results of the group and case studies in a general discussion in chapter 6.

Chapter 5
Case Studies

In this chapter we shall present nine case studies of patients with syntactic-comprehension disorders. In each case, we have studied the patient's ability to assign thematic roles to noun phrases and to coindex the various types of referentially dependent NPs described in chapter 1. We rely on Government and Binding theory (outlined in chapter 1) for a description of the nature and distribution of empty NPs and of the linguistic rules determining coindexation of all referentially dependent NPs, and on the Berwick-Weinberg parser (described briefly in chapter 2) for an account of the processes involved in the parsing of sentences.

This chapter is organized as follows. First, we present four research hypotheses, based on GB theory and the Berwick-Weinberg parser, that led to the construction of the materials on which our subjects were tested. Then we present aspects of the methodology we used to investigate these hypotheses and to formulate deficit analyses of each case. Then we present the individual cases. These fall into three groups. The first four patients have relatively mild deficits in parsing, with particular impairments in the coindexation of different types of empty categories. The next four patients have greater disturbances of parsing, and two show a double dissociation in the ability to coindex different types of overt referentially dependent NPs. The final case is that of a patient with a short-term memory deficit, whose comprehension deficit is analyzed as occurring after a parse has been achieved.

Research Predictions

Four hypotheses can be constructed on the basis of Berwick and Weinberg's formulation of the procedures for parsing referential dependencies within the model presented in chapter 2.

The first two hypotheses concern extra parsing operations involved in the parser's location of an empty NP in the incoming string and the creation of an empty NP position. The empirical predictions that follow from these hypotheses rest on an auxiliary assumption that extra parsing operations increase the processing load; therefore, it is predicted that the sentences containing extra processing operations will be the more difficult ones and that this will be reflected in dissociations in accuracy in the aphasic comprehension of particular sentence types.

The third and fourth hypotheses concern the parser's search for an antecedent for the various types of referential dependencies. The third hypothesis predicts that a double dissociation should be observed as a result of hypothesized independent procedures involved in searching for the antecedent of an NP, and makes claims about the independence rather than the relative complexity of the two processes. The fourth hypothesis predicts decreasing accuracy as the complexity of one particular operation—searching for an antecedent—increases.

The Location and Creation of Empty NPs

Hypothesis 1: Nodes for empty NPs are more difficult to construct than nodes for overt NPs.

Unlike the creation of an overt NP, the creation of an empty NP at a particular point in the structure occurs when top-down information indicates that a required NP is not present in the incoming string. As was discussed in chapter 2, the parser can determine the possible sites for an NP by using its knowledge of subcategorization information associated with the predicate, as well as by using its knowledge of correct phrase-structure configurations. However, deciding whether possible sites are correct is a complex process that relies on several sources of information and is subject to local ambiguity. For this reason, a node for an empty NP is predicted to be more difficult to construct than a noun phrase signaled by a lexical NP *in situ*.

The empirical prediction based on this hypothesis is that, when dissociations in accuracy occur, a sentence containing an empty NP should be lower in accuracy than a sentence containing an overt NP when matched for number of embeddings and overall length. For example, consider the following sentences.

(1) John promised Bill [PRO to shave]
(2) John promised Bill [that he would shave]

Sentence 2 contains an overt referential dependency with a strong pragmatic bias toward choosing the subject as the antecedent of the pronoun. Sentence 1 not only requires searching for an antecedent but also requires constructing an empty NP in embedded subject position. Thus, coindexation of the empty NP in sentence 1 requires everything involved in coindexation of the pronoun in sentence 2 plus the location and creation of the empty NP. Since sentence 1 requires the addition of an operation, it is predicted to be more difficult than sentence 2, and that any dissociation in accuracy in the two sentence types should be in this direction.

Hypothesis 2: Not all empty NPs are equally easy to create.

Some empty NPs may be more difficult to construct than others because of different sources of the information required to locate the empty NP (such as subcategorization information and phrase-structure rules—see chapter 2), and thus the location of an empty NP may not be equally difficult in every instance. In addition, certain types of empty NPs may become difficult because additional processing operations must co-occur with the creation of the empty NP. For example, consider the following structures:

(3) John$_i$ promised Bill [$_S$ PRO$_i$ to shave]
(4) John$_i$ seems to Bill [$_S$ t$_i$ to be shaving]

In each of these sentences the parser must locate an empty NP and search for an antecedent. One difference is that in sentence 3 the matrix subject NP *John* receives its own thematic role as soon as *promise* is encountered, whereas in sentence 4 the subject *John* must be held without a thematic role while other operations are occurring until the last word of the sentence is encountered. Thus, sentence 4 is predicted to have a heavier parsing load than sentence 3 at the point when the empty NP must be created in embedded subject position, and so would be predicted to be the more difficult structure when a dissociation is shown.

The Interpretation of Referential Dependencies

Hypothesis 3: [+pronominal] NPs may dissociate from [−pronominal] NPs

In the Berwick-Weinberg (1984) parser, [−pronominal] elements (reflexives, NP-trace, and *wh*-trace) are coindexed by looking back over the syntactic structure. Since lookback is limited, the reflexive or trace must be coindexed with its antecedent within a local domain. For [+pronominal] elements, the propositional list is searched in an essentially unbounded fashion.

This difference in the levels at which the search for an antecedent occurs leads to some immediate empirical predictions concerning dissociations that may be observed in aphasia.

First, reflexives would be expected to dissociate from pronouns in selected cases. Since two separate processes are hypothesized, a double dissociation is predicted, where one patient will have selective difficulty with reflexives and another patient will have selective difficulty with pronouns.

A second dissociation is predicted between [−pronominal] and [+pronominal] empty NPs, as in the following:

(5) John$_i$ promised Bill [PRO$_i$ to shave]   (subject control)
(6) John persuaded Bill$_i$ [PRO$_i$ to shave]   (object control)
(7) John$_i$ seems to Bill [t$_i$ to be shaving]   (NP raising)
(8) John$_i$ was shaved t$_i$ by Bill.   (simple passive)
(9) John$_i$ was introduced t$_i$ to Bill by Tom.   (dative passive)
(10) John$_i$ was believed by Bill [$_s$ t$_i$ to be shaving]   (passivized $\overline{S}$ deletion)

The finding of a double dissociation between [+ pronominal] and [− pronominal] empty NPs would be taken as evidence that the two types of empty NPs involve a different set of procedures in selecting an antecedent.

A third empirical prediction is that both overt and empty elements will occur in a pattern that preserves the [± pronominal] distinction. Thus, a patient who has difficulty with sentences containing pronouns, such as (11), would be predicted to have difficulty with a sentence containing an empty PRO, such as (12).

(11) John said that Bill hit him.
(12) John promised Bill to shave.

Similarly, a patient who has difficulty with sentences containing reflexives, such as (13), would be expected to have difficulty with a sentence containing an NP-trace, such as (14).

(13) John said that Bill shaved himself.
(14) John$_i$ seems to Bill [t$_i$ to be shaving]

Hypothesis 1 states that the empty NP should be more difficult than an overt element. This means that a patient could show difficulty with a particular type of empty NP but not with its overt counterpart. However, in the opposite direction, if the overt element causes difficulty, its empty counterpart should also be difficult.

Hypothesis 4. The greater the distance between a referentially dependent NP and its antecedent, the more difficult it is to interpret the referentially dependent NP.

If a notion of distance can be formalized in terms of parsing operations, it can be predicted that as the distance increases between the referentially dependent NP and its antecedent, the referentially dependent NP becomes more difficult to coindex correctly. There are several possible ways to define distance. At the syntactic level, it appears that the correct notion of distance is a hierarchical one. Hierarchically defined constraints within linguistic theory that serve to limit the distance over which an empty NP trace may be bound with an antecedent and remain grammatical were discussed in chapter 1. These constraints, known as the subjacency condition in GB theory, filter out all sentences in which two "bounding nodes"

(S and/or NP) intervene between the referentially dependent NP and its antecedent. The effects of the subjacency condition are produced in the Berwick-Weinberg parser by allowing lookback to occur only as far back as the adjacent pushdown stack that is dominated by NP or S. A measure of the number of nodes intervening between a [−pronominal] element and its antecedent may serve to define distance for the normal parser.

However, when a patient is unsuccessful at constructing a parse tree at the syntactic level, a linear notion of distance may become relevant to the coindexation of [−pronominal] NPs if the patient adopts a heuristic to coindex the referentially dependent NP with an antecedent. In this case the patient would be predicted to coindex the referentially dependent NP with the nearest NP. This means that patients will tend to choose *Bill* as the antecedent for the reflexive or NP-trace in sentences such as the following:

(15) John said that a friend of Bill's shaved himself.
(16) John$_i$ seems to Bill [t$_i$ to be stupid]

At the level of the propositional list, the correct formulation of distance is less clear-cut. The characterization cannot be hierarchical, since the syntactic structure is discarded once the NPs in a particular clause have been assigned their thematic roles and the clause has been transferred to the propositional list. Moreover, pronouns are not subject to a distance constraint, as is evidenced by the fact that the antecedent for a pronoun may lie an unbounded distance away. The selection of a preferred antecedent for a pronoun seems to depend on the "focus" of the discourse (Hirst 1981) and has very little to do with distance (aside from the constraint that it cannot be coindexed with a c-commanding NP in a particular domain; see chapter 1 above). If the parser were required to look back through the NPs in the propositional list in the reverse order of their occurrence in a sentence, or if the presence of intervening NPs increased the complexity of looking back for an antecedent at the level of the propositional list, then for a sentence like *John said that a friend of Bill's hit him* normal subjects would be expected to prefer *Bill* as the antecedent of *him*. In fact, the eleven normal controls tested as part of this study chose *John* as the antecedent 69% of the time, and *Bill* as the antecedent only 29% of the time. Thus, an initial prediction made by this hypothesis is that sentences containing NPs that are coindexed at the syntactic level (reflexives and trace) will decrease in accuracy as distance is increased between the referentially dependent NP and the antecedent, whereas this factor will not be relevant for NPs coindexed at the level of the propositional list (pronouns and PRO).

In the case studies of sentence-comprehension impairment to be reported, two aspects of the data will be analyzed with respect to these hypotheses. First, dissociations in accuracy will serve as evidence of overall relative complexity of sentence types for individual patients and will corroborate or disconfirm the predicted dissociations. Second, error patterns associated with each sentence type may reveal more details about the nature of the individual impairment. For some sentence types, more than one hypothesis can apply, and hence interpretation of an observed dissociation may be ambiguous. For example, a greater difficulty with sentences containing NP-trace, such as *John seems to Bill to be shaving*, than on sentences with empty PRO, such as *John promised Bill to shave*, could be due to the extra parsing operation required to maintain the antecedent *John* without a thematic role in the first sentence (hypothesis 2), or to a selective difficulty with coindexing NPs at the syntactic level (hypothesis 3), or to differences between the syntactic structure and the propositional list in terms of the distance required to search for an antecedent (hypothesis 4). One way to choose among possible explanations is to consider the dissociation within the overall pattern of performance on a large number of sentence types. For example, if performance on sentences containing *wh*-trace (i.e., another [−pronominal] NP that requires holding an antecedent without a thematic role) is good, then neither hypothesis 2 nor hypothesis 3 alone can account for the impairment. If performance on some sentence types with [−pronominal] empty NPs is good while performance on some sentence types with PRO is poor, then hypothesis 3 is not sufficient to account for the impairment. If performance on sentences with overt pronominals is good, then hypothesis 4 is not sufficient to account for the impairment. In this way, considering dissociations within the total response pattern may help us to choose among explanations of a patient's performance and to bring individual case studies to bear on these hypotheses.

In addition to the specific hypotheses, a deficit analysis is developed for each patient. Deficit analyses are important aspects of the interpretation of these cases because they allow us to establish single and double dissociations of affected functions. These dissociations bear on aspects of linguistic and parsing theory. The analyses take into account the possibility that some responses are generated by the use of heuristic interpretive strategies rather than by the normal parser, and that such heuristics may generate correct responses in certain sentence types. The task of developing a deficit analysis is essentially one of undertaking a linguistic analysis of the patient's pattern of responses and allocating responses either to the operation of normal parsing processes or to heuristics that occur after the failure of parsing operations. The deficit analyses we present here are not complete. For instance, they do not mention patients' abilities to attribute adjectives to nouns or to extend quantifier scope correctly. However, the database we need to investigate the hypotheses formulated above is adequate for at least a first-pass analysis of the deficits in our cases. Ideally, these deficit

analyses would be confirmed by testing each patient with specially designed materials, so that each analysis might rest on verified predictions
regarding individual performance. This could be done in several cases but
not in all (because of patient improvement, patient unavailability, and other
factors). In those cases in which testing with specially designed materials
was not possible, the deficit analyses we present are the most general
analyses consistent with the data that we have been able to provide. In
some instances in which two or more deficit analyses are equally plausible
for a single case, we select the one that is consistent with the deficit
analyses of the entire series of cases, on the assumption that all deficit
analyses must converge on a single theory of syntactic structure and
parsing.

Experimental Design

Materials
Each of five batteries included twelve sentences out of a total of 43
sentence types. The first battery was a longer form of the syntactic-
comprehension battery described in chapter 4. It consisted of twelve examples of the same eleven structures tested on the shorter form: actives,
passives and clefts of two-place and three-place verbs, conjoined sentences,
and sentences with relative clauses. All relative-clause structures (subject-
subject and object-object as well as those on the shorter battery) were
included. The nouns in each sentence were semantically reversible and
were drawn from a pool of six animal names. Lexical items were counterbalanced across grammatical positions to minimize pragmatic effects.

   The second through the fifth batteries tested various types of referential
dependencies in a more specific way. The structures were varied along
several syntactic and linear parameters. First, the sentences varied according to whether they contained a referential dependency and according to
the type of referential dependency. Sentences without a referential dependency were included as a baseline measure of the patient's ability to assign
structure. Thus, sentences of the following types were tested:

(17) *overt referential dependency:*
     John said that Bill kicked himself.
     John said that Bill kicked him.
     John said that Bill kicked Peter.   (baseline)
     empty referential dependency:
     John persuaded $Bill_i$ [PRO_i to wash]
     $John_i$ promised Bill [PRO_i to wash]
     $John_i$ seems to Bill [t_i to be washing]

John$_i$ was believed by Bill [t$_i$ to be washing]
John believed [Bill to be washing]   (baseline)

The group studies suggest that a common strategy that aphasic patients employ is to assign Agent to the NP immediately preceding the verb. If this were the case, a patient might select the nearest NP as the Agent and/or as the antecedent, leading to correct responses in many of these sentences. In order to be sure that patients were interpreting referential dependencies on the basis of hierarchical syntactic structure, and not merely choosing the nearest noun, we included complex NPs (e.g., *a friend of John's*). This methodology was suggested by a study by Jakubowicz (1984). The following sentence types are examples of these structures, in which "nonlinear" assignment of coreference is needed.

(18) John said that a friend of Bill's kicked himself.
    John said that a friend of Bill's kicked him.
    John persuaded a friend of Bill's to wash.
    John seems to a friend of Bill's to be washing.
    John believed a friend of Bill's to be washing.

Extra baseline sentences were added to test for the patients' ability to structure complex NPs and to interpret reflexives and pronouns in simple sentences such as the following:

(19) John kicked himself.
    John kicked him.
    A friend of John's kicked himself.
    A friend of John's kicked him.
    John's friend kicked himself.
    John's friend kicked him.
    A friend of John's kicked Bill.
    John's friend kicked Bill.

These sentence types allowed us to test several aspects of sentence-comprehension ability: the ability to assign structure to complex NPs and sentential complements, the ability to assign thematic roles to NPs in different syntactic positions, the ability to select the correct antecedent for a referentially dependent NP, and the ability to construct an empty NP position.

The sentence types were divided among the batteries as shown in tables 5.1–5.5. The fifth battery contained all the baseline sentences shown in (19). The second battery contained sentences with a sentential complement containing either a reflexive or a pronoun in the object position, and were compared with sentences with no referentially dependent element, as shown in (20).

Table 5.1
Sentence types in first syntactic-comprehension battery.

One-verb sentences

[01] Active (A2)
   The goat kicked the frog.

[21] Cleft-object (CO2)
   It was the goat that the frog kicked.
   It was the goat $[_{\bar{S}}$ that$_i$ $[_S$ the frog kicked $t_i]]$

[27] Passive (P2)
   The goat was kicked by the frog.
   The goat$_i$ was kicked t_i by the frog.

[02] Dative active (A3)
   The goat gave the frog to the cow.

[22] Dative cleft-object (CO3)
   It was the goat that the frog gave to the cow.
   It was the goat $[_{\bar{S}}$ that$_i$ $[_S$ the frog gave t_i to the cow]]

[28] Dative passive (P3)
   The goat was given to the frog by the cow.
   The goat$_i$ was given t_i to the frog by the cow.

Two-verb sentences

[03] Conjoined (CON)
   The goat kicked the frog and kissed the cow.

[23] Subject-object relative (S-O)
   The goat that the frog kicked kissed the cow.
   The goat $[_{\bar{S}}$ that$_i$ $[_S$ the frog kicked $t_i]]$ kissed the cow

[24] Object-subject relative (O-S)
   The goat kicked the frog that kissed the cow.
   The goat kicked the frog $[_{\bar{S}}$ that$_i$ $[_S$ t_i kissed the cow]]

[25] Object-object relative (O-O)
   The goat kicked the frog that the cow kissed.
   The goat kicked the frog $[_{\bar{S}}$ that$_i$ $[_S$ the goat kissed $t_i]]$

[26] Subject-subject relative (S-S)
   The goat that kicked the frog kissed the cow.
   The goat $[_{\bar{S}}$ that$_i$ $[_S$ t_i kicked the frog]] kissed the cow.

Table 5.2
Sentence types in second syntactic-comprehension battery.

[04] Baseline: Three overt NPs
Patrick knew that Joe kicked Eddie.

[06] Pronouns, simple NP
Patrick believed that Joe covered him.

[07] Pronouns, complex NP
Patrick knew that a friend of Joe's hit him.

[10] Reflexives, simple NP
Patrick said that Joe hit himself.

[11] Reflexives, complex NP
Patrick said that a friend of Joe's hit himself.

[13] Object control
Patrick persuaded Joe to wash.
Patrick persuaded Joe_i [PRO_i to wash]

[14] Object control, complex NP
Patrick allowed a friend of Joe's to wash.
Patrick allowed a $friend_i$ of Joe's [PRO_i to wash]

[17] Subject control
Patrick promised Joe to pray.
$Patrick_i$ promised Joe [PRO_i to pray]

[32] NP-raising
Patrick seems to Joe to be sleeping.
$Patrick_i$ seems to Joe [t_i to be sleeping]

Table 5.3
Sentence types in third syntactic-comprehension battery.

[05] $\overline{S}$ deletion, complex NP
Patrick expected a friend of Joe's to be praying.
Patrick expected [$_s$ a friend of Joe's to be praying]

[08] Embedded pronoun subject
Patrick promised Joe that he would kneel.

[18] Subject control
Patrick vowed to Joe to pray.
$Patrick_i$ vowed to Joe [$_s$ PRO_i to pray]

[29] Passivized $\overline{S}$ deletion
Patrick was believed by Joe to be eating.
$Patrick_i$ was believed by Joe [$_s$ t_i to be eating]

[30] Passivized object control
Patrick was told by Joe to run.
$Patrick_i$ was told t_{ij} by Joe [$_s$ PRO_j to run]

[33] NP-raising, complex postverbal NP
Patrick appears to a friend of Joe's to be eating.
$Patrick_i$ appears to a friend of Joe's [$_s$ t_i to be eating]

Table 5.4
Sentence types in fourth syntactic-comprehension battery.

[12] Baseline: 3 NPs + reflexive
Patrick told Joe that Eddie had scratched himself.

[09] Baseline: 3 NPs + pronoun
Patrick persuaded Joe that Eddie had patted him.

[15] Object control, reflexive embedded object
Patrick allowed Joe to pinch himself.
Patrick allowed Joe$_i$ [PRO$_{ij}$ to pinch himself$_j$]

[16] Object control, pronominal embedded object
Patrick forced Joe to hit him.
Patrick forced Joe$_i$ [PRO$_i$ to hit him]

[19] Subject control, reflexive embedded object
Patrick promised Joe to hit himself.
Patrick$_i$ promised Joe [PRO$_{ij}$ to hit himself$_j$]

[20] Subject control, pronominal embedded object
Patrick promised Joe to cover him.
Patrick$_i$ promised Joe [PRO$_i$ to cover him]

[31] Passivized $\overline{S}$ deletion, reflexive embedded object
Patrick was believed by Joe to have kicked himself.
Patrick$_i$ was believed by Joe [t$_{ij}$ to have kicked himself$_j$]

[34] NP-raising, reflexive embedded object
Patrick seems to Joe to have hit himself.
Patrick$_i$ seems to Joe [t$_{ij}$ to have hit himself$_j$]

Table 5.5
Sentence types in fifth (baseline) battery.

[40] John kicked him.   (simple active pronoun)

[41] A friend of John's kicked him.   ("friend of X" subject)

[42] John's friend kicked him.   ("X's friend" subject)

[37] John kicked himself.   (simple active reflexive)

[38] A friend of John's kicked himself.   ("friend of X" subject)

[39] John's friend kicked himself.   ("Y's friend" subject)

[35] A friend of John's kicked Bill.   ("friend of X" subject)

[36] John hit Bill's friend.   ("Y's friend" object)

[43] Subject control, complex NP object
Patrick promised a friend of Joe's to run.
Patrick$_i$ promised a friend of Joe's [PRO$_i$ to run]

(20) John said that Bill hit himself/him.
  John said that a friend of Bill's hit himself/him.
  John said that Bill hit Eddie.   (baseline)

The second battery also contained sentences with empty NPs of the types
PRO and NP-trace, such as those shown in (21).

(21) John promised/persuaded Bill [PRO to dance]
  John$_i$ seems to Bill [t$_i$ to be dancing]

These structures reappeared in the fourth battery, each with an added
reflexive or pronoun, along with some comparison sentences:

(22) John promised/persuaded Bill [PRO to kick himself]
  John$_i$ seems to Bill [t$_i$ to be kicking himself]
  John$_i$ is believed by Bill [t$_i$ to be kicking himself]
  John told Bill that Peter kicked himself/him.   (baseline)

Sentences 22 require two coindexing operations: Both the empty NP and
the reflexive or pronoun must be coindexed with an antecedent. For these
sentences, the source of error could lie in the choice of the wrong antecedent for the empty subject NP, in the choice of the wrong antecedent for
the overt reflexive or pronominal object, or in both.

  The third battery was originally designed to test certain empty categories more directly. It contained more types of sentences with empty
referentially dependent NPs with intransitive embedded verbs, such as
those in (23).

(23) John$_i$ vowed to Bill [PRO$_i$ to dance]
  John$_i$ seems to a friend of Bill's [t$_i$ to be dancing]
  John$_i$ was believed by Bill [t$_i$ to be dancing]
  John$_i$ was persuaded t$_{ij}$ by Bill [PRO$_j$ to dance]
  John believed [a friend of Bill's to be dancing]   (baseline)

In the second through the fifth battery, all sentences were semantically
reversible, and nouns were all of one gender so as to give no semantic or
pragmatic information as to the correct choice of antecedent for the overt
referentially dependent elements (*himself* and *him*). All nouns used in the
sentences were drawn from a pool of three proper nouns plus the word
friend and were balanced across positions in the sentence. For all five
batteries, sentences were arranged randomly with the constraint that no
three sentences of the same type occur consecutively, for the reasons given
in our description of the group studies.

Procedure
In the first battery, the experimenter followed the procedure for the object-
manipulation task described in chapter 4. He or she chose the relevant toy

animals out of a pool of six and displayed them in front of the patient in a counterbalanced array. The experimenter then read the sentence aloud to the subject. The task was to use the toy animals to enact the thematic roles in each sentence read by the examiner. Subjects were instructed that it was not important to demonstrate the action in the verb precisely, but rather that they should merely show who did what to whom.

In the second through the fifth battery, four or five male dolls and four or five female dolls (three dolls with tags displaying proper names plus one or two dolls labeled "friend," all of the same gender) were used. For each sentence, either male or female dolls were displayed in a fixed order, no matter how many names were mentioned in the sentence. The patient was trained to demonstrate only the action in the last part of the sentence, using dolls selected from the array. For example, for the sentence *John said that Bill hit him* the patient was expected to select the doll named Bill as the Agent of *hit* and to make that doll act on any other doll in the array. Patients were told that it was not necessary to demonstrate the details of the action. Testing with numerous patients and controls has shown that they are quite comfortable with acting out only the last action in a sentence. In addition, patients and controls give clues that they are attending to the initial part of a sentence even though they are not required to act it out: They repeat the whole sentence or portions of it, or they make eye movements toward the dolls in the order in which they were mentioned, or they make a small pointing movement toward the first-mentioned doll before initiating the action.

Scoring

The scoring procedure described in chapter 4 was used throughout. Referring nouns (R-expressions) in each sentence were numbered consecutively from left to right in their order of occurrence. Patients' responses were assigned to slots around each verb. The first slot denoted Agent and the second slot Theme, as (24) shows.

$$\overset{1}{} \qquad \overset{3}{} \quad \overset{3}{}$$

(24) John said that a friend of Bill's kicked himself.

Answer: $\dfrac{2}{\text{Agent}} \; V \dfrac{2}{\text{Theme}}$

In (24) the correct answer is 2V2 (V denotes the verb), since the friend is both the Agent and the Theme of the kicking action. For intransitive verbs there is a notation including only Agent, such as 1V.

In the second through the fifth battery, the entire set of dolls was present in the array for each sentence, and therefore it was possible for a subject to choose a doll not mentioned in the sentence. For a sentence with a pronoun, such a selection represents a correct response. Any doll not mentioned in the sentence was represented with the letter X. For example, a 2VX response would mean that the subject selected the second noun mentioned in the sentence as Agent and a doll not mentioned in the sentence as Theme. The response XVX would mean that the subject selected a doll not mentioned in the sentence as Agent and treated the Theme as a reflexive. The response XVY is used to denote the occasion where the patient chooses one doll not mentioned in the sentence as Agent and another doll not mentioned in the sentence as Theme.

Subjects
We selected aphasic patients who met minimal performance criteria of single-word comprehension and sentence comprehension. For single-word comprehension, a patient had to be able to point to the animals named in the first battery and to the dolls in subsequent batteries. Patients who met this criterion were then tested on the first syntactic-comprehension battery described above. Patients who showed some signs of difficulty on at least some of the sentence types were selected for further intensive testing. Patients were selected purely on these functional grounds; there was no consideration of location of lesion or clinical type of aphasia.

We shall present data on nine subjects who showed disturbances of syntactic comprehension that bear on the hypotheses enunciated above and on other theoretical issues in this field. The data we have collected on approximately 200 additional subjects have not all been analyzed; it is possible that these data will answer some of the remaining questions or that they will require modification of certain aspects of our interpretations and our formulations. The cases presented here were selected from this larger series as follows. Patients S.P. and R.L. had been studied before the present set of batteries was developed. These cases document interesting aspects of syntactic-comprehension impairments, despite the limited data-base. Six other cases were selected because the patients were the first to be studied on the set of materials described above. These six cases are therefore the first six consecutive cases for which data of the sort we have subsequently gathered on other patients were available. The final patient, G.S., was selected because he demonstrates an important double dissociation of deficits when compared with other cases in this series—K.G. and J.V. G.S. was the only patient who was especially selected from this larger population. No patient whose performance we examined in a cursory fashion was rejected for presentation because of performance that contradicted the hypotheses described above or the conclusions drawn from this study. We believe these cases are quite typical of patients with disorders of syntactic comprehension; further empirical study will determine whether we are correct in this belief.

The particular batteries we selected for use with an individual patient varied according to the overall proficiency level of the patient. For example, patients who appeared to be having difficulty understanding complex NPs, overt reflexives, or overt pronouns on the second battery were given the fifth (baseline) battery to test their understanding of the same linguistic objects in simpler sentences. On the other hand, patients who did poorly on the first screening battery and the baseline battery were not tested on every remaining battery.

Eleven control subjects, roughly matched for age, were tested with the identical materials to ensure that the comprehension difficulty could be interpreted as one specific to a pathological impairment. The average correct performance of each of the controls on all the tests was 91% or higher.

Data Analysis

Establishing Nonrandom Performance
In a case study, the object of interest is a dissociation between sentence types. However, the overall pattern of results must be considered from several points of view before an observed dissociation in accuracy can be attributed to an underlying functional impairment.

First, in order to claim that a patient shows a predicted deficit over a particular set of syntactic structures, it is necessary to show that the deficit is restricted to this set. Therefore, a variety of syntactic structures must be tested besides those specifically of interest within the theory being tested. In other words, it is important to show the set of unimpaired structures as well as the set of impaired structures.

Second, performance on individual sentence types cannot be considered in isolation from the totality of the data. It is always possible that highly accurate performance is the manifestation of the use of a nonlinguistic heuristic rather than of the use of normal parsing routines. For instance, a patient who consistently uses the nonlinguistic strategy of assigning Agent to the noun immediately preceding the verb and Theme to the noun immediately following it will achieve a high score on all structures where choice of this NP results in the correct answer. To choose among possible explanations of the data it is necessary to look at other sentence types for which such a strategy would result in the wrong answer. If a patient consistently chooses the immediately preceding noun as Agent and the immediately succeeding noun as Theme even when it results in the wrong answer, then it is safe to conclude that the correct interpretation is that the patient is using a heuristic, at least for these sentences.

Third, a deficit can be generalized from specific sentence types to linguistic entities if this deficit is consistent across sentence types containing the same contrastive linguistic entities. For example, a dissociation between the ability to interpret reflexives and the ability to interpret pronouns could be inferred only if a number of matched sentence types were to show the same dissociation.

Fourth, the responses for a given sentence type must be established as nonrandom before they can be interpreted as evidence for either syntactic processing or the use of a strategy. While this point may seem trivially obvious, studies of syntactic comprehension in aphasia have rarely used statistics to show that particular performance patterns on specific sentence types are significantly above chance in individual cases. In addition, the establishment of nonrandom performance is crucial to the valid attribution of an observed dissociation in accuracy to an underlying functional impairment. For example, suppose that a patient scores 68% on acting out the final verb of subject-control structures (*John promised Bill to jump*) and 8% on acting out the final verb of sentences like *John said that Bill shaved Eddie*. While it might appear that a difference in accuracy of 60% constitutes a valid dissociation, in fact neither of these scores would be significantly different from random if the patient were choosing randomly among nouns in the sentence to represent the required thematic roles. The reason is that a subject-control structure, which contains two overt NPs and an intransitive verb, has only two possible responses, and thus a random selection of responses would result in a score of 50%; a sentence with a transitive verb and three R-expressions, on the other hand, has nine possible responses, and so random selection of responses would result in a score of 11%. If performance is random for both structures, a dissociation of accuracy does not constitute an underlying dissociation of function.

In the single case study, the χ^2 statistic was chosen to reject the null hypothesis that the observed pattern of performance is random. In the analysis of the data to be presented here, the null hypothesis can be formulated on a number of increasingly restrictive levels. The patients discussed in this chapter were able to assign the correct number of thematic roles on nearly all the responses, and therefore it can be assumed that patients can assign the correct number of thematic roles. Therefore, for our purposes, the least restrictive assumption is the following.

Stage I: The patient is choosing randomly from among the objects in the array to act out the required number of thematic roles, regardless of the nouns mentioned in the sentence and regardless of syntactic structure or lexical properties of reflexives or pronouns.

To reject this null hypothesis, the total number of possible response types that meet the assumptions must first be calculated. When the sentence to be acted out has a single transitive action, for example, the set of possible responses would consist of any of the possible dolls in the array acting as Agent and Theme, including all possible reflexive interpretations. With four dolls in the array, the number of possible responses would be 16, and the expected frequency of occurrence of any one of these possible responses would be 6%. This way of calculating chance occurrence assumes that the patient extracts no particular information from either the words for the dolls or the syntax of the sentence but still assigns the correct number of thematic roles on the basis of lexical information associated with the verb. For instance, in a sentence like *John shaved himself*, the patient does not remember the names of the dolls mentioned, nor does he use the information that *himself* is a reflexive that must have a local antecedent, but he still acts out an Agent and a Theme.

The χ^2 measure compares the *observed distribution* of responses against a *chance distribution* of possible response types. A significant result would indicate that one or more responses were used by the patient at a level significantly greater than chance under the assumptions formulated above. Visual inspection would confirm whether this systematic pattern of response consists of correct or of incorrect responses, and whether this systematic pattern is limited to objects mentioned in the sentence. This, in turn, can be verified by further statistical means, if necessary.

If the data indicate that the patient uses only nouns mentioned in the sentence in his response, then a more restrictive hypothesis can be formulated, as follows.

Stage II: The patient is able to remember the objects mentioned in the sentence but chooses randomly among them without regard to syntactic structure or lexical properties of reflexives or pronouns.

To test this null hypothesis, we calculate the chance of random occurrence of the set of all possible responses involving objects mentioned in the sentence. For instance, in a sentence such as *John said that Peter hit him*, for which the patient is required to act out the last verb, there are four possible assignments of Agent and Theme to the nouns *Peter* and *John* mentioned in the sentence: John hit Peter, Peter hit John, John hit John, and Peter hit Peter. Therefore, the probability of random occurrence of any one of these responses would be 25%. If the actual distribution of responses is significantly different from this chance distribution, then it can be concluded that the patient systematically used one or more responses and in addition was able to hold the nouns presented in the sentence in memory. It is at this point that we can examine other features of the response pattern in order to determine the nature of this systematic response pattern.

Variations of the Stage I and Stage II assumptions can be formulated, as warranted by the data, for sentences that contain reflexives or pronouns. A patient might consistently assign reflexive and disjoint interpretations to reflexives and pronouns, respectively, but otherwise choose randomly among the objects in the array. Then the total set of responses that could occur randomly under these assumptions would consist of only reflexive interpretations for sentences with reflexives, and only disjoint interpretations for sentences with pronouns, for all combinations of the dolls in the array. This would constitute a more restrictive version of a Stage I hypothesis. If the χ^2 comparison of observed and expected patterns of response reaches significance, it shows not only that the referential dependency is systematically interpreted, but also that the thematic roles are systematically assigned to particular dolls in the array.

Alternatively, a patient might consistently assign reflexive and disjoint interpretations to reflexives and pronouns, respectively, and limit his responses to the nouns mentioned in the sentence, choosing randomly among these nouns. Then the set of random responses would contain only the appropriate reflexive or disjoint interpretation for only the nouns mentioned in the sentence. If the comparison reaches significance, it shows that thematic roles are consistently assigned to NPs in the sentence, and that a reflexive or disjoint interpretation is also consistently assigned. Further interpretation of the data would be necessary to establish whether this systematic assignment of thematic roles occurred on the basis of syntactic position or as a consequence of a nonlinguistic strategy, such as assigning Agent to the noun immediately preceding the verb.[1]

Test of Significance of Difference between Two Independent Proportions
Specific accuracy rates of sentence types with the same number of possible responses and number of verbs may be directly compared with one another to establish that this difference is greater than what would have occurred by chance, within reasonable confidence limits. The significance of the difference between two independent proportions (SDTIP) is used to determine whether a response for one sentence type occurs significantly more frequently than a response for a matched counterpart (Ferguson 1981, pp. 185–186). For example, suppose that a set of sentences with reflexives, such as *John said that Bill kicked himself*, showed the correct response ten out of twelve times whereas the same set of sentences with pronouns (e.g., *John said that Bill kicked him*) showed the correct response six times out of twelve. These two sentence types have the same number of possible responses on Stage II assumptions, so the SDTIP can be used to establish that the two proportions are not significantly different from each other. Thus, the possibility that this split in accuracy occurred by chance cannot be rejected, and the conclusion that there is a dissociation in accuracy cannot be drawn.

Case Studies

Patients with Minimal Disturbances of Parsing, Affecting Empty but Not Overt Referentially Dependent NPs

Patient J.V.

J.V. was a left-handed 65-year-old male who had suffered a cerebrovascular accident on April 8, 1985. The diagnosis was an occlusion of the left internal carotid artery. Positron emission tomography and a regional cerebral blood-flow study revealed a left posterior lesion.

J.V.'s speech was assessed in May 1985. At that time, J.V. showed mild paragrammatism, some phonemic paraphasias in repetition, and difficulty with repetition of single words but not sentences. Reading was intact except for some minor sentence-comprehension difficulties. Writing was normal. Digit span was seven oral and five pointing, within normal limits as compared with the controls who were tested.

J.V. was tested on the first four batteries over the course of several sessions between May 30, 1985, and June 6, 1985. Overall, J.V.'s performance was nearly perfect, as the summary of sentence accuracy in table 6.6 shows. However, he had specific difficulty with all three NP(*seems*)-raising structures and with two of the five passive structures. The feature common to all these sentence types is that they contain empty NPs that belong to the category [+ anaphoric, − pronominal]. This deficit cannot be due to an impairment of specific lexical items, since J.V. had equal difficulty with various verbs within the same sentence type. Nor can it be attributed to a sentence-length effect. A Pearson product-moment correlation between the number of words in the sentence and the error rate did not reach significance ($r = 0.10$, $p > 0.20$). Therefore, it appears that J.V.'s deficit must be accounted for in linguistic or processing terms.

J.V. has difficulty coindexing certain types of empty NPs over a sentence boundary (i.e., over an $\bar{S}$ node). All the sentences containing [+ anaphoric, − pronominal] empty NPs on which J.V. scored over 90% have the feature of being coindexed with an antecedent within the same sentence. All the sentences containing [+ anaphoric, − pronominal] empty NPs on which J.V. scored below 80% involve a trace in the embedded sentence coindexed with an NP in the matrix sentence.

We could state J.V.'s deficit simply in these terms—as an impairment affecting the coindexation of [+ anaphoric, − pronominal] empty NPs over an $\bar{S}$ node. This, however, is simply a redescription of the observations. We accept that some deficits may be very specific; however, we are unwilling to stop the analysis at this point, for two reasons. First, a statement of a deficit in these terms gives no explanation of the occurrence of the deficit. Though certain deficits do occur simply as the result of impairments in certain representations or processes, we would like to find reasons for the

Table 5.6
Results from all syntactic-comprehension batteries tested, patient J.V.

	Correct		Incorrect		
Sentence types with no referential dependencies					
[01] The bear kissed the donkey. (two-place active)	1,2	100%			(Stage II:† $E = 6$, d.f. $= 1$, $\chi^2 = 12.00$, $p < 0.001^*$)
[02] The bear gave the donkey to the goat. (dative active)	1,2,3	100%			(Stage II: $E = 2$, d.f. $= 5$, $\chi^2 = 60.00$, $p < 0.001^*$)
[03] The bear kissed the donkey and the goat. (conjoined)	1,2;1,3	100%			(Stage II: $E = 0.33$, d.f. $= 35$, $\chi^2 = 424.24$, $p < 0.001^*$)
[04] John said that Bill kicked Eddie. (baseline: three overt NPs)	2V3	100%			(Stage II: $E = 1.3$, d.f. $= 8$, $\chi^2 = 98.47$, $p < 0.001^*$)
[05] Patrick expected a friend of Joe's to be praying. ($\bar{S}$ deletion, complex NP object)	2V	92%	1V	8%	(Stage II: $E = 4$, d.f. $= 2$, $\chi^2 = 18.50$, $p < 0.001^*$)
Sentence types with pronouns					
[06] John said that Bill kicked him.	2V1	92%	1V2	8%	(Stage II: $E = 3$, d.f. $= 3$, $\chi^2 = 28.66$, $p < 0.001^*$)
[07] John said that a friend of Bill's kicked him.	2V1	83%			(Stage II: $E = 1.3$, d.f. $= 8$, $\chi^2 = 67.70$, $p < 0.001$)
	2V3	17%			
[08] Patrick promised Joe that he would kneel. (Overt pronoun embedded subject)	1V	83%			(Stage I: $E = 3$, d.f. $= 2$, $\chi^2 = 21.83$, $p < 0.001^*$)
	2V	8%			
	XV	8%			
[09] Patrick persuaded Joe that Eddie had patted him. (baseline: finite embedded clause, 3 NPs + pronoun)	3V1	100%			(Stage II: $E = 1.3$, d.f. $= 8$, $\chi^2 = 98.47$, $p < 0.001^*$)

Sentence types with reflexives

[10] John said that Bill kicked himself.	2V2	100%			(Stage II: $E = 3$, d.f. $= 3$, $\chi^2 = 36.00$, $p < 0.001^*$)
[11] John said that a friend of Bill's kicked himself.	2V2	100%			(Stage II: $E = 1.3$, d.f. $= 8$, $\chi^2 = 98.47$, $p < 0.001^*$)
[12] Patrick told Joe that Eddie had scratched himself. (baseline: finite embedded clause, 3 NPs + reflexive)	3V3	92%	1V1	8%	(Stage II: $E = 1.3$, d.f. $= 8$, $\chi^2 = 81.55$, $p < 0.001^*$)

Object-control sentence types

[13] Patrick persuaded Joe to wash. (object control)	2V	100%			(Stage II: $E = 6$, d.f. $= 1$, $\chi^2 = 12.00$, $p < 0.001^*$)
[14] Patrick persuaded a friend of Joe's to wash. (object control, complex NP)	2V	100%			(Stage II: $E = 4$, d.f. $= 2$, $\chi^2 = 24.00$, $p < 0.001^*$)
[15] Patrick asked Joe to pinch himself. (object control, reflexive embedded object)	2V2	100%			(Stage II: $E = 3$, d.f. $= 3$, $\chi^2 = 36.00$, $p < 0.001^*$)
[16] Patrick allowed Joe to hit him. (object control, pronominal embedded object)	2V1	92%	1V2	8%	(Stage II: $E = 3$, d.f. $= 3$, $\chi^2 = 28.66$, $p < 0.001^*$)

Subject-control sentence types

[17] Patrick promised Joe to wash. (subject control)	1V	100%			(Stage II: $E = 6$, d.f. $= 1$, $\chi^2 = 12.00$, $p < 0.001^*$)
[18] Patrick vowed to Joe to pray. (subject control)	1V	100%			(Stage II: $E = 6$, d.f. $= 1$, $\chi^2 = 12.00$, $p < 0.001^*$)
[19] Patrick promised Joe to hit himself. (subject control, reflexive embedded object)	1V1	92%	2V2	8%	(Stage II: $E = 3$, d.f. $= 3$, $\chi^2 = 28.66$, $p < 0.001^*$)
[20] Patrick promised Joe to cover him. (subject control, pronominal embedded object)	1V2	92%	2V1	8%	(Stage II: $E = 3$, d.f. $= 3$, $\chi^2 = 28.66$, $p < 0.001^*$)

Table 5.6 (continued)

	Correct		Incorrect		
Sentence types with wh-trace					
[21] It was the bear that the donkey kissed. (two-place cleft object)	2,1	100%			(Stage II: $E = 6$, d.f. $= 1$, $\chi^2 = 12.00$, $p < 0.001^*$)
[22] It was the bear that the donkey gave to the goat. (dative cleft object)	2,1,3	100%			(Stage II: $E = 2$, d.f. $= 5$, $\chi^2 = 60.00$, $p < 0.001^*$)
[23] The bear that the donkey kissed patted the goat. (subject-object)	2,1;1,3	92%	2,1;2,3	8%	(Stage II: $E = 0.33$, d.f. $= 35$, $\chi^2 = 357.58$, $p < 0.001^*$)
[24] The bear kissed the donkey that patted the goat. (object-subject)	1,2;2,3	100%			(Stage II: $E = 0.33$, d.f. $= 35$, $\chi^2 = 424.24$, $p < 0.001^*$)
[25] The bear kissed the donkey that the goat patted. (object-object)	1,2;3,2	100%			(Stage II: $E = 0.33$, d.f. $= 35$, $\chi^2 = 424.24$, $p < 0.001^*$)
[26] The bear that kissed the donkey patted the goat. (subject-subject)	1,2;1,3	92%	1,2;2,3	8%	(Stage II: $E = 0.33$, d.f. $= 35$, $\chi^2 = 357.58$, $p < 0.001^*$)
Passive sentence types					
[27] The bear was kissed by the donkey. (two-place passive)	2,1	100%			(Stage II: $E = 6$, d.f. $= 1$, $\chi^2 = 12.00$, $p < 0.001$)
[28] The bear was given to the donkey by the goat. (dative passive)	3,1,2	100%			(Stage II: $E = 2$, d.f. $= 5$, $\chi^2 = 60.00$, $p < 0.001^*$)
[29] Patrick was believed by Joe to be eating. (passivized S̄ deletion)	1V	75%	2V	25%	(Stage II: $E = 6$, d.f. $= 1$, $\chi^2 = 3.00$, $p < 0.10$) (Stage I: $E = 3$, d.f. $= 2$, $\chi^2 = 18.00$, $p < 0.001^*$)
[30] Patrick was told by Joe to run. (passivized object control)	1V	92%	2V	8%	(Stage II: $E = 6$, d.f. $= 1$, $\chi^2 = 8.34$, $p < 0.01^*$)
[31] Patrick was believed by Joe to have kicked himself. (passive S̄ deletion, reflexive embedded object)	1V1	58%	2V2	42%	(Stage II: $E = 3$, d.f. $= 3$, $\chi^2 = 12.66$, $p < 0.01^*$)

NP-raising sentence types

[32] Patrick seems to Joe to be praying. (NP-raising)	1V	25%	2V	75%	(Stage II: $E = 6$, d.f. $= 1$, $\chi^2 = 3.00$, $p < 0.10$) (Stage I: $E = 3$, d.f. $= 2$, $\chi^2 = 18.00$, $p < 0.001^*$)
[33] Patrick appears to a friend of Joe's to be eating. (NP-raising, complex postverbal NP)	1V	67%	2V	33%	(Stage II: $E = 4$, d.f. $= 2$, $\chi^2 = 8.00$, $p < 0.02^*$)
[34] Patrick seems to Joe to have kicked himself. (NP-raising, reflexive embedded object)	1V1	75%	2V2	25%	(Stage II: $E = 3$, d.f. $= 3$, $\chi^2 = 18.00$, $p < 0.001^*$)

$^+$ See Data Analysis section of present chapter for explanation of calculation of χ^2 values.

observed deficits, if that is possible. Second, we shall attempt to formulate the most general deficit analyses consistent with the data in each case. In the case of J.V., there are two such analyses. Each entails a commitment to certain linguistic and/or parsing analyses, and each "explains" the deficit by relating it to parsing operations that would be expected to occasion processing difficulty.

On the basis of the sentence types tested, this hypothesis can be stated in more general terms as the claim that J.V. had difficulty coindexing over a sentence boundary regardless of the type of referentially dependent NP. Then J.V.'s good performance on other sentence types containing referentially dependent NPs must be explained. J.V. did not have difficulty with the structures containing PRO, in which the empty NP in the embedded sentence is coindexed with an antecedent in the matrix sentence. However, if—as Berwick and Weinberg (1984) claim—PRO is coindexed with an antecedent in the propositional list, then, in terms of parsing, PRO is coindexed by looking back through a list of NPs at the propositional level, and therefore J.V.'s ability to coindex PRO should not be subject to syntactic hierarchical constraints. Hence, a difficulty involving hierarchical structure, such as coindexing over a sentence boundary, would not apply to the sentences containing PRO. The same is true of the coindexation of pronouns.

J.V. showed no difficulty with reflexives, which are [+anaphoric, −pronominal] elements and are hypothesized to be coindexed at the syntactic level. Reflexives may have been easier because they do not require the extra operations involved in locating and constructing an empty NP. In addition, for the particular sentences contained in these batteries, the binding conditions require that the reflexive have an antecedent within the embedded S node. Therefore, there was no instance in which J.V. was forced to coindex a reflexive in the embedded sentence with an antecedent outside the embedded sentence.

J.V. did not have difficulty with sentences containing relative clauses. Consider the linguistic analysis of the complex NP containing a relative clause, as shown in (25).

(25) [$_{NP}$ The goat [$_{\bar{S}}$ [$_{COMP}$ that$_i$] [$_S$ the frog hit t$_i$]

In Government and Binding theory, the empty NP (t) must be coindexed with a *wh*-element in COMP, and this *wh*-element is then semantically construed as coreferential with the head of the relative clause (the matrix NP). Translated into parsing terms, the coindexation of the trace would occur within the embedded sentence (accepting that the $\bar{S}$ position is entitled to be considered part of the sentence), and the construal of this *wh*-element in COMP as coreferential with the head of the matrix NP occurs at a semantic level. Therefore, the *wh*-trace does not necessitate looking back over the phrase marker for an antecedent lying outside of the embedded sentence. Thus, on the basis of the sentence types tested, it is possible to account for J.V.'s deficit by saying that he has difficulty choosing the correct antecedent for referentially dependent NPs in a syntactic structure outside the immediate sentence.

The second possible account is based on an operation that occurs only for [+anaphoric, −pronominal] empty NPs. In GB theory, the [+anaphoric, −pronominal] empty category requires the transmission of a thematic role from the empty NP position to the position of its antecedent. This transmission of a thematic role does not occur either in *wh*-movement (cleft sentences and relative clauses), in which the empty NP is treated as a variable that is bound to the *wh*-antecedent, or in sentences with PRO, where both the empty NP and the antecedent receive independent thematic roles. Thus, J.V. may have difficulty specifically with the operation of transmitting thematic roles. If Wasow's (1977) analysis of lexical passives is adopted, then the two-place and dative passives (types 27, 28, and 30) are formed by morphological processes in which their argument structure is changed before they are inserted into the syntax; they can then assign Theme directly to the subject position. Hence, sentences with these passives do not require empty NPs. The three sentence types hypothesized to contain lexical passives under Wasow's analysis are the [+anaphoric, −pronominal] sentences on which J.V. did well. Hence, if lexical passives are excluded, the sentence types on which J.V. had difficulty consist of the entire set of sentences that contain [+anaphoric, −pronominal] empty NPs (types 29, 31, 32, 33, 34). This account predicts that J.V. would have difficulty only with [+anaphoric, −pronominal] *empty* NPs, since only this set of elements (i.e., NP-trace) requires *transmission* of a thematic role to an antecedent.

This deficit in J.V. could be one affecting the transmission of a thematic role (i.e., affecting a parsing operation) or one affecting a syntactic category: [+anaphoric, −pronominal] empty NPs. If this category is absent from J.V.'s grammar, sentences into which it would be inserted by the parser would be incomplete, and those aspects of sentence meaning ordinarily assigned in reference to NP-trace would have to be assigned by a heuristic. Since the transmission of a thematic role is required if and only if an NP-trace is present in a sentence, these two forms of the second analysis are identical with respect to the sentence types in which difficulties arise. The linguistic analysis is less appealing, because it stipulates an unmotivated loss of a representation, whereas the parsing analysis identifies a particular operation, which would be expected to create processing demands, thus accounting for the deficit. However, formally either account is adequate. To the extent that a theory of deficits distinguishes an impairment affecting a parsing operation from one affecting a syntactic category on the basis of the frequency of occurrence of correct interpretations and errors in affected sentence types (see chapter 6), these two possible analyses may yet be distinguishable.

In summary: There are two possible accounts that are equally consistent with the data available for J.V. The first account is that he has difficulty at the syntactic level in choosing the correct antecedent of a referentially dependent NP when it lies outside the embedded sentence in which the referentially dependent NP occurs. The second account is that he suffers a specific processing impairment involving transmission of thematic roles, an operation that occurs only in sentences containing NP-trace. Both accounts entail commitments to particular aspects of linguistic and parsing theory. The first account implies that [+ pronominal] NPs are not affected because they are coindexed at the level of the propositional list. The second account implies a lexical analysis of simple passives. Both accounts require that *wh*-trace be distinguished from NP-trace with respect to its relationship to its antecedent. The next case bears on the selection of a preferred account, since the patient to be described has difficulty with the same structures that J.V. does, but the difficulty extends to sentences containing PRO.

Patient G.G.
G.G. was a 53-year-old right-handed male who had experienced transient global amnesia on July 15, 1985. Subsequent CT scanning revealed luxury perfusion in the region of the left anterior thalamus, and possibly the left putamen at the border of the external capsule. Etiology was inferred to be an embolic CVA, confirmed by subsequent CT and MRI scans.

Neurological mental-state examination revealed mild difficulties with word-finding and filled-delay difficulties with short-term memory. Digit span was six for oral repetition. G.G.'s performance on repetition of lists of semantically unrelated high- and low-frequency words revealed a reliable span of from four to five words. Fluency was observed to be slightly reduced in spontaneous speech.

G.G. was tested on the first four sentence-comprehension batteries on August 1 and August 23, 1985. A summary of his accuracy on all the sentence types tested is shown in table 5.7. His performance is within normal limits for all structures, with two striking exceptions on the second battery: He scored 17% on subject-control sentences (*John promised Bill to shave,* type 17) and zero on the NP(*seems*)-raising sentences (*John seems to Bill to be shaving,* type 32).

The data given in tables 5.8 and 5.9 suggest that G.G. improved between the two testing sessions. His poor performance on subject-control sentences (17%) in the first testing session stands in contrast to his perfect performance on the same structures in the second testing session. Similarly,

Table 5.7
Results from all syntactic-comprehension batteries tested, patient G.G.

Sentence	Correct		Incorrect		Statistics
[01] The bear kissed the donkey. (two-place active)	1,2	100%			(Stage II:[†] $E = 6$, d.f. $= 1$, $\chi^2 = 12.00$, $p < 0.001^*$)
[02] The bear gave the donkey to the goat. (dative active)	1,2,3	100%			(Stage II: $E = 2$, d.f. $= 5$, $\chi^2 = 60.00$, $p < 0.001^*$)
[03] The bear kissed the donkey and the goat. (conjoined)	1,2;1,3	100%			(Stage II: $E = 0.33$, d.f. $= 35$, $\chi^2 = 424.24$, $p < 0.001^*$)
[04] John said that Bill kicked Eddie. (baseline: three overt NPs)	2V3	100%			(Stage II: $E = 1.3$, d.f. $= 8$, $\chi^2 = 98.47$, $p < 0.001^*$)
[05] Patrick expected a friend of Joe's to be praying. (S̄ deletion, complex NP object)	2V	92%	1V	8%	(Stage II: $E = 4$, d.f. $= 2$, $\chi^2 = 18.50$, $p < 0.001^*$)
[06] John said that Bill kicked him.	2V1	100%			(Stage II: $E = 3$, d.f. $= 3$, $\chi^2 = 36.00$, $p < 0.001^*$)
[07] John said that a friend of Bill's kicked him.	2V1 2V3	17% 75%	3V1	8%	(Stage II: $E = 1.3$, d.f. $= 8$, $\chi^2 = 53.86$, $p < 0.001^*$)
[08] Patrick promised Joe that he would kneel. (overt pronoun embedded subject)	1V	100%			(Stage II: $E = 6$, d.f. $= 1$, $\chi^2 = 12.00$, $p < 0.001^*$)
[09] Patrick persuaded Joe that Eddie had patted him. (baseline: finite embedded clause, 3 NPs + pronoun)	3V1 3V2	83% 8%	1V2	8%	(Stage II: $E = 1.3$, d.f. $= 8$, $\chi^2 = 66.16$, $p < 0.001^*$)
[10] John said that Bill kicked himself.	2V2	100%			(Stage II: $E = 3$, d.f. $= 3$, $\chi^2 = 36.00$, $p < 0.001^*$)
[11] John said that a friend of Bill's kicked himself.	2V2	92%	2V3	8%	(Stage II: $E = 1.3$, d.f. $= 8$, $\chi^2 = 81.55$, $p < 0.001^*$)
[12] Patrick told Joe that Eddie had scratched himself. (baseline: finite embedded clause, 3 NPs + reflexive)	3V3	100%			(Stage II: $E = 1.3$, d.f. $= 8$, $\chi^2 = 98.47$, $p < 0.001^*$)

Table 5.7 (continued)

	Correct		Incorrect		
[13] Patrick persuaded Joe to wash. (object control)	2V	100%			(Stage II: $E = 6$, d.f. $= 1$, $\chi^2 = 12.00$, $p < 0.001^*$)
[14] Patrick persuaded a friend of Joe's to wash. (object control, complex NP)	2V	100%			(Stage II: $E = 4$, d.f. $= 2$, $\chi^2 = 24.00$, $p < 0.001^*$)
[15] Patrick asked Joe to pinch himself. (object control, reflexive embedded object)	2V2	100%			(Stage II: $E = 3$, d.f. $= 3$, $\chi^2 = 36.00$, $p < 0.001^*$)
[16] Patrick allowed Joe to hit him. (object control, pronominal embedded object)	2V1	92%	1V1	8%	(Stage II: $E = 3$, d.f. $= 3$, $\chi^2 = 28.66$, $p < 0.001^*$)
[17] Patrick promised Joe to wash. (subject control)	1V	17%	2V	83%	(Stage II: $E = 6$, d.f. $= 1$, $\chi^2 = 5.34$, $p < 0.05^*$)
[18] Patrick vowed to Joe to pray. (subject control)	1V	100%			(Stage II: $E = 6$, d.f. $= 1$, $\chi^2 = 12.00$, $p < 0.001^*$)
[19] Patrick promised Joe to hit himself. (subject control, reflexive embedded object)	1V1	75%	2V2	25%	(Stage II: $E = 3$, d.f. $= 3$, $\chi^2 = 18.00$, $p < 0.001^*$)
[20] Patrick promised Joe to cover him. (subject control, pronominal embedded object)	1V2	83%	2V1	17%	(Stage II: $E = 3$, d.f. $= 3$, $\chi^2 = 22.66$, $p < 0.001^*$)
[21] It was the bear that the donkey kissed. (two-place cleft object)	2,1	100%			(Stage II: $E = 6$, d.f. $= 1$, $\chi^2 = 12.00$, $p < 0.001^*$)
[22] It was the bear that the donkey gave to the goat. (dative cleft object)	2,1,3	100%			(Stage II: $E = 2$, d.f. $= 5$, $\chi^2 = 60.00$, $p < 0.001^*$)
[23] The bear that the donkey kissed patted the goat. (subject-object)	2,1;1,3	100%			(Stage II: $E = 0.33$, d.f. $= 35$, $\chi^2 = 424.24$, $p < 0.001^*$)
[24] The bear kissed the donkey that patted the goat. (object-subject)	1,2;2,3	100%			(Stage II: $E = 0.33$, d.f. $= 35$, $\chi^2 = 424.24$, $p < 0.001^*$)

[25] The bear kissed the donkey that the goat patted. (object-object)	1,2;3,2	100%			(Stage II: $E = 0.33$, d.f. $= 35$, $\chi^2 = 424.24$, $p < 0.001^*$)
[26] The bear that kissed the donkey patted the goat. (subject-subject)	1,2;1,3	92%	1,2;2,3	8%	(Stage II: $E = 0.33$, d.f. $= 35$, $\chi^2 = 357.58$, $p < 0.001^*$)
[27] The bear was kissed by the donkey. (two-place passive)	2,1	100%			(Stage II: $E = 6$, d.f. $= 1$, $\chi^2 = 12.00$, $p < 0.001^*$)
[28] The bear was given to the donkey by the goat. (dative passive)	3,1,2	100%			(Stage II: $E = 2$, d.f. $= 5$, $\chi^2 = 60.00$, $p < 0.001^*$)
[29] Patrick was believed by Joe to be eating. (passivized $\bar{S}$ deletion)	1V	100%			(Stage II: $E = 6$, d.f. $= 1$, $\chi^2 = 12.00$, $p < 0.001^*$)
[30] Patrick was told by Joe to run. (passivized object control)	1V	92%	2V	8%	(Stage II: $E = 6$, d.f. $= 1$, $\chi^2 = 8.34$, $p < 0.01^*$)
[31] Patrick was believed by Joe to have kicked himself. (passivized $\bar{S}$ deletion, reflexive embedded object)	1V1	75%	2V2	25%	(Stage II: $E = 3$, d.f. $= 3$, $\chi^2 = 18.00$, $p < 0.001^*$)
[32] Patrick seems to Joe to be praying. (NP-raising)	1V	0%	2V	100%	(Stage II: $E = 6$, d.f. $= 1$, $\chi^2 = 12.00$, $p < 0.001^*$)
[33] Patrick appears to a friend of Joe's to be eating. (NP-raising, complex postverbal NP)	1V	83%	2V	17%	(Stage II: $E = 4$, d.f. $= 2$, $\chi^2 = 14.00$, $p < 0.001^*$)
[34] Patrick seems to Joe to have kicked himself. (NP-raising, reflexive embedded object)	1V1	92%	2V2	8%	(Stage II: $E = 3$, d.f. $= 3$, $\chi^2 = 28.66$, $p < 0.001^*$)

† See Data Analysis section of present chapter for explanation of calculation of χ^2 values.

Table 5.8
Results from first testing session, patient G.G.

	Correct		Incorrect	
Sentence types with referential dependencies				
[01] The bear kissed the donkey. (two-place active)	1,2	100%		
[02] The bear gave the donkey to the goat. (dative active)	1,2,3	100%		
[03] The bear kissed the donkey and the goat. (conjoined)	1,2;1,3	100%		
[04] John said that Bill kicked Eddie. (baseline: three overt NPs)	2V3	100%		
Sentence types with pronouns				
[06] John said that Bill kicked him.	2V1	100%		
[07] John said that a friend of Bill's kicked him.	2V1 2V3	17% 75%	3V1	8%
Sentence types with reflexives				
[10] John said that Bill kicked himself.	2V2	100%		
[11] John said that a friend of Bill's kicked himself.	2V2	92%	2V3	8%
Object-control sentence types				
[13] Patrick persuaded Joe to wash. (object control)	2V	100%		
[14] Patrick persuaded a friend of Joe's to wash. (object control, complex NP)	2V	100%		
Subject-control sentence types				
[17] Patrick promised Joe to wash. (subject control)	1V	17%	2V	83%
Sentence types with wh-trace				
[21] It was the bear that the donkey kissed. (two-place cleft object)	2,1	100%		
[22] It was the bear that the donkey gave to the goat. (dative cleft object)	2,1,3	100%		
[23] The bear that the donkey kissed patted the goat. (subject-object)	2,1;1,3	100%		
[24] The bear kissed the donkey that patted the goat. (object-subject)	1,2;2,3	100%		
[25] The bear kissed the donkey that the goat patted. (object-object)	1,2;3,2	100%		
[26] The bear that kissed the donkey patted the goat. (subject-subject)	1,2;1,3	92%	1,2;2,3	8%

Table 5.8 (continued)

	Correct		Incorrect	
Passive sentence types				
[27] The bear was kissed by the donkey. (two-place passive)	2, 1	100%		
[28] The bear was given to the donkey by the goat. (dative passive)	3, 1, 2	100%		
NP-raising sentence types				
[32] Patrick seems to Joe to be praying. (NP-raising)	1V	0%	2V	100%

he failed completely on NP(*seems*)-raising sentences in the first session but scored nearly within normal limits on other NP(*seems*)-raising structures of at least equal complexity (types 33 and 34) in the second session. Improvement is not surprising. Spontaneous recovery is not unusual during the first month after a small stroke, and the initial testing session took place only two weeks after G.G.'s symptoms first appeared. In addition, patients with small thalamic lesions tend to suffer only transient aphasic disturbances (Benson 1979, p. 97). We will therefore consider only the sentence types tested in the first session, shown in table 5.8.

Several observations can be made regarding these data. First, all the sentences on which G.G. had difficulty contain empty NPs. Second, G.G. had difficulty with subject-control (type 17) and NP(*seems*)-raising structures (type 32), which involve coindexing between embedded subject and matrix subject. This deficit cannot be attributed to a difficulty with specific lexical items, since G.G. showed equal difficulty with the various verbs tested for each sentence type. Furthermore, G.G. showed no sentence-length effects; a Pearson product-moment correlation between number of words per sentence and error rate did not reach significance, and in fact was in the wrong direction ($r = -0.20, p > 0.20$). These facts invite the hypothesis of a linguistic or processing deficit at the syntactic level.

Like J.V., G.G. had difficulty with sentences containing [+ anaphoric, − pronominal] empty NPs but not with sentences containing *wh*-trace (relative-clause and cleft-object sentences) or passives (types 27 and 28). Unfortunately, passive sentences with an antecedent in embedded subject position were all tested in the second testing session, when G.G.'s performance on even the difficult structures had improved greatly, so a comparison between his performances on lexical and transformational passives is not possible. Unlike J.V., G.G. had difficulty with sentences with PRO. In other words, his impairment extended to all [+ anaphoric] empty NPs.

Table 5.9
Results from second testing session, patient G.G.

	Correct		Incorrect	
Sentence types with referential dependencies				
[05] Patrick expected a friend of Joe's to be praying. ($\overline{S}$ deletion, complex NP object)	2V	92%	1V	8%
Sentence types with pronouns				
[08] Patrick promised Joe that he would kneel. (overt pronoun embedded subject)	1V	100%		
[09] Patrick persuaded Joe that Eddie had patted him. (baseline: finite embedded clause, 3 NPs + pronoun)	3V1 3V2	83% 8%	1V2	8%
Sentence types with reflexives				
[12] Patrick told Joe that Eddie had scratched himself. (baseline: finite embedded clause, 3 NPs + reflexive)	3V3	100%		
Object-control sentence types				
[15] Patrick asked Joe to pinch himself. (object control, reflexive embedded object)	2V2	100%		
[16] Patrick allowed Joe to hit him. (object control, pronominal embedded object)	2V1	92%	1V1	8%
Subject-control sentence types				
[18] Patrick vowed to Joe to pray. (subject control)	1V	100%		
[19] Patrick promised Joe to hit himself. (subject control, reflexive embedded object)	1V1	75%	2V2	25%
[20] Patrick promised Joe to cover him. (subject control, pronominal embedded object)	1V2	83%	2V1	17%
Passive sentence types				
[29] Patrick was believed by Joe to be eating. (passivized $\overline{S}$ deletion)	1V	100%		
[30] Patrick was told by Joe to run. (passivized object control)	1V	92%	2V	8%
[31] Patrick was believed by Joe to have kicked himself. (passivized $\overline{S}$ deletion, reflexive embedded object)	1V1	75%	2V2	25%
NP-raising sentence types				
[33] Patrick appears to a friend of Joe's to be eating. (NP-raising, complex postverbal NP)	1V	83%	2V	17%
[34] Patrick seems to Joe to have kicked himself. (NP-raising, reflexive embedded object)	1V1	92%	2V2	8%

G.G.'s impairment, like J.V.'s, appears only when certain referentially dependent elements are coindexed with an antecedent over a sentence boundary. We may therefore postulate that his deficit is one of coindexation over an $\overline{S}$ node. The exclusion of pronouns and reflexives from this deficit is accounted for as was discussed in relation to the first deficit analysis considered for J.V. However, a variety of new questions arise regarding this analysis in G.G.'s case. First, it must be explained why an impairment based on hierarchical structure would extend to subject-control PRO, since there should be no hierarchical effects on the coindexation of this element at the level of propositional structure if the Berwick-Weinberg model is correct. Second, G.G.'s ability to coindex PRO in object-control sentences needs to be accounted for.

There are two ways to resolve the first question. One is to conclude that PRO is actually coindexed at the level of syntactic structure and thus is subject to hierarchical constraints. Bouchard (1982) has argued that subject-control and object-control structures such as those that were tested in this study are coindexed at the syntactic level. If this is the case, then the coindexation of the [+ anaphoric, + pronominal] PRO in these structures would constitute a different process than the coindexation of the [− anaphoric, + pronominal] overt pronouns, which occurs at the level of the propositional list.

If PRO is coindexed at the syntactic level, then it must be explained why J.V. did not have difficulty with PRO in these sentences. If J.V.'s impairment is also characterized as a difficulty in coindexing over a sentence boundary, then he should have difficulty with subject-control PRO sentences, just as G.G. does. If the alternate analysis for J.V. is adopted, namely that he has difficulty transmitting thematic roles, then PRO should not cause difficulty, even if it is coindexed at the level of syntactic structure, since PRO does not transmit a thematic role to its antecedent. Thus, considering the two cases together serves to narrow down the possible accounts for each case. The account that G.G. has difficulty coindexing over a sentence boundary requires that PRO be coindexed at the syntactic level in the obligatory-control structures we tested and that J.V.'s deficit be characterized as a difficulty in transmitting thematic roles from trace to antecedent. Further, if this is correct, Wasow's (1977) analysis of lexical passives must be correct to account for J.V.'s good performance on these sentences.

If this account of G.G.'s deficit is correct, we must also explain why object control is not also affected, since it too would involve coindexation over a sentence boundary. G.G.'s error patterns suggest that he could have performed well on object-control structures by using a heuristic. In the subject-control (type 17) and NP-raising (type 32) sentences on which G.G. performed poorly, his erroneous response in every case was to choose the

NP nearest to the empty NP. In other words, in sentences like *John promised Bill to shave* and *John seems to Bill to be shaving*, G.G. chose *Bill* as the Agent for 83% and 100% of the sentences, respectively. (In the few exceptions, his responses were correct.) This choice of the NP immediately preceding a verb as the Agent of that verb is a heuristic frequently seen in aphasia (see chapter 4 and other cases in the present chapter). Therefore, we may attribute G.G.'s good performance on object-control sentences to his use of this heuristic, which happened to produce the correct response.

The second way to solve the problem of why PRO and NP-trace are both affected in certain sentences is to conclude that the analysis that G.G. has difficulty coindexing over a sentence boundary is not the correct one. Then an alternative account must be proposed. One possible account is that G.G. has a selective linguistic impairment affecting coindexation of all [+ anaphoric] empty NPs, whether the coindexation occurs over a sentence boundary or not. If this is so, then it must be explained why his performance on particular sentences with [+ anaphoric] empty NPs, namely passives and object-control sentences, is good (see table 5.8). Both passive constructions on which G.G. was tested in the first session are analyzed as lexical passives (i.e., as containing no empty NP) by Wasow (1977), and therefore it is possible that these passive sentences are excluded as types that include [+ anaphoric] empty NPs. Object-control structures can be handled heuristically as described above.

This second account states the deficit in G.G. in purely linguistic terms: as a loss of a representation of the category "[+ anaphoric] empty NP." This loss cannot be lexical; empty NPs are not lexical items, and because G.G. had difficulty with all verbs involving NP-trace and PRO his disturbance cannot be stated in terms of selected lexical items. Nor does this loss include all [+ anaphoric] items; reflexives are not affected. This also indicates that the disturbance is not one of loss of lexical items.

A loss of the representation of the class of [+ anaphoric] empty NPs would create disturbances in parsing as follows: The parser would recognize the need to insert an empty NP in syntactic structures where members of this category ordinarily are inserted, but would have no element to insert into these positions. The result would be a structure without an NP in certain positions, such as the subject of embedded infinitives, as illustrated in (26) and (27).

(26) John promised Bill to jump.
(27) John seems to Bill to be jumping.

Heuristics that assign the NP immediately preceding a verb as the Agent of that verb would apply to assign Agency to *Bill* in both these structures.

G.G.'s deficit also cannot be one that disturbs his ability to apply a parsing procedure type-transparently related to principle A of the Binding theory (see chapter 1). There is no parsing procedure that affects only [+anaphoric] empty NPs. Gap-hunting is common to sentences containing NP-trace and *wh*-trace, and thus it cuts across the set of [+anaphoric] and [−anaphoric] empty NPs; however, it is not triggered by sentences containing PRO. Indeed, the next two cases to be presented show that sentences with PRO and those with NP-trace involve separate parsing steps. Thus, the generalization regarding [+anaphoric] empty NPs can be stated in linguistic terms but not in terms of parsing operations.

In contrast with the case of J.V., in which a linguistic analysis and a parsing analysis regarding NP-trace or transmission of thematic roles cannot be distinguished in terms of the structures that would be affected by one deficit and not the other, the two analyses we are considering for G.G. are distinguishable on empirical grounds; that is, there may be sentence types in which coindexation of a referentially dependent NP other than a [+anaphoric] empty NP occurs over an $\overline{S}$, and, conversely, there are structures in which coindexation of a [+anaphoric] empty NP does not take place over an $\overline{S}$. The first of these may be structures in which a *wh*-trace is bound by a series of (possibly deleted) *wh*-words, as in the following:

(28) The boy [(that)$_i$ [Susan knew [Mary likes t$_i$]]] lives in Maine.

If the binding of the trace (t) is accomplished without reference to the intervening chain of traces, such sentences involve coindexation of an empty NP (*wh*-trace) over an $\overline{S}$. Conversely, sentences such as (29) involve coindexation of an NP-trace within an $\overline{S}$ since the inner dative is not lexical.

(29) The elephant was given the donkey by the bear.

Because G.G. improved before his performance on these types of sentences could be tested, we were unable to decide between these two theories.

If this second account is correct, either of our two accounts of J.V.'s deficit may be correct. The conclusion we drew regarding the lexical analysis of passive suggested by Wasow (1977) still stands; it is needed for this analysis of G.G.'s performance, just as it is needed for the second of the two of our analyses of J.V. if this is not the accepted analysis of G.G. However, if this analysis and the second analysis of J.V. are both correct, we are not forced to conclude that PRO is coindexed in the syntax in obligatory-control structures.

This case is of value in several respects. First, it demonstrates the need for a linguistic or parsing analysis that accounts for the pattern of responses shown by G.G. and that is consistent with the data from other patients; several possibilities exist for such an analysis. Second, this case reveals the interdependence of linguistic theory and parsing models in the construction of accounts of language processing. For example, it is linguistic theory that provides the arguments in favor of subject-control and object-control PRO being coindexed either at the level of Logical Form (Chomsky 1981) or at the syntactic level (Bouchard 1982); the parser only mirrors these proposed distinctions in type. Third, this case illustrates the usefulness of this approach to the formulation of specific accounts of aphasic sentence comprehension. Even though there is more than one possible account of the data for G.G., each account requires a set of contingent assumptions derived from linguistic theory and from parsing models.

Patient K.G.

K.G. was a patient who had difficulty choosing the correct antecedent for an empty NP under certain conditions but never had difficulty interpreting overt referentially dependent NPs (reflexives or pronouns) correctly. In addition, there was a dissociation between different types of empty referentially dependent NPs, with trace impaired more severely than PRO. A previous report of K.G. appears in Hildebrandt, Caplan, and Evans 1987.

K.G. was a 74-year-old right-handed male who had suffered two embolic, hemorrhagic strokes in quick succession on October 18 and October 31, 1983. A left frontal hypodensity was noted on CT scanning after the hemorrhage had resorbed. One year after the stroke, K.G.'s speech pathologist diagnosed mild agrammatism, apraxia of speech, and marked anomia in spontaneous speech. Repetition was intact. Reading comprehension was difficult beyond the single-word level. K.G. also displayed difficulties with written language at both the word level and the sentence level. His digit span as measured on the Wechsler Adult Intelligence Scale was stable at seven for serial oral recall and five for serial pointing recall.

K.G. was tested on the first four batteries in November and December 1984, approximately one year after onset. Preliminary testing had shown that he was able to point to three objects in succession as requested by the examiner.

K.G.'s results on the first battery are shown in table 5.10. He performed almost perfectly on most sentences tested, but he showed some trouble with dative passives (67%), cleft object of the dative (58%), subject-object relative sentences (25%), and object-object relative sentences (58%). All responses were significantly different from random, as the χ^2 values in table 5.10 show.

K.G.'s results from the second battery are given in table 5.11. The χ^2 values appearing in this table show that all response patterns were interpreted correctly significantly more often than would occur by chance except for two structures: subject control with a direct object (*John promised Bill to shave*) and NP(*seems*)-raising (*John seems to Bill to be praying*). Subject-control structures with an indirect object (*John vowed to Bill to shave*) were interpreted correctly more often than would occur by chance on Stage II

Table 5.10
Results from first syntactic-comprehension battery, patient K.G.

	χ^2 values,[†] Stage II assumptions

One-verb sentences

[01] Active: 1   2
    The monkey kicked the elephant. $(E = 6,\ \text{d.f.} = 1,$
                                     $\chi^2 = 12.00,\ p < 0.001^*)$
    Correct: 1,2: 100%

[21] Cleft-object: 1   2
       It was the monkey that the elephant kicked. $(E = 6,\ \text{d.f.} = 1,$
                                      $\chi^2 = 8.34,\ p < 0.01^*)$
    Correct: 2,1: 92%   Incorrect: 1,2: 8%

[27] Passive: 1   2
    The monkey was kicked by the elephant. $(E = 6,\ \text{d.f.} = 1,$
                                       $\chi^2 = 12.00,\ p < 0.001^*)$
    Correct: 2,1: 100%

[ConThP] Conjoined-Theme passives: 1   2   3
               The monkey and the goat were pushed by the elephant.
    Correct: $3V\{1,2\}$: 92%   Incorrect: $\{1,2\}V3$: 8%

[ConAgP] Conjoined-Agent passives: 1   2   3
               The monkey was pushed by the frog and the rabbit.
    Correct: $\{2,3\}V1$: 100%

[02] Dative active: 1   2   3
        The monkey gave the elephant to the goat.
    Correct: 1,2,3: 92%   Incorrect: 1,3;2: 8% $(E = 2,\ \text{d.f.} = 5,$
                                      $\chi^2 = 49.00,\ p < 0.001^*)$

[22] Dative cleft-object: 1   2   3
       It was the monkey that the elephant gave to the goat.
    Correct: 2,1,3: 50%   Incorrect: 1,2,3: 42% $(E = 2,\ \text{d.f.} = 5,$
                                      1,3,2: 8% $\chi^2 = 19.00,\ p < 0.01^*)$

[28] Dative passive: 1   2   3
         The monkey was given to the elephant by the goat.
    Correct: 3,1,2: 67%   Incorrect: 1,2;3: 17% $(E = 2,\ \text{d.f.} = 5,$
                                      2,1,3: 17% $\chi^2 = 24.00,\ p < 0.001^*)$

Two-verb sentences

[03] Conjoined: 1   2   3
       The monkey kicked the elephant and kissed the goat.
    Correct: 1,2;1,3: 92%   Incorrect: 3,2;3,1: 8% $(E = 0.33,\ \text{d.f.} = 35,$
                                      $\chi^2 = 357.58,\ p < 0.001^*)$

[23] Subject-object relative: 1   2   3
       The monkey that the elephant kicked kissed the goat.
    Correct: 2,1;1,3: 25%   Incorrect: 1,2;1,3: 25% $(E = 0.33,\ \text{d.f.} = 35,$
                                      2,1;2,3: 25% $\chi^2 = 84.84,\ p < 0.001^*)$
                                      1,2;2,3: 17%
                                      1,3;1,2: 8%

Table 5.10 (continued)

		χ^2 values,[†] Stage II assumptions	
[24] Object-subject relative:	1	2	3
	The monkey kicked the elephant that kissed the goat.		
Correct: 1,2;2,3: 75%	Incorrect: 2,3;3,2: 8%	($E = 0.33$, d.f. $= 35$,	
2,3;1,2: 8%	1,3;2,1: 8%	$\chi^2 = 242.42$, $p < 0.001^*$)	
(Total correct: 83%)			
[25] Object-object relative:	1	2	3
	The monkey kicked the elephant that the goat kissed.		
Correct: 1,2;3,2: 50%	Incorrect: 1,2;2,3: 25%	($E = 0.33$, d.f. $= 35$,	
3,2;1,2: 8%	3,2;2,1: 8%	$\chi^2 = 133.33$, $p < 0.001^*$)	
(Total correct: 58%)	1,3;3,2: 8%		
[26] Subject-subject relative:	1	2	3
	The monkey that kicked the elephant kised the goat.		
Correct: 1,2;1,3: 83%	Incorrect: 1,2;2,3: 8%	($E = 0.33$, d.f. $= 35$,	
	3,2;3,1: 8%	$\chi^2 = 296.97$, $p < 0.001^*$)	

[†] See text for explanation of calculation of χ^2 values.

assumptions. The accuracy of responses to sentences in this second battery can be seen to form two groups: all sentences other than NP(*seems*)-raising ones were at least 75% correct, and NP(*seems*)-raising sentences were only 33% correct. The NP(*seems*)-raising structures were significantly lower in accuracy than the comparison subject-control and object-control structures ($p < 0.025$), using the test of significance of the difference between two independent proportions (Ferguson 1981).

In the first two batteries, the structures that gave K.G. significant difficulty—NP(*seems*)-raising structures, cleft object of the dative, subject-object relatives, and object-object relatives—are alike in that they contain a [−pronominal] empty NP (i.e., an NP-trace or a *wh*-trace) rather than the [+pronominal] empty NP (PRO) found in the subject-control and object-control structures. On the other hand, K.G. had performed well on sentences with two-place verbs in simple passive and cleft-object form. Though the former would follow from a lexical analysis of the passive (required in the previous two cases), the latter cannot come under this analysis; they required K.G. to assign structure correctly in cleft-object sentences or to employ a heuristic applicable to these but not to other object-relativization structures. K.G.'s difficulty therefore seemed to lie especially in coindexing trace with an antecedent in more difficult sentences.

Thus, it was predicted that K.G. would have difficulty with both passivized object control and passivized $\overline{S}$ deletion on the third battery, since both structures are analyzed as containing NP-trace. K.G.'s results on this battery are shown in table 5.12, along with the χ^2 values. The only two structures for which the number of correct responses reached significance

Table 5.11
Results from second syntactic-comprehension battery, patient K.G.

[04] Baseline: three overt NPs: 1   2   3
Patrick knew that Joe kicked Eddie.

Correct: 2V3: 83%   Incorrect: 3V2: 17%   (Stage II: $E = 1.3$, d.f. $= 8$,
$\chi^2 = 67.70$, $p < 0.001^*$)

[06] Pronouns, simple NP: 1   2
Patrick believed that Joe covered him.

Correct: 2V1: 83%   Incorrect: 1V2: 8%   (Stage II: $E = 3$, d.f. $= 3$,
                                  XV1: 8% $\chi^2 = 21.99$, $p < 0.001^*$)

[07] Pronouns, complex NP: 1   2   3
Patrick knew that a friend of Joe's hit him.

Correct: 2V1: 58%   (Stage II: $E = 1.3$, d.f. $= 8$,
2V3: 42%   (Total correct: 100%) $\chi^2 = 44.62$, $p < 0.001^*$)

[10] Reflexives, simple NP: 1   2
Patrick said that Joe hit himself.

Correct: 2V2: 83%   Incorrect: 2V−: 17%   (Stage II: $E = 3$, d.f. $= 3$,
$\chi^2 = 25.33$, $p < 0.001^*$)

[11] Reflexives, complex NP: 1   2   3
Patrick throught that a friend of Joe's pinched himself.

Correct: 2V2: 100%   (Stage II: $E = 1.3$, d.f. $= 8$,
$\chi^2 = 98.47$, $p < 0.001^*$)

[13] Object control: 1   2
Patrict persuaded Joe to wash.

Correct: 2V: 100%   (Stage II: $E = 6$, d.f. $= 1$,
$\chi^2 = 12.00$, $p < 0.001^*$)

[14] Object control, complex NP: 1   2   3
Patrick allowed a friend of Joe's to bend over.

Correct: 2V: 100%   (Stage II: $E = 4$, d.f. $= 2$,
$\chi^2 = 24$, $p < 0.001^*$)

[17] Subject control: 1   2
Patrick promised Joe to pray.   (Stage II: $E = 6$, d.f. $= 1$,
$\chi^2 = 3.00$, $p < 0.10$)

Correct: 1V: 75%   Incorrect: 2V: 25%   (Stage I: $E = 3$, d.f. $= 2$,
$\chi^2 = 18.00$, $p < 0.001^*$)

[32] NP-raising: 1   2
Patrick seems to Joe to be sleeping.

Correct: 1V: 33%   Incorrect: 2V: 58%   (Stage I: $E = 3$, d.f. $= 2$,
                                  XV: 8% $\chi^2 = 9.83$, $p < 0.05^*$)

Table 5.12
Results from third syntactic-comprehension battery, patient K.G.

[05] $\overline{\text{S}}$ deletion, complex NP: 1   2   3
                              Patrick expected a friend of Joe's to be praying.
        Correct: 2V: 92%   Incorrect: 3V: 8%   (Stage II: $E = 4$, d.f. $= 2$,
                                                                    $\chi^2 = 18.50$, $p < 0.001^*$)

[08] Embedded pronoun subject: 1   2
                              Patrick promised Joe that he would kneel.
        Correct: 1V: 75%   (Stage II: $E = 6$, d.f. $= 1$,
                2V: 25% $\chi^2 = 3.00$, $p < 0.10$)
                                                                    (Stage I: $E = 3$, d.f. $= 2$,
                                                                    $\chi^2 = 18.00$, $p < 0.001^*$)

[18] Subject control: 1   2
                    Patrick vowed to Joe to pray.
        Correct: 1V: 83%   Incorrect: 2V: 17%   (Stage II: $E = 6$, d.f. $= 1$,
                                                                    $\chi^2 = 5.34$, $p < 0.05^*$)

[29] Passivized $\overline{\text{S}}$ deletion: 1   2
                              Patrick was believed by Joe to be eating.
        Correct: 1V: 75%   Incorrect: 2V: 25%   (Stage II: $E = 6$, d.f. $= 1$,
                                                                    $\chi^2 = 3.00$, $p < 0.10$)
                                                                    (Stage I: $E = 3$, d.f. $= 2$,
                                                                    $\chi^2 = 18.00$, $p < 0.001^*$)

[30] Passivized object control: 1   2
                              Patrick was told by Joe to run.
        Correct: 1V: 67%   Incorrect: 2V: 33%   (Stage II: $E = 6$, d.f. $= 1$,
                                                                    $\chi^2 = 1.34$, $p > 0.20$)
                                                                    (Stage I: $E = 3$, d.f. $= 2$,
                                                                    $\chi^2 = 14.66$, $p < 0.001^*$)

[33] NP-raising, complex postverbal NP: 1   2   3
                              Patrick appears to a friend of Joe's to be eating.
        Correct: 1V: 17%   Incorrect: 2V: 42%   (Stage I: $E = 3$, d.f. $= 3$,
                                        3V: 33% $\chi^2 = 3.32$, $p > 0.20$)
                                        XV: 8%

under Stage II assumptions were $\overline{S}$ deletion sentences, which contain no empty NP (type 5), and subject-control sentences (type 18), which are identical in structure to the type 17 sentences tested in the second battery. In other words, it can be said that on this battery K.G. was using some systematic pattern of response only for the structures not containing a [−pronominal] NP. Individual comparisons between sentence types were again made using the test of the significance of the difference between two independent proportions. Passivized object-control sentences (type 30) were 67% correct, a significant drop ($p < 0.05$) from the previously tested nonpassivized object-control sentences (type 13). NP(*seems*)-raising sentences with a complex postverbal NP (type 33) were significantly worse than all other sentence types in the current test, at 17% ($p < 0.025$), but not significantly different from the NP(*seems*)-raising sentences previously tested (type 32). The results on this battery thus confirm the difficulty K.G. had with coindexation of traces in sentences with two verbs.

For the fourth battery, which contained both empty and overt referentially dependent NPs, our prediction was that if the ability to comprehend traces was selectively impaired, all the subject-control and object-control structures (which contain [+pronominal] empty NPs) should still be interpreted correctly. If, however, the additional complexity occasioned by the presence of a second referentially dependent NP—the overt reflexive or pronoun—disturbed K.G.'s abilities to accomplish parsing and/or interpretive operations that he could accomplish in simple sentences, the coindexation of PRO should have begun to be problematic for K.G. in these more complex sentences.

The results are shown in table 5.13. The χ^2 values, computed as above, show that the distribution of responses to all structural types was significantly above chance ($p < 0.05$). Visual inspection of the responses shows that for three of the structures with reflexive embedded objects—subject-control (type 19), NP-raising (type 34), and passivized $\overline{S}$ deletion (type 31)—the nonrandomness is due to the frequent occurrence of one or two erroneous responses. Consistent with the "complexity" prediction, K.G.'s performance on subject-control sentences deteriorated when a second coindexation operation was required.

Several generalizations can be drawn from K.G.'s performance on these four batteries.

First, he did not have difficulty with sentences that did not contain referential dependencies, as table 5.14 shows. All seven sentence types containing one overt referentially dependent element were interpreted correctly more than 75% of the time, as table 5.15 shows. Even in the sentences that contained both an empty NP and an overt referentially dependent element, the overt element was correctly interpreted as reflexive or disjoint at least 92% of the time, whether the antecedent for the empty

Table 5.13
Results from fourth syntactic-comprehension battery, patient K.G.

[12] Baseline: 3 NPs + reflexive:	1	2	3

Patrick told Joe that Eddie had scratched himself.

Correct: 3V3: 100%

(Stage II: $E = 1.3$, d.f. $= 8$, $\chi^2 = 98.47, p < 0.001^*$)

[09] Baseline: 3 NPs + pronoun:	1	2	3

Patrick persuaded Joe that Eddie had patted him.

Correct: 3V1: 42%   Incorrect: 2V1: 8%   (Stage II: $E = 1.3$, d.f. $= 8$,
3V2: 33%   1V3: 8% $\chi^2 = 21.55, p < 0.01^*$)
(Total correct $= 9$)   2V2: 8%

[15] Object control, reflexive embedded object: 1   2

Patrick asked Joe to pinch himself.

Correct: 2V2: 83%   Incorrect: 1V1: 8%   (Stage I: $E = 0.75$, d.f. $= 9$,
                                XVX: 8% $\chi^2 = 123.33, p < 0.001^*$)

[16] Object control, pronominal embedded object: 1   2

Patrick allowed Joe to hit him.

Correct: 2V1: 83%   Incorrect: 2V2: 8%   (Stage II: $E = 3$, d.f. $= 3$,
                                1V2: 8% $\chi^2 = 21.99, p < 0.001^*$)

[19] Subject control, reflexive embedded object: 1   2

Patrick promised Joe to hit himself.

Correct: 1V1: 33%   Incorrect: 2V2: 67%   (Stage II: $E = 3$, d.f. $= 3$,
                                                $\chi^2 = 14.66, p < 0.01^*$)

[20] Subject control, pronominal embedded object: 1   2

Patrick promised Joe to cover him.

Correct: 1V2: 58%   Incorrect: 2V1: 25%   (Stage I: $E = 0.75$, d.f. $= 9$,
                                2V2: 8% $\chi^2 = 67.33, p < 0.001^*$)
                                XV2: 8%

[31] Passivized $\overline{\text{S}}$ deletion, reflexive object: 1   2

Patrick was believed by Joe to have kicked himself.

Correct: 1V1: 33%   Incorrect: 2V2: 67%   (Stage II: $E = 3$, d.f. $= 3$,
                                                $\chi^2 = 14.66, p < 0.01^*$)

[34] NP-raising, reflexive embedded object: 1   2

Patrick seems to Joe to have kicked himself.

Correct: 1V1: 33%   Incorrect: 2V2: 58%   (Stage I: $E = 0.75$, d.f. $= 9$,
                                XVX: 8% $\chi^2 = 75.33, p < 0.001^*$)

Table 5.14
Summary of results on sentences without a referentially dependent NP, patient K.G.

Percent correct	Type
100	[1] Active The monkey kicked the elephant.
92	[2] Dative active The monkey gave the elephant to the goat.
92	[3] Conjoined The monkey kicked the elephant and kissed the goat.
92	[5] $\bar{\text{S}}$ deletion, complex NP Patrick expected a friend of Joe's to be praying.
83	[4] Baseline: three overt NPs Patrick knew that Joe kicked Eddie.

element was correct or not; in other words, the errors were due to the incorrect choice of Agent, not to the incorrect interpretation of the referential dependency related to the overt referentially dependent NP.

Second, among the empty NPs, traces were more difficult than PRO for sentences that were similar in word length, number of NPs, and surface linear order, as table 5.16 shows. For example, K.G. achieved 79% and 100% on subject-control and object-control sentences, respectively (*John vowed to Bill to pray*, types 17 and 18; *John persuaded Bill to pray*, type 13), but only 33% on NP(*seems*)-raising sentences (*John seems to Bill to be praying*, type 32).

Third, K.G. had difficulty with both NP-trace and *wh*-trace—i.e., with all [−pronominal] empty NPs. This contrasts with the linguistic analyses proposed as possible deficits for J.V. (disturbance of [+anaphoric, −pronominal] empty NPs) and G.G.(disturbance of [+anaphoric] empty NPs).

Fourth, as can be seen in table 5.16, not all sentences with [−pronominal] empty NPs were equally difficult for K.G. Among the NP-trace sentences, NP(*seems*)-raising sentence types were 33% correct or less under all conditions. On the other hand, the bulk of the passive sentences were approximately 70% accurate, and K.G. performed perfectly with passives of two-place verbs. Sentence types containing *wh*-trace also showed variability. K.G. had more difficulty with relative clauses when the empty NP was in object position than when the empty NP was in subject position, and he had no trouble with cleft objects of two-place verbs but got cleft objects of three-place verbs only 50% correct.

Fifth, K.G. had trouble with subject-control structures when a second coindexation operation was required.

What might account for K.G.'s impairment? His span, recall, and recog-

Table 5.15
Summary of results on sentences with overt referential dependencies, patient K.G.

Percent correct	Type
Overt pronouns [+ pronominal]	
100	[7] Pronouns, complex NP Patrick said that a friend of Joe's hit him.
83	[6] Pronouns, simple NP Patrick said that Joe hit him.
75	[8] Embedded pronoun subject Patrick promised Joe that he would kneel. (interpretation of antecedent = *Patrick*)
75	[9] Baseline: finite embedded clause, 3 NPs + pronoun Patrick told Joe that Eddie had hit him.
Overt reflexives [− pronominal]	
100	[11] Reflexives, complex NP Patrick said that a friend of Joe's hit himself.
100	[12] Baseline: finite embedded clause, 3 NPs + reflexive Patrick told Joe that Eddie had hit himself.
83	[10] Reflexives, simple NP Patrick said that Joe hit himself.

Table 5.16
Summary of results for sentences containing pronominal (PRO) versus nonpronominal (trace) empty NPs, patient K.G.

Percent correct	Type	
[+Pronominal] empty NPs		
Object control		
100	[13]	Object control
		Patrick persuaded Joe to wash.
100	[14]	Object control, complex NP
		Patrick persuaded a friend of Joe's to wash.
83	[15]	Object control, reflexive embedded object
		Patrick allowed Joe to hit himself.
83	[16]	Object control, pronominal embedded object
		Patrick forced Joe to hit him.
Subject control		
83	[18]	Subject control (third battery)
		Patrick promised Joe to pray.
75	[17]	Subject control (second battery)
		Patrick promised to Joe to pray.
58	[20]	Subject control, pronominal embedded object
		Patrick promised Joe to cover him.
33	[19]	Subject control, reflexive embedded object
		Patrick promised Joe to hit himself.
[−Pronominal] empty NPs		
100	[27]	Passive (P2)
		The goat was hit by the frog.
100	[ConAgP]	Conjoined Agent passives
		The monkey was pushed by the frog and the rabbit.
92	[ConThP]	Conjoined Theme passives
		The monkey and the goat were pushed by the rabbit.
92	[21]	Cleft object
		It was the goat that the frog hit.
83	[24]	Object-subject relative
		The goat hit the frog that kissed the cow.
83	[26]	Subject-subject relative
		The goat that hit the frog kissed the cow.
75	[29]	Passivized $\overline{S}$ deletion
		Patrick was believed by Joe to be praying.
67	[28]	Dative passive
		The goat was given to the frog by the cow.

Table 5.16 (continued)

Percent correct	Type	
67	[30]	Passivized object-control Patrick was persuaded by Joe to pray.
58	[25]	Object-object relative The goat hit the frog that the monkey kissed.
50	[22]	Dative cleft-object It was the goat that the frog gave to the cow.
33	[32]	NP-raising Patrick seems to Joe to be praying.
33	[34]	NP-raising, reflexive embedded object Patrick seems to Joe to have hit himself.
33	[31]	Passivized S̄ deletion, reflexive embedded object Patrick was believed by Joe to have kicked himself.
25	[23]	Subject-object relative The goat that the frog hit kissed the cow.
17	[33]	NP-raising, complex postverbal NP Patrick seems to a friend of Joe's to be praying.

nition performance, though not normal, were not so impaired that his sentence-processing deficit can be ascribed to an inability to recall or retrieve the words in the sentences presented. Furthermore, he showed no correlation between error rate and sentence length as measured by number of words per sentence ($r = 0.26$, $p < 0.20$). And his problem was not a lack of knowledge of aspects of syntactic structure (that is, a lack of "competence"). Since K.G.'s difficulties with trace and PRO arose only when the sentences were of a certain complexity, his deficit was not a simple loss of the representation of trace and PRO. We cannot rule out the existence of a complex set of heuristics that would yield correct interpretations of simple sentences, but we have not been able to devise such a set of heuristics that handles all the sentences that K.G. interpreted well. Thus, our proposed account of his deficit views it as a processing limitation that affects his ability to use his knowledge of the structures relevant to sentence interpretation when processing becomes complex.

K.G.'s difficulties with sentences containing trace were seen only where structure created a particular parsing demand. He failed to coindex traces when required to assign a thematic role to a second NP before he was able to assign a thematic role to the antecedent unambiguously (assuming that thematic roles are assigned as soon as they can be). In dative-passive sentences, the NP in subject position is locally ambiguous: It may be a Theme moved from the direct-object position (as it is for the structures tested), or it may be a Goal moved from the indirect-object position (as it is for passivized inner dative structures such as *The elephant was given the bear by the goat*). This disambiguation is resolved when the thematic role of the next NP is assigned. Thus, the trace cannot be assigned a thematic role until one is assigned to another NP, and the antecedent of the trace must be retained without a thematic role until a second NP is assigned its thematic role. In NP-raising structures, the NP following the matrix verb must be assigned a thematic role before one is assigned to the trace and transferred to the matrix subject antecedent. Similarly, in a relative clause with an empty NP in object position the intervening subject NP must be assigned a thematic role while the relative pronoun is awaiting a thematic role.

We have stated this generalization in terms of a difficulty in holding an NP without a thematic role in memory while another NP is assigned a thematic role before one is assigned to the trace, which will be coindexed with the first NP. This analysis must take into account the question of whether the passive forms of transitive and dative verbs involve trace. We have argued above that they do not. In this case, this formulation cannot account for K.G.'s relatively poor performance on dative-passive sentences (because they do not contain trace), though his good performance on passive sentences with two-argument-place verbs is expected. To be consistent with our previous cases, we must formulate a deficit analysis in K.G. without reference to trace to account for his performance on dative-passive sentences. This can be done easily: K.G.'s deficit can be seen as a difficulty that arises when he must hold an NP without a thematic role in memory while another NP is being assigned a thematic role. This covers all the cases that were difficult for K.G.; however, it also predicts difficulties with cleft-object and passive transitive sentences, which were not found.

Accordingly, we must consider the analysis that K.G. has trouble with sentences in which an NP is held in a memory system while another NP receives a thematic role in conjunction with other features of sentence structure to determine his performance on a sentence. For instance, there are only two thematic roles to be assigned in cleft-object sentences, and K.G. may assign the role of Agent to the embedded subject, leaving the role of Theme for the clefted NP by default. Though this heuristic could apply locally to object-relativized relative clauses, the longer sentences with two non-copula verbs make more processing demands, and this heuristic fails to be applied. Similarly, the assignment of Agent to the NP that is the object of the *by*-phrase leaves the subject NP to be assigned the thematic role of Theme by default in passive transitive structures, while more processing is required to assign the thematic role to the subject NP in dative-passive sentences. The fact that subject-object relatives are more difficult than object-object relatives also may be due to interactive factors leading to overall sentence complexity, since in subject-object relatives the matrix head NP of the relative can be assigned its thematic role by the matrix verb only after the relative clause has been presented (and processed), whereas in object-object relatives this NP has been assigned its thematic role around the matrix verb before the relative clause is presented (see also case R.L., below).

The difficulty that K.G. had with certain structures other than trace also tended to appear only in the presence of other factors (mentioned above) that caused increased complexity. PRO became difficult to interpret only in sentences that also contained an overt referentially dependent element and in which the PRO was subject to "long-distance" coindexing through subject control (*John promised Bill to shave himself/him*). This also suggests that K.G. is sensitive to the complexity of a sentence, which results from a cumulative interaction of a number of different parsing operations.

Though a lexical analysis of passive requires that we formulate one deficit for K.G. in terms that do not involve trace, there is also a possibility that K.G. has a second specific disturbance affecting his ability to locate and coindex empty [−pronominal] NPs—that is, affecting trace. His performance on NP(*seems*)-raising sentences was significantly worse than that on dative-passive sentences. If he has two specific deficits—one affecting the maintenance of an NP without a thematic role in memory and one affecting the coindexation of trace—this difference can be explicated as the result of the combination of these two deficits. K.G.'s extreme difficulties with NP(*seems*)-raising cannot be accounted for in any other way that we can think of; in particular, they cannot be stated as a loss of lexical knowledge regarding NP-raising verbs without missing a generalization, since the deficit occurred with all the verbs of this type that were tested.

The hypothesized processing impairments for K.G. and J.V. provide an account in processing terms for the observed differences in accuracy on sentences containing [−anaphoric, −pronominal] empty NPs (*wh*-trace) for these two patients. K.G. has difficulty on sentences with *wh*-trace in embedded object position because he must hold the *wh*-antecedent without a thematic role in a memory store while the embedded subject is assigned another thematic role. J.V. does not have difficulty on sentences with *wh*-trace because the thematic role of the *wh*-trace is not transmitted to its antecedent (see chapter 1).

We conclude that a processing impairment is responsible for K.G.'s pattern of difficulty in sentence comprehension. We can suggest two possible types of processing disturbance that may produce these deficits. The first is simply a limitation of the "capacity" or "space" that K.G. can devote to parsing and interpretation. The second possibility is that, in addition to such a limitation, K.G. has a specific disturbance affecting certain parsing processes (e.g., maintenance of an NP without a thematic role in a memory system or coindexation of empty NPs) that interacts with his ability to deploy processing resources in a task of syntactic comprehension. The allocation of the primary deficit to a capacity limitation or to a deficit specific to a particular type of empty NP will receive further discussion below.

Patient G.S.

G.S., a right-handed 69-year-old male with a secondary-school education, had suffered a right CVA on May 19, 1986. He was tested on July 8–9, 1986, with an expanded form of the first battery and with another battery containing selected sentence types from the second through the fifth battery. His results on all the sentence types on which he was tested are given in table 5.17.

G.S. had a digit span of six oral and six pointing. On an object-pointing pretest he was able to point to three to four objects reliably in the correct serial order out of an array of six objects.

Overall, G.S.'s sentence comprehension was quite good. He scored over 83% on all sentence types, with three notable exceptions: He had difficulty with all types of relative clauses and with three-place cleft-object sentences, and his performance on the subject-control structure was significantly poorer than his performance on either the object-control structure or the NP-raising structure.

There are several points that can be made about this case.

First, G.S. showed no difficulty on the object-control structures. Here it is difficult to know whether his good performance on these structures was due to his ability to parse the sentence or to his reliance on a heuristic of consistently choosing the noun nearest the verb.

Second, G.S.'s selective deficit on sentences containing *wh*-trace and PRO does not form a natural class within the linguistic typology of GB theory presented in chapter 1. Consistent with the linguistic analysis of *wh*-trace as [−anaphoric, −pronominal] and PRO as [+anaphoric, +pronominal], the Berwick-Weinberg parser has no procedures common to *wh*-trace and PRO and different from operations required for NP-trace. Thus, this linguistic analysis requires positing two independent selective deficits for G.S.: one for *wh*-trace and one for PRO.

Third G.S.'s good performance on NP-raising structures and his poorer performance on relative-clause structures presents a double dissociation with the pattern found for patient J.V. This suggests that the processes involved in interpreting NP-trace are at least partially separable from the processes involved in interpreting relative clauses. One linguistic difference between these two types is that at the level of Logical Form the *wh*-antecedent is treated as an operator that must be bound with a variable, the *wh*-trace. A syntactic difference between NP-trace and *wh*-trace is that the antecedent of a *wh*-trace must be held in a COMP position (a position to which a thematic role can never be directly assigned), whereas the ante-

Table 5.17
Results from all syntactic-comprehension batteries, patient G.S.

	Correct		Incorrect		
Sentence types with no referential dependency					
[01] The bear kissed the donkey. (two-place active)	1,2	100%			(Stage II:[†] $E = 6$, d.f. $= 1$, $\chi^2 = 12.00$, $p < 0.001*$)
[02] The bear gave the donkey to the goat. (dative active)	1,2,3	92%	1,3,–	8%	(Stage II: $E = 2$, d.f. $= 5$, $\chi^2 = 49.00$, $p < 0.001*$)
[03] The bear kissed the donkey and the goat. (conjoined)	1,2;1,3	92%	1,2;2,3	8%	(Stage II: $E = 0.33$, d.f. $= 35$, $\chi^2 = 357.58$, $p < 0.001*$)
[04] John said that Bill kicked Eddie. (baseline: three overt NPs)	2V3	75%	1V3	25%	(Stage II: $E = 1.3$, d.f. $= 8$, $\chi^2 = 56.93$, $p < 0.001*$)
[ACT] The frog patted the monkey and the elephant. (active conjoined Theme)	1,2 + 3	100%			(Stage II: $E = 0.67$, d.f. $= 17$, $\chi^2 = 202.99$, $p < 0.001*$)
Sentence types with pronouns					
[06] John said that Bill kicked him.	2V1	92%	1V2	8%	(Stage II: $E = 3$, d.f. $= 3$, $\chi^2 = 28.66$, $p < 0.001*$) (Stage II+:‡ $E = 6$, d.f. $= 1$, $\chi^2 = 8.34$, $p < 0.01*$)
Sentence types with reflexives					
[10] John said that Bill kicked himself.	2V2	92%	1V2	8%	(Stage II: $E = 3$, d.f. $= 3$, $\chi^2 = 28.66$, $p < 0.001*$) (Stage II+: $E = 6$, d.f. $= 1$, $\chi^2 = 8.34$, $p < 0.01*$)
Object-control sentence types					
[13] Patrick persuaded Joe to wash. (object control)	2V	92%	1V	8%	(Stage II: $E = 6$, d.f. $= 1$, $\chi^2 = 8.34$, $p < 0.01*$)

Subject-control sentence types

	1V	50%	2V	50%	
[17] Patrick promised Joe to wash. (subject control)		50%		50%	(Stage II: $E = 6$, d.f. $= 1$, $\chi^2 = 0$, $p > 0.20$)

Sentence types with wh-trace

	1V	50%	2V	50%	
[21] It was the bear that the donkey kissed. (two-place cleft object)	2, 1	92%	1, 2	8%	(Stage II: $E = 6$, d.f. $= 1$, $\chi^2 = 8.34$, $p < 0.01^*$)
[22] It was the bear that the donkey gave to the goat. (dative cleft object)	2, 1, 3	67%	2, 1, 2 1, 2, 3 2, 3, 1	8% 17% 8%	(Stage II: $E = 2$, d.f. $= 5$, $\chi^2 = 23.00$, $p < 0.001^*$)
[23] The bear that the donkey kissed patted the goat. (subject-object)	2, 1; 1, 3 1, 3; 2, 1	17% 8%	1, 3; –, – 1, 2; 1, 3 2, 3; –, – 2, 1; 2, 3 2, 1; –, –	17% 25% 17% 8% 8%	(Stage II: $E = 0.33$, d.f. $= 35$, $\chi^2 = 60.60$, $p < 0.01^*$)
[24] The bear kissed the donkey that patted the goat. (object-subject)	1, 2; 2, 3	58%	1, 2; 1, 3	42%	(Stage II: $E = 0.33$, d.f. $= 35$, $\chi^2 = 212.12$, $p < 0.001^*$)
[25] The bear kissed the donkey that the goat patted. (object-object)	1, 2; 3, 2	50%	1, 2; 1, 3 3, 1, 3, 2 1, 2; 3, 1	33% 8% 8%	(Stage II: $E = 0.33$, d.f. $= 35$, $\chi^2 = 151.51$, $p < 0.001^*$)
[26] The bear that kissed the donkey patted the goat. (subject-subject)	1, 2; 1, 3 1, 3; 1, 2	75% 8%	1, 2; 2, 3 1, 3; –, – 1, 2; 2, 3	8% 8% 8%	(Stage II: $E = 0.33$, d.f. $= 35$, $\chi^2 = 242.42$, $p < 0.001^*$)

Passive sentence types

	1V	50%	2V	50%	
[27] The bear was kissed by the donkey. (two-place passive)	2, 1	75%	1, 2	25%	(Stage II: $E = 6$, d.f. $= 1$, $\chi^2 = 3.00$, $p < 0.10$)
[28] The bear was given to the donkey by the goat. (dative passive)	3, 1, 2	83%	2, 1, 3 1, 2, 3	8% 8%	(Stage II: $E = 2$, d.f. $= 5$, $\chi^2 = 39.00$, $p < 0.001^*$)

Table 5.17 (continued)

	Correct		Incorrect		
[TP] The rabbit was patted. (truncated passive)	X,1	100%			(Stage I: $E = 6$, d.f. $= 1$, $\chi^2 = 12.00$, $p < 0.001^*$)
[PCA] The frog was patted by the goat and the cow. (passive conjoined Agent)	$2+3,1$	75%	$1,2+3$	25%	(Stage II: $E = 0.67$, d.f. $= 17$, $\chi^2 = 122.39$, $p < 0.001^*$)
NP-raising sentence types					
[32] Patrick seems to Joe to be praying. (NP-raising)	1V	92%	2V	8%	(Stage II: $E = 6$, d.f. $= 1$, $\chi^2 = 8.34$, $p < 0.01^*$)
Baseline sentences					
[35] A friend of John's kicked Bill.	1V3	100%			(Stage II: $E = 1.3$, d.f. $= 8$, $\chi^2 = 98.47$, $p < 0.001^*$)
[37] John kicked himself.	1V1	100%			
[38] A friend of John's kicked himself.	1V1	83%	1V2	17%	(Stage II: $E = 2$, d.f. $= 5$, $\chi^2 = 40.00$, $p < 0.001^*$) (Stage II+: $E = 6$, d.f. $= 1$, $\chi^2 = 5.34$, $p < 0.025^*$)
[40] John kicked him.	1VX	83%	XVY	17%	(Stage I: $E = 0.75$, d.f. $= 4$, $\chi^2 = 33.33$, $p < 0.001^*$) (Stage I+:§ $E = 1.3$, d.f. $= 2$, $\chi^2 = 14.37$, $p < 0.001^*$)
[41] A friend of John's kicked him.	1V2 1VX	67% 25%	2V1	8%	(Stage I: $E = 0.75$, d.f. $= 9$, $\chi^2 = 80.66$, $p < 0.001^*$)

† See Data Analysis section of present chapter for explanation of calculation of χ^2 values.
‡ Stage II+: Only appropriate reflexive or disjoint interpretations involving dolls mentioned in the sentence are counted as expected responses.
§ Stage I+: Only appropriate reflexive or disjoint interpretations involving dolls in the array are counted as expected responses.

cedent of an NP-trace must occur in an NP "argument" position (a position that can be assigned a thematic role if the predicate has one to assign). (See chapter 1.) How these differences might be realized in terms of different parsing operations remains to be specified in a particular parsing model.

Fourth, G.S.'s pattern of performance, along with those of J.V. and K.G., shows a double dissociation in the comprehension of NP-raising and subject-control structures. This double dissociation falsifies the analysis that NP-raising makes use of the same processing operations as subject-control structures but with the addition of the extra operation required for NP-raising of holding an NP without a thematic role while other operations occur. If the other operations were identical in both cases, a patient who does well on the NP-raising structure would always do well on the subject-control structure. Therefore, it can be concluded that NP-raising and subject-control each have operations not shared by the other.

The operations unique to NP-trace—the necessity of holding NPs without thematic roles and the necessity of transmitting theta roles from traces to their antecedent—have already been specified in connection with patients J.V. and K.G. Those operations related to PRO may have to do with the initiation of a gap-hunting procedure. We mentioned in chapter 2 that the parser may be alerted to search for a "gap" in the surface string that requires the construction of an empty NP, and that certain types of antecedents may activate this gap-hunting procedure. Psycholinguistic evidence shows that the position of a *wh*-word in the complementizer position will activate a gap-hunting procedure (Stowe 1983). Another possibility, not yet explored experimentally, is that a gap-hunting procedure will be initiated by the presence of an R-expression in an argument position that has not been assigned a thematic role by the following verb. In other words, the presence of an antecedent without a thematic role indicates unambiguously that there must be an empty NP elsewhere in the structure. For subject-control PRO structures, on the other hand, both the matrix subject and the matrix object are assigned thematic roles by the first verb, and therefore there is no unambiguous indicator that a gap will follow. For example, *John* cannot signal a gap in the sentence *John promised Bill to shave*, since at the local point at which the parser is dealing with *John* it cannot determine for every case—even with lookahead—whether an empty NP will occur at a later point in the sentence (viz., *John promised a friend of a friend of my cousin Bill's that he would shave*). For a deterministic parser, it would not be desirable to perform an operation that would lead to an incorrect structure in some cases. Therefore, for sentences with obligatory-control PRO we may hypothesize that the parser locates and constructs the empty NP subject of the lexically subjectless embedded infinitive purely on the basis of the knowledge that sentences must have subjects, and then establishes the antecedent of this empty NP subject,

PRO, through a combination of lookback and the lexical information associated with the verb.

Therefore, we hypothesize that G.S. has difficulty with structures containing an empty NP in which no gap-hunting procedure has been signaled. Under this analysis, his difficulty with *wh*-relative clauses is a separate impairment for which many analyses are possible—even nonlinguistic ones, such as a difficulty related to the number of propositions to be acted out in a sentence.

Discussion of the First Four Cases
The first four cases considered together allow several initial conclusions concerning the parsing of empty NPs. These conclusions will be discussed in more depth at the end of this chapter and in chapter 6.

First, in these mild cases, only sentences containing empty NPs are impaired. This finding supports the hypothesized reality of empty NPs as a parsing construct, since it is only the presence of the empty NP that unites the structures that were impaired in these cases.

Second, the finding that the mildly impaired patients showed difficulty only on sentences containing empty NPs stands in contrast to the findings on more severely impaired patients, who showed difficulty with both overt and empty referential dependencies. This finding can be accounted for by the hypothesis that empty NPs are more difficult to locate and to construct than overt NPs.

Third, even in the cases with mild impairment, the need to look back for an antecedent for an overt referentially dependent NP appears to add to the total processing load in sentences that contain both an empty and an overt referentially dependent NP. For example, although K.G. had no difficulty with sentences containing only one overt referential dependency, such as *John said that a friend of Bill's kicked himself/him*, he began to break down on the coindexation of PRO, but not on the interpretation of the pronoun or reflexive, in sentences with subject-control PRO when a reflexive or pronoun was added, such as *John promised Bill to kick himself/him*. This is evidence that the operations involved in coindexing reflexives and pronouns cause some complexity, and that the operations involved in constructing and coindexing empty NPs cause more.

Fourth, these cases reveal the specificity with which particular parsing operations may be impaired. In order to make the analyses of the four cases mutually consistent and to have them converge on a single model, it is necessary to postulate the impairment of such operations as holding an antecedent without a theta role (K.G.), transmitting a theta role from an NP-trace to its antecedent (J.V.), looking back for an antecedent beyond a particular domain (G.G.), and constructing an empty NP that has not been signaled by an antecedent (G.S.).

Fifth, several double dissociations have been found among the various types of empty NPs. This suggests that each different type of empty NP involves at least one unique operation. Thus, for example, the double dissociation between NP(*seems*)-raising and subject-control PRO is hypothesized to be due to the necessity of holding an antecedent without a thematic role in the former and the necessity of locating and constructing an empty NP in the absence of having been previously alerted that an empty NP would occur.

Finally, these cases illustrate the need to refer to detailed linguistic and parsing models in the specification of deficits, and the value of doing so. Though there is some uncertainty about the correct analysis of the deficit in some of these cases, all the deficits we have formulated are stated in terms of specific aspects of syntactic and parsing theory. Without these theories to refer to, the specific impairments seen in our subjects could not be stated; all these cases would simply be cases of unspecified, perhaps even undocumented, functional disturbances. For instance, J.V.'s and G.G.'s impairments would not have been discovered on the batteries used to test syntactic comprehension in any of the patients discussed in chapter 3. Reference to linguistic theory and parsing models also allows us to explain aspects of patients' performance such as the good performance of G.G. and J.V. on relative clauses.

The cases we shall now describe are ones in which syntactic-comprehension disturbances are more obvious than in the first four cases. Nonetheless, reference to specific aspects of syntactic structure and parsing is needed to account for the details of the performances of these patients as well.

Patients with More Severe Disturbances of Parsing, Which May Affect Both Empty and Overt Referentially Dependent NPs
The next four patients are more severely impaired, in terms of both lower overall accuracy on the batteries and lower accuracy on many of the sentence types within the batteries. In the two patients who were tested (A.B. and C.V.), overt referentially dependent NPs were selectively affected. A.B. and C.V. also showed difficulty with structures containing empty NPs, as predicted. All four cases further demonstrate the use of heuristics.

S.P. and R.L. were among the earliest patients to be studied using the object-manipulation paradigm. They are each the subject of other publications (Caplan and Futter 1986; Caplan, Vanier, and Baker 1986a,b; Caplan 1987b), to which the reader is referred for additional details. In this early stage of research, only a subset of the sentence types used in later work was presented to each patient. This subset consisted of active, passive, cleft-subject, and cleft-object versions of two-place one-verb sentences;

Table 5.18
Responses of patient S.P.

One-verb sentences

Response type	Two-place verbs			Three-place verbs		
	Active	Passive	Cleft-object	Active	Passive	Cleft-object
1,2	6/6*	3/6	4/6			
2,1		3/6*	2/6*			
1,2,3				6/6*	4/6	3/6
1,3,2					1/6	
2,1,3						3/6*
3,1,2					1/6*	

Two-verb sentences

	Conjoined	Subject-subject	Subject-object	Object-subject	Object-object
1,2;1,3	6/10*	5/10*	2/10	5/11	1/9
1,2;2,3	4/10	5/10	5/10	6/11*	1/9
1,2;3,2					7/9*
1,3;3,2			1/10		
2,1;1,3			2/10*		

* correct response

inner and outer active, passive, and cleft-object forms of three-place (dative) one-verb sentences; sentences with conjoined transitive verbs; and all four types of relative clauses that can be formed with two transitive verbs and three overt NPs: subject-subject, subject-object, object-subject, and object-object relatives. In the two cases we present here, the performances on this restricted set of sentence types were not as accurate as those of the patients described above. These patients differed from each other with respect to their ability to assign hierarchical syntactic structures, and both revealed aspects of the compensatory heuristics used by patients. R.L., a native speaker of Canadian French, was tested in his mother tongue. He was the only non-anglophone among our subjects in this series, but the sentences on which he was tested have identical structures in the two languages, and a direct comparison of the relevant aspects of his performance with that of other cases is thus not difficult.

Patient S.P.
S.P.'s performance is illustrated in table 5.18. It is possible to analyze S.P.'s response pattern linguistically and in terms of the operation of a parser/interpreter. We begin by considering one-verb sentences. We note that the only sentences that S.P. consistently interpreted correctly are the active forms of the two-place and three-place one-verb sentences. She

interpreted approximately half the passive and cleft-object forms correctly in both two-place and three-place one-verb sentences. These data suggest that S.P. is able to assign and interpret the basic N-V-N structure, including its extension to include a third noun in a prepositional phrase whose thematic role is Goal. She interprets this structure by assigning Agent, Theme, and Goal to N_1, N_2, and N_3 in sequences of the form N_1-V-N_2-(Prep-N_3). Moreover, she is sensitive to passive markings, to word order, and to other indications of object relativization found in cleft-object sentences. She interpreted sentences of both the above-mentioned types differently than the corresponding active and cleft-subject forms. However, she did not interpret these sentences normally. She treated the passive and cleft-object two-place verbs and the cleft-object three-place verbs as ambiguous between the normal meaning and the meaning these sentences would have had if nouns had been assigned their thematic roles in the linear fashion utilized in N-V-N-(Prep-N) structures.

This pattern suggests that S.P. recognizes N-V-N-(Prep-N) sequences and attempts to interpret them according to a principle that assigns the preverbal noun as Agent, the postverbal noun as Theme, and the post-prepositional noun as Goal. The presence of the passive morphology or some aspect of the object-relativization structure (perhaps simply the N-N-V sequence) renders the syntactic structure ambiguous. There are two ways to account for this ambiguity. The first is to hypothesize that S.P. occasionally interprets passive morphology and the cleft-object configuration correctly, and that she fails to do so on other occasions. When she fails to interpret these features in a normal, correct fashion, this account would postulate, she applies a heuristic interpretive algorithm to assign Agent, Theme, and Goal to the nouns of the sentence in the order in which she hears them. A second approach would be to account for S.P.'s ambiguous interpretations by postulating that she constructs a syntactic representation that is itself ambiguous with respect to its semantic interpretation. For instance, she could assign Agency to both the preverbal noun and the noun in the *by*-phrase in passive sentences, and to both the preverbal noun and the first noun in cleft-object structures. The data on the one-verb sentence types do not choose between these two analyses, but S.P.'s performance on two-verb sentences suggests that the latter analysis may apply to the cleft-object forms (see below).

S.P.'s performance on these one-verb sentences suggests that her parsing and interpretive processes operate on sequences longer than N-V strings. If her parsing and interpretive processes consisted of assigning Agency to the immediately preverbal noun regardless of the overall configuration of the sentence, she would assign Agency consistently to the correct noun in cleft-object forms. We note that this heuristic is one of two basic word-order-based interpretive strategies documented by MacWhinney et al.

(1984; see chapter 2 above). Its use would lead to consistently correct interpretations in two-place-verb cleft-object sentences, and to constant assignment of N_2 as Agent in three-place-verb cleft-object sentences, neither of which was observed. If, on the other hand, S.P. assigns the first noun she hears to the Agent role, she would have interpreted all these sentences and passives incorrectly. Thus, it seems that the "window" over which the parser and the interpreter operate in S.P. consists of more than just a verb with its immediately preceding noun. One possibility is that S.P. identifies the verb of each clause and attempts to assign a syntactic structure and an interpretation to as many NPs as are required by the argument structure of the verb, thus operating on two or three nouns plus the verb as the sentence and verb require. A mechanism of this sort was suggested on the basis of the group-study results presented in chapter 4.

Turning to S.P.'s performance on sentences with two verbs, we note that her interpretation of conjoined, subject-subject relative, and object-subject relative sentences is virtually identical. For her, each of these sentence types is ambiguous between an interpretation in which the first noun is Agent of both verbs and one in which the second noun is Agent of the second verb. As with the ambiguity of passive and cleft-object sentences, this pattern of interpretation might be due to an alternation between S.P.'s ability to assign a normal structure and her use of a compensatory strategy, or to her assignment of an inherently ambiguous structure. In the present case, there are two reasons to favor the second alternative.

First, if S.P. sometimes assigns a correct syntactic structure and interprets it normally and sometimes resorts to compensatory strategies, it must be the case that she uses a variety of compensatory strategies. Thus, in conjoined sentences, this analysis would claim, S.P. assigns the correct 1,2;1,2 interpretation half the time, after having constructed a normal phrase marker in which the VPs are conjoined, and, in the remaining cases, uses a 1,2;2,3 interpretive heuristic that assigns Agency to the preverbal noun and Theme to the postverbal noun. On the other hand, in the case of object-subject relatives this analysis would have to claim that S.P. assigns the 1,2;2,3 interpretation correctly in half the cases on the basis of having constructed a relative clause, and resorts to a 1,2;1,3 compensatory interpretation based on the use of a heuristic of assigning Agency to the first noun in the sentence in the other half of the sentences of this type. Though this is not impossible, this analysis is far from parsimonious.

Second, there is an analysis that can account for the observed alternation in responses and is consistent with other aspects of S.P.'s performance. The three sentence types that show this systematic alternation between 1,2;1,3 and 1,2;2,3 interpretations—the conjoined, subject-subject, and object-subject relatives—all have the structural property of containing the sequence N-V-N-V-N. Let us assume that S.P. represents the structure of these sentences as this linear string of lexical categories and interprets strings of this sort according to the interpretive principle suggested above (i.e., that she assigns Agency and Theme to the preverbal noun and the postverbal noun in a sequence of the form N-V-N). Suppose, further, that, having assigned a noun a thematic role in the argument structure of a verb, S.P. no longer considers that noun a candidate for the assignment of a thematic role around a second verb. On these assumptions, S.P. would assign N_1 as Agent of V_1, N_2 as Theme of V_1, and N_3 as Theme of V_2 in structures of the form N_1-V_1-N_2-V_2-N_3. She would be left with the problem of assigning the Agent of V_2. N_1 might be chosen for this function, either because of some special "saliency" attributable to the sentence-initial position (Goodglass 1968) or through an application of a "parallel function" interpretive strategy (Volin 1983). N_2 could be considered as Agent in this "second-pass" portion of the interpretive process because it is the immediately preverbal noun. S.P. chose both nouns equally frequently.

If we assume that S.P. assigns the simplified syntactic structure just described and uses the interpretive principles indicated above, we also can account for her performance on object-object and subject-subject relatives. The former present no problem; the first clause would be interpreted normally, and N_3 would be assigned as Agent of the second verb, leaving N_2 as Theme of the second verb. This pattern was found in seven of nine sentences of this type. The remaining interpretations must have been due to the application of a "linear order," a "parallel function," or a "salient first noun" strategy. Subject-object relatives, however, should present considerable difficulty with respect to assignment of thematic roles around the first verb (where they resemble cleft-object forms) and with respect to assignment of the Agent of V_2 (because of the presence of the sequence V-V-N). This was, in fact, observed.

At first glance, it seems possible that S.P. assigns the structure VP to sequences of the form V-N, since she almost always took the immediately postverbal noun as the Theme of a verb. However, if this were the case, sequences of the form N-V-N-V-N would be assigned a structure of the form N_1-$[_{VP1} V_1$-$N_2]$-$[_{VP2} V_2$-$N_3]$. If N_2 is part of a VP structure in such a sequence, there is no reason for it to be assigned the role of Agent around V_2. Since S.P. assigned a 1,2;1,3 and a 1,2;2,3 interpretation to sequences of this form with equal frequency, we conclude that this is not the way she structures such sequences. If she assigns hierarchical structure, we must assume that she sometimes structures N-V-N-V-N sequences as (30) and sometimes as (31).

(30) N_1-$[_{VP1} [_{VP2} V_1$-$N_2]$-$[_{VP3} V_2$-$N_3]]$
(31) N_1-$[_{VP1} V_1$-$[_{NP} N_2[_S[_{VP2} V_2N_3]]]]$

In (30), the two VPs are conjoined, and N_1 is the NP in subject position for both VPs and thus would be assigned the role of Agent around both verbs. In (31) the second VP is part of an S which is embedded under an NP whose head is N_2, and thus N_2 is the Agent of V_2. (30) is the structure of a conjoined sentence; (31) is that for an object-subject relative. This analysis would thus claim that S.P. alternately assigns the structure of conjoined and object-subject relatives to sequences of the form N-V-N-V-N. Like the first analysis we considered, this one, while not impossible, seems highly unlikely and is not parsimonious.

Overall, S.P.'s analysis of two-verb sentences suggests that she assigns linear strings of lexical categories and interprets these strings according to a simple interpretive strategy. This renders strings of the form N-V-N-V-N ambiguous for her. There is no evidence that S.P. organizes categories in hierarchies. Though the analysis is *post hoc*, it is supported by considerable internal argumentation.

The simplification of syntactic structure that we have suggested underlies S.P.'s interpretation of two-verb sentences helps decide between the two alternative accounts of her performance on one-verb passive and cleft-object sentences. Given the regularity of the assignment of thematic roles in more complex sentences, it seems unlikely that the alternation in assignment of agency between the two nouns in these simpler structures is due to S.P.'s failure to utilize any structure in the input string and to a random assignment of thematic roles to NPs. We had entertained two possibilities regarding how S.P. deals with these strings above: occasional correct assignment of structure and occasional use of a heuristic, and assignment of an ambiguous structure. If we were to accept that S.P. only assigns linear strings of major lexical categories to auditorily presented sentences, we would conclude that the structures she assigns to passive and cleft-object sentences are those in (32) and (33), respectively.

(32) N-V-Prep-N
(33) N-N-V

The heuristics outlined above apply to these structures in such a way that the immediately preverbal noun may be assigned the role of Agent but the noun in the *by*-phrase and the sentence-initial noun also may be assigned that role. Thus, the heuristics we postulated for two-verb sentences would render these strings ambiguous for S.P. We cannot exclude the possibility that S.P. can assign complete hierarchical structure to these simple sentences but fails to do so on some trials because of attentional and other factors. However, a parsimonious account of S.P.'s performance on all sentence types is available if we assume that she treats all strings as sequences of major lexical categories and that some very elementary aspects of syntactic structure trigger heuristic interpretive algorithms. If this analysis is correct, it suggests that the portion of S.P.'s parser that is defective is quite specific: it would consist of the operations that build phrasal and other nonlexical nodes.

It is possible that this particular failure could be related to S.P.'s expressive agrammatism, since, in the sentences we have tested, it could be the result of a failure to utilize function words and grammatical morphemes for structure-building purposes. Whether the failure to construct phrasal nodes extends to sentences where such structures are not marked overtly by function words, such as (34), was not tested.

(34) The elephant saw the monkey hit the frog.

If sentences such as (34) show the same ambiguity as all other sentences of the form N-V-N-V-N, despite the fact that the embedding in (34) is signaled by the subcategorization features of the main verb *saw* rather than the relative pronoun *that*, we would conclude that this impairment is not entirely secondary to a disturbance in the utilization of the function word/inflectional vocabulary, and that it is not related to S.P.'s agrammatism. Unfortunately, such structures were not examined when S.P. was available for testing. Whatever the resolution of this question, S.P. demonstrates a fairly severe impairment affecting the construction of a major aspect of syntactic form: hierarchical phrase structure.

Patient R.L.
R.L.'s performance is illustrated in table 5.19. His performance on one-verb sentences was strikingly similar to that of S.P. However, he showed quite a different pattern in interpreting two-verb sentences. R.L. interpreted conjoined sentences and object-subject relatives correctly in the majority of cases. Unlike S.P., he seemed to appreciate the differences in structure indicated by the coordinate conjunction *and* (*et* in French) and the relative pronoun *that* (*qui* in French); he took N_1 as Agent of V_2 in conjoined sentences and N_2 as Agent of V_2 in object-subject relatives. For R.L. these two sentence types did not have the ambiguity that they had for S.P. Subject-subject relatives were also interpreted differently by R.L. and S.P. These sentences were not ambiguous between two interpretations for R.L. He interpreted them correctly half the time, and the remaining responses showed a wide scatter of interpretations. This suggests that he sometimes assigned a correct structure to subject-subject relatives and interpreted that structure normally, and at other times failed to assign an interpretation to the sentence on the basis of its syntactic structure and resorted to random assignment of thematic roles to noun phases. However, the most common response for subject-subject relatives was the correct one, and it was a different response than the (correct) interpretation of object-subject relatives, which R.L. produced on seven of ten presentations. Moreover, R.L. was more accurate on conjoined sentences than on subject-subject

Table 5.19
Responses of patient R.L.

One-verb sentences

Response type	Two-place verbs			Three-place verbs		
	Active	Passive	Cleft-object	Active	Passive	Cleft-object
1, 2	6/6*	2/4	2/4			
2, 1		4/6*	4/6*			
1, 2, 3				6/6*	1/6	2/6
1, 3, 2					1/6	
2, 1, 3					1/6	4/6*
3, 1, 2					3/6*	

Two-verb sentences

	Conjoined	Subject-subject	Subject-object	Object-subject	Object-object
1, 2; 1, 3	8/10*	5/10*	2/10	2/10	
1, 2; 2, 3	2/10	2/10	2/10	7/10*	2/10
1, 2; 3, 2					8/10*
2, 1; 1, 3		1/10	2/10*		
2, 1; 2, 3			3/10		
1, 2; 1, 2		1/10		1/10	
1, 3; 2, 3		1/10			
2, 3; 1, 3			1/10		

*correct response

relatives. Thus, it appears that R.L. distinguished these three sentence types, unlike S.P., and that he had particular trouble interpreting subject-subject relative clauses. R.L. was quite accurate in the interpretation of object-object relatives. Subject-object relatives, however, produced almost random responses.

The fact that R.L. distinguished conjoined sentences from object-subject relatives and the fact that he interpreted both correctly in a majority of cases indicate that he appreciated the difference in structure signaled by the coordinate conjunction versus the relative pronoun. A similar conclusion can be reached on the basis of his superior performance on conjoined sentences versus subject-subject relatives. These differences would follow from R.L.'s appreciating the structural feature of embedding, signaled by the relative pronoun *that*. Thus, it appears that R.L. can construct phrase markers in which sentences are embedded under noun phases and VPs are conjoined. His grammar must therefore contain recursive rules elaborating phrase structures of the sort illustrated in (35)–(38).

(35) S → NP + VP
(36) VP → V + NP
(37) NP → NP + S
(38) VP → VP + VP

R.L.'s main difficulty lay in his ability to interpret relative clauses that occurred on the subject NP of the sentence. As noted, he was virtually random in interpreting subject-object relatives (he got only two of ten sentences correct), and he was worse on subject-subject relatives than on conjoined sentences or on object-subject relatives. This difficulty cannot be accounted for in terms of a loss of rules in R.L.'s grammar or an absence of the operations needed to construct relative clauses. There is no way to restrict the generative capacity of rules such as those above to NPs in object position. If we accept these rules as a characterization of R.L.'s knowledge of French, we must attribute his difficulty with relative clauses in subject position to performance factors. These factors do not preclude the construction and interpretation of relative clauses, but they do make the operations involved in this process difficult when relative clauses are in subject position.

The most obvious factor that may account for this pattern is an increase in memory load resulting from the presence of a relative clause on the subject NP. This NP is required for later assignment to a thematic role around a second verb, and must be stored in memory until the second verb is identified and its morphology ascertained. If this is the reason for R.L.'s difficulty with these sentence types, it is interesting that he did not show a similar difficulty with conjoined sentences, which also require the retention of the first NP in memory for assignment to a thematic role around the second verb. The difference between conjoined sentences and sentences with relative clauses in subject position may be that whereas relative clauses are marked by a relative pronoun and thus signal the need for retention of the first NP in memory, there is no such marking in conjoined sentences. A parsing operation that imposes memory demands of this sort is found in the HOLD operator of some Augmented Transitional Network parsers (see, e.g., Wanner 1980). As was noted in chapter 2 above, there is evidence that structures of this sort increase the local memory requirements of the parser (Wanner and Maratsos 1978). The suggestion is therefore that R.L. has difficulty in the processing of thematic roles around the verb of a relative clause in subject position because some portion of his parser/interpreter is devoted to the maintenance of the subject NP in memory, which diminishes his ability to process syntactic form and assign thematic roles within the relative clause. R.L.'s performance thus has certain similarities to that of K.G. with respect to the effect on performance of the increased memory load associated with relative-clause formation.

If this analysis is correct, it suggests that R.L.'s parser/interpreter is easily overburdened by sentences that impose certain types of memory loads. R.L.'s recognition memory functions were excellent (Caplan et al. 1986a), so it does not seem that his difficulty can be attributed to a failure of short-term-memory functions *per se*. This case thus establishes the partial independence of the memory system internal to the operation of the parser from that involved in recognition of words and nonwords in lists. Patient B.O. (see below) showed the opposite pattern: a severe limitation of STM functions but good comprehension of syntactic form. The implications of these two cases for the relationship between STM and syntactic comprehension will be discussed in chapter 6.

Patient A.B.
Patient A.B. had difficulty with syntactic operations such as interpreting reflexives and structuring complex NPs and sentential complements. From this and other evidence, we concluded that AB has difficulty constructing a syntactic tree. When processing demands exceed his limited ability to assign syntactic structure, he uses one of several heuristics to interpret the sentences he hears.

A.B. was a 56-year-old right-handed male who had suffered a right parietal CVA in February 1984. According to the assessment by the speech pathologist, his spontaneous speech was nonfluent and apraxic, and he had some word-finding difficulties and produced some semantic paraphasias. His single-word auditory comprehension was good. His confrontation naming ability was reduced. Word and sentence repetition was difficult, but his responses did not contain phonemic or semantic paraphasias. His digit span was four oral and three pointing. He was diagnosed as having a nonfluent aphasia with apraxia of speech.

A.B. was tested on the first, second, and fifth batteries between October 31 and December 19, 1984. His results on the first syntactic-comprehension battery are shown in table 5.20. Visual inspection shows that this battery was difficult overall, with a mean of 41%. A.B. scored well on active sentences, below 50% on passive sentences, and at 17% or less on both types of cleft constructions and on three of the four types of relative-clause constructions. The χ^2 values calculated under Stage II assumptions (see the Data Analysis section at the beginning of this chapter) are given in the table. The response pattern for two-place passives was not significantly different from random; all other sentence types reached significance ($p < 0.05$), although for six of eleven sentence types the nonrandomness was due to an incorrect response.

A.B.'s incorrect responses varied according to the number of verbs and nouns in the sentence. For sentences with one verb, A.B. tended to assign thematic roles in a canonical order: Agent to the first noun occurring in the

Table 5.20
Results from first syntactic-comprehension battery, patient A.B.

	Correct		Incorrect		χ^2 values,[†] Stage II assumptions
One-verb sentences					
[01] The bear kissed the donkey. (two-place active)	<u>1,2</u>	100%			$(E = 6, \text{d.f.} = 1,$ $\chi^2 = 12.00, p < 0.001^*)$
[27] The bear was kissed by the donkey. (two-place passive)	2,1	42%	<u>1,2</u>	58%	$(E = 6, \text{d.f.} = 1,$ $\chi^2 = 0.34, p > 0.20)$
[21] It was the bear that the donkey kissed. (two-place cleft object)	2,1	17%	<u>1,2</u>	83%	$(E = 6, \text{d.f.} = 1,$ $\chi^2 = 8.34, p < 0.01^*)$
[02] The bear gave the donkey to the goat. (dative active)	<u>1,2,3</u>	83%	1,3,2	17%	$(E = 2, \text{d.f.} = 5,$ $\chi^2 = 40.00, p < 0.001^*)$
[28] The bear was given to the donkey by the goat. (dative passive)	3,1,2	17%	<u>1,2,3</u> <u>1,3,2</u> 2,13	58% 17% 8%	$(E = 2, \text{d.f.} = 5,$ $\chi^2 = 17.00, p < 0.01^*)$
[22] It was the bear that the donkey gave to the goat. (dative cleft-object)	2,1,3	17%	<u>1,2,3</u> <u>1,3,2</u> 2,3,1	50% 25% 8%	$(E = 2, \text{d.f.} = 5,$ $\chi^2 = 13.00, p < 0.05^*)$
Two-verb sentences					
[03] The bear kissed the donkey and the goat. (conjoined)	<u>1,2;1,3</u>	75%	2,1;2,3 1,2;2,3 2,1;1,3	8% 8% 8%	$(E = 0.33, \text{d.f.} = 35,$ $\chi^2 = 242.42, p < 0.001^*)$
[23] The bear that the donkey kissed patted the goat. (subject-object)	2,1;1,3	17%	<u>1,2;1,3</u> <u>2,1;2,3</u> 1,3;3,2 1,2;2,3	50% 17% 8% 8%	$(E = 0.33, \text{d.f.} = 35,$ $\chi^2 = 127.27, p < 0.001^*)$

Table 5.20 (continued)

	Correct		Incorrect		χ^2 values,[†] Stage II assumptions
[24] The bear kissed the donkey that patted the goat. (object-subject)	1,2;2,3	0%	1,2;1,3	75%	($E = 0.33$, d.f. $= 35$,
			1,3;1,2	17%	$\chi^2 = 248.48$, $p < 0.001^*$)
			3,1;3,2	8%	
[25] The bear kissed the donkey that the goat patted. (object-object)	1,2;3,2	0%	1,2;1,3	75%	($E = 0.33$, d.f. $= 35$,
			3,1;3,2	8%	$\chi^2 = 242.42$, $p < 0.001^*$)
			1,3;3,2	8%	
			1,3;1,2	8%	
[26] The bear that kissed the donkey patted the goat. (subject-subject)	1,2;1,3	75%	1,2;2,3	8%	($E = 0.33$, d.f. $= 35$,
	1,3;1,2	8%	3,1;3,2	8%	$\chi^2 = 242.42$, $p < 0.001^*$)

[†] See text for explanation of calculation of χ^2 values.

sentence, Theme to the second noun, and Goal to the third noun (when present). The frequency of occurrence of this response pattern varied from 50% to 100% across the sentence types with one verb (a 1,2 response for two-place verbs and a 1,2,3 response for three-place verbs), showing some sensitivity to differences between active, passive, and cleft-object structures.

For sentences in the first battery with two verbs to be acted out, A.B. chose the Agent of the first verb as the Agent of the second verb (a 1,2;1,3 response) 75% of the time for nearly every sentence type. This fact suggests that A.B. was not sensitive to structural differences in the two-verb sentences and was using some heuristic strategy to assign thematic roles to NPs in these sentences. This response happened to be the correct one for the conjoined sentences (type 3) and the subject-subject relatives (type 26); thus, A.B. may have scored relatively well on these structures without being able to structure them syntactically.

A.B. also performed poorly overall on the second battery, scoring an average of 53%. On the basis of his poor overall performance on the first two batteries, he was given the fifth (baseline) battery but not the more difficult fourth and fifth batteries. A.B. had difficulty interpreting even the simple sentences on the baseline battery. His accuracy ranged from zero to 100%, with a mean accuracy of 53% (excluding the type 43 sentences, such as *John promised a friend of Bill's to shave*, which were also difficult for some control subjects).

The results for the fifth and the second battery are presented in table 5.21, along with the χ^2 value for each sentence type. The χ^2 values for sentences containing no referential dependency (types 4, 35, 36) were calculated under Stage II assumptions, because A.B. always assigned thematic roles to dolls mentioned in these sentences. For each of thirteen of the fifteen sentence types containing referential dependencies, the χ^2 values were calculated on the weaker Stage I assumption because A.B. assigned a thematic role to a noun not mentioned in the sentence at least once. Only 42% of these responses involving objects not mentioned in the sentence constituted correct responses (i.e., in sentences with pronouns).

On the fifth battery, all eight calculated sentence-response patterns were significantly different from random. For six of these eight structures, the correct response occurred with a frequency greater than chance ($p < 0.001$). The two sentence types for which the correct response did not occur significantly more often than chance were the two sentence types containing both a reflexive and a complex NP (types 38 and 39). On the second battery, the response patterns for all three sentence types without referential dependencies (types 4, 35, 36), calculated under the more restrictive Stage II assumptions, reached significance ($p < 0.05$), and the correct response occurred significantly above chance ($p < 0.001$). The response

Table 5.21
Results from second and fifth batteries, patient A.B.

	Correct		Incorrect		
Fifth (baseline) battery					
[40] John kicked him.	1VX	58%	1V1	42%	(Stage I: $E = 0.75$, d.f. $= 4$, $\chi^2 = 43.11$, $p < 0.001^*$)
[41] A friend of John's kicked him.	1V2	67%	2V1 XV1	25% 8%	(Stage I: $E = 0.75$, d.f. $= 9$, $\chi^2 = 86.00$, $p < 0.001^*$)
[42] John's friend kicked him.	2V1 2VX	67% 8%	1V2	25%	(Stage I: $E = 0.75$, d.f. $= 9$, $\chi^2 = 86.00$, $p < 0.001^*$)
[37] John kicked himself.	1V1	100%			(Stage I: $E = 0.75$, d.f. $= 4$, $\chi^2 = 180.00$, $p < 0.001^*$)
[38] A friend of John's kicked himself.	1V1	0%	2V2 2V1 1VX 1V2	8% 33% 17% 42%	(Stage I: $E = 0.75$, d.f. $= 9$, $\chi^2 = 46.66$, $p < 0.001^*$)
[39] John's friend kicked himself.	2V2	8%	1V1 2V1 1V2 XV2	8% 58% 17% 8%	(Stage I: $E = 0.75$, d.f. $= 9$, $\chi^2 = 61.99$, $p < 0.001^*$)
[35] A friend of John's kicked Bill.	1V3	67%	2V3 2V1	25% 8%	(Stage II: $E = 1.3$, d.f. $= 8$, $\chi^2 = 44.62$, $p < 0.001^*$)
[36] John hit Bill's friend.	1V3	50%	2V3 3V1	17% 33%	(Stage II: $E = 1.3$, d.f. $= 8$, $\chi^2 = 30.78$, $p < 0.001^*$)
Second battery					
[06] John said that Bill kicked him.	2V1 2VX	75% 8%	1V2 XV2	8% 8%	(Stage I: $E = 0.75$, d.f. $= 9$, $\chi^2 = 98.67$, $p < 0.001^*$)

Sentence					Statistics
[07] John said that a friend of Bill's kicked him.	2V1 25% 2V3 25% 2VX 8%	3V2 17% 1V2 8% XV3 8% 1VX 8%			(Stage I: $E = 0.75$, d.f. $= 15$, $\chi^2 = 22.65$, $p < 0.10$)
[10] John said that Bill kicked himself.	2V2 42%	XVX 8% 2V1 42% 1VX 8%			(Stage I: $E = 0.75$, d.f. $= 9$, $\chi^2 = 56.00$, $p < 0.001^*$)
[11] John said that a friend of Bill's kicked himself.	2V2 25%	3V3 8% 1V2 17% 2V1 17% 3V2 25% 3VX 8%			(Stage I: $E = 0.75$, d.f. $= 15$, $\chi^2 = 25.32$, $p < 0.05^*$)
[04] John said that Bill kicked Eddie. (baseline: three overt NPs)	2V3 42%	1V3 8% 2V1 17% 3V1 17% 3V2 17%			(Stage II: $E = 1.3$, d.f. $= 8$, $\chi^2 = 16.94$, $p < 0.05^*$)
[13] Patrick persuaded Joe to wash. (object control)	2V 100%				(Stage II: $E = 6$, d.f. $= 1$, $\chi^2 = 12.00$, $p < 0.001^*$)
[14] Patrick persuaded a friend of Joe's to wash. (object control, complex NP)	2V 50%	3V 33% XV 8% 1V2 8%			(Stage I: $E = 3$, d.f. $= 3$, $\chi^2 = 7.66$, $p < 0.10$)
[17] Patrick promised Joe to wash. (subject control)	1V 33%	2V 58% XV 8%			(Stage I: $E = 3$, d.f. $= 2$, $\chi^2 = 9.83$, $p < 0.05^*$)
[32] Patrick seems to Joe to be praying. (NP-raising)	1V 42%	2V 50% XV 8%			(Stage I: $E = 3$, d.f. $= 2$, $\chi^2 = 8.50$, $p < 0.02^*$)

patterns for two of the sentence types on the second battery— pronouns with a complex NP (*John said that a friend of Bill's hit him*) and object-control with a complex NP (*John persuaded a friend of Bill's to shave*)—did not reach significance, even under the weak Stage I assumptions. In summary: both of the sentence types on the second battery on which A.B. seems to be performing randomly contain complex NPs. In addition, A.B.'s response patterns discriminate between sentences with and sentences without referential dependencies.

As table 5.21 shows, in four out of five cases A.B.'s performance was worse on structures with complex NPs than on matched structures with simple NPs. In the one exceptional case—the sentence type containing a simple NP subject and a pronoun object (*Patrick hit him*, type 40)—the pronoun has no linguistic antecedent, and the patient is thus forced to select an antecedent from among the dolls in the array. On these sentences, A.B. often chose the only overt noun mentioned in the sentence as the antecedent of the pronoun, which led to a reflexive interpretation. Although the normal controls never treated these sentences as reflexive, in our experience it is not uncommon for aphasic patients to do so. This means that A.B. preferred to choose an antecedent from among nouns mentioned in the sentence, which led to the correct answer more often for the sentence type with the complex NP (*A friend of John's kicked him*, type 41) than for the matched sentence type with the simple NP (*John kicked him*, type 40).

A.B.'s ability to structure complex NPs depended on the sentence type. In sentences like *A friend of John's kicked Bill* (type 35) and *A friend of John's kicked him* (type 41), he chose the head of the complex NP as Agent 67% of the time—significantly above chance ($p < 0.001$). However, in more complex sentences (*John said that a friend of Bill's kicked himself*, type 11), his accuracy dropped to 42%.

This reduction in A.B.'s ability to construct a complex NP in a sentence containing a reflexive suggested that sentences with reflexives might also be particularly difficult for him. As table 5.21 shows, A.B. scored lower on four of five structures containing a reflexive, relative to the matched structure with a pronoun. The one exception again involved a sentences containing a pronoun without a linguistic antecedent (*Patrick hit him*, type 40). Since there are more possible correct response types for sentences with pronouns, it is important to establish that A.B.'s better performance on sentences with pronouns was not merely due to a greater probability that chance performance would produce the correct interpretation in these sentences. For sentences with sentential complements and complex NPs, such as *John said that a friend of Bill's kicked himself/him* (types 11 and 7), it does indeed appear that A.B.'s better performance on pronouns was due to the higher likelihood of a correct response, since the response patterns are nearly identical for the two structures. (The response pattern for the sentence with the reflexive just reaches significance; that for the sentence with the pronoun does not.) However, this factor cannot explain A.B.'s better performance with the pronoun form of three other matched structures: *A friend of John's kicked himself/him* (types 38 and 41); *John's friend kicked himself/him* (types 39 and 42), and *John said that Bill kicked himself/him* (types 10 and 6). For the structures with a pronoun, the set of A.B.'s correct responses included a doll not mentioned in the sentence only twice out of 36 trials; therefore, A.B.'s better performance on the structures with pronouns must have been due to his consistent selection of the one correct response in which a sentence-internal antecedent is assigned for the pronoun or the reflexive. In summary: A.B. appears to be less accurate on sentences with reflexives, except in the shortest and the longest sentences. He tends to choose a linguistic antecedent for pronoun sentences such as *John kicked him*, resulting in an incorrect answer. Both the reflexive and pronoun forms of sentences like *John said that a friend of Bill's kicked himself/him* are so difficult that he responds nearly randomly.

A.B.'s error patterns also reveal differences between his interpretations of reflexives and pronouns, as table 5.21 shows. Except on sentences like *Patrick kicked him*, A.B. consistently chose a disjoint interpretation (correct or incorrect) for sentences with pronouns. On sentences with reflexives, on the other hand, A.B. often also assigned an erroneous disjoint interpretation rather than an incorrect reflexive interpretation. For instance, on sentences with a complex NP plus a reflexive, such as *John said that a friend of Bill's kicked himself* (type 11), all nine errors out of twelve trials involved choosing a disjoint rather than reflexive interpretation.

A.B.'s difficulty with both the structuring of complex NPs and the interpretation of reflexives is evidence of some type of impairment in the handling of syntactic operations, if one assumes (as do Berwick and Weinberg [1985]) that the coindexing of a reflexive with its antecedent occurs at the syntactic level, and if it can be shown that A.B.'s difficulty with reflexives is specifically a syntactic impairment in the ability to find an antecedent and not a lexical loss of knowledge of the properties of a reflexive. It appears that A.B. is able to recognize a difference between reflexives and pronouns when other processing demands are low. He always chose a reflexive interpretation for *Patrick hugged himself* (type 37), whereas he chose a disjoint interpretation 58% of the time for *Patrick hugged him* (type 40). If A.B. retained no lexical knowledge of pronouns or reflexives, he would have assigned the same interpretation to both sentences with equal frequency. The difference in accuracy between these two matched sentence types with reflexives and pronouns is significant ($p < 0.025$), using the test of the significance of the difference between two independent proportions (Ferguson 1981). This suggests that A.B. has an understanding of the lexical properties of reflexives and pronouns, and therefore that his impairment must lie in the ability to make use of this knowledge when the demands of syntactic processing become more complex.

These facts suggest that for A.B. there is an interaction between syntactic complexity and the ability to make use of lexical knowledge regarding reflexives. It would be of interest to see whether there are any other syntactic effects on A.B.'s ability to use lexical knowledge. Consider his knowledge of the number of thematic roles associated with each predicate. If A.B. has access to this type of information, he would be expected to consistently act out transitive verbs with an Agent and a Theme, to act out intransitive verbs with an Agent only, and to act out dative verbs with an Agent, a Theme, and a Goal. On the other hand, if he does not have the use of this information, he would be expected either to assign a random number of thematic roles around a verb or else to assign a canonical number of thematic roles around a verb (say, Agent and Theme). If increasing syntactic demands impinge on his ability to use lexical information, he should show errors in thematic-role assignment only on more difficult sentences, especially sentences with complex NPs and sentences with reflexives.

There is some evidence that A.B. did not always utilize his lexical knowledge of thematic roles. On the second and fifth batteries, there were six instances in which he interpreted intransitive verbs as transitive, acting them out with an Agent and a Theme. Five of these six instances occurred on a sentence type that, as mentioned above, has been eliminated from the analysis because three of eight control subjects scored below 80% on it (*Patrick promised a friend of Joe's to shave*, type 43). A.B. may have made this error because all the other sentence types in that particular battery contained transitive verbs (although the control subjects never made this type of error). Notice also, however, that this sentence type contains a complex NP and thus is predicted to be particularly difficult for A.B. The sixth error involved incorrectly acting out an Agent and a Theme for an intransitive verb in an object-control sentence with a complex NP (*John persuaded a friend of Joe's to shave*).

A.B. also appears to have had difficulty assigning the correct number of thematic roles to the dative structures in the first battery. For the dative active, dative passive, and dative cleft-object sentences, the responses were scored as indicating Agent, Theme, and Goal; however, three separate observers were unable to decide whether A.B. was acting out one action, with Agent, Theme, and Goal, or two separate transitive actions, each with Agent and Theme. We attempted to disambiguate A.B.'s responses to these structures in a variety of ways, including asking him to verbally

Table 5.22
Results of sentence-verification task, patient A.B.

		Judgment by A.B.	
		True	False
Dative active			
Correct: 1,2,3			
Response used by examiner:	1,2,3	3/6	3/6
	3,1,2	4/6	2/6
	1,2;1,3	1/6	5/6
Dative passive			
Correct: 3,1,2			
Response used by examiner:	1,2,3	4/6	2/6
	3,1,2	3/6	3/6
	1,2;1,3	3/6	3/6
Dative cleft-object			
Correct: 2,1,3			
Response used by examiner:	1,2,3	2/6	4/6
	2,1,3	0/6	6/6
	1,2;1,3	1/6	5/6

paraphrase his response and retraining him to act out an unambiguous response. A.B. continued to give ambiguous responses.

We decided to give A.B. a sentence-verification task that included various dative structures, along with other filler sentences. A.B.'s task was to listen to the sentence and then judge whether the experimenter had acted out the sentence correctly. Foils were chosen from the predominant pattern of A.B.'s responses on the object-manipulation battery for these sentence types. The results are listed in table 5.22.

For dative active sentences, A.B. correctly rejected the two-verb interpretation five out of six times. However, he was unable to discriminate between correct and incorrect enactments of the dative interpretations at a level significantly above chance. This finding suggests that A.B. is capable of accessing the lexical information about thematic roles associated with dative verbs but cannot assign the thematic roles to the correct grammatical positions. For cleft-object constructions of the dative, A.B. tended to respond No to the correct response and to both types of foils. For dative passive sentences, A.B. chose randomly among the two-verb foil, the single-action dative foil, and the single-action dative correct answer. Therefore, it appears that although A.B. recognized differences in the dative active, dative passive, and dative cleft-object constructions, he was not able to assign the correct structure to any of the dative constructions, and he was able reject a two-action response as incorrect only for the dative active and possibly the dative cleft-object constructions. The fact that A.B. could not reject the two-action response on the more complex dative sentences suggests that he loses the ability to utilize the lexically encoded information specifying the number of thematic roles a verb requires when parsing becomes more complex. Since A.B. tended to accept answers other than the one he had acted out as correct, he may have been aware in some way that his heuristic was merely a substitute for the correct answer.

A.B. adopted certain canonical responses for certain types of sentences. One-verb sentences in the first battery tended to receive a "linear" interpretation, with the first NP occurring in the sentence assigned Agent, the second NP assigned Theme, and the third NP (when present) assigned Goal. In the second and fifth batteries, for sentences containing a referential dependency plus either a complex NP or a sentential complement, such as *A friend of John's kicked himself* (type 38), *John's friend kicked himself* (type 39), and *John said that Bill kicked himself* (type 10), A.B.'s most frequent response was to choose the subject as Agent and the other NP as Theme. However, in the sentences containing a complex NP, a sentential complement, and a referential dependency—e.g. *John said that a friend of Bill's kicked himself* (type 11)—A.B. resorted to a random assignment of Agent and Theme to any two of the NPs mentioned in the sentence. In other words, the disjoint interpretation was maintained, but the assignment of thematic roles no longer depended on the order of occurrence of the NPs in the sentence.

Whereas the more complex sentences on the second and fifth batteries caused A.B.'s response pattern to become more random, the more complex sentences on the first battery evidently caused A.B. to use the 1,2;1,3 response in an invariant fashion (see table 5.20). There are several differences between the batteries that may account for A.B.'s use of highly different heuristics for the most complex sentences. First, the presence of a referential dependency may have alerted A.B. that a strictly linear heuristic was not appropriate. Second, in the first battery the verbs assign all the thematic roles, which is not the case for sentences containing a complex NP in the other batteries. A.B. maintained a consistent interpretation as long as there were only two overt NPs to which he could assign Agent and Theme (*A friend of John's kicked himself/him, John's friend kicked himself/him,* or *John said that Bill kicked himself/him*), but when he had to select Agent and Theme from among three NPs (*Patrick said that a friend of Joe's kicked Eddie*) his performance became random. Third, the size of the array differed among the batteries. In the first battery the array of objects contained only the NPs that had been mentioned in the sentence; in the other batteries the entire array was present, and A.B. had to select dolls from it to fill the thematic roles of the sentence.

A.B.'s error patterns shows some sensitivity to differences in the lexical properties of the verb in the sentences with intransitive verbs shown in table 5.21. He scored 100% on the object-control sentences, such as *Patrick persuaded Joe to shave* (type 13). For sentences with a complex NP, such as *Patrick persuaded a friend of Joe's to shave* (type 14), he chose nearly equally between the head of the nearest NP (*friend*), which was the correct response, and the nearest noun (*Joe's*). In sentences for which the matrix subject was the correct response (*Patrick promised Joe to shave, Patrick seems to Joe to be shaving*), A.B. again selected the nearest noun half of the time. This suggests that A.B. resorted to choosing the NP immediately preceding the verb as Agent of that verb when his ability to assign syntactic structure failed for particular sentences. In addition, the varying frequency of his use of this response shows that A.B. did recognize differences among the verbs *persuade*, *promise*, and *seem*.

In summary: A.B. has difficulty with several types of operations at the syntactic level as processing load increases. In simple sentences he is able to access and use lexical knowledge of thematic roles, to correctly interpret reflexives, and to build syntactic structure for complex NPs and sentential complements; however, these abilities begin to break down when several of these operations are combined in a single sentence. It therefore appears that A.B. suffers from a severe limitation of his processing capacity, which affects the assignment of syntactic structure. The breakdown of his ability to use lexical knowledge of verb-argument structure and the properties of reflexives is of interest because a strong form of the modularity hypothesis (Fodor 1983) would predict that impairments on the syntactic level should not affect the use of knowledge at the lexical level. However, while the assignment of thematic roles and the interpretation of reflexives make use of lexical properties of the verb or the reflexive, respectively, the operations themselves occur at the syntactic level. We have argued that, as processing demands increase, A.B. loses the ability to use his knowledge of the lexical knowledge of the lexical properties of the verb or reflexive to perform the appropriate syntactic operations.

A.B. makes use of several heuristics to interpret complex sentences. These heuristics vary in type and frequency of use as a function of A.B.'s ability to assign syntactic structure in the particular sentence being parsed and as a function of his sensitivity to the lexical properties of certain items, such as number of verbs, number of thematic roles assigned by the verb, and the existence of a referential dependency. Other possible factors influencing A.B.'s use of a particular heuristic are the size of the array and the number of NPs in the sentence from which he must choose.

Patient C.V.
C.V. was a 28-year-old right-handed female who had suffered a hemorrhagic stroke in August 1983. A CT scan revealed a hyperdensity in the

left parietal area, hypodensities in the left frontal area, and left atrophy. An EEG indicated focal slowing over both the left and the right temporal lobe. In January 1984 she showed worsening symptoms and was diagnosed as having moyamoya disease, a syndrome causing progressive deterioration of cerebral blood vessels and leading to multiple strokes. An extracranial/intracranial bypass was performed in June 1984. A neurological examination revealed a right hemianopsia, mild bilateral hearing loss, and right-sided anesthesia.

C.V. was given a diagnostic aphasia examination by a speech pathologist in July 1984. Her comprehension of single words was good, but her comprehension of more complex material was judged abnormal. Her spontaneous speech was generally nonfluent and anomic, with agrammatic and paragrammatic utterances and phonemic and semantic paraphasias. No dysarthria or dyspraxia was noted.

C.V.'s sentence comprehension was initially tested with the first, second, and fifth syntactic-comprehension batteries in December 1984. Her digit span was five oral and five pointing. In order to get a more complete picture of C.V.'s performance, we tested her sentence comprehension on the third, fourth, and fifth syntactic-comprehension batteries one year later. At that time her digit span was five oral and four pointing. The data are marked to indicate whether the testing took place in the first session or the second.

First Battery, First Session
C.V.'s results on the first syntactic-comprehension battery are summarized in table 5.23. The χ^2 values were calculated under the more restrictive assumptions discussed at the beginning of the chapter. Nine of eleven response patterns were significantly above chance. However, for six of these nine structures, the most frequent response was an incorrect one. For the two-place passives (type 27) and the two-place cleft objects (type 21) that did not reach significance, the possibility cannot be rejected that C.V. was randomly assigning thematic roles to dolls mentioned in the sentence.

C.V.'s performance on this first battery is like that of A.B. in two respects. First, her mean overall accuracy was 39%, nearly identical to that of A.B. Second, she tended to use a "linear" response. For the sentences with two-place verbs, she assigned Agent to the first noun and Theme to the second noun mentioned in the sentence (a 1,2 response). For dative sentences, she assigned Agent, Theme, and Goal to the first, the second, and the third noun, respectively (a 1,2,3 response). For sentences with two verbs, as table 5.23 shows, the linear response pattern consisted of assigning Agent and Theme of the first verb to the first and second nouns mentioned in the sentence, and Agent and Theme of the second verb to the second and third nouns mentioned in the sentence (a 1,2;2,3 response).

Table 5.23
Results from first syntactic-comprehension battery (first testing), patient C.V.

	Correct		Incorrect		χ^2 values, Stage II assumptions
One-verb sentences					
[01] The bear kissed the donkey. (two-place active)	<u>1,2</u>	100%			$(E = 6, \text{d.f.} = 1,$ $\chi^2 = 12.00, p < 0.001^*)$
[27] The bear was kissed by the donkey. (two-place passive)	2,1	58%	1,2	42%	$(E = 6, \text{d.f.} = 1,$ $\chi^2 = 0.34, p > 0.20)$
[21] It was the bear that the donkey kissed. (two-place cleft-object)	2,1	42%	1,2	58%	$(E = 6, \text{d.f.} = 1,$ $\chi^2 = 0.34, p > 0.20)$
[02] The bear gave the donkey to the goat. (dative active)	1,2,3	92%	3,2,1	8%	$(E = 2, \text{d.f.} = 5,$ $\chi^2 = 49.00, p < 0.001^*)$
[28] The bear was given to the donkey by the goat. (dative passive)	3,1,2	0%	<u>1,2,3</u>	100%	$(E = 2, \text{d.f.} = 5,$ $\chi^2 = 60.00, p < 0.001^*)$
[22] It was the bear that the donkey gave to the goat. (dative cleft-object)	2,1,3	8%	<u>1,2,3</u> 3,2,1	83% 8%	$(E = 2, \text{d.f.} = 5,$ $\chi^2 = 39.00, p < 0.001^*)$
Two-verb sentences					
[03] The bear kissed the donkey and the goat. (conjoined)	1,2;1,3	8%	1,2;2,3 <u>2,1;2,3</u>	83% 8%	$(E = 0.33, \text{d.f.} = 35,$ $\chi^2 = 296.97, p < 0.001^*)$
[23] The bear that the donkey kissed patted the goat. (subject-object)	2,1;1,3	0%	1,2;2,3 <u>2,1;2,3</u> 1,2;1,3 1,3;3,2	50% 25% 17% 8%	$(E = 0.33, \text{d.f.} = 35,$ $\chi^2 = 139.39, p < 0.001^*)$
[24] The bear kissed the donkey that patted the goat. (object-subject)	<u>1,2;2,3</u>	92%	1,2;1,3	8%	$(E = 0.33, \text{d.f.} = 35,$ $\chi^2 = 357.58, p < 0.001^*)$

Table 5.23 (continued)

	Correct		Incorrect		χ^2 values, Stage II assumptions
[25] The bear kissed the donkey that the goat patted. (object-object)	1, 2; 3, 2	17%	1, 2; 2, 3	33%	($E = 0.33$, d.f. = 35, $\chi^2 = 84.84$, $p < 0.001^*$)
			2, 1; 2, 3	25%	
			2, 1; 3, 2	8%	
			1, 2; 1, 3	8%	
			1, 2; 3, 1	8%	
[26] The bear that kissed the donkey patted the goat. (subject-subject)	1, 2; 1, 3	17%	1, 2; 2, 3	58%	($E = 0.33$, d.f. = 35, $\chi^2 = 163.63$, $p < 0.001^*$)
			2, 1; 2, 3	17%	
			1, 2; 3, 1	8%	

Table 5.24
Results from first syntactic-comprehension battery (first testing), patient C.V.: frequency of occurrence of most common response pattern for sentences with two verbs.

Type	1, 2; 2, 3 response	Order of occurrence of nouns and verbs
[24] Object-subject	92%*	N-V-N-V-N
[3] Conjoined	83%	N-V-N-V-N
[26] Subject-subject	58%	N-V-N-V-N
[23] Subject-object	50%	N-N-V-V-N
[25] Object-object	33%	N-V-N-N-V

* correct answer

This response was different from that used by A.B. on the sentences with two verbs, but like A.B.'s response it reflects the use of a heuristic based on the linear sequence of nouns and verbs in these sentences (see below). The only sentence with two verbs on which C.V. achieved high accuracy was the one for which this response constituted the correct answer. Hence, her performance on object-subject relatives (type 24) was nearly perfect, but her performance on the other sentences with two verbs was close to zero.

C.V.'s use of these "linear" responses in sentences with one verb varied from 42% to 100%, which suggests that she was able to recognize structural differences in these sentences. For the sentences with two verbs, C.V.'s use of the 1,2;2,3 response varied from 33% to 92%, whereas A.B. used that response pattern 75% of the time on those sentence types. These facts suggest that C.V. was somewhat sensitive to structural differences in the sentences, even when she could not achieve the correct answer. One aspect of the sentences with two verbs to which C.V. may have been sensitive is the order of occurrence of nouns and verbs. As table 5.24 shows, she used the 1,2;2,3 response most often in sentences with an N-V-N-V-N order. However, C.V. must use information other than order of occurrence of nouns and verbs, since otherwise she should use the 1,2;2,3 response more frequently with the subject-subject relatives. In subject-subject relatives, the complementizer *that* signals the presence of a relative clause before the matrix subject can be assigned a thematic role. The presence of this relative pronoun may have alerted C.V. to aspects of the structure beyond the simple N-V-N-V-N order and induced her to use another response, such as 1,2;1,3.

If sentences with two verbs are difficult for C.V. because of their length or their more complex structure, she might be expected to assign local structure on the basis of a canonical order of occurrence of nouns and verbs within one clause. For example, she would be expected to assign a 1,2

Table 5.25
Results from first syntactic-comprehension battery (first testing), patient C.V.: frequency of
occurrence of most common response pattern for sentences with one verb.

Type	1,2 or 1,2,3 response	Order of occurrence of nouns and verbs
[01] Two-place active	100%*	N-V-N
[28] Dative passive	100%	N-V-N-N
[02] Dative active	92%*	N-V-N-N
[22] Dative cleft-object	83%	N-N-V-N
[21] Two-place cleft-object	58%	N-N-V
[27] Two-place passive	42%	N-V-N

* correct answer

interpretation to the first clause of the object-object relatives (type 25),
since the order of occurrence of nouns and verbs in the first clause is a
canonical N-V-N. However, this was not the case. Not only did C.V. use
the 1,2;2,3 response least often in the object-object relatives, she assigned
a 1,2 interpretation to the first clause only 67% of the time—exactly the
same frequency as for subject-object relatives, whose order of occurrence
of nouns and verbs in the first clause is N-N-V. Therefore, it appears to be
the entire N-V-N-V-N pattern that encourages C.V. to use the 1,2;2,3
response.

If a canonical word order determines the frequency of C.V.'s use of a
heuristic, yielding 1,2 interpretations, then two-place passives should show
a high frequency of use of the 1,2 response in the sentences with one verb
in the first battery. However, can be seen in table 5.25, two-place passives
showed the lowest occurrence of the 1,2 response. This may have been due
to C.V.'s ability to assign some syntactic structure to a sentence with only
two thematic roles. However, since C.V.'s performance was not significantly different from random on these two structures, it is not possible to
distinguish between the possibility that she correctly interpreted the two-
place passive and cleft-object sentences correctly half the time and the
possibility that she was assigning thematic roles randomly to the two
animals on display in the array.

In summary: C.V. appears to be sensitive to certain differences among
sentence types, as is evidenced by her preference for particular responses
and by the frequency with which she applied them. She is apparently able
to identify a noncanonical order of occurrence of nouns and verbs in a
sentence and to identify relative pronouns as markers of embedded clauses.
These differences, in turn, affect her choice and her frequency of use of a
heuristic.

Second and Fifth Batteries, First Session
In the first testing session two more batteries were administered: the second battery and the fifth (baseline) battery. The results are listed in table 5.26. C.V.'s mean overall accuracy on the fifth (baseline) battery was 62%, with a range of 33% to 100% on particular sentence types. On the second battery her mean overall accuracy was 59%, with a range of 25% to 100%.

The results show that C.V. had greater difficulty with pronouns than with reflexives. As the table shows, in four out of five cases C.V. scored better on the sentence with a reflexive than on the matched sentence with a pronoun. Three of these four differences reached significance (SDTIP, $p <$ 0.05). For one matched pair, the sentence containing the pronoun was higher in accuracy than the sentence containing the reflexive form (*Patrick said that a friend of Joe's kicked himself/him*, types 11 and 7). The pronoun forms of these sentences include three correct responses, with the result that there is a higher probability of obtaining the correct answer on this type, and in fact C.V.'s overall accuracy of 75% is evenly divided among these three responses.

C.V. tended to assign reflexive interpretations to sentences with pronouns, as table 5.27 shows. This tendency was the opposite of A.B.'s tendency to interpret reflexives as pronouns. C.V. was, however, evidently sensitive to differences between reflexives and pronouns; she assigned reflexive interpretations more often to sentences with reflexives than to sentences with pronouns. C.V. assigned reflexive interpretations 100% of the time to four of the five sentences containing a reflexive, whereas her use of a reflexive interpretation for the matched sentences with pronouns varied from 25% to 58%. For the fifth matched comparison, containing both a sentential complement and a complex NP, her use of a reflexive interpretation dropped to 67% for the reflexive form (*John said that a friend of Bill's kicked himself*, type 11) and to 8% for the pronoun form (*John said that a friend of Bill's kicked him*, type 7). These findings show that C.V. continued to distinguish between reflexives and pronouns even in the most difficult sentences with these elements.

In summary: C.V. showed greater difficulty with the coindexation of pronouns than with that of reflexives. Although her error patterns indicate that she can distinguish pronouns from reflexives, she was apparently unsure of how to treat them and she gave them a reflexive interpretation up to half of the time. For sentences containing a complex NP, a sentential complement, and a referential dependency, C.V.'s responses became more random; she sometimes assigned a disjoint interpretation to a reflexive, and a reflexive interpretation to a pronoun.

Sentences with Intransitive Verbs
C.V.'s response patterns for the structures with intransitive embedded verbs are listed in table 5.26. She did well on structures in which the correct

Table 5.26
Results from second and fifth batteries (first testing), patient C.V.

	Correct		Incorrect		(stats)
Fifth (baseline) battery					
[40] John kicked him.	1VX	58%	1V1	17%	(Stage I: $E = 0.75$, d.f. $= 4$, $\chi^2 = 19.58$, $p < 0.001^*$)
			XV1	17%	
			XVX	8%	
[41] A friend of John's kicked him.	1V2	33%	1V1	25%	(Stage I: $E = 0.75$, d.f. $= 9$, $\chi^2 = 35.33$, $p < 0.001^*$)
	1VX	8%	2V2	8%	
			2V1	25%	
[42] John's friend kicked him.	2V1	33%	1V2	8%	(Stage II: $E = 3$, d.f. $= 3$, $\chi^2 = 9.99$, $p < 0.02^*$)
			2V2	58%	
[37] John kicked himself.	1V1	100%			(Stage I: $E = 0.75$, d.f. $= 4$, $\chi^2 = 180.00$, $p < 0.001^*$)
[38] A friend of John's kicked himself.	1V1	83%	2V2	17%	(Stage II: $E = 3$, d.f. $= 3$, $\chi^2 = 22.66$, $p < 0.001^*$)
[39] John's friend kicked himself.	2V2	83%	1V1	17%	(Stage II: $E = 3$, d.f. $= 3$, $\chi^2 = 22.66$, $p < 0.001^*$)
[35] A friend of John's kicked Bill.	1V3	67%	2V3	8%	(Stage II: $E = 1.3$, d.f. $= 8$, $\chi^2 = 41.55$, $p < 0.001^*$)
			3V1	17%	
			2V1	8%	
[36] John hit Bill's friend.	1V3	33%	2V3	42%	(Stage II: $E = 1.3$, d.f. $= 8$, $\chi^2 = 21.55$, $p < 0.01^*$)
			3V1	8%	
			1V2	8%	
			3V2	8%	

Second battery

Sentence					Statistics
[06] John said that Bill kicked him.	2V1 17% 2VX 8%		1V2 8% 2V2 67%		(Stage I: $E = 0.75$, d.f. $= 9$, $\chi^2 = 80.66$, $p < 0.001^*$)
[07] John said that a friend of Bill's kicked him.	2V1 25% 2V3 25% 2VX 25%		3V2 17% 2V2 8%		(Stage I: $E = 0.75$, d.f. $= 15$, $\chi^2 = 30.66$, $p < 0.01^*$)
[10] John said that Bill kicked himself.	2V2 100%				(Stage II: $E = 3$, d.f. $= 3$, $\chi^2 = 36.00$, $p < 0.001^*$)
[11] John said that a friend of Bill's kicked himself.	2V2 42%		3V3 25% 1V2 8% 2V3 8% 3V2 17%		(Stage II: $E = 1.3$, d.f. $= 8$, $\chi^2 = 18.47$, $p < 0.02^*$)
[04] John said that Bill kicked Eddie.	2V3 100%				(Stage II: $E = 1.3$, d.f. $= 8$, $\chi^2 = 98.47$, $p < 0.001^*$)
[13] Patrick persuaded Joe to wash. (object control)	2V 83%		1V 17%		(Stage II: $E = 6$, d.f. $= 1$, $\chi^2 = 5.34$, $p < 0.05^*$)
[14] Patrick persuaded a friend of Joe's to wash. (object control, complex NP)	2V 42%		3V 50% 2V3 8%		(Stage II: $E = 4$, d.f. $= 2$, $\chi^2 = 5.25$, $p < 0.10$) (Stage I: $E = 3$, d.f. $= 3$, $\chi^2 = 8.66$, $p < 0.05^*$)
[17] Patrick promised Joe to wash. (subject-control)	1V 25%		2V 75%		(Stage II: $E = 6$, d.f. $= 1$, $\chi^2 = 3.00$, $p < 0.10$) (Stage I: $E = 3$, d.f. $= 2$, $\chi^2 = 18.00$, $p < 0.001^*$)
[32] Patrick seems to Joe to be praying. (NP-raising)	1V 42%		2V 58%		(Stage II: $E = 6$, d.f. $= 1$, $\chi^2 = 0.34$, $p > 0.20$) (Stage I: $E = 3$, d.f. $= 2$, $\chi^2 = 12.66$, $p < 0.01^*$)

Table 5.27
Results from fifth and second batteries (first testing), patient C.V.: frequency of use of reflexive and disjoint interpretations on sentences containing reflexives and pronouns.

	Reflexive interpretation	Disjoint interpretation
Fifth battery		
[37] John kicked himself.	100%	0
[40] John kicked him.	25%	75%
[38] A friend of John's kicked himself.	100%	0
[41] A friend of John's kicked him.	33%	67%
[39] John's friend kicked himself.	100%	0
[42] John's friend kicked him.	58%	42%
Second battery		
[10] John said that Bill kicked himself.	100%	0
[06] John said that Bill kicked him.	67%	33%
[11] John said that a friend of Bill's kicked himself.	67%	33%
[07] John said that a friend of Bill's kicked him.	8%	92%

choice of Agent was the proper noun nearest the embedded verb, such as *John persuaded Bill to shave*; however, she assigned Agent randomly to either of the two proper nouns in sentences in which the correct choice of Agent was the doll named in the matrix subject, such as *John promised Bill to shave* and *John seems to Bill to be shaving*. For sentences in which the correct choice of Agent was the head of a complex NP in object position, such as *John persuaded a friend of Bill's to shave*, C.V. chose randomly between the head of the complex NP (*friend*) and the NP nearest the verb (*Bill*). The fact that C.V. chose the matrix-subject NP as Agent more often in sentences in which it was the correct answer shows that she was aware of lexical differences between verbs such as *promise* and verbs such as *persuade*. However, it is impossible to tell from the data whether C.V.'s high accuracy on the object-control sentences was due to her ability to parse these structures normally or to her use of the heuristic of assigning Agent to the NP immediately preceding the verb, or to both.

Second Session
One year later, C.V. was tested on the third and fourth batteries and retested on the fifth (baseline) battery. Table 5.28 shows the results from the retesting of the baseline battery. C.V.'s mean score on this battery was 56%—close to that on the first testing (62%). As the table shows, her overall accuracy for reflexives was still better than that for pronouns. In

Table 5.28
Results from fifth battery (second testing), patient C.V.

	Correct		Incorrect		
[40] John kicked him.	1VX	0	1V1	100%	(Stage I: $E = 0.75$, d.f. $= 4$, $\chi^2 = 180.00$, $p < 0.001^*$)
[41] A friend of John's kicked him.	1V2	8%	1V1	50%	(Stage II: $E = 3$, d.f. $= 3$, $\chi^2 = 5.99$, $p < 0.20$)
			2V2	33%	(Stage I: $E = 0.75$, d.f. $= 9$,
			2V1	8%	$\chi^2 = 59.99$, $p < 0.001^*$)
[42] John's friend kicked him.	2V1	17%	1V2	17%	(Stage II: $E = 3$, d.f. $= 3$,
			2V2	67%	$\chi^2 = 11.99$, $p < 0.01^*$)
[37] John kicked himself.	1V1	100%			(Stage I: $E = 0.75$, d.f. $= 4$, $\chi^2 = 180.00$, $p < 0.001^*$)
[38] A friend of John's kicked himself.	1V1	67%	2V2	33%	(Stage II: $E = 3$, d.f. $= 3$, $\chi^2 = 14.66$, $p < 0.01^*$)
[39] John's friend kicked himself.	2V2	100%			(Stage II: $E = 3$, d.f. $= 3$, $\chi^2 = 36.00$, $p < 0.001^*$)
[35] A friend of John's kicked Bill.	1V3	33%	2V3	17%	(Stage II: $E = 1.3$, d.f. $= 8$,
			3V1	8%	$\chi^2 = 10.79$, $p > 0.20$)
			1V2	8%	(Stage I: $E = 0.75$, d.f. $= 15$,
			3V3	17%	$\chi^2 = 27.98$, $p < 0.05^*$)
			2V2	17%	
[36] John hit Bill's friend.	1V3	25%	2V3	42%	(Stage II: $E = 1.3$, d.f. $= 8$,
			3V3	33%	$\chi^2 = 26.16$, $p < 0.001^*$)

Table 5.29
Results from fifth battery (second testing), patient C.V.: frequency of use of reflexive and
disjoint interpretations on sentences containing reflexives and pronouns.

	Reflexive interpretation	Disjoint interpretation
[37] John kicked himself.	100%	0
[40] John kicked him.	100%	0
[38] A friend of John's kicked himself.	100%	0
[41] A friend of John's kicked him.	83%	17%
[39] John's friend kicked himself.	100%	0
[42] John's friend kicked him.	67%	33%

this testing session, C.V. showed more frequent use of a reflexive interpretation for sentences with pronouns. For example, she assigned reflexive
interpretation to sentences like *Patrick kicked him* (type 40) 100% of the
time. As table 5.28 shows, she even assigned a reflexive interpretation 33%
of the time to two sentence types with no referential dependencies: sentences such as *A friend of Patrick's kicked Joe* (type 35), and *Patrick kicked Joe's
friend* (type 36). However, she had not totally lost her residual knowledge
of the properties of pronouns, since on some sentence types she still used a
reflexive interpretation more often on sentences with reflexives than on
sentences with pronouns. For one matched comparison, involving sentences like *John's friend kicked himself/him* (type 39 and 42), this difference
reached significance (SDTIP, $p < 0.05$). Thus, it appears that by the time of
the second testing session C.V. had solidified a heuristic of assigning
reflexive interpretations to the extent that she sometimes used them even
on sentences that contained no referential dependency.

C.V.'s use of a reflexive interpretation as a heuristic is further revealed
by the results from the fourth battery (table 5.30). Her mean score on this
battery was only 25%, and she assigned a reflexive interpretation at least
75% of the time for each sentence type, whether the sentence contained a
reflexive or whether it contained a pronoun instead. Thus, for these very
difficult sentences containing both an overt and an empty referential dependency, C.V. was no longer able to distinguish between reflexives and
pronouns.

C.V.'s performance on sentences with empty NPs was still poor, as the
results for the sentences from the third battery (table 5.31) show. As before,
C.V. assigned Agent randomly to one of the two proper nouns in the
subject-control sentences. For the two passivized structures, she most often
assigned Agent incorrectly to the object position. For the two structures
containing a complex NP (*Patrick expected a friend of Joe's to be shaving*, type

Table 5.30
Results from fourth battery (second testing session), patient C.V.

	Correct		Incorrect		
[12] Patrick told Joe that Eddie had scratched himself. (baseline: finite embedded clause, 3 NPs + reflexive)	3V3	50%	2V2 1V1	33% 17%	(Stage II: $E = 1.3$, d.f. $= 8$, $\chi^2 = 30.78$, $p < 0.001^*$)
[09] Patrick persuaded Joe that Eddie had patted him. (baseline: finite embedded clause, 3 NPs + pronoun)		0	3V3 2V2 1V1 1V2	42% 33% 17% 8%	(Stage II: $E = 1.3$, d.f. $= 8$, $\chi^2 = 23.09$, $p < 0.01^*$)
[19] Patrick promised Joe to hit himself. (subject control, reflexive embedded object)	1V1	33%	2V2 XVX	58% 8%	(Stage I: $E = 0.75$, d.f. $= 9$, $\chi^2 = 75.33$, $p < 0.001^*$)
[20] Patrick promised Joe to cover him. (subject control, pronominal embedded object)	1V2	25%	2V2 1V1	67% 8%	(Stage II: $E = 3$, d.f. $= 3$, $\chi^2 = 12.66$, $p < 0.01^*$)
[15] Patrick asked Joe to pinch himself. (object control, reflexive embedded object)	2V2	50%	1V1 1V2	42% 8%	(Stage II: $E = 3$, d.f. $= 3$, $\chi^2 = 8.66$, $p < 0.05^*$)
[16] Patrick allowed Joe to hit him. (object control, pronominal embedded object)	2V1	8%	2V2 XVX 1V1 1V2	58% 17% 8% 8%	(Stage I: $E = 0.75$, d.f. $= 9$, $\chi^2 = 59.99$, $p < 0.001^*$)
[34] Patrick seems to Joe to have kicked himself. (NP-raising, reflexive embedded object)	1V1	17%	2V2 1V2	75% 8%	(Stage II: $E = 3$, d.f. $= 3$, $\chi^2 = 16.66$, $p < 0.001^*$)
[31] Patrick was believed by Joe to have kicked himself. (passivized $\bar{S}$ deletion, reflexive embedded object)	1V1	17%	2V2	83%	(Stage II: $E = 3$, d.f. $= 3$, $\chi^2 = 22.66$, $p < 0.001^*$)

Table 5.31
Results from third battery (second testing session), patient C.V.

	Correct		Incorrect		
[18] Patrick vowed to Joe to pray. (subject control)	1V	42%	2V	58%	(Stage II: $E = 6$, d.f. $= 1$, $\chi^2 = 0.34$, $p > 0.20$) (Stage I: $E = 3$, d.f. $= 2$, $\chi^2 = 12.66$, $p < 0.01^*$)
[08] Patrick promised Joe that he would kneel. (overt pronoun embedded subject)	1V 2V XV	58% 33% 8%			(Stage I: $E = 3$, d.f. $= 2$, $\chi^2 = 9.83$, $p < 0.01^*$)
[05] Patrick expected a friend of Joe's to be praying. ($\bar{S}$ deletion, complex NP object)	2V	92%	3V	8%	(Stage II: $E = 4$, d.f. $= 2$, $\chi^2 = 18.5$, $p < 0.001^*$)
[29] Patrick was believed by Joe to be eating. (passivized $\bar{S}$ deletion)	1V	0	2V XV	92% 8%	(Stage I: $E = 3$, d.f. $= 2$, $\chi^2 = 28.5$, $p < 0.001^*$)
[30] Patrick was told by Joe to run. (passivized object control)	1V	17%	2V XV	67% 17%	(Stage I: $E = 3$, d.f. $= 2$, $\chi^2 = 11.33$, $p < 0.01^*$)
[33] Patrick appears to a friend of Joe's to be eating. (NP-raising, complex postverbal NP)	1V	0	2V	100%	(Stage II: $E = 4$, d.f. $= 2$, $\chi^2 = 24.00$, $p < 0.001^*$)

5; *Patrick appears to a friend of Joe's to be shaving*, type 33), she selected the head of the complex NP most of the time (resulting in the correct answer in the case of type 5 and the incorrect answer in the case of type 33). However, it is probably not correct to conclude from these data that C.V.'s ability to choose the head of a complex NP had improved since the first session. It appears, rather, that C.V. had begun to use a nonlinguistic strategy of selecting *friend* as Agent whenever it occurred. Even for sentences containing no referential dependency, such as *Patrick kicked Joe's friend* (type 36, table 5.28), C.V. chose *friend* as Agent, and gave it a reflexive interpretation, 33% of the time. This propensity to choose *friend* as Agent wherever it occurs may have developed as a test-specific strategy, since *friend* does happen to be the correct choice of Agent in a majority of the sentences tested on this battery. Alternatively, *friend* may be more salient for C.V. because it has semantic features associated with it, whereas the proper nouns used in other NP positions in the sentence do not.

In summary: C.V. could recognize differences between verbs like *promise* (type 18) and verbs like *expect* (type 5), but she seemed unsure of what the correct interpretations of sentences containing these verbs might be. Her overall level of accuracy over the two testing sessions was approximately the same; however, in the second session she showed an increased tendency to assign a reflexive interpretation to sentences with pronouns and to select *friend* as Agent.

Summary
C.V. had difficulty with several types of operations at the syntactic level. Her overall accuracy on the sentence batteries was low, and she had particular difficulty with sentences containing complex NPs and sentential complements. She had difficulty with all sentences containing empty NPs except in cases where the correct answer coincided with one of her heuristics.

Overall, C.V. appeared to rely heavily on heuristics to interpret sentences. Nevertheless, she appeared to parse structures to the extent that she could. Her choice and frequency of use of a heuristic depended on her recognition of features of the sentence, such as the passive morphology, a *by*-phrase, the order of occurrence of nouns and verbs, structural features such as the presence of a relative pronoun, and, possibly, an NP without a thematic role.

In addition, C.V. had difficulty with pronouns. She tended to assign (incorrect) reflexive interpretations to pronouns, although less frequently than she assigned (correct) reflexive interpretations to reflexives. Anecdotally, during the second testing session C.V. mentioned that during conversations she was always getting confused about to whom *he, she, it,* and so on were referring.

The difficulty that C.V. showed with operations at the syntactic level is similar to that of A.B. However, A.B. was worse at reflexives than at pronouns, whereas C.V. was worse at pronouns than at reflexives. These two cases considered together thus present a double dissociation for reflexives and pronouns. This finding will be dealt with in the general discussion of the research hypotheses at the end of this chapter.[2]

A Patient with a Limited Short-Term Memory: B.O.
B.O. was a 64-year-old right-handed female who had suffered a cerebral infarction of unknown etiology on June 22, 1982. On neurological examination, she showed significant left-hemisphere impairment, with motor and sensory signs indicating cortical as well as subcortical involvement. A CT scan showed hypodensities indicating infarction in the left internal capsule and left middle cerebral artery territory. B.O. was diagnosed as mildly dysarthric, dyspraxic, and anomic. Auditory comprehension of single words was intact, although she did have some difficulties with confrontation naming.

Pretesting revealed a significant limitation of short-term memory. The patient's digit span was three oral and four pointing. On recall tests for lists of words and letters with a pointing response, she showed a consistent ability to repeat or point to only three words reliably. Because of our interest in the nature of short-term memory and the claims in the literature regarding the relationship between short-term-memory impairments and syntactic-comprehension deficits (see chapter 3), we documented B.O.'s short-term-memory function in detail for later comparison with her syntactic-comprehension performance.

Assessment of Short-Term Memory

Experiment 1: Phonological Processing
B.O.'s short-term memory was assessed within the theoretical framework of Baddeley's "working memory" model (see chapter 3). In the first part of the assessment, we established her ability to decode phonological segments normally in order to eliminate the possibility that a disturbance at this antecedent level of function was the cause of her STM impairment.

In the *phoneme-discrimination* task, the experimenter read aloud pairs of CV syllables, one immediately after the other, and B.O. was required to judge whether the two syllables were the same or different. She scored 100% on this task.

In the *word-discrimination* experiment, B.O. was presented with seventy pairs of words and required to indicate whether the two words were the same or different. On half of the trials the words were the same, and on half they were minimally different phonologically. B.O.'s score on this task was 97%.

Table 5.32
Percentage of trials correct on memory-span task (oral presentation).

	Span size					
	2	3	4	5	6	7
High-frequency words						
B.O.	100	80	20			
Controls			98	90	63	23
Low-frequency words						
B.O.	100	40	20			
Controls			98	82	50	21

In the *lexical-decision* test, the experimenter read aloud a word or a minimally phonologically different nonword, and B.O.'s task was to indicate whether the item was a real English word. Her score for the forty items (twenty words and twenty nonwords) on this task was perfect.

Experiment 2: STM Span
In the second set of investigations, B.O.'s span was established for different types of stimuli.

In the *digit-span* task, the experimenter read digits aloud at the rate of one digit per second. After all the digits on a given trial had been presented, B.O. pointed sequentially on a response card to the digits she had heard. The digits 1 to 10 were printed in ascending order on the response card. Testing began at span size 2 and continued until she could not recall the items in the correct serial order on four of the five trials. B.O. recalled the digits in the correct serial order on four of five trials at span size 3 but on only one of five trials at span size 4. Thus, B.O.'s digit span was 3. On the four-digit sequences, she showed a primacy effect but not a recency effect.

B.O.'s *word span* for high- and low-frequency words was tested with both oral and visual presentations, because of specific predictions made by Baddeley's theory regarding the effect of particular deficits in components of a working memory system on written-list recall performances. Previous testing had established good single-word reading capacities in B.O. Items were presented at the rate of one per second. Table 5.32 shows the percentage of trials correct with oral presentation at each of the span sizes from 2 to 7 for B.O. and the twelve control subjects. If span sizes at which subjects performed correctly on at least 60% of the trials are considered to be within the subject's memory span, then B.O.'s memory span was 3 for high-frequency words and 2 for low-frequency words. The control subjects had a span of 6 for high-frequency words and 5 for low-frequency words.

Table 5.33
Percentage of trials correct on memory-span task (print presentation).

	Span size					
	2	3	4	5	6	7
High-frequency words						
B.O.	100	20	20			
Controls			92	84	58	40
Low-frequency words						
B.O.	60	40	0			
Controls			95	62	40	31

Table 5.34
Percentage of trials correct on phonologically similar and dissimilar words (oral presentation).

	Span size					
	2	3	4	5	6	7
Patient B.O.						
Phonologically similar	60	40	0			
Phonologically dissimilar	100	60	0			
Controls						
Phonologically similar			66	46	24	
Phonologically dissimilar			98	86	70	

The data from the visual-presentation condition are shown in table 5.33. B.O.'s memory span was 2 for both high- and low-frequency words in print; that of the control subjects was 5.

Experiment 3: Effects of Phonological Similarity and Word Length on STM
Baddeley's theory specifies that the phonological-similarity effect found with auditorily presented lists (span decreases if monosyllabic items in a list rhyme) is due to confusion of items in the "phonological store," whereas the occurrence of this effect with visually presented stimuli and the presence of a word-length effect with both auditorily and visually presented lists (span is reduced when items have more or longer syllables) are due to the effects of subvocal rehearsal in the articulatory loop. We therefore tested B.O. for these effects.

Our test of the phonological-similarity effect examined B.O.'s memory span for phonologically similar and dissimilar words with both oral and print presentation. Table 5.34 gives the data for B.O. and the control subjects on this task for oral presentation; table 5.35 gives the data for print

Table 5.35
Percentage of trials correct on phonologically similar and dissimilar words (print presentation).

	Span size					
	2	3	4	5	6	7
Patient B.O.						
Phonologically similar	60	60	0			
Phonologically dissimilar	60	20	0			
Controls						
Phonologically similar			68	40	22	
Phonologically dissimilar			95	68	38	

Table 5.36
Percentage of trials correct on phonologically similar and dissimilar letters (print presentation).

	Span size					
	2	3	4	5	6	7
Patient B.O.						
Phonologically similar	100	50				
Phonologically dissimilar	100	12				
Controls						
Phonologically similar			94	56	45	
Phonologically dissimilar			95	82	59	

presentation. The performance of the control subjects was better with dissimilar than with similar sequences for both oral and print presentation, but B.O. showed this effect only when the items were presented orally. This finding suggests that B.O. does not subvocalize the items to be remembered. We replicated this finding with a second set of stimulus materials, which consisted of phonologically similar (P,D,B,T,C,V) and dissimilar (R,X,K,F,Z,W) letters. The data obtained with these materials are given in table 5.36. Again, unlike the control subjects, B.O. did not do better on phonologically dissimilar items with visual presentation.

Our procedure for testing the word-length effect was identical to that for the phonological-similarity effect with the exception that the stimuli consisted of short and long rather than phonologically similar and dissimilar words. The results are presented in tables 5.37 and 5.38. B.O. did not show a clear advantage for short words on this task with either oral or

Table 5.37
Percentage of trials correct on short and long words (oral presentation).

	Span size				
	2	3	4	5	6
Patient B.O.					
Short words	100	0	0		
Long words	100	80	20		
Controls					
Short words			100	72	58
Long words			90	60	22

Table 5.38
Percentage of trials correct on short and long words (print presentation).

	Span size				
	2	3	4	5	6
Patient B.O.					
Short words	60	0	0		
Long words	40	0	0		
Controls					
Short words			82	45	28
Long words			80	33	11

print presentation. The control subjects did, however, show a word-length effect.

These results are consistent with B.O.'s having an impairment in the articulatory loop (AL), according to Baddeley's theory of working memory. The articulatory loop is said to be critical in creating the length effect in list recall with both visual and oral presentation and in creating the phonological-similarity effect with visual presentation. That B.O. showed neither of these effects is consistent with an abnormality in the AL. On the other hand, the AL is not thought to be involved in creating the phonological-similarity effect normally seen with auditorily presented lists, since these stimuli are thought to enter the phonological store (PS) directly. That B.O. showed this effect indicates normal functioning of this aspect of the PS. The location of B.O.'s functional deficit in the articulatory loop is also consistent with her apraxia of speech, which leads to a very reduced articulatory rate. Thus, this case is consistent with the theory of working memory developed by Baddeley (see, e.g., Vallar and Baddeley 1984a), and

B.O.'s short-term-memory impairment can be located within a component of the memory system postulated in this theory.

Assessment of Syntactic Comprehension

B.O.'s syntactic comprehension was tested on the first four batteries and on half of the fifth battery between May 1 and June 12, 1985 (3 years after onset). The results are given in tables 5.39–5.43.

In spite of her poor short-term-memory span, B.O.'s sentence comprehension was remarkably good. Her mean score on each battery ranged from 68% to 89%. All other patients whose digit spans were lower than 6 had considerably more severe syntactic problems, as the reports on A.B. and C.V. illustrate.

A striking thing about B.O.'s pattern of results is her good performance on some sentence types that the performance of other subjects and the group data in chapter 4 have shown to be difficult. Whereas aphasic patients tend to have more difficulty with relative-clause sentences when the empty NP is in object position (types 23 and 25), B.O. performed at the same level on all types of relative clauses on the first battery (table 5.39). Whereas aphasic patients tend to do better on sentences with a canonical order of thematic-role assignment (i.e., sentences in which Agent, Theme, and Goal are assigned to the first, second, and third nouns, such as *The goat gave the elephant to the monkey*), B.O. performed below normal on such sentences. And whereas aphasic patients can be expected to perform more poorly on dative passive sentences (type 28) and dative cleft-object sentences (type 22) than on dative active sentences (type 2), B.O. performed with equal accuracy on all three types.

On the second battery (table 5.40), B.O. had some difficulty with structures that other cases reported here have shown to be difficult, namely subject-control sentences (type 17) and NP-raising sentences (type 32). However, B.O. showed some unpredicted patterns of performance. She performed significantly worse on sentences with no empty NP (type 4) than on sentences containing reflexives (type 10). Also, for two matched pairs of sentence types, she performed better on sentences containing a complex NP (types 7 and 14) than on matched sentences with a simple NP (types 6 and 13).

B.O.'s good performance on sentences with complex NPs appears to be due to a preference to select as Agent the noun with semantic content (*friend*). This preference is also revealed by her errors on a sentence type for which the choice of *friend* as Agent is not the correct answer: the NP-raising sentences on the third battery (*Patrick appears to a friend of Joe's to be eating*, type 33, table 5.41). For this sentence type, four of her five errors involved selecting *friend* to be Agent.

B.O.'s good performance on sentence types for which *friend* was the

Table 5.39
Results from first syntactic-comprehension battery, patient B.O.

	Correct		Incorrect		χ^2 values, Stage II assumptions
One-verb sentences					
[01] The bear kissed the donkey. (two-place active)	1, 2	100%			$(E = 6, \text{d.f.} = 1,$ $\chi^2 = 12.00, p < 0.001^*)$
[27] The bear was kissed by the donkey. (two-place passive)	2, 1	92%	1, 2	8%	$(E = 6, \text{d.f.} = 1,$ $\chi^2 = 8.34, p < 0.01^*)$
[21] It was the bear that the donkey kissed. (two-place cleft-object)	2, 1	100%			$(E = 6, \text{d.f.} = 1,$ $\chi^2 = 12.00, p < 0.001^*)$
[02] The bear gave the donkey to the goat. (dative active)	1, 2, 3	75%	2, 1, 3	25%	$(E = 2, \text{d.f.} = 5,$ $\chi^2 = 33.00, p < 0.001^*)$
[28] The bear was given to the donkey by the goat. (dative passive)	3, 1, 2	83%	3, 2, 1	17%	$(E = 2, \text{d.f.} = 5,$ $\chi^2 = 40.00, p < 0.001^*)$
[22] It was the bear that the donkey gave to the goat. (dative cleft-object)	2, 1, 3	75%	1, 3, 2 3, 1, 2 3, 2, 1	8% 8% 8%	$(E = 2, \text{d.f.} = 5,$ $\chi^2 = 30.00, p < 0.001^*)$
Two-verb sentences					
[03] The bear kissed the donkey and the goat. (conjoined)	1, 2; 1, 3	100%			$(E = 0.33, \text{d.f.} = 35,$ $\chi^2 = 424.24, p < 0.001^*)$
[23] The bear that the donkey kissed patted the goat. (subject-object)	2, 1; 1, 3	75%	1, 2; 1, 3 2, 3; 1, 2	17% 8%	$(E = 0.33, \text{d.f.} = 35,$ $\chi^2 = 248.48, p < 0.001^*)$

[24] The bear kissed the donkey that patted the goat. (object-subject)	1,2;2,3	67%	2,1;3,1	8%
			1,3;3,2	8%
			1,2;1,3	8%
			1,2;3,2	8%
			$(E = 0.33$, d.f. $= 35$, $\chi^2 = 193.94$, $p < 0.001^*$)	
[25] The bear kissed the donkey that the goat patted. (object-object)	1,2;3,2	83%	1,2;2,3	8%
			2,3;1,2	8%
			$(E = 0.33$, d.f. $= 35$, $\chi^2 = 296.97$, $p < 0.001^*$)	
[26] The bear that kissed the donkey patted the goat. (subject-subject)	1,2;1,3	92%	1,2;2,3	8%
			$(E = 0.33$, d.f. $= 35$, $\chi^2 = 357.58$, $p < 0.001^*$)	

Table 5.40
Results from second battery, patient B.O.

	Correct		Incorrect		
[06] John said that Bill kicked him.	2V1	58%	1V2 XV1	8% 33%	(Stage I: $E = 0.75$, d.f. $= 9$, $\chi^2 = 65.33$, $p < 0.001$*)
[07] John said that a friend of Bill's kicked him.	2V1 2V3 2VX	67% 25% 8%			(Stage I: $E = 0.75$, d.f. $= 15$, $\chi^2 = 86.66$, $p < 0.001$*)
[10] John said that Bill kicked himself.	2V2	100%			(Stage II: $E = 3$, d.f. $= 3$, $\chi^2 = 36.00$, $p < 0.001$*)
[11] John said that a friend of Bill's kicked himself.	2V2	100%			(Stage II: $E = 1.3$, d.f. $= 8$, $\chi^2 = 98.47$, $p < 0.001$*)
[04] John said that Bill kicked Eddie.	2V3	42%	3V2 1VX 1V3	42% 8% 8%	(Stage I: $E = 0.75$, d.f. $= 15$, $\chi^2 = 57.32$, $p < 0.001$*)
[13] Patrick persuaded Joe to wash. (object control)	2V	83%	1V XV	8% 8%	(Stage I: $E = 3$, d.f. $= 2$, $\chi^2 = 21.83$, $p < 0.001$*)
[14] Patrick persuaded a friend of Joe's to wash. (object control, complex NP)	2V	100%			(Stage II: $E = 4$, d.f. $= 2$, $\chi^2 = 24.00$, $p < 0.001$*)
[17] Patrick promised Joe to wash. (subject control)	1V	58%	2V XV XV1	17% 17% 8%	(Stage I: $E = 3$, d.f. $= 2$, $\chi^2 = 8.33$, $p < 0.02$*)
[32] Patrick seems to Joe to be praying. (NP-raising)	1V	67%	2V XV	25% 8%	(Stage I: $E = 3$, d.f. $= 2$, $\chi^2 = 12.50$, $p < 0.01$*)

Table 5.41
Results from third battery, patient B.O.

	Correct		Incorrect		
[18] Patrick vowed to Joe to pray. (subject control)	1V	100%			(Stage II: $E = 6$, d.f. $= 1$, $\chi^2 = 12.00$, $p < 0.001^*$)
[08] Patrick promised Joe that he would kneel. (overt pronoun embedded subject)	1V 2V XV	75% 17% 8%			(Stage I: $E = 3$, d.f. $= 2$, $\chi^2 = 16.50$, $p < 0.001^*$)
[05] Patrick expected a friend of Joe's to be praying. ($\bar{S}$ deletion, complex NP object)	2V	100%			(Stage II: $E = 4$, d.f. $= 2$, $\chi^2 = 24.00$, $p < 0.001^*$)
[29] Patrick was believed by Joe to be eating. (passivized $\bar{S}$ deletion)	1V	92%	2V	8%	(Stage II: $E = 6$, d.f. $= 1$, $\chi^2 = 8.34$, $p < 0.01^*$)
[30] Patrick was told by Joe to run. (passivized object control)	1V	83%	2V XV	8% 8%	(Stage I: $E = 3$, d.f. $= 2$, $\chi^2 = 21.83$, $p < 0.001^*$)
[33] Patrick appears to a friend of Joe's to be eating. (NP-raising, complex postverbal NP)	1V	58%	2V 3V	33% 8%	(Stage II: $E = 4$, d.f. $= 2$, $\chi^2 = 4.50$, $p < 0.20$)

Table 5.42
Results from fourth battery, patient B.O.

	Correct		Incorrect		Statistics
[12] Patrick told Joe that Eddie had scratched himself. (baseline: finite embedded clause, 3 NPs + reflexive)	3V3	67%	1V1 2V2 2V3	17% 8% 8%	(Stage II: $E = 1.3$, d.f. $= 8$, $\chi^2 = 41.55$, $p < 0.001^*$)
[09] Patrick persuaded Joe that Eddie had patted him. (baseline: finite embedded clause, 3 NPs + pronoun)	3V1 3V2	42% 33%	3V3 2V1 2V3	8% 8% 8%	(Stage II: $E = 1.3$, d.f. $= 8$, $\chi^2 = 21.55$, $p < 0.01^*$)
[19] Patrick promised Joe to hit himself. (subject control, reflexive embedded object)	1V1	75%	2V2 XVX	17% 8%	(Stage I: $E = 0.75$, d.f. $= 9$, $\chi^2 = 102.00$, $p < 0.001^*$)
[20] Patrick promised Joe to cover him. (subject control, pronominal embedded object)	1V2 1VX	50% 17%	1V1 2V1 XV2	17% 8% 8%	(Stage I: $E = 0.75$, d.f. $= 9$, $\chi^2 = 46.00$, $p < 0.001^*$)
[15] Patrick asked Joe to pinch himself. (object control, reflexive embedded object)	2V2	75%	1V1 XVX	8% 17%	(Stage I: $E = 0.75$, d.f. $= 9$, $\chi^2 = 100.00$, $p < 0.001^*$)
[16] Patrick allowed Joe to hit him. (object control, pronominal embedded object)	2V1	50%	2V2 XV1 1V2	8% 25% 17%	(Stage I: $E = 0.75$, d.f. $= 9$, $\chi^2 = 48.66$, $p < 0.001^*$)
[34] Patrick seems to Joe to have kicked himself. (NP-raising, reflexive embedded object)	1V1	67%	2V2	33%	(restricted Stage II: $E = 3$, d.f. $= 3$, $\chi^2 = 14.66$, $p < 0.01^*$)
[31] Patrick was believed by Joe to have kicked himself. (passivized $\bar{S}$ deletion, reflexive embedded object)	1V1	67%	2V2 XVX	8% 25%	(Stage I: $E = 0.75$, d.f. $= 9$, $\chi^2 = 80.66$, $p < 0.001^*$)

Table 5.43
Results from fifth (baseline) battery (first half), patient B.O.

	Correct		Incorrect	
[40] John kicked him.	1VX	4/6	XVY	2/6
[41] A friend of John's kicked him.	1V2	5/6		
	1VX	1/6		
[42] John's friend kicked him.	2V1	6/6		
[37] John kicked himself.	1V1	6/6		
[38] A friend of John's kicked himself.	1V1	6/6		
[39] John's friend kicked himself.	2V2	6/6		
[35] A friend of John's kicked Bill.	1V3	6/6		
[36] John hit Bill's friend.	1V3	5/6	2V3	1/6

correct answer follows from a more general finding of better performance on sentences containing nouns with semantic content than on sentences containing proper nouns. Her lowest score on all of the sentence types tested was that for structures with three proper nouns (*John said that Bill kicked Eddie*, type 4). Also, she did somewhat better on sentences with three animal names (e.g., *The monkey gave the elephant to the frog*, type 2; *The monkey that kissed the elephant scratched the frog*, type 26) than on sentences with three proper nouns (*Patrick said that Joe kicked Eddie*, type 4).

This pattern suggests that B.O.'s difficulty lies not in parsing a sentence but in holding proper nouns in memory after a sentence has been parsed. If this difficulty with proper nouns were occurring at a syntactic level, B.O. would be expected to have much more difficulty achieving the correct parse, and hence would be expected to show effects of syntactic complexity. Since she did not show such effects, we hypothesize that she has difficulty maintaining proper nouns with the correct thematic-role assignment at the level of the propositional list, or that she errs in transferring the thematic roles from arguments in the proposition to actual referents in the array in the process of acting out the sentence.

These observations and this account of B.O.'s deficit are reflected in the correlations between different features of the stimulus sentences and B.O.'s error rate on each sentence type. B.O. showed no significant correlation between the number of words in a sentence and her error rate ($r = 0.13$, $p > 0.20$). Likewise, correlations between the number of words in the sentence and her error rate did not reach significance when the sentences were divided into those with an empty NP ($r = -0.03$, $p > 0.20$) and those without an empty NP ($r = 0.07$, $p > 0.20$). Thus, in spite of a severe imitation on her short-term-memory span, B.O. was able to assign the correct structure to long sentences, even sentences containing empty NPs that have proved difficult for other patients. On the other hand, there was a significant correlation between number of NPs (overt and empty) in a sentence and the error rate ($r = 0.33$, $p < 0.05$). The correlation between number of proper nouns mentioned in a sentence and error rate is even stronger than the correlation between total number of NPs and the error rate, at 0.59 (df = 27; $p < 0.001$). This fact lends further support to the claim that B.O. has difficulty with NPs in general and with proper nouns in particular, and is consistent with the hypothesis that B.O.'s deficit arises from a difficulty with holding NPs in memory rather than from one with the assignment of syntactic structure.

An analysis of B.O.'s errors provides another line of evidence that her deficit arises at a postsyntactic level. The errors are mainly of two types. The first involves reversals of the two thematic roles to be acted out in applicable sentences. In other words, the correct dolls are chosen, but the doll that should be Theme is incorrectly taken to be Agent and the correct Agent is incorrectly taken to be Theme. Reversals are possible in sentences with transitive verbs and without reflexive objects. In these sentence types, reversals accounted for 44% of the errors (11 of 25 instances). This type of error is consistent with the analysis that B.O. assigns thematic roles correctly during the syntactic parse and later forgets which NP was assigned which thematic role. The second type of error involves the incorrect choice of a doll not mentioned in the sentence to act out the response. Patients J.V. and K.G. consistently chose only among the dolls mentioned in the sentence, but more than one-third of B.O.'s errors on the last four batteries (25 of 67 instances) involved the incorrect assignment of thematic roles to dolls not mentioned in the sentence. Moreover, these mistaken assignments nearly always involved a doll labeled with a proper name rather than the "friend." Conversely, for sentences containing the NP *a friend*, B.O. almost never erroneously selected a doll not mentioned. For the eight sentence types with transitive embedded verbs without reflexive objects, in which both error types (reversal and incorrect assignment of a thematic role to an object not mentioned in the sentence) are possible, these two types of errors accounted for 80% of the total errors (20 of 25 instances). These two error types provide evidence that B.O. cannot hold proper nouns in memory and cannot retain the thematic roles assigned to particular proper nouns.

This analysis generates a verifiable prediction based on the Berwick-Weinberg parser's distinction between finding antecedents for reflexives and pronouns: If B.O. has no syntactic deficit, then she should have little difficulty looking back over the parse tree to choose the nearest c-commanding NP, and therefore she should do well on sentences with reflexives. However, to find the antecedent for the pronoun would require

Table 5.44
Comparative accuracy on matched sentences with both proper nouns and reflexives or pronouns, patient B.O.

[37] John kicked himself.	1V1	100%		
[40] John kicked him.	1VX	83%	XVY	17%
[10] John said that Bill kicked himself.	2V2	100%		
[06] John said that Bill kicked him.	2V1	58%	1V2	8%
			XV1	33%
[15] Patrick asked Joe to pinch himself.	2V2	75%	1V1	8%
(object control, reflexive embedded object)			XVX	17%
[16] Patrick allowed Joe to hit him.	2V1	50%	2V2	8%
(object control, pronominal embedded object)			XV1	25%
			1V2	17%
[19] Patrick promised Joe to hit himself.	1V1	75%	2V2	17%
(subject control, reflexive embedded object)			XVX	8%
[20] Patrick promised Joe to cover him.	1V2	50%	1V1	17%
(subject control, pronominal embedded object)	1VX	17%	2V1	8%
			XV2	8%
[12] Patrick told Joe that Eddie had scratched himself.	3V3	67%	1V1	17%
(baseline: finite embedded clause, 3 NPs + reflexive)			2V2	8%
			2V3	8%
[09] Patrick persuaded Joe that Eddie had patted him.	3V1	42%	3V3	8%
(baseline: finite embedded clause, 3 NPs + pronoun)	3V2	33%	2V1	8%
			2V3	8%

searching for an NP at the postsyntactic level of the propositional list. Therefore, sentences with pronouns should be more difficult for B.O. than sentences with reflexives.

The data are consistent with this prediction. As mentioned above, B.O. consistently assigns a reflexive or a disjoint interpretation to reflexives and pronouns, respectively, showing that there is no impairment in her lexical knowledge of pronouns and reflexives. For three sentence types with the complex NP *a friend of X's*, B.O. performed perfectly on both sentences with reflexives and sentences with pronouns; because of her good performance on NPs with semantic content, as described above, these three types were removed from the analysis. Her performances on five other matched pairs of sentences containing only proper nouns (not *a friend*) plus the reflexive or pronoun are compared in table 5.44. B.O.'s performance on sentences with a reflexive were more accurate on average (83%) than her performances on their counterparts with a pronoun (63%). Though this difference was significant in only one case (type 6 versus type 10, *John said that Bill kicked himself/him*), the direction of the difference was the same with four of the five contrasting structures. The exceptional pair of structures contained three proper nouns plus a reflexive or a pronoun (*Patrick told Joe that Eddie had hit himself/him*; types 9 versus 12), on which B.O. scored 8% higher on the sentences with the pronoun (a difference which is not significant). B.O. would be expected to have some difficulty with *Patrick told Joe that Eddie had hit himself* and *Patrick told Joe that Eddie had hit him* because they each contain three proper nouns; thus, it may be that B.O.'s difficulty with proper nouns is masking a difficulty with pronouns relative to reflexives in this one sentence type.

In conclusion: Several lines of evidence suggest that B.O.'s sentence-comprehension difficulties are attributable to a difficulty with holding NPs—particularly proper nouns—in memory at a postsyntactic level. First, B.O.'s ability to assign a correct parse tree to the sentences that she hears is shown by her good overall performance and by the lack of sentence-complexity effects upon accuracy. Second, the correlation between the number of proper nouns in a sentence and the error rate suggests a problem related to memory for proper nouns. Third, B.O.'s errors largely consist of incorrect selections of dolls with proper names (despite excellent single-item selection performance) and of reversals of thematic roles between two dolls with proper names. These errors are consistent with a difficulty in retaining or retrieving proper nouns associated with thematic roles. Finally, when floor and ceiling effects are eliminated, B.O. can be seen to have more difficulty with sentences having pronouns than with sentences having reflexives. This is consistent with a postsyntactic deficit in a parser in which pronouns are coindexed in a postsyntactic propositional list and reflexives at the syntactic level.

This analysis not only accounts for B.O.'s performance but also leads to a consistent picture of the determinants of parsing complexity seen in the performances of our other subjects. For instance, at first glance it appears that B.O.'s pattern of results falsifies the hypothesis that empty NPs are more difficult to parse than overt NPs, which is otherwise verified. However, if B.O. does not suffer from any impairment in her ability to assign syntactic structure but rather from a post-parsing limitation on the ability to hold NPs in memory, then her poorer performance on sentences containing R-expressions results from a post-parsing deficit and has no bearing on the relative complexity of parsing empty and lexical NPs. This case thus documents the independence of parsing from short-term-memory functions and indicates that short-term-memory limitations can affect post-interpretive stages of the processing of propositional content.

Discussion

Of the nine cases presented in this chapter, eight have been analyzed as involving disorders that affect parsing operations or syntactic representations—that is, as occurring at the syntactic level of sentence processing. We generally refer to these as impairments of *parsing*, by which term we mean the operations described by Berwick and Weinberg that complete constituents before transferring them to the propositional list. These operations assign coreference to all [−pronominal] NPs and label each NP—overt or empty—as receiving a theta role from a predicate, either by direct assignment or by linking. Operations involving the propositional list (e.g., the assignment of coreference to [−pronominal] elements and thematic roles to NPs) are not considered parsing processes. Such operations are affected in at least one of our subjects (C.V.) and may be involved in other cases as well, depending on whether obligatory-control PRO is considered to be [+pronominal] or [−pronominal] (see above and chapter 6). However, in all our subjects except B.O., even if there is a problem in coindexation of items in the propositional list there is also a disturbance of parsing. In the case of our subject B.O. we have argued that no disturbance affecting parsing exists, but that there is some impairment in the ability to maintain NPs (especially proper nouns) in the propositional list along with their thematic roles.

The eight patients we have analyzed as having parsing deficits show patterns of syntactic comprehension attributable to disturbances affecting particular parsing operations, particular linguistic representations, and combinations of particular parsing operations. It is for these reasons that we attribute disturbances in parsing functions to these patients. It has been suggested to us that ours is an inadequate database upon which to found a deficit analysis claiming that a parsing disturbance exists because the task of comprehension cannot by itself establish a parsing impairment, as opposed to an interpretive impairment. On this view, poor performance on a grammaticality-judgment task is required to document a parsing disturbance. We disagree strongly with this argument. First, as we have indicated in our discussion of the results of Linebarger et al. (1983a), good performance on the grammaticality-judgment task does not guarantee that a parser is operating normally. We argued in that, if a patient is sensitive to lexical information about theta roles associated with a predicate, he can reject sentences with extra NPs that have not been assigned thematic roles and sentences in which not enough NPs are present to complete the theta grid without constructing a great deal of syntactic structure. For instance, though Linebarger et al. (1983a) take good performance on stimuli such as (39) and (40) to indicate sensitivity to displaced constituents, such performance may result from the appreciation that there are too many NPs in the sentence for the number of theta roles the verb has to assign, without any appreciation of displacement of constituents (or their hierarchical organization).

(39) How many did you see birds in the park?
(40) The cake that the boy ate the pie was good.

Without a detailed set of observations converging on the syntactic structures which must be the basis for an entire pattern of grammaticality judgments in a patient, good performance on grammaticality judgments in general is uninterpretable with respect to what aspects of parsing are retained. It is simplistic to consider that "parsing" is tested in grammaticality-judgment tasks and "interpretation" in comprehension tasks.

The patterns of comprehension we have presented here require description and explanation, and we have described and (to some extent) explained them by postulating deficits in parsing processes. We have taken great pains to distinguish parsing from post-parsing processes, by reference to linguistic and parsing theories. We cannot find any operations in post-parsing parts of the sentence-interpretation system that could be disturbed to yield the patterns of performance seen in these eight cases. What disturbance affecting representations in the propositional list would disrupt comprehension of NP(seems)-raising sentences but not subject-control sentences in patient J.V. and vice versa in patient G.S.? Disturbances affecting NPs in the propositional list would not be expected to be sensitive to syntactic structures, since these are not maintained in that level of representation. However, they would be expected to be sensitive to factors such as the number of nouns and the semantic content of nouns, as was observed in patient B.O. It is the entirety of a patient's performance on large sets of theoretically focused sentence types (including the types of errors he makes) that, in relation to well-defined theories of parsing and post-parsing operations specifying what representations are available at each of these processing stages, allows us to ascribe a deficit to the parsing, the post-parsing, or the pre-parsing stage of sentence processing—not simply the overall level of a patient's performance on a "comprehension" task, a grammaticality-judgment task, or any other task.

With these considerations in mind, we now turn to the empirical predictions made by the hypotheses enunciated at the outset of this chapter.

Hypothesis 1: Empty NPs Are More Difficult to Construct than Overt NPs
The empirical prediction from the first hypothesis is that whenever there is a dissociation in matched sentence types, it is the sentence with the empty NP that will be more difficult. This prediction can be examined from two perspectives: the total pattern of dissociations shown by particular patients

and the direction of dissociations shown on specific matched sentence types. It is supported both between and within cases.

Four of the eight patients analyzed as having deficits in syntactic comprehension—J.V., G.G., K.G., and G.S.—showed relatively good comprehension overall, with selective difficulties on particular sentence types containing empty NPs. The other four patients who showed deficits in syntactic comprehension were more severely impaired; they had difficulty with several aspects of assigning syntactic structure and coreference. In each of these cases, certain sentence types with empty NPs were the most severely impaired, with either very poor or random performance on at least some sentence types with empty NPs. Thus, the eight cases of syntactic-comprehension deficit, considered together, support the hypothesis that at least certain types of empty NPs are more difficult to parse than overt NPs.

To further test the hypothesis that empty NPs are more difficult than overt NPs, we made specific comparisons among matched sentence types for each of the eight patients showing a deficit at the syntactic level. The specific prediction from the first hypothesis is that no sentence type with an empty NP should be significantly higher in accuracy than any matched sentence type without an empty NP. In some cases, performance on the sentence type with an empty NP is predicted to be significantly worse than performance on the matched sentence type without an empty NP.

Comparison 1: Embedded Clauses with Intransitive Verbs
The test batteries contained a set of sentences with the surface order Noun-Verb-Noun-Infinitival verb, so that a comparison could be made between sentences with empty NPs and sentences without empty NPs among sentences matched for number of words and order of occurrence of nouns and verbs. In a sentence without an empty NP, such as *John believes Joe to be shaving*, the postverbal noun *Joe* lies in the embedded-subject position. In a sentence with an empty NP, the postverbal noun is analyzed as part of the main clause, and the empty NP lies in embedded-subject position. For these sentences, either the postverbal noun or the subject noun of the main clause is the correct antecedent, depending on the sentence type.

There is an additional complication in the comparison, due to the potential effects of the use of heuristics. In our individual case studies, the most common error involved choosing the noun nearest the verb as Agent. Thus, if a sentence such as *John believes Bill to be shaving* is correct, it is difficult to know whether a patient assigned the correct structure to the sentence or whether the patient arrived at the correct answer fortuitously because of a nonlinguistic strategy of assigning Agent to the nearest NP. In order to eliminate this possibility, we chose a structure with a complex NP—*John believes a friend of Bill's to be shaving*—as the baseline sentence. A patient who was assigning Agent to the nearest NP would respond incorrectly on this type as well as on sentences such as *John persuaded a friend of Bill's to shave* (type 14). Hence, all the sentence types to be compared (with the exception of object control, type 13) involve either assigning Agent to the head of a complex NP or coindexing the embedded subject NP with the matrix subject; both operations must occur over an intervening NP.

The comparisons, for the six patients who were tested on these structures, are shown in table 5.45. The probability of occurrence of a particular response as a result of a random assignment of Agent to any of the overt nouns mentioned in the sentence is included for each sentence type.

In spite of the potentially increased complexity due to the complex NP, the baseline structure *John believed a friend of Bill's to be jumping* (type 5) was interpreted nearly perfectly by every patient tested. No sentence type with an empty NP could be significantly more accurate than this structure. On the other hand, at least one structure for every patient was significantly lower in accuracy than the baseline structure on the test of the significance of the difference between independent proportions (see Methodology section). In general, the sentence types with empty NPs coindexed with matrix subject positions (types 17, 32, 33) dissociated from the sentence type without an empty NP (type 5), as well as from the sentence types with empty NPs coindexed with the matrix object (types 13 and 14).

For the matched structures in table 5.45, the most meaningful comparison to show that *all* sentences with empty NPs are more difficult is the matched comparison between object control with a complex NP (type 14) and $\bar{S}$ deletion with a complex NP (type 5), since in both cases the referent of the postverbal NP must be chosen to act out the Agent of the intransitive verb. Patient C.V. shows a significant dissociation between object-control and $\bar{S}$-deletion structures. However, it must be noted in this particular case that the baseline structure was administered in the second testing session, a year after the object-control sentences were tested. In the second testing session C.V. developed a tendency to choose *friend* as the Agent, so she might have improved her accuracy on object-control structures with complex NPs had she been tested on them in the second testing session. Therefore, it must be concluded that no evidence for distinguishing object-control structures from $\bar{S}$-deletion structures was found in the initial data.

Comparison 2: Embedded Clauses with Transitive Verbs Plus an Overt Referential Dependency

A second matched comparison was made between sentence types with a surface order of Noun-Verb-Noun-Infinitival verb-Noun. The final noun was either a reflexive or a pronoun, such as in the sentence *John ordered Bill to cover himself/him*. These comparisons are valuable because they show

Table 5.45
Aphasic patients' scores on matched structures with and without empty NPs (embedded clauses with intransitive verbs and complex NPs).

| | Patient | | | | | | Chance |
	J.V.	G.G.	K.G.	G.S.	A.B.	C.V.	
[+ empty NP]							
[13] Object control: Patrick persuaded Eddie to dance.	100%	100%	100%	92%	100%	83%	50%
[14] Object control, complex NP object: Patrick persuaded a friend of Eddie's to dance.	100%	100%	100%	—	50%	42%*	33%
[17] Subject control: Patrick promised Eddie to dance.	100%	17%*	75%	50%	33%	25%*	50%
[32] NP-raising: Patrick seems to Eddie to be dancing.	25%*	0%*	33%*	92%	42%	42%*	50%
[33] NP-raising, complex postverbal NP: Patrick seems to a friend of Eddie's to be dancing.	67%	83%	17%*	—	—	0%*	33%
[− empty NP]							
[05] S̄ deletion, complex object NP: Patrick believes a friend of Eddie's to be dancing.	92%	92%	92%	—	—	92%	33%

* Score is significantly below that of type 5 (SDTIP, $p < 0.05$).

whether the prediction is verified when the baseline sentences become longer and more difficult with the addition of the transitive action as well as an overt referential dependency. The results for these sentences are listed in table 5.46 for each patient tested on these sentence types. Sentences with reflexives and those with pronouns are considered separately, since for the pronoun sentences it is possible to choose an antecedent not mentioned in the sentence, and thus the set of possible responses is larger and cannot be compared statistically. For reflexives, the probability of the chance occurrence of a particular response is calculated as a function of the possible responses involving the nouns mentioned in the sentence. For pronouns, the set of possible responses also includes the correct response, in which the pronoun refers to a doll not mentioned in the sentence. The probability of chance occurrence of each response is listed in table 5.46 for each sentence type.

For this set of sentence types, only patient K.G. showed significantly lower accuracy on the sentence types with an empty NP than on those without one. On the other hand, even though for some patients the scores on the baseline sentences were low enough to allow significantly higher scores to occur among the sentences with empty NPs, no such scores occurred. Thus, the data from our patients are again consistent with the prediction that empty NPs are more difficult to parse than overt NPs; however, only the sentences in which the antecedent for the empty NP lies in matrix *subject* position showed a dissociation from the comparison sentence.

Comparison 3: Relative-Clause and Conjoined Sentences
The four types of relative-clause sentences tested on the first battery can be compared with the conjoined sentences, which have no empty NP. Each patient's accuracy on these sentence types is given in table 5.47. The expected random frequency of occurrence of any particular response is 3%.

For the relative-clause and conjoined sentences, a dissociation in accuracy in the predicted direction appears for five of the eight patients who showed impairments at the syntactic level. C.V. presents the first contradiction to the predicted direction of dissociation; her score on object-subject relatives is significantly higher than her score on conjoined sentences. However, C.V. used a strategy that happened to result in the correct answer for object-subject relatives and the incorrect answer on all other sentences with two verbs. Since this is a nonlinguistic strategy, the data on C.V. are not taken as evidence against a prediction about difficulty in assigning structure. By the same token, patient A.B. happened to perform well on subject-subject relatives and conjoined sentences and poorly on all other types of relative-clause sentences, but this was probably due to his use of a nonsyntactic strategy. Similarly, G.S. showed better performance

Table 5.46
Aphasic patients' scores on matched structures with and without empty NPs (structures with two referential dependencies).

Sentence type	Patient					Chance
	J.V.	G.G.	K.G.	A.B.	C.V.	
[+empty NP, +reflexive]						
[15] Object control Patrick persuaded Eddie to kick himself.	100%	100%	83%	—	50%	25%
[19] Subject control Patrick promised Eddie to kick himself.	92%	75%	33%*	—	33%	25%
[31] Passivized $\overline{S}$ deletion Patrick was believed by Eddie to be kicking himself.	58%	75%	33%*	—	17%	25%
[34] NP-raising Patrick seems to Eddie to be kicking himself.	75%	92%	33%*	—	17%	25%
[−empty NP, +reflexive]						
[12] Three R-expressions Patrick told Joe that Eddie had kicked himself.	92%	100%	100%	—	50%	11%
[+empty NP, +pronoun]						
[16] Object control Patrick persuaded Eddie to kick him.	92%	92%	83%	—	8%	20%
[20] Subject control Patrick promised Eddie to kick him.	92%	83%	58%	—	25%	20%
[−empty NP, +pronoun]						
[09] Three R-expressions Patrick told Joe that Eddie had kicked him.	100%	92%	75%	—	0%	10%

*Score is significantly below that of type 12 (SDTIP, $p < 0.05$)

Table 5.47
Aphasic patients' scores on matched structures with and without empty NPs (relative clauses versus conjoined sentences).

Sentence type	Patient								
	J.V.	G.G.	K.G.	G.S.	A.B.	C.V.	R.L.(1)	R.L.(2)	S.P.
[+ empty NP]									
[23] Subject-object relative The frog that the goat hit kissed the cow.	92%	100%	25%*	25%*	17%*	0%	20%* (2/10)	50% (5/10)	10%* (1/10)
[24] Object-subject relative The frog hit the goat that kissed the cow.	100%	100%	83%	64%	0%*	92%	70% (7/10)	60% (6/10)	54% (6/11)
[25] Object-object relative The frog hit the goat that the cow kissed.	100%	100%	58%	50%*	0%*	17%	80% (8/10)	100% (10/10)	67% (6/9)
[26] Subject-subject relative The frog that hit the goat kissed the cow.	92%	92%	83%	83%	83%	17%	50% (5/10)	80% (8/10)	50% (5/10)
[− empty NP]									
[03] Conjoined The frog hit the goat and kissed the cow.	100%	100%	92%	92%	75%	8%	80% (8/10)	90% (9/10)	60% (6/10)

*Score is significantly below that of type 3.

on sentences for which a 1,2;1,3 response was the correct answer, and this response also constituted his most common error pattern. Therefore, the dissociations in accuracy observed for these two patients are not taken as evidence in support of the prediction.

The significant dissociations among the remaining patients (K.G., R.L., and S.P.) cannot be so easily attributed to the use of a particular non-syntactic strategy, and these dissociations are therefore taken as evidence that a sentence with an empty NP is more difficult than the matched sentence without an empty NP. Once again it can be seen that only certain of the sentence types with empty NPs (specifically, object relatives) have shown a dissociation.

Comparison 4: PRO and Overt Pronouns
Our initial hypothesis entailed the prediction that sentences with PRO should be more difficult than sentences with overt pronouns. Both were hypothesized to require the same process of looking back through the propositional list for an appropriate antecedent, but PRO additionally requires the parser to seek and construct an empty NP. We have revised our parsing model on the basis of our data so that PRO is coindexed in the syntax in the obligatory-control structures we tested (see below). None-theless, we have compared the coindexation of these empty NPs with that of overt pronouns. Table 5.48 shows the breakdown of correct responses for sentences with pronouns in comparison with that for subject-control sentences (the only sentences with PRO that caused difficulty) for the patients who were tested on these structures. General comparisons in this case require consideration of the differences in number of possible responses and in number of correct answers. However, a few specific points can be made.

No patient who did well on subject-control sentences did poorly on the sentences with overt pronouns. J.V., the only patient who did not have any difficulty with subject-control sentences, also performed nearly perfectly on the sentences with pronouns. K.G., whose performance on pronouns was slightly below normal on sentences like *John said that Bill kicked him* (type 6), showed identical accuracy on sentences with subject control of PRO; in both types of sentences, the matrix subject is the antecedent. Two patients showed dissociations in the predicted direction: G.G. scored only 17% on subject-control sentences but scored perfectly on the type 6 pro-nominal sentences, and G.S. scored 50% on subject-control sentences but 92% on the pronominal sentences. (These sentence types cannot be directly compared statistically, but the chance probability of achieving the correct response is higher for the subject-control sentences, in contrast with the observed dissociation.) Therefore, the data are consistent with the hypo-thesis that empty NPs are more difficult to parse than overt NPs.

Table 5.48
Aphasic patients' scores on matched structures with and without empty NPs (structures with subject-control PRO versus structures with pronouns).

Sentence type		Patient					
		J.V.	G.G.	K.G.	G.S.	A.B.	C.V.
[17] Subject control John promised Bill to shave.	1V:	100%	17%	75%	50%	33%	25%
[6] Pronouns, simple NP John said that Bill hit him.	2V1:	92%	100%	83%	92%	75%	17%
	2VX:	0	0	0	0	8%	8%
[8] Embedded pronoun subject John promised Bill that he would shave.	1V:	83%	100%*	75%	—	—	58%*
	2V:	8%	0	25%			33%
	XV:	8%	0	0			8%
[7] Pronouns, complex NP John said that a friend of Bill's kicked him.	2V1:	83%	17%	58%	—	25%	25%
	2V3:	17%	83%	42%		25%	25%
	2VX:	0	0	0		8%	25%
[9] Three NPs plus pronoun John told Bill that Peter kicked him.	3V1:	100%	83%*	42%	—	—	0*
	3V2:	0	8%	33%			0
	3VX:	0	0	0			0

* second testing session

Summary
The initial evidence from eight cases is consistent with the hypothesis that sentences with empty NPs are more difficult to parse than sentences without empty NPs. Patients J.V., G.G., K.G., and G.S. provide evidence that particular structures from the total set of structures containing empty NPs can be selectively impaired, without a disturbance affecting sentences with pronouns or reflexives. Patients A.B. and C.V. document the co-occurrence of disturbances of overt and empty referentially dependent NPs. Investigation of specific matched sentence types reveals that significant dissociations in accuracy between matched structures with and without empty NPs are consistently in the direction of lower accuracy for the sentence with the empty NP. However, only certain types of structures showed dissociation both between and within subjects, namely subject-control structures, NP-raising structures, certain types of passive structures, and object-relative structures. The strongest dissociation between object-control structures and S̄-deletion structures, which would show that *all* structures with empty NPs are more difficult than structures without empty NPs, has not yet presented itself in the cases reported here.

Hypotheses 2 and 4: Some Empty NPs Are More Difficult to Construct and/or to Interpret Than Others
The data just reviewed indicate that not all syntactic structures containing empty NPs are equally difficult. There are two possible accounts for why subject-control structures, NP-raising structures, object-relative structures, and certain passive structures dissociated from the comparison structure without an empty NP, whereas object-control and subject-relative structures did not.

The first account is based on the observation that subject-control, NP-raising, and object-relative structures and certain passive structures share the property of being coindexed over an intervening NP and verb. This fact could be considered support for hypothesis 4, the hypothesis that "long-distance" coindexing is difficult and led to a decrease in accuracy on just these sentence types. However, this account is unappealing in two respects. First, "intervening NP" and "intervening verb" are *linear* notions that are not considered relevant at the syntactic level. A syntactic definition of distance should be stated in hierarchical terms, such as G.G.'s putative difficulty in coindexing over a sentence boundary. Second, difficulty with "long-distance" coindexing cannot be the deficit underlying every observed dissociation. If it were, every patient would have had the same relative difficulty with these sentences; however, that was not the case. For example, G.G. was equally impaired on subject-control and NP-raising sentences, K.G. did worse on NP-raising than on subject-control sentences, and G.S. did worse on subject-control than on NP-raising sentences. This suggests that a different underlying deficit was the cause of the observed difficulties in each of these cases.

A second possible account is that subject-control, NP-raising, and object-relative structures, and certain passive structures, are *not* selectively impaired, but rather that the impairments on the object-control and subject-relative structures are masked by the use of heuristics that happen to generate the correct response. For example, the account of G.G.'s deficit included a hypothesized difficulty with object-control sentences, but it was suggested that he performed well on these structures because of his use of a heuristic of selecting the head of the nearest NP as Agent. The attribution of G.G.'s perfect performance on object-control sentences to the use of a heuristic is reasonable in light of the fact that he also used this response pattern 92% of the time on subject-control and NP-raising sentences. Though this may account for some of the difference between those structures with empty NPs that are more difficult and those that are less difficult, this cannot be the entire explanation of these discrepancies in every case. R.L., for instance, did worse on subject-subject relatives than on conjoined sentences because of the memory load imposed by the relative clause in the former. Similarly, K.G. did well on conjoined sentences, on subject-subject relatives, and on object-subject relatives. No single heuristic could provide correct interpretations for all three of these sentence types; it is unlikely that this mildly impaired patient's correct responses on these sentence types were due to the application of different heuristics to each sentence type rather than to the normal operation of the parser.

Another feature of these cases related to the hypothesis that some empty NPs are more difficult to construct or interpret than others concerns the fact, just cited, that the subject-control, NP-raising, passive, and object-relative structures dissociate from one another. As table 5.49 shows, two double dissociations were shown between the NP(*seems*)-raising sentences and those with another type of empty NP: subject-control structures and object relatives. Three patients performed significantly better on the subject-control structures than on the NP(*seems*)-raising structures, though for G.S. the opposite was the case. J.V. showed higher accuracy on relative clauses than on the NP(*seems*)-raising sentences; G.S. showed the reverse pattern. C.V. also scored lower on subject-object relatives (0%) than on NP(*seems*)-raising structures (42%), but her performance on either type was not significantly different from random. Therefore, this dissociation cannot be taken as evidence for an underlying dissociation of function.

In summary: In the cases studied so far, NP-raising sentences (type 32) have shown a double dissociation with subject-control structures and with object relatives. The possibility of double dissociation occurring between NP-raising structures and other sentence types cannot be ruled out. The double dissociations uncovered so far show that the processes for NP-

Table 5.49
Dissociations between NP(*seems*)-raising sentences (type 32) and other sentence types.

seems	Subject-control PRO
Ex.: John seems to Bill to be dancing.	John promised Bill to dance.
K.G. 33%	75% ($p < 0.05$)*
J.V. 25%	100% ($p < 0.01$)*
G.S. 92%	50% ($p < 0.05$)*

seems	Passivized $\overline{\text{S}}$ Deletion
Ex.: John seems to Bill to be dancing.	John was believed by Bill to be dancing.
K.G. 33%	75% ($p < 0.05$)*

seems	Dative passive
Ex.: John seems to Bill to be dancing.	The frog was given to the goat by the monkey.
J.V. 25%	100%[†]
G.G. 0%	100%

seems	Relative clause (*wh*-trace)
Ex.: John seems to Bill to be dancing.	The frog hit the goat that kissed the monkey.
J.V. 25%	(S-O) 92%[†]
	(O-S) 100%
	(O-O) 100%
	(S-S) 92%
G.S. 92%	(S-O) 25%[†]
	(O-O) 50%

*significantly different using the test of the significance of the different between two independent proportions (SDTIP)
[†] SDTIP not applicable

raising structures, subject-control structures, and object relatives are at least partially independent.

The dissociation that occurred between passives and *seems* sentences must be addressed, as these structures both contain NP-trace and therefore would be expected to be equally impaired. There are several possible explanations of this pattern. Under Wasow's (1977) analysis, among the sentences we tested only the passivized $\overline{\text{S}}$-deletion sentences (type 29) are considered examples of syntactic passives that undergo NP-movement; the other types are lexically formed passives that do not have an empty NP in the syntax. Excluding the sentences that can be analyzed as lexical passives, the only comparison is between the passivized $\overline{\text{S}}$-deletion sentences (such as *John is believed by Bill to be shaving*) and the NP-raising structures. These two types appeared on separate batteries, and there are several reasons why the cases presented here provide little evidence of a dissociation in the

Table 5.50
Comparison of NP(*seems*)-raising and passivized S̄-deletion sentences on the fourth battery.

Patient*	NP(*seems*)-raising plus reflexive, type 34	Passivized S̄-deletion plus reflexive, type 31
C.V.	17%	17%
J.V.	75%	58%
G.G.	92%	75%
K.G.	33%	33%

*G.S., R.L., A.B. not tested
(Chance = 25% on Stage II assumptions)

ability to parse and interpret these two sentence types. Patient A.B. was not tested on the passivized S̄-deletion structures. Patient C.V. was tested on each of the sentence types, but the two sessions were separated by a one-year interval. Patients J.V. and G.G. both showed signs of an improvement over the course of testing, and therefore their higher scores on passivized S̄-deletion structures could be due to spontaneous recovery. Only patient K.G. showed significantly better responses on the S̄-deletion structures within an otherwise stable set of response patterns, but in the analysis of the data on this subject it was suggested that the *by*-phrase was a cue to the assignment of Agent, and therefore that the passive sentences were slightly easier for K.G. because of the use of this cue rather than because of his abilities to assign a complete structure to this sentence. Thus, these data do not demonstrate a dissociation in the *parsing* of these two sentence types.

There is one more pair of sentence types that can be used to compare performance on NP-raising and passives: the NP-raising and passivized S̄-deletion sentences with a reflexive object in the embedded clause, which were tested in the fourth battery. There are no significant differences in degree of accuracy between the two sentence types, and not even a suggestion of a trend that NP-raising sentences were harder. Future studies will determine whether these findings are consistent. If they are, we may take that as evidence for a similarity of structure and parsing operations in these sentence types.

The comparison between sentences with subject-control PRO and sentences with relative clauses (*wh*-trace) revealed dissociations in both directions, as table 5.51 shows. G.G. showed poor accuracy on subject-control sentences but nearly perfect performance on sentences with relative clauses. K.G. did better on subject-control sentences than on relatives with an empty NP in object position. (His performance on both was nonrandom.) These findings suggest that for K.G. and G.G. there must be other sources of complexity besides coindexing over an intervening NP and

Table 5.51
Comparison of sentences with subject-control PRO, sentences with relative clauses, and cleft sentences (*wh*-trace).

Patient	Subject-control PRO Ex.: John promised Bill to dance.	Relative clause (*wh*-trace) The frog hit the goat that kissed the monkey.		Cleft object (*wh*-trace) It was the frog that the goat hit.	
G.G.	17%	(S-O)	100%	(CO2)	100%
		(O-S)	100%	(CO3)	100%
		(O-O)	100%		
		(S-S)	92%		
K.G.	75%	(S-O)	25%	(CO2)	92%
	83%	(O-S)	83%	(CO3)	50%
		(O-O)	58%		
		(S-S)	83%		

verb, since these patients did not perform equally poorly on the two structures compared. We suggested that the source of K.G.'s difficulty with the object relatives lay in his diminished ability to hold the relative pronoun without a thematic role in memory while other thematic roles were assigned, an operation not necessary in subject-control sentences. For G.G. we suggested that the presence of the relative pronoun in a position dominated by $\bar{S}$ (and therefore within the same embedded sentence as the empty NP) may have allowed him to coindex *wh*-trace. Other differences in complexity exist for these two sentence types, which may have nothing to do with the empty NP; however, the total pattern of performance by K.G. and G.G. shows that these differences are not relevant to this particular dissociation. For example, for the object-relative sentences, subjects must act out two separate transitive actions, while for subject-control sentences they must act out only one intransitive action; however, K.G.'s good performance on subject-relative sentences shows that he was quite able to act out two transitive actions correctly.

In the remaining comparisons among sentence types with empty NPs, no dissociations were uncovered.

In summary: Three double dissociations emerged among the various types of empty NPs. There was a double dissociation between NP(*seems*)-raising structures and subject-control PRO structures, one between NP(*seems*)-raising structures and object-relative sentences, and one between object-relative and subject-control sentences. These dissociations are explained on the basis of the analysis of each case. No other dissociations emerged, with the possible exception of K.G.'s differential performance on the NP(*seems*)-raising and passivized $\bar{S}$-deletion structures, which may reflect his use of a heuristic to interpret the latter.

Hypothesis 3: [+ pronominal] and [− pronominal] Referential
Dependencies May Pattern Separately
The Berwick-Weinberg parser allocates different searching operations to [+ pronominal] and [− pronominal] referential dependencies: [− pronominal] elements are coindexed by a tree-searching operation at the syntactic level, whereas [+ pronominal] elements (including PRO) are coindexed by searching through the part of the sentence that has already been syntactically analyzed and transferred to the propositional list. For overt NPs, this hypothesized difference predicts that reflexives and pronouns should doubly dissociate. This prediction is borne out by the data: A.B. and C.V. showed a double dissociation between reflexives and pronouns, which constitutes evidence that the coindexation of reflexives and the coindexation of pronouns are at least partially independent processes. In the context of the Berwick-Weinberg parser, this dissociation can be

explained by reference to the separate levels at which coindexation occurs for reflexives and pronouns.

For empty NPs, if PRO is coindexed at the propositional level just as pronouns are, one might expect that subject-control sentences would not cause difficulty when other empty NPs do cause difficulty, or else that the search for an antecedent of PRO in a subject-control sentence would involve a complexity metric not based on hierarchical structure. The data do not support this prediction in two respects. First, for most patients, the sentences with empty NPs that caused difficulty include sentences with subject-control PRO. Second, one account of G.G.'s deficit (that he has difficulty coindexing over a sentence boundary) requires that PRO be coindexed at the syntactic level, and the alternate account (that he has difficulty with [+ anaphoric] empty NPs) has a more parsimonious parsing explanation if all [+ anaphoric] NPs are coindexed at the same level.

As we indicated in chapter 2, there is some linguistic basis for believing that, in the obligatory-control sentences that were used in this study, the empty PRO is coindexed at the syntactic level. In subject-control and object-control structures, the empty PRO in the embedded subject position is obligatorily coindexed with either the subject or the object in the matrix sentence, as stipulated by the lexical information associated with the verb, and the antecedent always c-commands the PRO. If the c-command relationship is relevant to the coindexation of subject-control and object-control PRO, then the syntactic level is the appropriate level at which to coindex these structures.

Bouchard (1982) has argued on linguistic grounds that there is not a single category of [+ anaphoric, + pronominal] PRO but that, rather, obligatory (subject- and object-) control PRO is [+ anaphoric] and co-indexed at the syntactic level whereas arbitrary PRO, for which an antecedent is not determined by the predicate (e.g, PRO *feeding lions is dangerous*), is [+ pronominal] and coindexed at the level of Logical Form (or, in parsing terminology, at the level of the propositional list). The sentences containing PRO that we used to test our patients are all of the obligatory-control type and hence, under Bouchard's analysis, are coindexed at the syntactic level.

The one case that may be an exception to the analysis of PRO being coindexed at the syntactic level is that of J.V., who did well on subject-control and object-control sentences but poorly on NP-raising sentences. One of the accounts offered for J.V. was that he had difficulty coindexing over a sentence boundary, which requires that PRO be coindexed at the propositional level in order to account for the fact that J.V. had no difficulty in coindexing over a sentence boundary in sentences with PRO. As was discussed above, adopting this account for J.V. forces us to adopt the account for G.G. in which the impairment is characterized as one for all

[+ anaphoric] NPs, since G.G.'s impairment on both subject-control and NP-raising sentences cannot be explained by a difficulty with long-distance coindexation (over a sentence boundary) affecting both structures. However, if [+ anaphoric, − pronominal] NPs are coindexed at the syntactic level and [+ anaphoric, + pronominal] NPs are coindexed at the level of the propositional list, there is no way to formulate the set of [+ anaphoric] NPs as a natural class in terms of parsing operations, and this second account of G.G.'s problem is no more than a description of the data. The alternate account for J.V., namely that he has difficulty transmitting a thematic role, would predict that he should have no difficulty on sentences with PRO even if it is coindexed at the syntactic level, and this account allows for the analysis of G.G. that maintains that he has difficulty coindexing over a sentence boundary, which includes sentences with PRO. These two accounts are thus preferred, and they lead to the conclusion that obligatory-control PRO is coindexed in the syntax.

A further prediction from the third hypothesis was that, if PRO and pronouns are coindexed at the level of the propositional list, and trace and reflexives in the syntax, then a patient showing a selective difficulty with one type of overt referentially dependent NP should show a similar difficulty with its empty counterpart. In other words, patients showing difficulty with overt pronouns would be expected to show difficulty with PRO, and patients showing difficulty with reflexives would be expected to show difficulty with NP-trace. The data are not clear regarding this prediction. The two patients who had difficulty with reflexives or pronouns, A.B. and C.V., had difficulty with both [+ pronominal] and [− pronominal] empty NPs (e.g., subject-control and NP-raising structures). Thus, there was no case in which a patient showed an impairment on [+ pronominal] empty and overt NPs but not on [− pronominal] empty and overt NPs, or vice versa.

Summary

In this chapter, the original predictions concerning the relative processing complexity of empty and overt referentially dependent NPs were evaluated. Evidence from several matched-sentence comparisons and several patients showed that, when dissociations occurred, certain sentence types with empty NPs were consistently more difficult than sentence types without referential dependencies. This fact supports the hypothesis that empty NPs exist as entities that play a role in parsing operations.

The accounts of the deficits in the three patients showing selective impairments (K.G., J.V., and G.G.) appear to favor a model in which all types of empty NPs except arbitrary PRO are coindexed at the syntactic level. Individual differences in accuracy for various types of empty NPs across patients are attributed to additional processes associated with the particular type of empty NP. For K.G., the construction of the NP itself causes some difficulty, which is compounded by the necessity of holding an NP without a thematic role in memory when the empty NP is [— pronominal] (*wh*-trace or NP-trace). For J.V., transmission of a thematic role is difficult, and this operation is necessary only when the empty NP is an NP-trace. For G.G., coindexing over a sentence boundary is difficult for all empty NPs, and thus subject-control and NP(*seems*)-raising sentences are affected equally.

Cases A.B. and C.V. present a double dissociation of reflexives and pronouns, allowing us to conclude that independent operations are involved with these elements, which in the context of the Berwick-Weinberg parser can be attributed to the distinction between levels of searching for an antecedent for these two types of elements. The data do not show a predicted parallel selective breakdown in overt and empty referential dependencies of the same category. This could be because the additional complexity involved in parsing all empty NPs created either a ceiling effect or a floor effect in each of the patients tested, or, in the case of [+ pronominal] categories, because the structures used here involve coindexation of overt and empty NPs (pronouns and PRO) at different levels (the propositional list and the syntax, respectively).

Aside from the results that bear on the predictions made in chapter 3, several other findings have emerged. First, some specific parsing procedures have been identified, and some generalizations have been made concerning their interactive effect on sentence complexity. Second, most of the impairments of our subjects must be attributed to a primary deficit of syntactic comprehension that interacts with a capacity limitation to produce the observed pattern of responses. The evidence for this is that particular parsing operations can be carried out when the total processing load of the sentence is low but break down as the processing load increases, and these operations differ in different patients. Third, some initial observations have been made concerning the use of heuristics by particular patients. Finally, though digit-recall and word-recall span was generally correlated with overall sentence-comprehension accuracy, there was not a strict relationship. This is demonstrated by patient B.O., who showed relatively good comprehension with a digit- and word-recall span of 3.

Our results have implications for certain aspects of linguistic analysis and certain models of parsing. They are consistent with a parsing model in which obligatorily controlled PRO is coindexed at the syntactic level, and with Wasow's lexical analysis of passives. Overall, these results indicate that theoretical linguistics, parsing models, and theoretical linguistic aphasiology can interact to describe and partially explain aphasic impairments of syntactic comprehension in individual cases in considerable detail.

Chapter 6
Conclusions and Discussion

We have presented a study of syntactic comprehension in an unselected aphasic population and more detailed investigations of nine selected aphasic patients, along with preliminary analyses of our findings. In this chapter, we shall review the most important aspects of these investigations and draw conclusions regarding the breakdown of syntactic-comprehension processes in aphasia, the compensations patients make for their impairments, and the implications of our research for linguistic theory, parsing models, and the neural basis of language. We shall draw upon the results of both the group and the case studies in formulating and justifying our views.

The Nature of Syntactic-Comprehension Disturbances in Aphasia

We indicated in the introduction that the overt performance of a patient on a task of syntactic comprehension is a result of his primary disorder affecting syntactic processing and of the adaptive heuristics he uses to assign and interpret structure in sentences he does not process normally. We indicated that the characterization of the primary deficit would be in terms of a theory of normal language structure and processing (a grammar and a parser) and a theory of possible deficits in these mental representations and processes. We begin this chapter with a number of specific suggestions regarding the last of these theories—that of aphasic impairments in this domain. Our suggestions emerge from consideration of both the group and the case studies, which we consider to be mutually confirmatory with respect to the major aspects of our theory. The fact that this is the case despite the considerable differences in methodology and analytic approach between these two types of studies increases our confidence in the framework we are proposing.

Stated in very broad and general terms, we envision syntactic-comprehension disorders as arising from two separate types of primary impairments. The first are specific disturbances patients have with particular parsing processes and/or linguistic representations. The second is a reduction in the computational resources available to a patient for the task of syntactic comprehension.

The evidence that one aspect of the primary deficit in aphasic patients is a disturbance of specific parsing functions comes from two sources: the performance of subgroups of patients in the group studies, and the specific nature of impairments in individual patients. Having presented the relevant data in chapters 4 and 5, we will review and discuss the implications of these results here.

In every patient population tested, with both the object-manipulation test and the sentence-picture matching test, subgroups of patients identified by clustering analyses were distinguished from one another along an axis reflecting the overall level of impairment and along one or more axes reflecting performance on particular sentence types. This clearly emerges from the principal-components analyses, which all contain a first vector reflecting overall severity and other vectors reflecting performance on particular sentence types. These latter vectors account for between 35% and 50% of the variance in patient clustering, with the largest contributions of these vectors arising in the sentence-picture matching test, in which the sentence groupings on which the patient clustering was based are maximally different from one another with respect to the features of syntactic form and the semantic representations that were tested. Although the second and third vectors of the PCAs, which contribute most significantly to patient classification, assign roughly equal scores of similar polarity to sentence types that are structurally similar (in the object-manipulation test, where there are enough sentence-type factors to allow factor weightings to be analyzed in this fashion), the PCA vectors are not themselves directly interpretable as reflections of particular impairments in parsing. However, to some extent, review of the mean correct scores per sentence type and the errors made by each of the subgroups identified in the object-manipulation test does suggest some specific impairments in parsing in particular subgroups of patients. Similarly, the pattern of performance on each of the sentence groupings by different subgroups in the sentence-picture matching test suggests particular disturbances in different aspects of the construction and the interpretation of sentence form.

We do not wish to overemphasize these data and analyses because of the level of detail of the survey work, which was not designed to answer questions regarding the detailed nature of parsing impairments in individual cases. We noted in the introduction that deficit analyses could be revised in light of analyses of patients' compensatory heuristics, and we gave examples of such analyses in chapter 5 (for example, patient G.G.'s correct interpretation of object-control sentences and patient A.B.'s correct interpretation of subject-subject relatives are attributed to heuristic interpretive strategies, and the analyses of the deficits in these patients are stated accordingly). We do not have enough data on the patients in the survey studies to be confident of our deficit analyses. We have noted the extent to which details of deficit analyses have not been supported with adequate data in studies in the literature, and we do not wish to follow a path we have criticized others for taking.

Despite these reservations, the results are at least suggestive that aphasic patients have specific difficulties with assigning and interpreting specific aspects of syntactic form. The factors that emerge from the survey studies as possible loci of specific impairments include the functional argument structure of a verb, the number of verbs in a sentence, the assignment of lexical grammatical categories to category-ambiguous lexical items and of phrasal categories to sequences of lexical items as a function of local syntactic cues, the presence of pronouns and possessive adjectives requiring coindexation, the presence of noncanonical orders of NP constituents in a sentence, and (though the supporting data were not presented in chapter 4) the extension of quantifier scope over an adjective. Different groups of patients show particular difficulties with sentence types in which the processing of these different aspects of sentence structure is required. These results lead to two further research topics: the need to demonstrate conclusively that specific impairments in parsing processes occur in patients, and the need to develop a theory of the nature of and the constraints on these specific impairments.

The first of these needs can be addressed by considering the performance of the patients discussed in chapter 5. Each of these cases presents a pattern of comprehension that is unique in some respect. The fact that these different patterns of comprehension exist proves the existence of specific deficits, as follows.

For any patient considered in isolation, an account could be developed in which the observed sentence-comprehension impairments occur as a secondary effect of reduced resources available for parsing. For instance, it could be argued that for patient K.G. all individual parsing operations and linguistic representations are intact and that performance breaks down on the sentences that have the greatest processing load. However, if this is correct, then the same pattern of impairment will occur in any patient suffering exclusively from an equivalent reduction in resources available for parsing. In general, if the pattern seen in any one of the cases in chapter 5 is due entirely to a primary deficit in resource availability, then any deviation from this pattern must reflect a different degree of resource availability or a specific deficit.

The possibility that the different patterns seen in the cases presented in chapter 5 are due entirely to variation in the reduction of resources available for parsing in different cases is ruled out by the existence of double and *n*-way dissociations in performance among the cases. For instance, if failure to coindex PRO but retention of the ability to coindex NP-trace (seen in patient G.S.) is due solely to reduced resources in G.S., then the coindexation of PRO must require more resources than the coindexation of NP-trace. In that case, the deficit in K.G., which spares PRO and affects NP-trace, cannot solely be secondary to a different degree of limitation of parsing resources but must involve a specific deficit affecting NP-trace. Conversely, if K.G.'s deficit is due solely to resource reduction, G.S.'s impairment must include a specific deficit. Similar considerations apply to the coindexation of pronouns and reflexives in the cases of A.B. and C.V. Though all or most of our patients may have some reduction in resources available for parsing, logically such a limitation must interact with specific deficits in all but one case. In all probability, there is an interaction between specific deficits and resource limitations in all the patients we have studied.

A theory of deficits in this area must specify what these specific impairments are. We suggested in the introduction that specific impairments (as opposed to reductions in the resources available for parsing) could take two basic forms: a loss of knowledge pertaining to a particular representation and a loss of the ability to perform a particular parsing operation. We suggested that these could be distinguished in the following way. Loss of knowledge regarding a linguistic item would result in misutilization of that item in every context in which it occurred. Impairments in the ability to perform specific parsing operations were thought to produce disturbances affecting the representations upon which those procedures operated in such a way as to yield disturbances when other processing demands were high. In retrospect, this bipartite division of specific impairments appears too simple and conflates two different aspects of breakdown. We would now suggest that the issue of whether representations or operations are affected should be separated from the issue of variability as a function of processing load. Thus, we now would recognize four types of specific impairments in aphasic patients: loss or utilization difficulty affecting either linguistic representations or parsing operations. The basic types of specific impairments should be distinguished as follows.

Loss of either a linguistic representation or a parsing operation would affect specific items in all the linguistic contexts in which they occur. Loss of a linguistic representation would be distinguishable from loss of a parsing operation only in cases in which the linguistic representational system and the parsing system made different "cuts" with respect to linguistic items. For instance, if a parsing system had a single gap-hunting operation, which was obligatorily triggered by all cues to the existence of a gap in a sentence, different patterns of impairment would result from a loss of the representations of specific empty categories and a loss of this general gap-hunting procedure. Or, to take another possibility, if the parsing system has a single process for searching for the antecedent of all [+ anaphoric,

—pronominal] NPs, loss of this process would affect both NP-trace and reflexives, each of which could be separately lost at the level of linguistic representations. We do not necessarily expect parsing processes to be more general than linguistic representations, as in the examples just given. Higher-order groupings of linguistic representations—such as Kean's (1977) phonological clitics, Grodzinsky's (1984) items without phonological specification at S-structure, Rizzi's (1985) theta-role assignees and assigners, and many other sets of representations—are, in principle, subject to individual loss, and are more general than many parsing processes related to subsets of the items within these categories.

Variability in performance always results from a utilization impairment, according to our theory. Either representations or operations may be subject to this type of specific impairment. This aspect of our theory differs from other theoretical formulations in the literature regarding the nature of loss and utilization disorders in other domains of aphasic impairments, such as Warrington and Shallice's discussion of "storage" and "access" impairments in the area of lexical semantic representations (Warrington and Shallice 1979; Warrington and MacCarthy, 1983; Shallice 1987; for criticism of these formulations on theoretical grounds, see Caplan in 1987d). In the area of utilization impairments as well as that of actual loss of representations and operations, the distinction between a parsing deficit and a representation deficit depends on which linguistic items are affected in a particular patient and on whether these items are grouped together by the parser, the grammar, or both.

Operationally, we can distinguish a loss from a utilization impairment as follows. If every sentence type containing a particular linguistic representation (or requiring a particular parsing operation) produces a pattern of responses that is not distinguishable from chance on Stage II assumptions regarding random performance (see chapter 5), we can conclude that it is possible that the linguistic representation (or parsing operation) in question is lost. If even one sentence type containing the representation (or parsing operation) in question is interpreted at above-chance rates on a Stage II assumption, we are dealing with a utilization deficit.[3]

This framework explicitly asserts that any particular linguistic representation or any set of representations that constitutes a natural class in a grammar, or any process specified by the parser, can be impaired in aphasia. Formulations of this sort have appeared in other theoretical papers on aphasia (e.g., Badecker and Caramazza 1985; Caplan 1986a).

Most of the specific deficits we have documented fall into the realm of utilization impairments. K.G.'s difficulties with retention of an NP without a theta role in memory while other theta roles are being assigned, A.B.'s difficulty with reflexives, C.V.'s difficulty with pronouns, and R.L.'s difficulty with relative clauses in subject position are all clearly specific utilization deficits, on our theory. Some of these deficits, such as that described in K.G., affect parsing operations; others apparently affect linguistic representations, such as those in A.B. and C.V. A few specific deficits may be classed as losses of representations or operations. We have argued that S.P. cannot construct hierarchical structure; this could to due to a specific loss of linguistic representations (the rules representing hierarchical structure) or of structure-building operations in the parser.

Patient J.V. is an interesting example of how establishing a specific deficit affecting representations or parsing operations requires commitment to specific theories of representations and parsing operations. We have argued that his deficit is best described as an inability to transmit thematic roles from a trace to an antecedent. Phrased in these terms, J.V.'s disturbance is in the domain of parsing. It is possible to rephrase this analysis in linguistic terms: J.V. could have an impaired ability to utilize the category NP-trace. We cannot distinguish the linguistic and the parsing account of J.V.'s impairment, because the parsing operation that may be affected affects all and only the representations specified as NP-traces in linguistic theory. This analysis is predicated upon the existence of NP-traces in syntactic representations and upon the existence of a parsing operation that effects the transmission of theta roles from traces to antecedents. If Lexical-Functional Grammar is correct, neither of these analyses can be entertained, since this theory does not involve transmission of a theta role from a trace to an antecedent. On this theory, it would be possible to formulate a single specific deficit in terms of the linguistic structures affected: these consist of functional control structures in which the matrix-subject NP is not assigned a theta role by the matrix verb. It is also possible to formulate the specific deficit in J.V. in terms of an operation in a parser type-transparently related to an LFG grammar that searches for a referentially dependent element at f-structure with which to coindex an NP in a matrix clause that has not received a theta role. We shall discuss the relationship between our data and different theories of syntactic structures in greater detail below.

Thus case analyses proposed here begin to illustrate and document the basic types of specific impairments seen in syntactic-comprehension disturbances in aphasic patients.

We close this discussion of specific deficits by emphasizing how specific these deficits may be. The patterns of impairments affecting empty categories and the double dissociation between coindexation of pronouns and reflexives illustrate both how sensitive isolated parsing operations and linguistic representations are to brain damage and how operations and representations quite similar to those that are affected can be spared in a single patient. A major research topic that emerges from this study is the documentation of the complete set of specific impairments in linguistic representations and parsing processes in brain-damaged patients. Seen in the light of the specific deficits we have documented, formulations of a deficit in terms of an inability to utilize the function-word vocabulary or the inflectional vocabulary to construct syntactic structure, the inability to map syntactic structures onto semantic representations, or the failure of a parser (see chapter 3) are extensive specific deficits indeed. We also note that the results of our studies give no support to the hypotheses (outlined in chapter 3) that maintain that specific parsing deficits are in some way related to other aphasic impairments, such as agrammatism or short-term-memory limitations. We shall return to the specific question of short-term-memory and parsing deficits later in this chapter.

The second major type of impairment seen in the patients we studied is what we term a decrease in the overall resources that can be applied to the task of syntactic comprehension. We shall refer to this component of the impairment as a decrease in the work space available to a patient, recognizing that this term is merely an analogy (we could easily recast the terminology in terms of computational time, for instance). It would be possible to develop a formal account of this aspect of an impairment in terms of the number of elementary computational operations that can be accomplished in a specified period of time (perhaps simultaneously) in a particular patient. Such an account would entail a commitment to the detailed computations accomplished by a parser. Although such an account is possible in principle for an implemented parser of the type we have been using as the basis for our analyses, we have not attempted to describe the degree of reduction of a parsing work space in a patient in quantitative terms because the algorithms specified in these parsers are compatible with several computational instantiations, and we are not in a position to choose between different instantiations. Thus, we have restricted ourselves to the use of an informal term, *parsing work space*, to capture this potentially formal concept. As with the specific deficits found in patients, evidence that one component of the impairment leading to syntactic-comprehension disturbances is a reduction in the parsing work space comes from both the group studies and the case studies. We shall review and comment on this aspect of the deficit as it emerges in these different studies in turn.

The evidence for the operation of a decrease of parsing work space in creating impairments in the comprehension of syntactic structure in the group studies consists of the determinants of patient grouping and those of sentence complexity. As noted just above and at many points in chapter 4, patients are clustered into groups primarily as a function of how they do on all sentence types, and performance on any particular sentence type is no more important than performance on any other in determining these clusters in the first vectors of all the PCAs. This is true of all clustering analyses of all patient groups, on both the object-manipulation protocol and the sentence-picture-matching protocol. It is not possible for a series of differ-ent specific impairments to produce this pattern. Impairments as specific as those we have described in chapter 5 do not affect performance on all sentence types.

Another way to look at these results is to note that the performance of successive clusters of patients deteriorates on almost all sentence types as one goes from the best-performing to the worst-performing subgroups and that, within each subgroup and across the set of subgroups, more difficult sentences are usually more affected than simpler sentences (where difficulty is judged by mean performance of the entire population). These patterns would directly result from greater decreases in work space in more affected patients. Specific processing impairments would not be expected to pro-duce these regularities, but would be expected to affect different sentence types in different patients. With sufficiently great diminutions in work space, one would expect even simple sentences to be misinterpreted at times, as was observed in our worst-performing group. Variable interpre-tation of sentences of a single type may be due to the assignment of an ambiguous structure to such sentences or to the interaction of the limited resources available to the parser or of specific deficits with attentional control and other psychological factors. Again, if extraprocessing factors only affected or interacted with disturbances of specific operations, the regular deterioration of progressively more impaired subgroups on almost all sentence types and the presence of complexity effects within almost all groups would not be expected.

The second type of evidence from the group studies that indicates that one component of the primary deficit in syntactic comprehension is a diminution of a patient's parsing work space is the nature of the determi-nants of sentence complexity in the object-manipulation task. We have noted that a noncanonical thematic-role order, a third argument to be assigned around a verb, and a second verb are individual sources of sen-tence complexity which are, to a considerable degree, additive in their effects on performance. In chapter 4 we attributed this additivity to the effect of a decrease in the work space on sentence comprehension; such a decrease would lead to more difficulty with sentence types incorporating more of these features, just as variability in the degree of diminution of a work space would lead to the aspects of the pattern of performance in different subgroups of patients discussed above. Once again, an expla-nation of this pattern of sentence complexity phrased solely in terms of specific impairments of processing operations does not seem possible.

More evidence that a decrease in the work space available to a patient is a factor in creating an impairment in syntactic comprehension comes from the results of the case studies we have presented. In these studies, we have also documented specific syntactic features that contribute to the complexity of processing a sentence. These include the following:

• complexity due to the demands of building hierarchical structure—
specifically, complex NPs (patients A.B. and C.V.),

• complexity due to the demands of holding an NP in the syntactic
structure without a thematic role (patient K.G.),

• complexity due to transmission of a thematic role from an empty
[+ anaphoric, − pronomial] NP to its antecedent (patient J.V.),

• complexity due to searching for an antecedent (patients A.B. and C.V.),

• complexity due to searching for an antecedent over a sentence
boundary (patient G.G.),

• postsyntactic complexity due to the need to hold propositions in
memory and assign thematic roles to real-world referents (patient B.O.).

In several cases, one or more features of a patient's performance appeared to result from a capacity limitation, since the patient could perform
the operations listed above when the overall complexity of the sentence
was low but not when other operations also had to be carried out. For
example, K.G. was able to hold an NP in the syntactic structure without a
thematic role as long as no other thematic roles were assigned in the
meantime. A.B. and C.V. were able to interpret pronouns and reflexives
correctly as well as to construct complex NPs in very simple active sentences, but not in sentences that required both the construction of a complex NP and a coindexation operation. These facts highlight the interactive
nature of processing complexity. When the combined complexity of concurrent parsing operations exceeds the processing capacity of a patient, the
ability to perform the particular operations breaks down.

This interaction extends to functions outside of assigning phrase structure or coindexation. That B.O. began to mix up her assignment of thematic roles to dolls in the array when the number of NPs in the proposition
equaled her digit span indicates that the post-interpretive stage of sentence
processing can be affected by the overall processing load. Increased complexity has even been demonstrated to affect the ability to make use of
lexical information necessary for operations at the syntactic level. That A.B.
began to assign the wrong number of thematic roles to verbs in sentences
with complex syntactic form, which were particularly difficult for him,
showed that, under conditions of processing load, either he did not access
lexical information about thematic roles or that he could not make use of
this information. Both A.B. and C.V. lost their ability to use their lexical
knowledge of the referential nature of the reflexive or pronoun when a
complex NP was added to a sentence with a sentential complement.

The relationship between reduced parsing work space and specific impairments emerges in an interesting feature of the performance of our patients. We have invariably found that small reductions in the parsing work space occur in patients with less severe specific deficits, and larger reductions in patients with more severe specific deficits. For instance, we have argued that a reduction in work space is responsible for K.G.'s difficulties in sentences with both subject control of PRO and a pronoun in embedded object position. This must be a smaller reduction in work space than that which we have claimed leads to C.V.'s difficulties in constructing complex NPs in sentences with both a complex NP and a pronoun, since K.G. has no trouble with such sentences and since C.V. also fails (badly) on sentences with subject control and a referentially dependent NP in embedded object position. We also maintain that K.G.'s specific deficit (inability to maintain an NP without a thematic role in memory while another NP is being assigned a thematic role) is milder than C.V's (a difficulty affecting, among other things, coindexation of pronouns). The observation upon which this conclusion is based is that a deficit in constructing and coindexing an empty NP may occur without a corresponding deficit in coindexing an overt referentially dependent item, but not *vice versa*; this would follow from the fact that the former function is more difficult than the latter. In every case we have presented, and in all the other patients we have seen in our laboratory, this correlation between the size of a reduction in the parsing work space and the difficulty of the operations in which a patient shows specific deficits has held.

This suggests that there is some functional connection between the size of a reduction in the parsing work space and the occurrence of a specific functional deficit. We have argued above, on the basis of double and n-way dissociations in these deficits, that a work-space limitation cannot lead to all the specific deficits we have documented; these dissociations imply that reductions in work space must be independent of specific deficits to some extent. Thus, it is, in principle, possible for a patient with a mild diminution of work space to have a specific deficit in a simpler operation. For instance, in principle it is possible for a patient with a relatively mild reduction in work space to have a specific deficit in coindexation of pronouns but no deficit in coindexation of empty NPs. We have not yet found such co-occurrences of mild decreases in work space and specific deficits in simpler functions in any of the patients we have tested to date. We have also found empirically that there is a relationship between specific deficits: a disturbance affecting even one overt referentially dependent NP always entails a disturbance affecting all empty NPs. Since our parsing theory maintains that the parsing of some overt referentially dependent NPs contains operations not present in that of some empty NPs, this also presents a problem. For instance, the coindexation of a pronoun involves lookback over the propositional list, whereas the coindexation of trace does not.

Therefore, one would expect that a deficit could affect the coindexation of pronouns at the stage of lookback over the propositional list and not affect trace. We have not found such dissociations of impairments in the cases presented or in any other patient we have studied.

There is an analysis that resolves both these problems. The impairments in simpler processes seen in our patients (e.g., difficulties in the coindexation of pronouns) may be due to the interaction of specific deficits and a diminution in work space great enough to disrupt functionally independent, more complex processes (e.g., coindexation of trace). This suggestion remains speculative. The allocation of aspects of disturbed performance to specific deficits, diminution of the parsing work space, and the interaction of these two factors will require a commitment to specific models of the instantiation of the algorithms of the parser and a formal computational statement of the nature of what we may term their "local computational environment"—the parsing work space. We hope to explore this topic in future research.

These considerations lead to the conclusion that most and possibly all of the patients described here have both utilization impairments affecting specific parsing operations and some degree of reduction in overall processing capacity, since all show different patterns of interpretations attributable to specific deficits and since all but J.V. and possibly S.P. show some influence of processing load on their ability to carry out particular operations.

Our notion of a work space is not easily related to the concept of "working memory" developed by Baddeley and his colleagues, outlined in chapter 3. The parsing work space is not the entire working-memory system. The differences between the two are related to the connection that the central computational system in the Baddeley system (the "central executive") has to a phonological storage device (the "phonological store") and to a device for articulatory rehearsal (the "articulatory loop"). Baddeley's theory maintains that the central executive utilizes these systems as "slave systems" to retain material when processing exceeds it capacity and makes use of material so maintained. Our interpretation of the results in the literature (chapter 3) and of our own cases indicates that the parsing system does not make use of such slave systems (at the very least, they can be severely impaired without consequences for the parser, as in B.O.) and that the intactness of these systems does not help the parser overcome limitations affecting its operations (as in K.G. and J.V.). Thus, we see no evidence that these systems are utilized by the parser itself, though they may be used at stages of processing that arise after a parse has already been assigned (see below). Thus, the parsing work space is not the entire working-memory system, since it excludes the articulatory loop and the phonological store. This leaves the possibility that the parsing work space is the same as the central executive in this model. We doubt that the parsing work space is the equivalent of Baddeley's central executive, since he considers the central executive to be involved in a very large number of mental functions that have nothing to do with parsing, such as those impaired in the "frontal-lobe syndrome" (Baddeley 1985). Though the overlap of the parsing work space with the resources utilized in other mental functions is unclear, a conservative view, consistent with a modularity hypothesis that extends to resources as well as to representations and operations, would posit that the central processing system is fractionated to a greater degree than Baddeley's theory seems to allow in its present formulation. In other words, our concept of a parsing work space is considerably more circumscribed than Baddeley's concept of a central executive in terms of its operations and representations.

In connection with the issue of what mental functions share processing resources with the parser, we note that we may also disagree with Baddeley regarding the overlap of working space between the PS/AL system and central computational functions. Despite the fact that Baddeley envisages the central executive as a computational system involved in almost every mental function (from parsing through high-level control of attention and action), he presents the working-memory model in terms that lead to us believe that he considers the CE, the AL, and the PS to be independent systems. Though we do not believe that the parser makes the special use of the AL and the PS that Baddeley's CE is said to, we also are not prepared to accept that the resource space utilized for parsing and for memory of the phonological form of lexical items is non-overlapping. On our view, though no special connections exist between the parsing work space and these memory-system components that would allow the parser to use items in phonological form, the parsing work space may share processing resources with these systems, such that a decrease in computational resources could affect all three of these functional systems: the parsing work space, a passive-decay memory system for the phonological form of lexical items (the PS), and an articulatory-based rehearsal mechanism that maintains representations in the passive-decay system (the AL). We remain agnostic regarding these possibilities, and our inability to decide between them is part of a large domain of ignorance regarding which mental functions share processing resources with the parser—the problem that we term that of the "external computational environment" of the parser. This is a large and complex area in which little research has been undertaken. Studies of associations and dissociations of deficits in other functional systems and those affecting the parser, coupled with dual-task experiments involving the parser in normals (Wanner and Maratsos 1978; Waters, Caplan, and Hildebrandt 1987) will be necessary to determine this aspect of mental architecture.

A Theory of Compensatory Heuristics

Errors patients make reflect failures of normal parsing and the use of compensatory heuristics for sentence interpretation. In the survey studies, we have repeatedly emphasized the occurrence of what we have called "strictly linear interpretations," in which thematic roles are assigned in the order Agent, Theme, and Goal to sequential NPs regardless of the syntactic structure of a sentence. Though these strictly linear interpretations are predominant in errors, patients in the survey studies also may be sensitive to what may be called "local" aspects of sentence form. For instance, many patient groups show equal numbers of 1,2 and 2,1 responses to passive sentences. This may simply reflect random performance, but, as noted by Grodzinsky (1986), it is also possible that sensitivity to the consequences of a *by*-phrase for thematic-role assignment leads to the 2,1 response whereas sensitivity to the global sequence of nouns and verbs leads to the 1,2 response.

Additional features of heuristics and their use emerge from the case studies. Besides the features of heuristics described above on the basis of the survey study, these cases show that the heuristics used by these patients usually respect basic aspects of sentence structure and meaning, such as the number of thematic roles assigned by a verb, the number of propositions expressed in a sentence, and the distinction between referentially dependent noun phrases and R-expressions. When these basic aspects of sentence form are not preserved, there is a strong tendency for the substitution of what may be considered unmarked values of the parameter in which the error occurs. For instance, A.B.'s change of three thematic roles to two sets of two in dative sentences is consistent with the notion that the unmarked functional structure for verbs involves two argument places.

The case studies also bear on the heuristics governing the assignment of antecedents to overt referentially dependent NPs, which were not explored in the materials used in the group studies. There is evidence that most of our patients prefer to assign antecedents locally when heuristics are used. Patients tended to assign Agent incorrectly to the preverbal noun in sentences like *John promised Bill to shave* and *John seems to Bill to be shaving*. In sentences containing a complex postverbal NP, such as *John persuaded a friend of Bill's to shave*, the most common error was to assign Agent to *Bill*. Furthermore, this tendency seems to be reflected in the choice of antecedents for overt pronouns. As table 6.1 shows, there is a correlation between accuracy in the subject-control structure and choice of the matrix subject as the antecedent of a pronoun in the embedded sentence. For patient G.G., two of the sentence types should be excluded from the correlation because of his great improvement between testing sessions. With these data excluded, there is a perfect rank-order correlation between accuracy on

Table 6.1
Rank order of accuracy on subject-control sentences and choice of matrix subject in sentences with pronouns.

Sentence type		Patient					
		J.V.	K.G.	A.B.	C.V.	G.G.
[17] Subject control John promised Bill to shave.	1V:	100%	75%	33%	25%	17%
[8] Embedded pronoun subject John promised Bill that he would shave.	1V:	83%	75%	—	58%	100%*
[7] Pronouns, complex NP John said that a friend of Bill's kicked him.	2V1:	83%	58%	25%	25%	17%
[9] Three NPs plus pronoun John told Bill that Peter kicked him.	3V1:	100%	42%	—	0	83%*

(Patients G.S., S.P., and R.L. were not tested on the relevant sentence types.)
* second testing session

subject-control sentences and frequency of choice of the matrix subject as antecedent of the pronoun, even though the selection of a different antecedent for the pronoun does not necessarily constitute a wrong answer.

This distance effect for pronouns stands in contradiction to the prediction, from hypothesis 4 of chapter 5, that the distance between an empty NP and its antecedent is not relevant at the level of the propositional list. However, it may be that linear distance becomes relevant during the use of a heuristic rather than as a factor making for complexity in the search through the propositional list for an antecedent during a normal parse. It is of interest, for example, that, unlike the aphasic patients, the normal control subjects did not show a consistent tendency across sentence types to choose a closer legal antecedent for pronouns, as table 6.2 shows.

Several questions may be raised about these error patterns. One regards their basic nature: What syntactic structures are assigned, and what rules govern the interpretation of these structures? Do the structures and processes that lead to these interpretations arise from residual language-specific knowledge, from language-universal factors, or from nonlinguistic causes? Are the processes responsible for these patterns obligatory (in the sense that patients have no option but to apply them to sentence interpretation when normal mechanisms fail), and are they related to task-internal and subject-internal variables? We shall discuss each issue in turn.

We begin with a linguistic analysis of the structures that underlie these errors. We divide the linguistic analysis into one part that is related to the syntactic structures assigned and one part that is related to the rules that interpret these structures. The error patterns we have documented can all be accounted for by the application of simple interpretive rules to linear sequences of major lexical categories. The 1,2 and 1,2,3 responses in one-verb sentences and the 1,2;1,3 and 1,2;2,3 responses in two-verb sentences can result from the application of the following rules to the sequence of nouns and verbs in a sentence:

1. In sequences of the form N-V-N or N-N-V, assign either the immediately preverbal noun or the first noun in the sentence the role of Agent, and assign the remaining noun the role of Theme.

2. In sentences with a verb requiring three arguments, assign the first noun the role of Agent, the second noun the role of Theme, and the third noun the role of Goal.

3. In a sentence with two verbs each of which has two argument places, use rule 1 iteratively around each verb.

The 2,1 responses in passive sentences could arise from a rule such as the following:

4. Assign the noun in the sequence by-N the thematic role of Agent.

Table 6.2
Comparison of normal subjects' selection of antecedents for pronouns and accuracy on subject-control sentences.

Sentence type		Subject A.C.	B.J.	D.S.	E.J.	H.G.	K.W.	K.W.2	M.F.	N.T.	P.G.	S.B.
[17] Subject control												
John promised Bill to shave.	1V:	100%	100%	100%	100%	100%	100%	83%	100%	100%	100%	92%
[6] Pronouns, simple NP												
John said that Bill hit him.	2V1:	100%	92%	100%	100%	100%	100%	92%	100%	92%	83%	100%
	2VX:	0	0	0	0	0	0	0	0	0	0	0
[8] Embedded pronoun subject												
John promised Bill that he would shave.	1V:	100%	100%	—	100%	100%	100%	83%	100%	100%	100%	75%
	2V:	0	0		0	0	0	17%	0	0	0	25%
	XV:	0	0		0	0	0	0	0	0	0	0
[7] Pronouns, complex NP												
John said that a friend of Bill's kicked him.	2V1:	92%	92%	50%	75%	67%	75%	50%	83%	67%	33%	75%
	2V3:	8%	8%	50%	8%	33%	25%	42%	17%	33%	67%	25%
	2VX:	0	0	0	8%	0	0	8%	0	0	0	0
[9] Three NPs plus pronoun												
John told Bill that Peter kicked him.	3V1:	92%	83%	—	42%	100%	92%	42%	92%	25%	67%	100%
	3V2:	8%	8%		50%	0	8%	50%	8%	50%	25%	0
	3VX:	0	0		0	0	0	0	0	0	0	0

Linear sequences of categories also are the basis for the heuristic assignment of antecedents of referentially dependent NPs.

Rules 1–4 mention only the linear sequences of major lexical categories (nouns and verbs) and one lexically specified preposition (*by*) as the syntactic structures to which interpretive algorithms apply. It is possible that other features of sentence form may also be used to assign thematic roles; for instance, the passive morphology may be important in recognizing a *by*-phrase as relevant to the assignment of the thematic role of Agent as opposed to being interpreted as a locative, and it may also be important in determining the verb whose argument structure is filled by the noun in the *by*-phrase. Even if these additional features of sentence form slightly complicate these very simple rules, the structures to which interpretive rules apply are still linear sequences of major lexical categories and associated morphological forms. We have not found it necessary to postulate hierarchically organized phrase markers as the structures to which interpretive rules apply to yield erroneous interpretations. Moreover, the interpretive rules themselves are very simple; they assign thematic roles on the basis of the absolute position of a noun in a sentence, simple precedence relations among items specified in a linear sequence of categories, and a few lexical items (such as *by*). These features of heuristics even apply to operations, such as coindexation of pronouns, that are usually sensitive to neither hierarchical nor sequential features of categories. Pending empirical evidence to the contrary, we conclude that the structures and interpretive rules that underlie erroneous responses have these properties of linearity and simplicity of interpretive mapping. We also conclude that patients who have disturbances of parsing utilize a mechanism that yields these structures and interprets them in this way. We shall refer to the use of this mechanism (or different mechanisms with these properties) as the use of a heuristic (or a set of heuristics) to interpret sentences.

In considering the psychological sources of such a mechanism, we first consider the structures themselves. These structures would result from the operation of lexical identification processes in conjunction with a memory system that maintains lexical items and their associated grammatical categories in linear sequences. Such a system is not part of the "central" operations and memory stores of the parser, since the parser stores constituents, not linear sequences of lexical categories, in its pushdown stacks. Nor is this system clearly the same as the short-term-memory system that underlies recall of items in lists, since the maintenance of category information is crucial to the mechanism postulated here and does not appear to be relevant to list recall (there is no evidence that N-V-N-V-N lists are better or worse recalled than N-V-V-V-N lists, for instance). We are reluctant to ascribe this mechanism to what we conceive of as "perceptual" operations, for several reasons. First, lexical access intuitively involves more than just "perception." Second, one part of this mechanism maintains categorized items in memory for at least the time needed to identify the nouns required by the argument structure of a verb, and we assume that the memory component of this mechanism falls outside the bounds of "perceptual" processes.

The linear sequences of major lexical categories and associated morphological markings are precisely those representations that we indicated were the input to the parser (see chapter 2). One possibility is that the mechanism that generates these structures is related to the operation of the earliest, "peripheral," or "pre-parsing" parts of a parser, which feed the lookahead buffer in the Berwick-Weinberg parser. Chomsky has suggested a possible source for this mechanism in his account of the nature of Universal Grammar. He suggests that Universal Grammar may be considered to be "a set of concepts and a set of theorems stated in terms of these concepts." "We may," he continues, "select a primitive basis of concepts in terms of which the others are definable ... perhaps subject to simplicity conditions of some sort.... In the case of Universal Grammar,... the primitive basis must meet a condition of epistemological priority.... we want the primitives to be concepts that can plausibly be assumed to provide a preliminary, pre-linguistic analysis of a reasonable selection of presented data; that is, to provide the primary linguistic data that are mapped by the language faculty onto a grammar.... It would, for example, be reasonable to suppose that concepts such as 'precedes' ... enter into the primitive basis.... But it would be unreasonable to incorporate, for instance, such notions as 'subject of a sentence' or other grammatical relations [i.e., concepts involving hierarchical structures—D.C. and N.H.] within the class of primitive notions, since it is unreasonable to suppose that these notions can be applied to linguistically unanalyzed data." (Chomsky 1981, p. 10)

Both the mechanism for assignment of structure and the interpretive rules that we have suggested underlie the errors on the object-manipulation test make use of primitive concepts, such as linear sequences of lexical categories and precedence, and not derived concepts, such as hierarchical structure, and thus can been seen as relying upon what Chomsky suggests may be one aspect of the primitive conceptual basis for language. Chomsky's use of the term *epistemological priority* to describe the character of these concepts captures the notion, with which we agree, that the aspect of cognition which provides the intrinsic content of these concepts is not derived from perceptual function, memory capacities, or general knowledge, but from general elementary cognitive analytic capacities of the human, which are present in the developing child. It is reasonable to suppose that such capacities are retained after brain demage and that they can form the basis for structuring linguistic input in a way that allows interpretive heuristics to be applied to input so analyzed, just as in children these primitive structuring processes feed the "theorems" of the language faculty.

Whether or not the mechanism that yields linear strings of category-labeled lexical items and maintains them in memory is derived from the pre-parsing segmentation mechanism of a deterministic parser and/or from some component of human cognition related to primitive processing of linguistic representations, it appears to be related to linguistic processing and to occur prior to parsing operations. It yields representations upon which the parser operates, if it can, and which are interpreted heuristically if the parser fails.

The interpretive aspects of the heuristics we have described are quite different from the algorithms of the parser. First, they utilize linear rather than hierarchical structure, as can be seen in the use of terms such as "immediately preverbal noun" in rule 1 above. Second, they use structure-independent notions, such as the absolute position of a lexical category in a sentence (e.g., "first noun" in rule 1), that are also not utilized by any other part of the language faculty (including the parser, which only makes use of structure-dependent concepts). These features testify that nonlinguistic factors are at work in the determination of the interpretive aspects of the compensatory mechanisms employed by aphasic patients. These features of the interpretive portions of heuristics are also simple (in ways that require careful characterization), and suggest that the interpretive aspects of heuristics may also arise from elementary cognitive capacities applied to the interpretation of simple structures.

We may indeed ask whether there is any truly linguistic aspect to the heuristic rules we have described, or whether they are entirely due to a pre-linguistic portion of human cognition that provides primitive structures and simple interpretive algorithms. At first glance, it seems reasonable to account for the fact that N-V-N(-Prep-N) sequences are most easily interpreted, and for the fact that they are interpreted as Agent-V-Theme(-Goal), by invoking language-specific features of English and French as part of the interpretive portion of the compensatory heuristics used by patients. However, the relative ease of assignment of the thematic roles of Agent, Theme, and Goal to nouns in N-V-N(-Prep-N) sequences may also result from pre-linguistic cognitive operations. It has been argued (Lightfoot 1982) that the drift from Subject-Object-Verb to Subject-Verb-Object as the canonical word order for human languages is due to the increased simplicity of the latter for parsing/interpretive operations on general epistemological grounds. Thus, based on our observations from these studies of English- and French-speaking aphasic patients alone, we must conclude that we have no convincing evidence that *any* purely linguistic factors are responsible for the heuristics used by aphasic patients in compensating for disorders of syntactic comprehension.

This, however, appears to be too strong a conclusion. Studies of syntactic comprehension using the object-manipulation technique with Japanese aphasics (Hagiwara and Caplan, in preparation) show a pattern of interpretations that differs in several important respects from that seen in the French and English patients studied here. Japanese is an S-O-V language, with postpositional Case markings, which allows N-V-N structures in right-dislocation and pseudo-cleft structures in which either the subject or the object may be N_2, as well as O-S-V constituent order (marked by Case). Japanese aphasics interpret Case-marked S-O-V sentences correctly significantly more often than Case-marked O-S-V or right-dislocation or pseudo-cleft structures, thus demonstrating that, unlike English and French aphasics, they interpret N-N-V word order most easily, and that they apply a language-specific word-order-based interpretive algorithm to this sequence of categories. Moreover, they assign thematic roles in the order Theme-Agent significantly more often than in the order Agent-Theme to N_1 and N_2 in N_1-V-N_2 sequences, regardless of construction type (right dislocation or pseudo-clefting) or Case marking. This is likely to result from language-specific topicalization processes. These results indicate considerable retention of language-specific parameters in the heuristics used by Japanese aphasics with respect to the interpretive algorithms applied to sequences of nouns and verbs. A parsimonious account of the origins of heuristics would thus ascribe the N-V-N(-Prep-N) mapping onto Agent-Theme(-Goal) to language-specific features of English and French.

The language-specific features of syntactic structure that determine basic word order and the direction of assignment of thematic roles in configurational languages include the direction of theta-mapping and the direction specified for headedness. The heuristic interpretive algorithms we have described cannot make use of these aspects of syntactic structure, since these language-specific parameters operate over hierarchically organized phrase markers not utilized by heuristics (as pointed out to us by L. Travis, 1986). Our hypothesis, therefore, is that language-specific parameters such as the direction of Case and theta-role assignment and headedness, which determine features such as the direction of branching and thus the basic word order of a language, serve to establish the frequency of the co-occurrence of semantic values, such as Agency, with superficial aspects of sentence form, such as preverbal or sentence-initial position. The frequency of these co-occurrences, in turn, serves as the basis for the interpretive aspect of the heuristics utilized by aphasic patients with parsing disorders.

The source of the interpretive aspect of these heuristics thus appears to be similar, if not identical, to that of the "mappings" which Bates and MacWhinney suggest underlie normal sentence comprehension. There is, however, evidence from our studies that the particular mappings involved in syntactic comprehension specified by these authors are not used by aphasic patients. In the Bates-MacWhinney paradigm, English sequences of the form N-N-V were most frequently interpreted as Theme-Agent sequences in structures controlled for animacy, whereas we have found that English and French aphasics assign Agent-Theme interpretations as often as Theme-Agent interpretations to these sequences. The relative unimportance of Case cues to thematic roles in the Japanese aphasics whose performance is cited above contrasts with the reliance of Bates and MacWhinney's German and Italian subjects on declension and agreement. These discrepancies indicate that the particular mappings identified by Bates and MacWhinney do not give rise to the heuristics used by aphasic patients. In turn, this suggests that the mappings identified by these authors may be artifacts of the particular experimental paradigm they utilized.[4]

Bates and MacWhinney also suggest (Bates et al. 1982) that the "mappings" used by normal subjects to assign sentential semantic features may be divided into one set based on "local" properties of lexical items and a second set based on more "global" properties of sentence structure. Case markings directly realized as morphological features on nouns are paradigmatic examples of the first type of input into a mapping, and the "word order" of a sentence is a paradigmatic example of the input into the second type of mapping; subject-verb-agreement phenomena and case markings carried on determiners occupy an intermediate position. Though we do not accept the notion of mappings as relevant to normal sentence interpretation, it has been suggested to us (D. Bub, personal communication, 1986) that a similar division of heuristics into those based on local cues (such as the presence of a *by*-phrase) and those based on larger structures (such as category sequences) may be relevant to aphasic performances. We have, so far, not found dissociations between the use of "local" and "general" or "global" structural cues in the heuristics applied by aphasic patients. Nor have we found dissociations among the various local cues that might be used heuristically by individual cases (such as the presence of a *by*-phrase or the attachment of the possessive morpheme to a proper noun in certain sentences used in the cases studies). However, we shall continue to look for such dissociations, and to seek natural-kind groupings of dissociations among heuristics, as part of the effort to further constrain the theory of the heuristics utilized by aphasic patients.

The final questions regarding these heuristics are whether they are obligatory and whether they are affected by subject-related or task-related variables. The survey studies suggest that the use of heuristics of the sort we have just described is obligatory. In the object-manipulation test, patients in all groups made similar errors. The level of proficiency in syntactic interpretation was related to an ability to achieve partially correct responses, thus affecting the errors patients make, but a tendency to produce strictly linear interpretations was ubiquitous and dominant in aphasics' assignment of erroneous thematic roles, regardless of sentence type or patient impairment, until patients were so impaired that no consistent pattern of sentence interpretation was found. Neither intrinsic pragmatic factors nor the spatial array of objects before the patients significantly determined patients' responses to the sentences presented in this task, though either could easily have done so. These two latter findings were also true of all patient groups and all sentence types. The ubiquity of these responses, based upon the heuristics we have outlined, would be explained by these heuristics being obligatory. A reasonable working hypothesis that emerges from the survey study is that the application of a heuristic with the properties described above is obligatory when normal sentence-comprehension mechanisms fail.

The relationship of the use of heuristics to the failure of the parser is further clarified by the study of individual cases. First, the data suggest that parsing itself is an obligatory, automatic process, even when it is impaired. For instance, patient C.V., who showed evidence of the use of a set of heuristics in generating a large number of their responses, attempted to structure sentences syntactically before applying a heuristic. This is evidenced by the fact that particular heuristics were not applied equally often to every sentence type, suggesting that C.V. was at least able to recognize certain features of the surface string. C.V.'s frequency of use of one heuristic was apparently dependent upon the presence of a relative pronoun, or possibly an NP without a thematic role, suggesting that C.V. was able to structure these sentences at least partially. These findings are consistent with the notion that syntactic parsing is itself an automatic process. If a syntactic parse occurs automatically, then the parser is automatically assigning structure to the extent that it can in each patient.

When the parser does not entirely succeed, patients obligatorily employ heuristics to complete the semantic properties of sentences. (In severely impaired patients, even the use of heuristics breaks down, and random responses are made.) However, though they are both obligatory and highly constrained as to their content, interpretive heuristics are not completely invariant. C.V. and A.B. do not use the same set of heuristics. For example, C.V. assigns a 1,2;2,3 interpretation to relative-clause sentences, while A.B. assigns a 1,2;1,3 interpretation. In sentences with referentially dependent NPs, C.V. tends to assign reflexive interpretations as a heuristic, while A.B. tends to assign disjoint interpretations as a heuristic. In addition, there is some variation in the heuristics each patient used, with the opposite response pattern occurring for the occasional two-verb sentence in each case. There is also evidence for some sensitivity to task-specific factors in the emergence of a heuristic. C.V. probably chose *a friend* as Agent of the embedded verb in sentences such as *Patrick expected a friend of Joe's to be shaving* and *Patrick appears to a friend of Joe's to be shaving* on the second testing session because of a task-specific strategy to assign Agency to *a friend* wherever this NP occurred on one battery.

At this time it cannot be predicted which heuristic a particular patient will select for a particular sentence type on a particular task. However, some sentential features have been identified that partially account for changes in the use of a heuristic by a particular patient. These factors include the order of nouns and verbs in a sentence, the presence of a referentially dependent element, the presence of a relative pronoun, the presence of the passive morphology and/or a *by*-phrase, and the presence of a word with semantic content (*friend*) in a sentence with proper nouns. We suggest that the variation in the use of heuristics as a function of the presence of these features of sentence form is the result of two factors. First, the parser itself can at times make use of these features to structure and interpret parts of a sentence, thus obviating the use of a heuristic at all. Second, some of these features of sentence form are themselves the basis for interpretive heuristics, such as the presence of a *by*-phrase in a passive sentence, which could alternate with word order to determine sentence interpretation.

If this theory is correct, two aspects of variation must be explained. The first is the variation in the use of particular heuristics. Though surface features of sentences constrain the set of the heuristics that are applicable in a given sentence, they do not determine the choice among the members of this set by a particular patient on a particular trial. We have no account of this variation at present. The second variation is in the adequacy of the parsing process, which, this theory maintains, fails intermittently. Again, we have no evidence upon which to base an account of this variation. An explanation of this variation is properly part of the theory of deficits, not of the theory of compensations to deficits, and we indicated in our previous discussion of deficits that we are inclined to the view that this variation reflects the effects of other mental functions (deployment of attention, variable proactive memory effects due to list composition, fatigue, etc.) on the resources available for parsing at a particular moment. We would be interested in other accounts of this variation and in evidence supporting any theory of the origin of this variation.

One feature of our data is potentially damaging to the analysis we have just presented: A.B.'s failure to accept his own erroneous interpretations of dative passive and dative cleft-object sentences as correct. If heuristics are obligatory and are constrained to apply uniformly in a given subject for a given syntactic structure, this result would not be expected. There are two possible explanations of this performance which merit investigation. Both ascribe A.B.'s failure to accept his own responses to differences between the object-manipulation task and the verification task. One is that the heuristics we have outlined are influenced by the manipulation aspects of the task, in addition to their reliance upon general cognitive and language-specific mechanisms. This seems extremely unlikely, given the absence of spatial effects on these heuristics. The second is that the enactment task requires not a judgment regarding the correctness of an interpretation but rather the patient's enactment of what he considers to be the best interpretation of a presented sentence, while the verification task requires a judgment as to the correctness of a response. Though the heuristics we have outlined generate interpretations for these sentences, it may be that the confidence a patient has in the correctness of these interpretations is not absolute in some cases. We are inclined to ascribe A.B.'s performance to the relationship between a judgment task and the output of heuristic interpretive mechanisms. This, too, deserves further investigation.

We have avoided discussing the occurrence of heuristics in relation to the concepts of "automatic" and "controlled" processes developed by Schneider and Shiffrin (1977), Shiffrin and Dumais (1981), and others, because we do not think these concepts are easily applied to the use of heuristics or to parsing itself. Shiffrin and Dumais (1981, p. 116) define an automatic process as one that does not decrease processing capacity and/or that is involuntarily initiated by particular external stimuli. Parsing does not fall into the category of automatic processes according to the first of these criteria, since it requires processing capacity (see discussion of the parsing work space above and in chapter 2); but it falls into this category according to the second criterion, since it is involuntarily initiated by the presentation of a sentence under ordinary circumstances. Heuristics are also obligatory, but they show task and subject variability which we believe is not under conscious control. For instance, C.V. erroneously took *a friend* as the Agent of the embedded verb in sentences of the form *Patrick appears to a friend of Joe's to be shaving* in the third battery on the second testing session, possibly because *a friend* is the correct choice for Agency in many sentences in this and other batteries used in that testing session. If this heuristic is triggered by these task-specific features, its use is not automatic according to the second criterion above, inasmuch as particular external stimuli independent of task-specific factors do not necessarily trigger its operation. On the other hand, the use of this heuristic is not likely to be under C.V.'s conscious control. We may thus say that heuristics are automatically engaged by the same linguistic stimuli that engage the parser, if the latter fails, but are under unconscious (including some task-specific) control. Exploration of the effects of stimulus list composition upon the frequency of occurrence of particular heuristics may shed further light on the nature of this unconscious control. Until further data are available, we cannot further develop this aspect of the theory of heuristic usage.

Thus, heuristics play important roles in determining interpretations of syntactic structures in these patients. They are responsible for errors and can also produce correct responses. The type and frequency of use of a heuristic is determined by lexical features, such as the number of thematic roles associated with the verb and the presence of an overt referentially dependent NP, and by surface features of the sentence, such as the order of nouns and verbs or the passive morphology. The use of a heuristic can also be observed to vary as sentences increase in complexity. On the basis of the results we have presented, we are prepared to advance a hypothesis regarding the nature of heuristics utilized by aphasic patients in the task of syntactic comprehension. We suggest that the structures on which interpretive heuristics are based all meet a criterion of epistemological priority, and that they consist of strings that are usually the input to the parser. The interpretive algorithms used by heuristics are also primitive, in that they specify simple mappings between linear sequences of categories and semantic features. These features of heuristics apply even for operations, such as coindexation of pronouns, that are usually sensitive to neither hierarchical nor sequential features of categories. It is also possible for the interpretive portion of a heuristic to apply to a structure created by the parser. Language-specific values of syntactic parameters, such as the direction of theta-role assignment and of headedness, the presence of Case marking, and the richness of inflectional agreement, influence the heuristics seen in a particular language. Heuristics are obligatorily activated, but they vary as a function of subject and task factors in ways that are not yet completely understood.

Syntactic Comprehension and Short-Term Memory

Although this study did not specifically compare detailed measures of short-term memory with a measure of sentence comprehension in most cases, it is clear that the nature of a syntactic-comprehension impairment is not predictable from digit or word recall span. Patients J.V. and K.G. each had a digit span of seven items, which was comparable to the average of the normal controls tested; and yet both patients scored less than 50% on particular sentence types, well below two standard deviations beneath normal performance. Patient B.O., who showed the shortest recall span of all of the patients reported here (three words and digits), showed relatively good comprehension—much better than A.B. and C.V., who had roughly comparable spans. The qualitative nature of impairments is also not predictable from span. B.O. was quite different from A.B. and C.V., and J.V. and K.G. also differed. Finally, heuristics are not determined by span. Patients A.B. and C.V., who both had low digit spans, adopted different heuristics of choosing the first noun as Agent of both the first and the second verb of a two-verb sentence, or of picking the NP appearing directly in front of each verb as the Agent of that verb, while B.O., with an equally low digit span, did not need to adopt this strategy.

This finding is of interest because of studies, such as that by Albert (1976), which have found a correlation between sentence comprehension and short-term-memory span. In our case studies, there was a correlation between digit and word recall span and overall sentence-comprehension accuracy. However, even though patients with high digit span may tend to perform better than patients with low digit span, this correlation is not invariant; specific deficits in syntactic processing ability can occur independent of a reduction in digit span. Conversely, low digit span may reflect a reduced short-term-memory capacity not directly related to the capacity needed for syntactic parsing and storage operations.

Reduced span may, however, entail post-interpretive difficulties. We argued that patient B.O.'s low digit span caused her difficulty in holding a list of NPs in memory at the post-syntactic level. It is also possible that A.B. suffered from a post-syntactic impairment in addition to his impairments in syntactic processing. His digit and word recall span was nearly as low as B.O.'s and he showed as many "reversal" errors (in which two thematic roles shown in a transitive action would be correct if reversed) as B.O. Future work must determine if a reduced digit or word recall span necessarily entails a reduction in this post-syntactic storage or in other post-interpretive operations (Waters, Caplan, and Hildebrandt 1987).

Implications for Linguistic Theory and Parsing Processes

We have interpreted the significant differences in mean correct score per sentence type in the group studies with the object-manipulation test as due to the effects of variable degrees of diminution in a work space devoted to syntactic comprehension on the ability to assign and interpret various aspects of syntactic structure. The aspects of syntactic structure that distinguish sentence types with significantly different mean correct scores must, therefore, be related to parsing mechanisms that take up parsing work space in normal subjects, on this view. We can suggest several aspects of the parsing process on the basis of these patterns.

The suggestion we can make with the greatest confidence on the basis of the group studies relates to the upper and lower bounds of the string on which some part of the parser operates. The low limit of the string is suggested by the greater ease all patient groups had with cleft-subject and active sentences than with cleft-object sentences This strongly suggests that the parser is sensitive to the entire noun-verb-noun or noun-noun-verb sequence; if it were able only to consider the noun-verb portion of these sentences, accurate assignment of Agency to the immediately preverbal noun in cleft-object sentences should result. The upper bound to the string examined by some part of the parser may be the number of nouns needed to fill the argument positions of a verb, along with the verb that determines the argument structure. The evidence for this upper bound is the patients' greater difficulty with two-verb sentences than with one-verb sentences (equated for word order). This greater difficulty suggests that one aspect of the parser operates on strings of nouns needed to fill the thematic roles to be assigned around the verb, and that when two verbs both require processing within one sentence unit, two such "buffers" are activated, increasing the resources required to structure and interpret the sentence. There are numerous ways in which the parsing of two-verb sentences might impose additional work-space requirements, such as triggering a new stack in the type of pushdown storage system outlined in chapter 2.

That there is increased difficulty in sentences with noncanonical thematic-role orders and in those with more arguments to be assigned around a verb suggests that extra computational space is required in sentences with these features at some point in the parsing/interpretive process.

The case studies we have presented also suggest features of syntactic structures and parsing operations. A primary assumption within both linguistic theory and parsing theory is that all evidence must converge on one model. Therefore, an account of one case must be consistent with the accounts of all other cases. When the possible accounts of the four cases showing a selective deficit with empty NPs (namely those of patients K.G., J.V., G.S., and G.G.) are considered together, several implications for linguistic and parsing models emerge.

First, as mentioned in the discussion concerning hypothesis 3 in chapter 5, there is some suggestion that PRO is coindexed at the syntactic level in obligatory-control structures. This analysis is needed if G.G.'s impairment is characterized as a difficulty in coindexing over a sentence boundary, and it is consistent with J.V.'s proposed impairment in transmitting thematic roles and K.G.'s difficulty related to holding an NP without a thematic role in memory.

Second, each of the proposed accounts is either supportive of or neutral toward Wasow's (1977) analysis of certain passives as lexical, with no empty NP at the syntactic level (see also Levin and Rappaport 1986). Taken together, the cases support this analysis, since the lexical passive analysis is required for at least one patient for the deficit analyses in all the cases to converge upon a single theory of syntactic structure. If J.V.'s deficit is characterized as a difficulty in coindexing over a sentence boundary, it forces the selection of the account in which G.G. has difficulty with [+ anaphoric] NPs, for which the lexical analysis of passives is required. Alternatively, the account that G.G. has difficulty in coindexing over a sentence boundary forces the selection of the account that J.V. has difficulty transmitting a thematic role, for which lexical analysis of the passive is required. Hence, no matter which analysis is adopted, the lexical analysis of the passive will be necessary for either J.V. or G.G.

Finally, the deficit analyses we have presented provide some support for Chomsky's Government and Binding (GB) theory of syntactic structure over Bresnan's (1982b) Lexical Functional Grammar (LFG). The argument stems from the double dissociation between disturbances affecting NP-raising seen in J.V. and K.G. and those affecting subject control of PRO seen in G.S. This double dissociation proves that each of these sentence types involves a representation and/or an operation that the other does not.

In GB theory, the assignment of the empty category PRO on the basis of the overtly subjectless infinitive in subject-control sentences would qualify as the operation unique to that structure, and the maintenance of the matrix-subject NP without a theta role assigned by its own verb, the creation of the NP trace in embedded subject position, and/or the transmission of the theta role from the NP trace to the matrix subject would qualify as the unique operation(s) in the NP-raising structures. Parsers based on LFG could specify several processes in NP-raising structures that are not found in the control structures, such as the maintenance in memory of the matrix NP in subject position without a theta role or a type of gap-hunting process searching for a referential dependency at the level of f-structure in sentences in which the matrix-subject NP is not assigned a theta role by the matrix NP. These processes could be impaired in J.V. and K.G. However, characterizing the deficit in G.S. is problematic for LFG and a type-transparently related parser. Suppose that the lexically specified marker that specifies subject control, which marks a verb as exempt from the usual hierarchy of functional control (see chapter 1), is the locus of the deficit in G.S. In that case, the deficit should affect only the verb *promise*, since the remaining subject-control verbs (*learn from, vow to*) take prepositional-phrase complements which do not c-command the embedded VP and thus, for these verbs, the subject NP is the only possible controller of the embedded VP, so G.S. should interpret sentences with these verbs correctly even if this lexically specified marker is unavailable (as was pointed out to us by C. Jakubowicz and D. Saddy). If the general process of functional control of an embedded VP complement by a matrix subject is the locus of the independent deficit in G.S., this deficit should also affect the NP-raising structures. Though we can characterize the verbs affected as those that require functional control of an embedded VP by the matrix-subject NP and do not assign a thematic role to the matrix-subject NP, we have no parsing account of why this class of verbs is affected. Thus, the second deficit in LFG must be one that applies to the lexical entry of each "subject-control" verb (*promise, vow to, learn from*) and not the lexical entries for NP-raising verbs (*appear, seem*). Clearly this account is missing a significant generalization, which can be stated only in a parsing theory that recognizes a parsing operation in the subject-control cases that is not present in the NP-raising cases. A parser that is type-transparently related to GB theory allows for the existence of such an operation (the Berwick-Weinberg parser contains one related to the construction of PRO as subject of the embedded infinitive); a parser that is type-transparently related to LFG cannot formulate such an operation in any way we can think of.[5]

Thus, these cases provide evidence relevant to several aspects of linguistic theory, including the choice among competing theories of syntactic structure.

Implications for the Neural Basis for Language Functions

A widely accepted model of the functional neuroanatomy of the perisylvian cortex for language maintains that narrow and invariant localization of language-processing subcomponents exists within this area. According to this model, the permanent representations for the sounds of words are stored in Wernicke's area, the association cortex of the second temporal gyrus. These auditory representations are accessed after auditory presentation of language stimuli. They, in turn, evoke the concepts associated with words in the "concept center." According to Geschwind (1965), a critical part of this process involves the inferior parietal lobe. In spoken-language production, concepts access the phonological representations of words in Wernicke's area, which are then transmitted to the motor-programming areas for speech in Broca's area, the association cortex of the pars triangularis and opercularis of the third frontal gyrus and possibly that of the Rolandic (frontal) operculum. Simultaneously, according to Lichtheim (1885), the concept center activates Broca's area. The proper execution of the speech act depends upon Broca's area receiving input from both these different cortical areas, each conveying different types of linguistically relevant representations. The principal evidence in favor of this model is said to be the occurrence of specific syndromes of language disorders that can be accounted for by lesions of these centers and the connections between them (Wernicke 1874; Lichtheim 1885; Geschwind 1965; Benson and Geschwind 1971; Benson 1979).

This theory incorporates two claims common to all the traditional neurolinguistic theories that postulate localization of components of the language-processing sysem. First, all these theories claim that, if one ignores the lateralization of language functions, the localization of components of the language system is the same in all normal adults. Second, they all derive the specific functions of the subareas of language-related cortex from the relationship of these subareas to motor and sensory areas of the brain. For instance, Geschwind (1965) relates the language functions of the inferior parietal lobe to its connections, as well as to its intrinsic elements and organization, indicating that prefrontal cortex, which does not have similar connections, has no language functions despite its equally advanced structural character. Similarly, Luria (1947) explicitly derives the particular role of areas of cortex in language from the role of adjacent cortex in motor and sensory function.

The empirical evidence for this theory is very weak. Numerous exceptions and counterexamples to the localization of the classical aphasic syndromes were documented in the era of clinico-pathological studies (Freud 1891; Marie 1906; Moutier 1908; see Bogen and Bogen 1976 for a review of one syndrome). The correlation of lesion site with aphasic syndrome in more recent studies of both selected and unselected aphasic groups using CT scanning also does not confirm this theory. Mohr, Pessin, Finkelstein, Funkenstein, Duncan, and Davis (1978) showed that a permanent Broca's aphasia requires a large lesion, which they throught occupied the entire upper bank of the perisylvian cortex. Kertesz, Sheppard, and Mackenzie showed that auditory comprehension is disturbed not by a lesion disconnecting Wernicke's area from the inferior parietal lobe but rather by a lesion at the junction of the parietal and occipital lobes. Basso, Lecours, Moraschini, and Vanier (1985) found that at least 15% of cases in a large unselected series of aphasics with vascular lesions involved lesion sites that violated even the basic anterior/posterior lesion-deficit correlations predicted by this theory.

Though advocates of the classical theory rely on syndrome-lesion correlations for support, one could argue that the theory may be correct despite the failure of these correlations to emerge in many studies. This is because the heterogeneity of symptoms in a given case and the polytypical nature of classical aphasic syndromes (Schwartz 1984) makes syndrome-lesion correlations difficult to use as a database for localizing specific language functions. This suggests that a better way to approach the issue of the neural basis for language would be to study deficit-lesion correlates in groups of patients with more narrowly delineated deficits. Our group study is one of a number of recent studies that have taken the next step in this area of research by correlating more specific impairments with lesions (see also McFarling, Rothi, and Heilman 1982; Roeltgen, Sevush, and Heilman 1983; Vanier and Caplan 1985; in press; Niccum, Speaks, Rubens, Knopman, York, and Larson 1986).

We have argued that one important component of the functional deficit in patients in the survey study is the degree of diminution of the work space available for syntactic comprehension in a given patient. This factor was the most important determinant of the level of correct performance of the patients tested on our battery. The subgroups that we have identified by means of clustering analyses primarily reflect overall severity and, we have argued, therefore represent groups of patients with roughly similar, and progressively greater, diminutions in the work space available for syntactic-comprehension processes. Though we cannot correlate specific parsing deficits with lesions, because we do not yet have large enough numbers of patients with specific deficits, our study allows us to examine the lesion correlates of different degrees of reduction in the parsing work space.

Thus, the fact that lesions confined to different portions of the perisylvian cortex are found in all the subgroups identified in the survey study has important implications for a theory of the neurological basis for language. Since patients in the poorest-performing groups have an extremely reduced syntactic work space, and since patients in these groups can have lesions affecting a single lobe within the perisylvian association cortex, we may conclude that this work space can be localized in a single lobe of the perisylvian cortex in some patients. However, this localization varies across all the lobes of the perisylvian cortex. We do not have enough patients to be certain, but this variable localization of the work space relevant to syntactic comprehension does not seem to be constrained in any way by sex, age, or educational level, since there are no obvious tendencies for patients in any of the identified subgroups to have lesions in particular lobes of perisylvian cortex as a function of these parameters. Thus, it appears that the variability in localization of the syntactic work space is not constrained by these factors. A reasonable hypothesis is that it is under direct genetic control, through a mechanism yet to be elucidated.

The fact that a lesion within any particular lobe of the perisylvian cortex may also produce a level of impairment that classifies the patient in the best-performing group or leads to a performance that is indistinguishable from normal indicates that syntactic comprehension may also be largely or entirely spared by a lesion in any lobe of the perisylvian cortex. This rules out another theory of the representation of language in the brain: the theory that the neural basis for syntactic comprehension involves "mass action" (Lashley 1950). On this theory, the amount of neural tissue removed—perhaps from a critical area of the brain—determines the extent of a functional impairment. The fact that tissue in a single lobe within the perisylvian cortex can be associated with all degrees of syntactic impairment, including the absence of any demonstrable disturbance, indicates that this principle does not pertain to the cerebral basis for syntactic-comprehension functions.

Our survey study shows that the degree of impairment of syntactic comprehension is independent of lesion location within the perisylvian cortex. This pattern also rules out "equipotentiality" (Lashley 1950) as the neural basis for syntactic-comprehension functions. Equipotentiality holds that areas of the brain may substitute for a damaged area to accomplish a function. If equipotentiality were true of the neural basis for syntactic comprehension, lesions in a single lobe would never result in impairments of this function, (or, at least, should not result in severe impairments in this function). The results presented in chapter 4 indicate that, though spared syntactic comprehension is possible after lesions in a single lobe, it is the exception and not the rule.

Thus, our data indicate that invariant localization of the functions involved in syntactic comprehension in a single lobe of the perisylvian cortex, mass action, and equipotentiality are all inadequate models for describing the neural basis for syntactic comprehension. It appears that the work space responsible for the comprehension of syntactic structures is variably localized within the perisylvian cortex, with considerable individual variation in the exact location of the neural tissue that supports this function. Moreover, though there are no direct measurements of lesion size in the present study, the data suggest that the amount of cortex responsible for syntactic-comprehension functions is also highly variable across the population. This suggestion follows from the fact that lesions in a particular area are found in patients with varying degrees of impairment in syntactic comprehension. One simple way of accounting for the variation in severity of syntactic-comprehension impairments in patients with lesions within a single lobe would be to postulate that this variability is directly correlated with the amount of syntactic work space located in that lobe in an individual patient. Variability in the amount of syntactic work space located in an individual lobe would be an immediate consequence of variability in the extent of the neural tissue in the perisylvian association cortex in which such a work space was located. Thus, we tentatively suggest that both the site and the amount of cortex in the perisylvian region devoted to the function of syntactic comprehension are highly variable across adult humans.

The extent of individual variation of this and other portions of the language-processing sysem within the perisylvian association cortex remains a matter for further investigation. The genetic, organic environmental, and environmental psychological determinants of any constraints on such variation in the localization of subcomponents of the language-processing system also remain to be determined. Our study of the lesions in patients with syntactic-comprehension impairments indicates that the neural basis of the "local computational environments" of this function varies in different adults, and that this variation is not constrained by such factors. If this is the case, the exact location of the neural tissue responsible for this operating system in an individual is likely to be under direct control of the genome of that individual. This may be true of the neural substrate responsible for all central language-computation operations. This theory of the neural basis for language contrasts with the classical clinically derived model in that it emphasizes the contribution of the genome to the neural basis of language and the independence of the neural basis of central language processing from motor and sensory influences. This theory thus begins to explore the issues regarding the neural basis for language raised by nativist and modular theories of language structure, acquisition, and processing (see, e.g., Chomsky 1965, 1981; Klein 1978; Fodor 1983; Caplan 1984).

Final Considerations

We have presented the results of several detailed analyses of disturbances affecting the interpretation of syntactic form in aphasic patients, and made a number of suggestions on the basis of our findings regarding the general form of a theory of deficits of this function and regarding normal structures and processes. We shall conclude by presenting a capsule analysis of what we think we have done, what we know we have not done, and what we think is worth doing in the future.

We believe we have shown that disturbances of syntactic comprehension can be described and, to some extent, explained by reference to theories of normal language structure and processing. Detailed analyses of the deficits in syntactic comprehension in individual aphasic patients can be related to quite abstract and specific constructs in recent models of syntactic structure and parsing. We believe that we have documented the feasibility of accomplishing detailed empirical studies into this aspect of aphasia with the theoretical tools of modern linguistics, psycholinguistics, and artificial intelligence, and that we have shown that the use of these tools leads to far clearer descriptions and explanations of the details of the performance of aphasic patients on syntactic-comprehension tasks than can be acheived without their use. We also believe we have shown that the pattern of performance of aphasic patients can be used to generate evidence relevant to the choice between competing linguistic analyses and parsing models.

We are aware that our study is heavily dependent on one model of syntactic structure and a related parser. Clearly, the requirement that one model of aphasic disturbances of syntactic comprehension in reference to a theory of linguistic structure and parsing does not allow one to pick a theory of normal function arbitrarily. We chose the model we did for the reasons outlined in chapter 1. As it turns out, the analyses we consider to best describe and explain these data are analyses that we believe support the theory with which we began. We are anxious to know whether other researchers agree with our specific analyses of these data, and to learn of other detailed case studies that support or refute the theories of normal function upon which our analyses are based.

We believe we have shown that quite a lot can reasonably be inferred about disturbances affecting unconscious aspects of parsing processes from the use of "off-line" dependent variables, such as error rates on the comprehension tests we used. One of the things we know we have not done is provide evidence from other sources that these analyses of deficits are correct. Such evidence could come from performances of patients on tasks that utilize off-line dependent variables (such as grammaticality judgments) and tasks that utilize on-line dependent variables (such as phoneme monitoring, click detection, and word monitoring). We wish to stress, however, that the use of such tests to verify hypotheses stated at the level of detail presented here for single cases requires detailed, systematic, and principled analyses of how patients perform on linguistic structures on each task, and that without such detailed linguistic analyses the utility of these tests for ascertaining the functional locus of a deficit is much reduced. For instance, patients' performances on grammaticality-judgment tasks in which the specific structures a patient constructs to achieve a particular pattern of performance can be ascertained would be an extremely useful method to apply simultaneously with comprehension tests of the type we used. Together, they could provide converging evidence regarding the functional locus of a parsing impairment, as could various on-line measures of local processing load in particular structures in patients in whom processing load is inferred to create specific parsing difficulties on the basis of the results of comprehension tests. However, broadly formulated deficit analyses and those not supported by a sufficiently large and adequately focused database do not advance the analysis of individual patients' deficits in detail, no matter what type of task is used. This area of linguistic aphasiology requires models of subject and patient performance in relation to the details of linguistic structure in any task in which performance is used to bear on deficits in the syntactic-comprehension process.

The reason we emphasize these requirements is that it seems to us that the greatest challenge in this area of linguistic aphasiology—and probably in other areas of this field—is to set justified constraints on the types of constructs that can enter into descriptions and explanations of the data provided by aphasics' performances. Clearly, linguistic theory and parsing models are rich sources of such constraints, and we have attempted to take advantage of their existence by describing specific deficits in relation to identified structures and operations in such models. We are aware, however, that we are just groping toward the outlines of a theory of deficits and compensations. For instance, though we have classified specific deficits into those producing loss and misutilization of representations and processes in the manner described earlier in this chapter, we are left at this point with the very general claim that every natural kind in parsing or syntactic theory could be subject to individual disruption—a claim that "everything dissociates," which has been heard elsewhere in aphasiology.

This may be true, but it leads to many problems; how, for instance, could one distinguish a disturbance affecting a natural-kind grouping of structures or operations from a set of disturbances affecting each of the members of such a set? The basic theoretical question is whether the "everything dissociates" assumption is correct in this functional domain (and elsewhere in aphasiology). To take another example: The notion of a syntactic work space, crucial to our theory of deficits in this area, is almost completely undefined. We have argued that it is distinct from other constructs in the psychological literature, such as Baddeley's concept of working memory, but this is hardly surprising given that the two concepts emerged from the study of very different psychological processes, and not very helpful in determining what the work space *is*. More work into the manner in which parsing algorithms are instantiated will be needed to explore deficits of this sort in a formal way. Similarly, we have only begun to explore the constraints on the heuristics patients use to compensate for their disorders in this functional sphere. Though we have constrained ourselves as much as possible by relating specific deficits to aspects of linguistic and parsing theory, the task of justifying constraints on the descriptions and explanations that can appear in this area of linguistic aphasiology is far from completed.

We take this as the major challenge in theoretical linguistic aphasiology in the immediate future. It suggests that real progress will be made through more detailed analyses of individual cases, based on linguistic and parsing theory, in which the nature of postulated deficits and compensations will be considered at the highest possible level of linguistic detail, and through studies of normal subjects that will clarify the nature of some of the constructs that these analyses of aphasic phenomena suggest (such as that of a syntactic work space).

Another subject for future research is that of the neuropathological correlates of these disturbances, which, as we described above, have implications for the neural basis of normal language functions. It is unlikely that large series of patients with specific deficits will be collected in which any observed variation in the loci of neural lesions will be related to the endogenous and exogenous factors of interest to a theory of the neural basis of language and its genetic and environmental determinants. However, if the concept of a reduction in syntactic work space is valid, it is not unrealistic to expect the radiologic study of series of patients with similar degrees of reduction in this space. Since different modern imaging techniques reveal different aspects of lesions, much correlational work could be done, even in cases of vascular pathology. If we broaden the population to include patients with nonvascular pathology, both the opportunities and the challenges of such correlational studies increase.

In fine, we believe that the work we have presented here is part of an approximately decade-old approach to the empirical study of the details of acquired neurogenic language breakdown in relation to rich and principled theories of language structure and processing. We believe that we are beginning to see that studies in many areas of linguistic aphasiology are possible at this level of detail, and that we are beginning to amass evidence that concepts from linguistics, psycholinguistics, and artificial intelligence contribute to—indeed are essential to—the description and explanation of regularities in the details of aphasic performance. Though the most important questions about this breakdown remain unanswered, we believe we are now beginning to see more clearly what they are.

Appendix
Detailed Description of Patient Clusters

Experiment 1

The mean correct responses and standard deviations for all subgroups are given in table 4.4. The first three groups performed extremely well on all one-verb sentences. They differed in their performance on two-verb sentences. Group 1 interpreted all two-verb sentences quite well; group 2 interpreted object-subject sentences well and conjoined and subject-object sentences poorly; group 3 interpreted conjoined sentences well and subject-object and object-subject sentences poorly. The standard deviations for each of these subgroups' performances on each of these sentence types are low, even when the mean correct score is low on a sentence type, indicating considerable homogeneity of patient performance within each group. We conclude that these patients were all capable of interpreting one-verb sentences well, but that they began to break down on certain types of sentences containing two verbs. Since all our two-verb sentences were of identical length and contained the same numbers of nouns, verbs, and function words, we conclude that the differences in the patterns of interpretation of these sentences reflect differences in the syntactic structure of the sentences. Here we have the first indication that different groups of patients differ with respect to their ability to interpret different syntactic structures.

Groups 4 and 5 showed much higher error rates for certain one-verb sentences than groups 1, 2, and 3. With a noncanonical thematic-role order, as in passive, cleft-object, and dative passive sentences, these groups' perfomances dropped dramatically. Performance on dative sentences, in which three noun phrases must be assigned thematic roles around a single verb, was not as good as performance on active and cleft-subject sentences, which require only the assignment of two thematic roles around a verb, and also not as good as the near-perfect performance of groups 1, 2, and 3 on these sentences. Performance on sentences with two verbs was quite poor, although responses were provided for most of the two-verb sentences. It thus appears that patients in groups 4 and 5 began to have considerable trouble with sentences containing two verbs and sentences containing a noncanonical order of thematic roles, and some difficulty with sentences in which three thematic roles must be assigned around a single verb even in canonical order.

There are several differences between groups 4 and 5. Because of the small number of subjects in these groups, statistical analyses of these differences were not undertaken; however, it is apparent that patients in group 4 interpreted passive and cleft-object sentences more accurately than patients in group 5 and that patients in group 5 interpreted conjoined sentences more accurately than those in group 4. These differences are reflected in the ratings of the different sentence types in the third eigen-vector of the PCA: the high values of passive, cleft-object, and conjoined sentence types on this eigenvector (see table 4.4) serve to separate groups 4 and 5 (see figure 4.2).

Groups 6 and 7 consisted of patients who were able to provide re-sponses to sentences containing one verb with two thematic roles but who failed to provide responses to the majority of sentences with three thematic roles to be assigned by a single verb and to sentences with two verbs. Again, statistical analysis of significant differences in mean correct scores between these two groups is difficult because of the small number of subjects in each group, but there were more correct responses for active and cleft-subject sentences in group 7 than in group 6, and more correct responses for passive sentences in group 6 than in group 7. Patients in group 6 assigned Agency and Theme with roughly equal frequency to both nouns in all one-verb, two-argument-place sentences, whereas pa-tients in group 7 provided more correct responses when both word order and thematic-role order were canonical. The high loading of active and cleft-subject sentences on the second eigenvector of the PCA reflects these patterns and leads to a complete separation of groups 6 and 7 by this factor (figure 4.1). Patients in group 8 could not perform this task.

Experiment 2

Complete data on the performance of patients in each group in experiment 2 on each sentence type, including all erroneous responses, are given in tables A1–A5.

Patients in group 1 were minimally impaired with respect to their ability to assign and interpret syntactic structure. All one-verb sentences, with the exception of the dative passive, were interpreted almost perfectly. There were slightly more errors on dative passive than on two-verb sentences; however, given the large number of possible responses for each of these sentence types, the correct response occurred more frequently than would be expected by chance on all. It does appear that, for patients in this group, the presence of a second verb or a third thematic role in combination with a noncanonical order of thematic roles led to difficulty in sentence interpre-

Table A1
Responses to two-place verb sentences by subgroup, experiment 2.

Sentence type	Response	Subgroup				
		I	II	III	IV	V
Active	0	—	—	—	—	10
	*12	45	71	25	22	—
	21	—	4	—	8	—
Passive	0	—	—	—	—	10
	12	2	32	22	10	—
	*21	43	43	3	20	—
Cleft-subject	0	—	—	—	1	10
	*12	45	72	23	17	—
	21	—	3	2	12	0
Cleft-object	0	—	—	—	—	10
	12	1	38	24	16	—
	*21	44	37	1	14	—

*correct response

Table A2
Responses to three-place verb sentences by subgroup, experiment 2.

Sentence type	Response	Subgroup				
		I	II	III	IV	V
Dative	0	—	2	8	15	10
	*123	43	58	11	5	—
	132	1	5	5	5	—
	213	1	5	1	1	—
	231	—	2	—	2	—
	312	—	1	—	1	—
	321	—	2	—	1	—
Dative passive	0	—	5	7	14	10
	123	4	20	10	6	—
	132	1	2	1	5	—
	213	—	8	2	3	—
	231	—	2	1	—	—
	*312	39	31	2	2	—
	321	1	7	2	—	—

*correct response

Table A3
Responses to conjoined sentences by subgroup, experiment 2.

Response	Subgroup				
	I	II	III	IV	V
1212			2		
*1213	37	49	12	3	
1221					
1223	6	14	2	6	
1231		1			
1232		2			
1312	1	1		1	
1313					
1321			1		
1323		1			
1331					
1332					
2112					
2113		2	1		
2121					
2123		2	1	3	
2131		1			
2132					
2312					
2313					
2321			1		
2323					
2331					
2332					
3112					
3113					
3121					
3123				1	
3131					
3132		1			
3212					
3213					
3221					
3223					
3231	1				
3232					
NR		1	5	16	10

*correct response

Table A4
Responses to subject-object sentences by subgroup, experiment 2.

Response	Subgroup				
	I	II	III	IV	V
1212					
1213	2	10	10	1	
1221					
1223	7	20	2	5	
1231		1	1		
1232		1			
1312	1	3	1		
1313					
1321					
1323				1	
1331					
1332		1		1	
2112					
*2113	33	11	3		
2121			1		
2123		12	1		
2131		3	1	1	
2132		1			
2312					
2313		2			
2321				1	
2323					
2331					
2332					
3112	1	3		1	
3113					
3121		1			
3123		1			
3131					
3132					
3212					
3213					
3221				2	
3223					
3231		1			
3232					
NR	1	4	5	17	10

*correct response

Table A5
Responses for object-subject sentences by subgroup, experiment 2.

Response	Subgroup				
	I	II	III	IV	V
1212			2		
1213	3	16	9	2	
1221		1		1	
*1223	41	38	3	4	
1231		2			
1232		4	2		
1312	1	1	1	2	
1313					
1321		1			
1323		1		1	
1331					
1332		4			
2112					
2113		3			
2121					
2123			1		
2131			1		
2312					
2313					
2321					
2323					
2331					
2332					
3112		1		1	
3113					
3121				2	
3123					
3131					
3132					
3212					
3213					
3221		1			
3223					
3231		1			
NR		1	6	17	10

*correct response

tation. Under these circumstances, the patients in this group assigned thematic roles in a strictly linear fashion to the nouns in the presented sentences, interpreting the first noun as Agent, the second as Theme, and the third as Goal, as appropriate to the argument structure of the verb.

Patients in group 2 showed strong word-order and thematic-role-order effects. For sentence types matched for the number of theta roles (active versus passive, cleft-subject versus cleft-object, dative active versus dative passive, and conjoined and object-subject versus subject-object), the latter sentence types, with noncanonical word order or thematic-role order, were more difficult to interpret. In addition, there were effects upon correct performance of the number of theta roles assigned by a verb (manifest by the increased difficulty of dative over active and cleft-subject sentences) and of the number of verbs in a sentence (manifest by the increased difficulty of two-verb sentences over one-verb sentences) when sentences with either canonical or noncanonical word order were compared. The majority of errors made by patients in this group consisted of linear assignments of thematic roles to nouns. It thus appears that patients in group 2 were able to assign and interpret all aspects of syntactic structure but were extremely sensitive to processing load: the presence of a third thematic role, a second verb, or a noncanonical word or thematic-role order occasioned difficulty, and these factors were, to some extent, additive in their effects on parsing and interpretation. When the parser failed, patients in group 2 used a linear interpretive heuristic to assign meaning to sentences.

Patients in group 3 also showed effects of word order and thematic-role order, number of theta roles, and number of verbs upon their ability to interpret sentences, but unlike the patients in group 2 they showed little evidence of any retained ability to interpret noncanonical thematic-role order. Patients in this group achieved the lowest scores on passive and cleft-object sentences of any patient group identified (except group 5). Patients in this group produced primarily 1,2;1,3 responses as errors. If a heuristic generated this response to two-verb sentences, the higher number of correct responses on conjoined versus object-subject sentences could also result from its use. Thus, given the possible existence of this heuristic, we cannot conclude that patients in this group were conjoining clauses or verb-phrases rather than embedding them. The correct responses for active, cleft-subject, and dative sentences may also reflect the operation of a strictly linear interpretive strategy, not any structure-building operations that the patients accomplished.

Superficially, patients in group 4 seem to have performed better than those in group 3 on passive and cleft-object sentences; however, it is clear from the overall performance of this group that this improved performance should be taken not as an indication of these patients' abilities to interpret these noncanonical word and thematic-role orders but, rather, as the result of a completely random assignment of thematic roles to noun phrases in all sentence types. Examination of the distribution of error types in patients in this group clearly shows that all but two-place one-verb sentences produced a large number of nonresponses, and that, though linear interpretive patterns were marginally more frequent than other error patterns, they were not as predominant in this group for the three-place and two-verb sentences as they were in other groups. Thus, patients in this group were not attempting to assign syntactic structure or to interpret the linear sequence of nouns and verbs in sentences; they were simply assigning thematic roles randomly to nouns in two-place verb sentences.

Patients in group 5 were unable to perform the test.

Experiment 3

The data from experiment 3 are given in tables A6–A10.

Group 1 consists of seven subjects, all of whom did extremely well on all sentence types.

Cluster 2 consists of nine patients whose scores were almost perfect on all but subject-object and object-subject sentence types. Though correct responses constitute the most frequent response to this sentence type, only 17 of 45 subject-object sentences were interpreted correctly. There are two errors which occurred with any frequency for subject-object relatives: the strictly linear 1,2;1,3 response and the partially correct 2,1;2,3 response. Patients in this group interpreted 26 of 45 object-subject sentences correctly, and made fourteen 1,2;1,3 erroneous responses to sentences of this type.

Cluster 3 consists of seven patients who made a large number of errors in one-verb sentences with noncanonical thematic-role order. Approximately one-third of the passive and cleft-object sentences were misinterpreted. The patients in this group also made six errors in 35 dative sentences, and only five out of 35 dative-passive sentences were interpreted correctly. For dative and dative-passive sentences there is a wide scatter of error types; the most frequent error type on dative-passive sentences was strictly linear (15/35). Conjoined sentences evoked 22/35 correct responses and 8/35 1,2;2,3 responses. Subject-object sentences produced 24/35 errors, of which 18 were strictly linear (10 of the form 1,2;1,3 and 8 of the form 1,2;2,3). Object-subject sentences were interpreted well: 28 of 35 responses were correct, and 5 were of the form 1,2;1,3. Patients in cluster 3 were best able to interpret sentences that were in canonical form, making for more errors on passive, cleft-object, dative-passive, and subject-object sentences than on corresponding sentence types with equivalent numbers of verbs and argument positions around verbs. They applied strictly linear interpretations when interpreting two-verb sentences.

Table A6
Responses to two-place verb sentences by subgroup, experiment 3.

Sentence type	Response	Subgroup						
		I	II	III	IV	V	VI	VII
Active	*12	35	44	33	36	35	19	1
	21	—	1	2	4	5	6	6
	NR	—	—	—	—	—	—	18
Passive	12	—	—	10	28	20	9	4
	*21	35	45	25	12	20	16	3
	NR	—	—	—	—	—	—	18
Cleft-subject	*12	35	45	32	39	34	6	5
	21	—	—	3	1	6	19	2
	NR	—	—	—	—	—	—	18
Cleft-object	12	4	5	12	33	23	13	4
	*21	31	40	22	7	17	12	3
	NR	—	—	—	—	—	—	18

* correct response

Table A7
Responses to three-place verb sentences by subgroup, experiment 3.

Sentence type	Response	Subgroup						
		I	II	III	IV	V	VI	VII
Dative	NR	—	—	—	12	15	18	24
	*123	35	33	29	21	13	4	—
	132	—	1	5	3	5	—	—
	213	—	1	1	2	5	1	1
	231	—	—	—	—	1	2	—
	312	—	—	—	1	0	—	—
	321	—	—	—	1	1	—	—
Dative passive	NR	—	—	2	17	16	18	25
	123	—	1	15	12	10	2	—
	132	—	1	3	2	1	—	—
	213	—	3	5	1	5	1	—
	231	—	—	1	—	1	—	—
	*312	35	35	5	7	4	4	—
	321	—	—	4	1	3	—	—

* correct response

Table A8
Responses to conjoined sentences by subgroup, experiment 3.

Response	Subgroup						
	I	II	III	IV	V	VI	VII
1212			1				
*1213	34	32	27	29	6	6	
1221							
1223	1	1	8	4	1	1	
1231						1	
1232			1		2	1	
1312				1	4	1	
1313							
1321							
1323						1	
1331							
1332				1		1	
2112							
2113		1			1	1	
2121							
2123					5		
2131						1	
2132				1	1	1	
2312						1	
2313			1			1	
2321					1		
2323							
2331							
2332							
3112					1	1	
3113							
3121							
3123							
3131							
3132					3		
3212						1	
3213							
3221				1			
3223							
3231		1		1	4		
3232							
NR			3	2	11	6	25

*correct response

Table A9
Responses to subject-object sentences by subgroup, experiment 3.

Response	Subgroup						
	I	II	III	IV	V	VI	VII
1212							
1213		9	10	17	7		
1221						1	
1223		1	8	7	1	1	
1231							
1232							
1312		1	1	2	1	1	
1313							
1321							
1323							
1331							
1332							
2112		2			1		
*2113	32	17	11	2	2	4	
2121							
2123	3	10	2	1	3		
2131				2		1	
2132		1			1		
2312							1
2313						1	
2321		1	1				
2323							
2331							
2332							
3112		1					
3113							
3121						2	
3123							
3131							
3132		2			4		
3212							
3213							
3221					1	2	
3223							
3231							
3232							
NR		1	2	9	14	12	24

*correct response

Table A10
Responses to object-subject sentences by subgroup, experiment 3.

Response	Subgroup						
	I	II	III	IV	V	VI	VII
1212							
1213	1	14	5	17	8	4	
1221							
*1223	33	26	28	12	2	3	
1231				1			
1232					1	3	
1312				1	4		
1313							
1321							
1323							
1331							
1332			2				
2112							
2113		1			3		
2121							
2123				1	3		
2131						1	
2132						1	
2312	1			1			
2313							
2321		1			2		
2323							
2331							
2332							
3112				1	1		
3113							
3121						1	
3123							
3131							
3132		1					
3212							
3213		2					
3221				1	1	1	
3223							
3231					2		
3232							
NR				4	14	11	25

*correct response

Cluster 4 consists of eight patients who failed to provide responses to some sentences of certain types. Most two-place verb sentences received the 1,2 interpretation. Dative and dative-passive sentences evoked a considerable number of nonresponses; there were more nonresponses to either of these sentence types than to any of the two-verb sentences. There were also noticeable numbers of errors on dative sentences (7/40) and on dative-passive sentences (15/40). Twelve of the responses to dative-passive sentences were of the form 1,2,3. Conjoined sentences were relatively well interpreted (29 of 40 correct responses). Subject-object sentences were rarely interpreted correctly (2/40), with a majority of the errors strictly linear—17 of the form 1,2;1,3 and 7 of the form 1,2;2,3. There are nine subject-object sentences that were not interpreted by patients in this group. Object-subject sentences were correctly interpreted only 13 of 40 times, with 17 misinterpretations of the form 1,2;1,3.

Cluster 5 consists of eight patients who had significant difficulty on all but active and cleft-subject sentences. Thirty-five active sentences and 34 cleft-subject sentences were interpreted correctly. Performance on passive and cleft-object sentences was essentially random. Fifteen of 40 dative and 16 of 40 dative-passive sentences produced no responses. Twelve of 40 dative and 20 of 40 dative-passive sentences were misinterpreted. The majority of the errors on dative sentences were of the form 1,3,2 and 2,1,3, while ten and five errors in dative-passive sentences were of the forms 1,2,3 and 2,1,3, respectively. Only six conjoined sentences were interpreted correctly, and ten different types of errors were made on sentences of this form. Only two subject-object sentences were interpreted correctly, and, though the largest number of errors were of the form 1,2;1,3, nine different types of errors were seen. Object-subject sentences were interpreted correctly only twice, and nine error types arose. Eight errors were of the form 1,2;1,3. Thus, patients in cluster 5 had considerable difficulty with all but two-place verb sentences in canonical form. Responses to two-place verb sentences in noncanonical form were random, and there was less reliance on a strictly linear interpretive strategy to produce erroneous responses in two-verb sentences.

Cluster 6 consists of five patients. The majority of dative and dative-passive sentences did not elicit responses from these patients, nor did many conjoined, subject-object, and object-subject sentences. With two-place verbs, these patients did less well than those in group 5 on active and cleft-subject sentences; the latter were reversed to yield a 2,1 interpretation in 19 of 25 instances. Though it is noteworthy that patients in this group applied a nonlinear interpretive strategy more frequently than a correct linear strategy for this sentence type, this pattern may have arisen by chance (binomial expansion, $p > 0.05$). Interpretation of passive and cleft-object sentences was random. There were very few responses to dative and dative-passive sentences, but the majority of the responses to sentences of these types were correct. For conjoined and subject-object sentences, the most frequent responses were correct; however, very few correct responses were provided. Patients in group 6 were obviously significantly impaired in interpreting even the simplest syntactic structures. No consistent pattern of responses emerges for the group as a whole or for individual patients on any sentence type.

Group 7 consists of five patients: three who provided no responses at all, one who provided eight responses for 20 one-place verb sentences (six correct), and one who consistently misinterpreted active and passive sentences and performed randomly on cleft-subject and cleft-object sentences.

Notes

1. The question whether responses to the twelve examples of each sentence type are independent events has been raised by several commentators. For single case studies of the sort we present here, we address this issue as follows. Assume that all twelve examples of each sentence type are independent events for a given subject. Suppose, further, that the application of the χ^2 measure shows that the distribution of responses across the twelve examples of a given sentence type is not random (on some assumption regarding the determinants of random performance, such as the Stage I or II assumptions outlined). Then we conclude that our original assumption was incorrect: The twelve responses to the sentence type are not independent, but rather are all related in some way. This is a perfectly acceptable conclusion; what we now need to know is *in what way* the responses are related. They may be related (a) through the application of the subject's residual grammatical knowledge and parsing capacities, or (b) through his use of heuristic interpretive mechanisms, or (c) in some other way. Analysis of the total pattern of responses will indicate whether (a) or (b) is correct. One possibility of type (c)—that the subject bases his responses to later instances of a sentence type on his responses to earlier instances of that sentence type—cannot be completely ruled out, but is rendered less likely by the pseudo-randomization of sentences on each battery and the inclusion of many different sentence types on each battery. It does not seem likely that a subject will recall how he responded to a previous sentence, such as (i) below, when presented with sentence (ii), especially when many sentences, including ones like (iii), (iv), and (v), occur between (i) and (ii).

(i)   Patrick seemed to Eddie to be jumping.
(ii) Joe appeared to Patrick to be shaving.
(iii) Patrick persuaded Eddie to run.
(iv) Eddie promised Joe to jump.
(v)   Eddie promised Patrick that he would run.

2. Amy Weinberg (personal communication) has suggested that both A.B. and C.V. have the same deficit. On this analysis, A.B. compensates by adopting a heuristic appropriate for pronouns and C.V. by adopting one appropriate for reflexives. If this were correct, response patterns for matched sentence pairs with pronouns and reflexives, such as (i) and (ii) or (ii) and (iv) below, should be the same within each subject.

(i)   Eddie believed that Joe kicked him.
(ii) Eddie believed that Joe kicked himself.
(iii) A friend of John's kicked him.
(iv) A friend of John's kicked himself.

This is not the case. The distribution of responses to all these pairs differs in C.V.'s performance, and it differs for the pair (i) and (ii) in A.B.'s performance. This, in addition to the arguments presented in the text, indicates that both A.B. and C.V. distinguish reflexives from pronouns and have selective disturbances affecting the first and the second of these items, respectively.

3. An interesting question is whether significant differences in the production of the correct response on two sentence types, each containing a particular linguistic representation (or requiring a particular parsing operation), can be considered evidence for a utilization deficit, as opposed to a loss, when the pattern of performance on each sentence type is not distinguishable from random performance on Stage II assumptions. We do not consider such differences evidence for a utilization deficit (see chapter 5, where we claim that such differences are uninterpretable in terms of deficit analyses), but there may be arguments in favor of relaxing these criteria along these lines.

4. Bates et al (in press) report that, using the paradigms described in chapter 2, English Broca's aphasics show the same tendency as normals to take N_2 as Agent of V in sequences of the form N_1-N_2-V. However, this tendency was not observed in conduction aphasics. These data do not help determine whether this tendency is a consequence of the particular stimuli used in these experiments in both normals and aphasics, or what the relationship is between this "mapping" and normal sentence comprehension or between this "mapping" and the heuristics used by aphasics to interpret real sentences with object relativization.

5. In recent formulations of Lexical Functional Grammar, Bresnan analyzes control relations for "subject-control" verbs with a direct object (*promise*) as verbs of anaphoric control, in distinction to those without a direct object (*vow to, learn from*), which are analyzed as verbs of functional control (Bresnan, lectures at Linguistic Society of America Summer Institute, Stanford University, 1987). However, the data on G.S. are equally problematic for this new formulation, since they do not explain why the functional-control structures with *vow to* and *learn from* were impaired to the same extent as the anaphoric-control structures with *promise* while the functional-control NP-raising structures were not affected.

Bibliography

Albert, M. L. 1976. Short-term memory and aphasia. *Brain and Language* 3: 28–33.

Atkinson, R. C., and R. M. Shiffrin. 1968. Human memory: A proposed system and its control processes. In K. W. Spence and J. T. Spence (eds.), *The Psychology of Learning and Motivation: Advances in Research and Theory*, volume 1 (New York: Academic).

Atkinson, R. C., and R. M. Shiffrin. 1971. The control of short-term memory. *Scientific American* 225: 82–90.

Baddeley, A. D. 1966a. The influence of acoustic and semantic similarity on long-term memory for word sequences. *Quarterly Journal of Experimental Psychology* 18: 302–309.

Baddeley, A. D. 1966b. Short-term memory for word sequences as a function of acoustic, semantic and formal similarity. *Quarterly Journal of Experimental Psychology* 18: 362–365.

Baddeley, A. D. 1981. The concept of working memory: A view of its current state and probable future development. *Cognition* 10: 17–24.

Baddeley, A. D. 1985. The Dis-Executive Syndrome. Presented at Second International Conference on Cognitive Neuropsychology, Venice.

Baddeley, A. D., and G. Hitch. 1974. Working memory. In G. H. Bower (ed.), *The Psychology of Learning and Motivation: Advances in Research and Theory*, volume 8 (New York: Academic).

Baddeley, A. D., N. Thomson, and M. Buchanan. 1975. Word length and the structure of short-term memory. *Journal of Verbal Learning and Verbal Behavior* 14: 575–589.

Badecker, W., and A. Caramazza. 1985. On considerations of method and theory governing the use of clinical categories in neurolinguistics and cognitive neuropsychology: The case against agrammatism. *Cognition* 20: 97–125.

Basso, A., A. R. Lecours, S. Moraschini, and M. Vanier. 1985. Anatomicoclinical correlations of the aphasias as defined through computerized tomography: Exceptions. *Brain and Language* 16: 201–230.

Bates, E., A. Friederici, G. Miceli, and B. Wulfeck. In press. Comprehension in aphasia: A cross-linguistic study. *Brain and Language*.

Bates, E., S. McNew, B. MacWhinney, A. Devescovi, and S. Smith. 1982. Functional constraints on sentence processing. *Cognition* 11: 245–299.

Benson, D. F. 1979. *Aphasia, alexia, and agraphia*. New York: Churchill Livingstone.

Benson, D. F., and N. Geschwind. 1971. Aphasia and related cortical disturbances. In A. B. Baker and L. H. Baker (eds.), *Clinical Neurology* (New York: Harper and Row).

Berndt, R., and A. Caramazza. 1980. A redefinition of the syndrome of Broca's aphasia. *Applied Psycholinguistics* 1: 225–278.

Berndt, R., and A. Caramazza. 1982. Psycholinguistic aspects of aphasia: Syntax. In M. T. Sarno (ed.), *Acquired Aphasia* (New York: Academic).

Berwick, R. C., and A. Weinberg. 1984. *The Grammatical Basis of Linguistic Performance: Language Use and Acquisition*. Cambridge: MIT Press.

Berwick, R. C., and A. Weinberg. 1985. Deterministic parsing and linguistic explanation. *Language and Cognitive Processes* 1: 109–134.

Bever, T. G. 1970. The cognitive basis for linguistic structures. In J. R. Hayes (ed.), *Cognition and the Development of Language* (New York: Wiley).

Bogen, J. E., and G. M. Bogen. 1976. Wernicke's region: Where is it? *Annals of the New York Academy of Sciences* 280: 834–843.

Boller, F., and L. A. Vignolo. 1966. Latent sensory aphasia in hemisphere-damaged patients: An experimental study with the Token Test. *Brain* 89: 815–830.

Bouchard, D. 1982. On the Content of Empty Categories. Ph.D. dissertation, Massachusetts Institute of Technology.

Bradley, D. C., M. F. Garrett, and E. B. Zurif. 1980. Syntactic deficits in Broca's aphasia. In D. Caplan (ed.), *Biological Studies of Mental Processes* (Cambridge: MIT Press).

Bresnan, J. 1982a. Control and complementation. In J. Bresnan (ed.), *The Mental Representation of Grammatical Relations* (Cambridge: MIT Press).

Bresnan, J. (ed.). 1982b. *The Mental Representation of Grammatical Relations*. Cambridge: MIT Press.

Bresnan, J. 1982c. The passive in lexical theory. In J. Bresnan (ed.), *The Mental Representation of Grammatical Relations* (Cambridge: MIT Press).

Caplan, D. 1981. On the cerebral localization of linguistic functions: Logical and empirical issues surrounding deficit analysis and functional localization. *Brain and Language* 14: 120–137.

Caplan, D. 1983a. A note on the "word order problem" in agrammatism. *Brain and Language* 20: 155–165.

Caplan, D. 1983b. Syntactic competence in agrammatism: A lexical hypothesis. In M. Studdert-Kennedy (ed.), *The Neurobiology of Language* (Cambridge: MIT Press).

Caplan, D. 1984. The mental organ for language. In D. Caplan, A. R. Lecours, and A. Smith (eds.), *Biological Perspectives on Language* (Cambridge: MIT Press).

Caplan, D. 1985. Syntactic and semantic structures in agrammatism. In M.-L. Kean (ed.), *Agrammatism* (New York: Academic).

Caplan, D. 1986a. In defense of agrammatism. *Cognition* 24: 263–276.

Caplan, D. 1986b. Patterns of Syntactic Comprehension in Aphasia. Unpublished manuscript.

Caplan, D. 1987a. Agrammatism and the coindexation of traces: Comments on Grodzinsky's reply. *Brain and Language* 30: 191–193.

Caplan, D. 1987b. Contrasting patterns of sentence comprehension deficits in aphasia. In M. Coltheart, G. Sartori, and R. Job (eds.), *The Cognitive Neuropsychology of Language* (London: Erlbaum).

Caplan, D. 1987c. Discrimination of normal and aphasic subjects on a test of syntactic comprehension. *Neuropsychologia* 25: 173–184.

Caplan, D. 1987d. *Neurolinguistics and Linguistic Aphasiology: An Introduction*. Cambridge University Press.

Caplan, D. In press. On the role of group studies in neuropsychological and pathopsychological research. *Cognitive Neuropsychology*.

Caplan, D., C. Baker, and F. Dehaut. 1985. Syntactic determinants of sentence comprehension in aphasia. *Cognition* 21: 117–175.

Caplan, D., and C. Futter. 1986. Assignment of thematic roles to nouns in sentence comprehension by an agrammatic patient. *Brain and Language* 27: 117–134.

Caplan, D., and N. Hildebrandt. 1986. Language deficits and the theory of syntax: A reply to Grodzinsky. *Brain and Language* 27: 168–177.

Caplan, D., E. Matthei, and H. Gigley. 1981. Comprehension of gerundive constructions by Broca's aphasics. *Brain and Language* 13: 145–160.

Caplan, D., M. Vanier, and C. Baker. 1986a. A case study of reproduction conduction aphasia: I. Word production. *Cognitive Neuropsychology* 3: 99–128.

Caplan, D., M. Vanier, and C. Baker. 1986a. A case study of reproduction conduction aphasia: II. Sentence comprehension. *Cognitive Neuropsychology* 3: 129–146.

Caramazza, A. 1986. On drawing inferences about the structure of normal cognitive systems from the analysis of impaired performance: The case for single patient studies. *Brain and Cognition* 5: 45–66.

Caramazza, A. In press, a. Valid inferences regarding normal symptoms from pathological performances can only be drawn on the basis of single case studies. In Proceedings of the Clinical Aphasiology Conference.

Caramazza, A. In press, b. On inferring the structure of normal cognitive systems from patterns of impaired performance consequent to brain damage. *Cognitive Neuropsychology*.

Caramazza, A., A. Basili, J. J. Koller, and R. S. Berndt. 1981. An investigation of repetition and language processing in a case of conduction aphasia. *Brain and Language* 14: 234–271.

Caramazza, A., and R. S. Berndt. 1985. A multicomponent view of agrammatic Broca's aphasia. In M.-L. Kean (ed.), *Agrammatism* (New York: Academic).

Caramazza, A., R. S. Berndt, A. G. Basili, and J. J. Koller. 1981. Syntactic processing deficits in aphasia. *Cortex* 17: 333–348.

Caramazza, A., and E. Zurif. 1976. Dissociation of algorithmic and heuristic processes in language comprehension: Evidence from aphasia. *Brain and Language* 3: 572–582.

Chomsky, N. 1957. *Syntactic Structures*. The Hague: Mouton.

Chomsky, N. 1965. *Aspects of the Theory of Syntax*. Cambridge: MIT Press.

Chomsky, N. 1981. *Lectures in Government and Binding*. Dordrecht: Foris.

Chomsky, N. 1982. *Some Concepts and Consequences of the Theory of Government and Binding*. Cambridge: MIT Press.

Conrad, R., and A. J. Hull. 1964. Information, acoustic confusion and memory span. *Journal of Psychology* 55: 429–432.

Crain, S., and J. D. Fodor. 1985. How can grammars help parsers? In D. R. Dowty, L. Karttunen, and A. Zwicky (eds.), *Natural Language Parsing: Psychological, Computational, and Theoretical Perspectives* (Cambridge University Press).

Daneman, M., and P. A. Carpenter. 1980. Individual differences in working memory and reading. *Journal of Verbal Learning and Verbal Behavior* 19: 450–466.

Daneman, M., and P. A. Carpenter. 1983. Individual differences in integrating information between and within sentences. *Journal of Experimental Psychology: Learning, Memory, and Cognition* 9: 561–584.

Daneman, M., and I. Green. 1986. Individual differences in comprehending and producing words in context. *Journal of Memory and Language* 25: 1–18.

DeRenzi, E., and L. Vignolo. 1962. The Token Test: A sensitive test to detect receptive disturbances in aphasics. *Brain* 85: 665–678.

Ehrlich, K. 1983. Eye movements in pronoun assignment: A study of sentence integration. In K. Rayner (ed.), *Eye Movements in Reading* (New York: Academic).

Ehrlich, K., and K. Rayner. 1983. Pronoun assignment and semantic integration during reading. Eye movements and immediacy of processing. *Journal of Verbal Learning and Verbal Behavior* 22: 75–87.

Ferguson, G. A. 1981. *Statistical Analysis in Psychology and Education*. Fifth edition. New York: McGraw-Hill.

Fodor, J. A. 1983. *The Modularity of Mind*. Cambridge: MIT Press.

Fodor, J. A., T. G. Bever, and M. F. Garrett. 1974. *The Psychology of Language: An Introduction to Psycholinguistics and Generative Grammar*. New York: McGraw-Hill.

Fodor, J. A., and M. Garrett. 1967. Some syntactic determinants of sentential complexity. *Perception and Psychophysics* 2: 289—296.

Fodor, J. A., M. Garrett, and T. G. Bever. 1968. Some syntactic determinants of sentential complexity: II. Verb structure. *Perception and Psychophysics* 3: 453—461.

Ford, M. 1983. A method for obtaining measures of local parsing complexity throughout sentences. *Journal of Verbal Learning and Verbal Behavior* 22: 203—218.

Forster, K. I., and I. Olbrei. 1973. Semantic heuristics and syntactic analysis. *Cognition* 2: 319—347.

Frazier, L. 1978. On Comprehending Sentences: Syntactic Parsing Strategies. Ph.D. dissertation, University of Connecticut, Storrs.

Frazier, L. 1983. Processing sentence structure. In K. Rayner (ed.), *Eye Movements in Reading* (New York: Academic).

Frazier, L., C. Clifton, and J. Randall. 1983. Filling gaps: Decision principles and structure in sentence comprehension. *Cognition* 13: 187—222.

Frazier, L., and J. D. Fodor. 1978. The sausage machine: A new two-stage parsing model. *Cognition* 6: 291—325.

Freud, S. 1891. *On Aphasia* (New York: International Universities Press, 1953).

Friedrich, F. J., R. Martin, and S. J. Kemper. 1985. Consequences of a phonological coding deficit on sentence processing. *Cognitive Neuropsychology* 2: 385—412.

Geschwind, N. 1965. Disconnection syndromes in animals and man. *Brain* 88: 237—294, 585—644.

Glanzer, M., L. Koppenaal, and R. Nelson. 1972. Effects of relations between words on short-term storage and long-term storage. *Journal of Verbal Learning and Verbal Behavior* 8: 435—447.

Goldstein, K. 1948. *Language and Language Disturbances*. New York: Grune and Stratton.

Goodglass, H. 1968. Studies on the grammar of aphasics. In S. Rosenberg and J. H. Koplin (eds.), *Developments in Applied Psycholinguistic Research* (New York: Macmillan).

Goodglass, H., and E. Kaplan. 1972. *The Assessment of Aphasia and Related Disorders*. Philadelphia: Lea and Febiger.

Goodglass, H., and E. Kaplan. 1982. *The Assessment of Aphasia and Related Disorders*. Second edition. Philadelphia: Lea and Febiger.

Gordon, B., and A. Caramazza. 1982. Lexical decision for open- and closed-class words: Failure to replicate differential frequency sensitivity. *Brain and Language* 15: 143—160.

Grodzinsky, Y. 1984. The syntactic characterization of agrammatism. *Cognition* 16: 99—120.

Grodzinsky, Y. 1986. Language deficits and the theory of syntax. *Brain and Language* 27: 135—159.

Hagiwara, H., and D. Caplan. In preparation. Syntactic comprehension in Japanese aphasics.

Heilman, K. M., and R. J. Scholes. 1976. The nature of comprehension errors in Broca's, Conduction, and Wernicke's aphasics. *Cortex* 12: 258—265.

Hildebrandt, N., D. Caplan, and K. Evans. 1987. The man$_i$ left t$_i$ without a trace: A case study of aphasic processing of empty categories. *Cognitive Neuropsychology* 4: 257—302.

Hirst, G. 1981. *Anaphora in Natural Language Understanding: A Survey*. Berlin: Springer-Verlag.

Jackson, J. H. 1874. On the nature of the duality of the brain. In J. Taylor (ed.), *Selected Writings of John Hughlings Jackson*, volume 2 (New York: Basic Books, 1958).

Jakubowicz, C. 1984. On markedness and binding principles. In *NELS 14* (Amherst: GLSA, University of Massachusetts).

Just, M. A., and P. A. Carpenter. 1980. A theory of reading: From eye-fixations to comprehension. *Psychological Review* 87: 329—354.

Kean, M.-L. 1977. The linguistic interpretation of aphasic syndromes: Agrammatism in Broca's aphasia, an example. *Cognition* 5: 9–46.

Kean, M.-L. 1980. Grammatical representations and the description of language processing. In D. Caplan (ed.), *Biological studies of mental processes* (Cambridge: MIT Press).

Kean, M.-L. 1982. Three perspectives for the analysis of aphasic syndromes. In M. A. Arbib, D. Caplan, and J. C. Marshall (eds.), *Neural Models of Language Processes* (New York: Academic).

Kertesz, A. 1979. *Aphasia and Associated Disorders: Taxonomy, Localization and Recovery.* New York: Grune and Stratton.

Kertesz, A., and E. Poole. 1974. The Aphasia Quotient: The taxonomic approach to measurement of aphasic disability. *Canadian Journal of Neurological Sciences* 1: 7–16.

Kertesz, A., A. Sheppard, and R. MacKenzie. 1982. Localization in transcortical sensory aphasia. *Archives of Neurology* 39: 475–478.

Klein, B. von Eckardt. 1978. On inferring functional localization from neurological evidence. In E. Walker (ed.), *Explorations in the Biology of Language* (Montgomery, Vermont: Bradford).

Kolk, H. H., and M. J. F. van Grunsven. 1985. Agrammatism as a variable phenomenon. *Cognitive Neuropsychology* 2: 347–384.

Lapointe, S. G. 1983. Some issues in the linguistic description of agrammatism. *Cognition* 14: 1–39.

Lashley, K. S. 1950. In search of the engran. *Symposia for the Society for Experimental Biology* 4: 454–482.

Lesser, V. R., R. D. Fennel, L. D. Erman, and D. R. Reddy. 1975. Organization of the HEARSAY-II speech understanding system. *IEEE Transactions on Acoustics, Speech and Signal Processing* 23: 11–23.

Levin, B., and M. Rappaport. 1986. The formation of lexical passives. *Linguistic Inquiry* 17: 623–661.

Lichtheim, L. 1885. On aphasia. *Brain* 7: 433–484.

Lightfoot, D. 1982. *The Language Lottery: Towards a Biology of Grammars.* Cambridge: MIT Press.

Linebarger, M. C., M. F. Schwartz, and E. M. Saffran. 1983a. Sensitivity to grammatical structure in so-called agrammatic aphasics. *Cognition* 13: 361–392.

Linebarger, M. C., M. F. Schwartz, and E. M. Saffran. 1983b. Syntactic processing in agrammatism: A reply to Zurif and Grodzinsky. *Cognition* 15: 207–214.

Luria, A. R. 1947. *Traumatic aphasia.* Translation. The Hague: Mouton, 1970.

MacWhinney, B., E. Bates, and R. Kliegl. 1984. Cue validity and sentence interpretation in English German, and Italian. *Journal of Verbal Learning and Verbal Behavior* 23: 127–150.

Marcus, M. P. 1980. *A Theory of Syntactic Recognition for Natural Language.* Cambridge: MIT Press.

Marcus, M. P. 1982. Consequences of functional deficits in a parsing model: Implications for Broca's aphasia. In M. A. Arbib, D. Caplan, and J. C. Marshall (eds.), *Neural models of language processes* (New York: Academic).

Marie, P. 1906. Révision de la question de l'aphasie: La troisième convolution frontale gauche ne joue aucun rôle spécial dans la fonction du langage. *Semaine Medicale* 26: 241–247.

Marshall, J. C. 1986. The description and interpretation of language disorder. *Neuropsychologia* 24: 5–24.

Marslen-Wilson, W., and L. K. Tyler. 1980. The temporal structure of spoken language understanding. *Cognition* 8: 1–71.

Marslen-Wilson, W. D., and A. Welsh. 1978. Processing interactions and lexical access during word-recognition in continuous speech. *Cognitive Psychology* 10: 29–63.

Matthei, E. H. 1982. The acquisition of prenominal modifier sequences. *Cognition* 11: 301–332.

McFarling, D., L. J. Rothi, and K. Heilman. 1982. Transcortical aphasia from ischaemic infarcts of the thalamus: A report of two cases. *Journal of Neurology, Neurosurgery, and Psychiatry* 45: 107–112.

Miceli, G., A. Mazzucchi, L. Menn, and H. Goodglass. 1983. Contrasting cases of Italian agrammatic aphasia without comprehension disorder. *Brain and Language* 19: 65–97.

Miller, G. A. 1956. The magic number seven plus or minus two, or, some limits on our capacity for processing information. *Psychological Review* 63: 81–96.

Mohr, J. P., M. S. Pessin, S. Finkelstein, H. H. Funkenstein, G. W. Duncan, and K. R. Davis. 1978. Broca's aphasia: Pathologic and clinical. *Neurology* 28: 311–324.

Moutier, F. 1908. *L'aphasie de Broca*. Paris: Steinheil.

Nespoulous, J. C., C. Perron, M. Dordain, D. Caplan, D. Bub, J. Mehler, and A. Lecours. 1985. A Case of Agrammatism without Comprehension Impairment. Unpublished manuscript.

Niccum, N., C. Speaks, A. B. Rubens, D. S. Knopman, D. Yock, and D. Larson. 1986. Longitudinal dichotic listening patterns for aphasic patients: II. Relationship with lesion variables. *Brain and Language* 28: 289–303.

Nie, H. H., C. H. Hull, J. G. Jenkins, K. Steinbrenner, and D. M. Bent. 1975. *Statistical Package for the Social Sciences*. Second edition. New York: McGraw-Hill.

Parisi, D., and L. Pizzamiglio. 1970. Syntactic comprehension in aphasia. *Cortex* 6: 204–215.

Pinker, S. 1982. A theory of the acquisition of lexical interpretive grammars. In J. Bresnan (ed.), *The Mental Representation of Grammatical Relations* (Cambridge: MIT Press).

Reinhart, T. 1983. *Anaphora and Semantic Interpretation*. London: Croom Helm.

Rizzi, L. 1978. Violations of the *wh*-island constraint in Italian and the subjacency condition. In C. Dubisson, D. Lightfoot, and Y. C. Morin (eds.), *Montreal Working Papers in Linguistics*, volume 11 (University of Montreal).

Rizzi, L. 1985. Two notes on the linguistic interpretation of Broca's aphasia. In M.-L. Kean (ed.), *Agrammatism* (New York: Academic).

Roeltgen, D., S. Sevush, and K. Heilman. 1983. Phonological agraphia: Writing by the lexical-semantic route. *Neurology* 33: 755–765.

Roeper, T. 1978. On the acquisition of gerunds. *UMass Working Papers in Linguistics*, volume 1. Amherst: University of Massachusetts.

Rosenberg, B., E. Zurif, H. Brownell, M. Garrett, and D. Bradley. 1985. Grammatical class effects in relation to normal and aphasic sentence processing. *Brain and Language* 26: 287–303.

Rundus, D. 1971. Analysis of rehearsal processes in free recall. *Journal of Experimental Psychology* 89: 63–77.

Saffran, E. 1985. Working memory and auditory sentence comprehension. Presented at the Second International Conference on Cognitive Neuropsychology, Venice.

Saffran, E. M., and O. S. M. Marin. 1975. Immediate memory for word lists and sentences in a patient with deficient auditory short-term memory. *Brain and Language* 2: 420–433.

Saffran, E. M., M. F. Schwartz, and O. Marin. 1980. The word order problem in agrammatism: II. Production. *Brain and Language* 10: 263–280.

Salamé, P., and A. D. Baddeley. 1982. Disruption of short-term memory by unattended speech: Implications for the structure of working memory. *Journal of Verbal Learning and Verbal Behavior* 21: 150–164.

Schneider, W., and R. M. Shiffrin. 1977. Automatic and controlled information processing in vision. In D. LaBerge and S. J. Samuels (eds.), *Basic Processes in Reading: Perception and Comprehension* (Hillsdale, N. J.: Erlbaum).

Schwartz, M. 1984. What the classical aphasia categories can't do for us, and why. *Brain and Language* 21: 3–8.

Schwartz, M. F., M. C. Linebarger, E. M. Saffran, and D. S. Pate. 1987. Syntactic transparency and sentence interpretation in aphasia. *Language and Cognitive Processes* 2: 85–113.

Schwartz, M., E. Saffran, and O. Marin. 1980. The word order problem in agrammatism: I. Comprehension. *Brain and Language* 10: 249–262.

Segui, J., J. Mehler, U. Frauenfelder and J. Morton. 1982. The word frequency effect and lexical access. *Neuropsychologia* 20: 615–627.

Shallice, T. 1987. Impairments of semantic processing: Multiple dissociations. In M. Coltheart, G. Sartori, and R. Job (eds.), *The Cognitive Neuropsychology of Language* (London: Erlbaum).

Shiffrin, R. M., and S. T. Dumais. 1981. The development of automatism. In J. R. Anderson (ed.), *Cognitive Skills and Their Acquisition* (Hillsdale, N. J.: Erlbaum).

Slobin, D. I. 1966. Grammatical transformations and sentence comprehension in childhood and adulthood. *Journal of Verbal Learning and Verbal Behavior* 2: 219–227.

Stowe, L. 1983. Models of Gap-Location in the Human Language Processor. Ph.D. dissertation, University of Wisconsin, Madison.

Stowe, L. 1986. Parsing WH-constructions: Evidence for on-line gap location. *Language and Cognitive Processes* 1: 227–245.

Thomas, A. 1908. Discussion sur l'aphasie. *Revue Neurologigue* 16: 611–636.

Tzeng, O. J. L. 1973. Positive recency effect in delayed free recall. *Journal of Verbal Learning and Verbal Behavior* 12: 436–439.

Vallar, G. 1985. Strategic Determination of the Recency Effect in an STM Patient. Presented at Second International Conference on Cognitive Neuropsychology, Venice.

Vallar, G., and A. D. Baddeley. 1984a. Fractionation of working memory: Neuropsychological evidence for a phonological short-term store. *Journal of Verbal Learning and Verbal Behavior* 23: 151–161.

Vallar, G., and A. D. Baddeley. 1984b. Phonological short-term store, phonological processing and sentence comprehension: A neuropsychological case study. *Cognitive Neuropsychology* 1: 121–142.

Vanier, M., and D. Caplan. 1985. CT scan correlates of surface dyslexia. In K. Patterson, J. C. Marshall, and M. Coltheart (eds.), *Surface Dyslexia* (London: Erlbaum).

Vanier, M., and D. Caplan. In press. CT-scan correlates of agrammatism. In L. Obler, L. Menn, and H. Goodglass (eds.), *A Cross-Language Study of Agrammatism* (New York: Benjamin).

Volin, R. A. 1983. Characterization of Aphasic Disruption of Syntax: The Perception of Grammatical Relations in Relative Clauses. Ph.D. dissertation, City University of New York.

Wanner, E. 1980. The ATN and the Sausage Machine: Which one is baloney? *Cognition* 8: 209–225.

Wanner, E., and M. Maratsos. 1978. An ATN approach to comprehension. In M. Halle, J. Bresnan, and G. Miller (eds.), *Linguistic Theory and Psychological Reality* (Cambridge: MIT Press).

Ward, J. 1963. Hierarchical grouping to optimize on function. *American Statistical Association Journal* 58: 236–244.

Warrington, E. K., and R. McCarthy. 1983. Category specific access dysphasia. *Brain* 106: 859–878.

Warrington, E. K., and T. Shallice. 1969. The selective impairment of auditory verbal short-term memory. *Brain* 92: 885–896.

Warrington, E. K., and T. Shallice. 1972. Neuropsychological evidence of visual storage in short-term memory tasks. *Quarterly Journal of Experimental Psychology* 24: 30–40.

Warrington, E. K., and T. Shallice. 1979. Semantic access dyslexia. *Brain* 102: 43–63.

Warrington, E. K., and L. Weiskrantz. 1973. An analysis of short-term and long-term memory deficits in man. In J. A. Deutsch (ed.), *The Physiological Basis of Memory* (New York: Academic).

Wasow, T. 1977. Transformations and the lexicon. In P. W. Culicover, T. Wasow, and A. Akmajian (eds.), *Formal Syntax* (New York: Academic).

Waters, G., D. Caplan, and N. Hildebrandt. 1987. Working memory and written sentence comprehension. In M. Coltheart (ed.), *Attention and Performance XII* (London: Erlbaum).

Wernicke, C. 1874. *The Aphasic Symptom Complex: A Psychological Study on a Neurological Basis*. Breslau: Kohn and Weigert. Reprinted in R. S. Cohen and M. W. Wartofsky (eds.), *Boston Studies in the Philosophy of Science*, volume 4 (Boston: Reidel).

Williams, E. 1980. Predication. *Linguistic Inquiry* 11: 203–238.

Williams, E. 1981. Argument structure and morphology. *Linguistic Review* 1: 81–114.

Winer, B. J. 1971. *Statistical Principles in Experimental Design*. Second edition. New York: McGraw-Hill.

Wishart, D. 1978. *CLUSTAN User Manual*. Third edition. Research Councils Series Report No. 47. Edinburgh: Inter-University Press.

Woods, W. A. 1970. Transition network grammars for natural language analysis. *Communications of the ACM* 13: 591–606.

Woods, W. A. 1982. HWIM: A speech understanding system on a computer. In M. A. Arbib, D. Caplan, and J. C. Marshall (eds.), *Neural Models of Language Processes* (New York: Academic).

Zurif, E. B. 1982. The use of data from aphasia in constructing a performance model of language. In M. A. Arbib, D. Caplan, and J. C. Marshall (eds.), *Neural Models of Language Processes* (New York: Academic).

Zurif, E. B. 1984. Psycholinguistic interpretation of the aphasias. In D. Caplan, A. R. Lecours, and A. Smith (eds.), *Biological Perspectives on Language* (Cambridge: MIT Press).

Zurif, E. B., and A. Caramazza. 1976. Psycholinguistic structures in aphasia: Studies in syntax and semantics. In H. Whitaker and H. A. Whitaker (eds.), *Studies in Neurolinguistics*, volume 1 (New York: Academic).

Zurif, E. B., A. Caramazza, and D. Myerson. 1972. Grammatical judgements of agrammatic aphasics. *Neuropsychologia* 10: 405–417.

Zurif, E. B., E. Green, A. Caramazza, and C. Goodenough. 1976. Grammatical intuitions of aphasic patients: Sensitivity to functors. *Cortex* 12: 183–186.

Zurif, E. B., and Y. Grodzinsky. 1983. Sensitivity to grammatical structure in agrammatic aphasics: A reply to Linebarger, Schwartz, and Saffran. *Cognition* 15: 207–214.

Author Index

Subject Index